Executive
Wisdom

Executive Wisdom

Coaching and the Emergence of Virtuous Leaders

Richard R. Kilburg

American Psychological Association • Washington, DC

Published by
American Psychological Association
750 First Street, NE
Washington, DC 20002
www.apa.org

To order
APA Order Department
P.O. Box 92984
Washington, DC 20090-2984
Tel: (800) 374-2721
Direct: (202) 336-5510
Fax: (202) 336-5502
TDD/TTY: (202) 336-6123
Online: www.apa.org/books/
E-mail: order@apa.org

In the U.K., Europe, Africa, and the Middle East, copies may be ordered from
American Psychological Association
3 Henrietta Street
Covent Garden, London
WC2E 8LU England

Typeset in Goudy by World Composition Services, Inc., Sterling, VA

Printer: Edwards Brothers, Ann Arbor, MI
Cover Designer: Naylor Design, Washington, DC
Technical/Production Editor: Harriet Kaplan

The opinions and statements published are the responsibility of the authors, and such opinions and statements do not necessarily represent the policies of the American Psychological Association.

Library of Congress Cataloging-in-Publication Data

Kilburg, Richard R., 1946–
    Executive wisdom : coaching and the emergence of virtuous leaders / Richard R. Kilburg.
        p. cm.
    Includes bibliographical references and index.
    ISBN 1-59147-402-7
    1. Executive coaching. 2. Leadership—Psychological aspects. I. Title.

    HD30.4.K542   2006
    658.4'092—dc22   2005032199

British Library Cataloguing-in-Publication Data
A CIP record is available from the British Library.

Printed in the United States of America
First Edition

I dedicate this book to my brother and two sisters,
James Kilburg, Amy Kilburg Majetic, and Jane Kilburg Alcorn,
who have been my constant, loving, and joyful companions in life.

CONTENTS

PREFACE

Stepping across the intellectual and emotional threshold of a scholarly subject such as human wisdom requires a blend of furious curiosity, innocence, and hubris. One knows with complete confidence that many, many others have made significant efforts to extend humanity's understanding of this most important topic and welcomes the opportunity to explore their passions, ideas, and perspectives. One also hopes that a new set of eyes, a different heart, and a fresh perspective might open some new pathways into a dense yet well-traveled forest. To be sure, wisdom has at one time or another occupied the minds of the vast majority of what we could call the major intellectual figures in human history. I set off on this journey in an effort to learn something about it and arrived at a point where I believe those explorations may be useful to share with people leading human organizations and professionals who try to help those executives.

SOME RELEVANT PERSONAL HISTORY

For over 30 years, I have been a student of psychology, individuals, organizations, communities, and leadership. During that time, I have always had leadership responsibilities in organizations of various sizes and with different goals. I began my career as a faculty member in the Department of Psychiatry at the University of Pittsburgh, where John Hitchcock, one of my graduate school mentors, gave me my professional start by offering me his job when he was promoted. At the ripe age of 26, with a newly minted PhD, I defended my dissertation on a Friday and assumed the responsibility for mental health services in two Pittsburgh neighborhoods comprising 26,000 people the following Monday. I went from being a graduate student working on an internship with a talented group of full-time professionals to being their leader.

I shall never forget the lessons my colleagues taught me and those we learned together while trying to improve the well-being of those communities. It was there and then that I cut my leadership and consulting teeth in the trenches of inner-city Pittsburgh and in the aftermath of the Martin Luther King assassination and the subsequent riots. It was during the madness of the Vietnam War and the height of the civil rights revolution. Those events then led directly to the women's liberation movement of the 1970s. In such a crucible, my initial ideas about and experiences with leaders of various sorts were created.

In the decades since, I have held a number of other jobs, and they have all involved trying to lead groups of talented people to create services and solve problems. Those positions have spanned leading a small for-profit business and a multicounty agency and management roles in several organizations, including my current job at The Johns Hopkins University. In all of them, I have learned huge lessons about leadership from the events, projects, and actions taken by myself and others, especially boards of directors, committees, superiors, subordinates, and clients. Over the past 10 years or so, my work has increasingly focused on the challenges of helping managers and leaders develop themselves and their organizations. I now direct a multidisciplinary team of extraordinary professionals who are devoted to creating a life span human development capacity in the Human Resources Department at The Johns Hopkins University. We have been continuously supported by four university presidents and five vice presidents for Human Resources. Our collective work has built a unique capacity into the organization for addressing the developmental needs of its faculty, staff, students, and family members. In addition, I have had greater opportunities to coach leaders in other organizations as a result of our collective work at the university and some of the writing I have done about that activity. The content of this book has evolved from that history.

Five years ago, I published *Executive Coaching: Developing Managerial Wisdom in a World of Chaos* (Kilburg, 2000) with the American Psychological Association. A major subtheme of that volume attempted to place the development of wisdom in leaders at all levels of organizations at the heart of the practice of coaching. As my work with individuals in senior leadership positions has continued in the years since, I have increasingly been asking myself hard questions about what I am really trying to accomplish in the hours that I spend with them. These leaders continue to tell me that the discussions we have and the time we spend together is very helpful. Most often, that feedback is sufficient for me, because the pace of life and work is such that consistent, in-depth reflection on every transaction I have with clients and others remains beyond my capacity. However, there are moments and situations that force me to ponder deeply how a client, a subordinate, or someone else is reacting to what is happening in his or her life, who they are as people, what I have said or done, or who I am. In many of those moments, I have asked myself the question "Just what am I trying to do here?"

Now, after more years of reading, writing, teaching, working, and living, I have begun to understand more fully what I have been trying to achieve personally and consistently pushing others to stretch toward. It is a simple, one-word answer: wisdom. I have been trying to be wise in my life and to encourage, lead, and coach others to create wisdom in their lives and organizations. An equally simple but somewhat more sarcastic version of the same answer is that I have been trying not to be stupid and to help others avoid the experience of choosing folly in their lives or for their organizations.

I have also asked myself what makes me an arbiter of what is wise and foolish in life. Why have organizations hired me to provide leadership? Why have individuals contracted with me to coach them? The answers generate complex streams of associations, but eventually they can all be reduced to two concepts. One is that organizations and individuals expect consistently wise assessments, decisions, and actions from me. The other is that they also implicitly expect me to conduct myself in a consistently virtuous manner. They want me to be honest, sincere, kind, temperate, courageous when it is called for, and fair in the way I treat them. In other words, they expect me both to know how to be a good person and to behave as one in a consistent fashion. If they did not believe they were receiving those two things from me, they would eventually turn away.

During the decades of my career, I have also watched many, many people derail in their jobs and lives. Indeed, as a leader myself, I have had to fire a number of individuals for incompetence, consistently bad behavior, and other forms of human folly. I often receive coaching assignments to work with individuals to try to prevent them from blowing up their careers or their organizations. In all of these experiences, I have found consistently absent in the individuals who are failing the ability to make good assessments of their situations, to develop plans that really make sense, and to take actions that have good outcomes over long periods of time. The understanding of human wisdom and, more broadly, virtuous behavior that I have currently achieved is also based on such experiences. It is what I try to share with you in the chapters that follow.

I believe that the professional coaches who read this volume will find it a natural sequel to my previous book. However, the emphasis here is shifted significantly. In the first volume on coaching, I explicitly focused on conceptual foundations and the how-tos of coaching and a delineation of the complex set of ideas that guide the actions that I take with my clients—that is, some of the means that I believed should be used to help develop leaders. In this volume, I am trying to emphasize the ends to which we coach and develop. I have included a number of practical suggestions and ideas about actions development professionals can take with clients and that leaders themselves can take. I have made a special point of trying to emphasize complex forms of inquiry that can push both leaders and coaches into more reflective states of mind about their situations, alternatives, and actions. However, the primary outcome I would like to create for you, my readers, is that by the end of your efforts, you will have a much better set of ideas about how wisdom is manifested by leaders; what kinds of things can get in the way of its development and implementation; and what individuals, be they coaches or executives themselves, can do to improve the likelihood that they will think, decide, and act wisely.

CASES AND CONFIDENTIALITY

As you work your way through the book, you will find a number of case studies that have been drawn from some of my experiences in coaching various leaders. All of them have been heavily disguised to protect the privacy of the individuals and organizations involved.

GRATITUDE

Any book represents the culmination of a lot of effort on the part of a lot of people. Although I cannot and do not know everyone who has had a hand in its production, I want to thank several for their special support. To Catherine Fitzgerald, I owe a permanent debt of intellectual gratitude for introducing me to the work of Robert Sternberg, Robert Kegan, and others. To my colleagues at The Johns Hopkins University, I am constantly thankful for their professional and personal support, their intellectual and practice challenges, and their good company. Chanda Marvin, my executive assistant, helps me stay sane, controls my constant impulse to complicate my life, and keeps me as organized as I will let her. Bob Wilson, Jimmy Jones, Ed Rouhlac, Audrey Smith, my past leadership partners, and Charlene Moore Hayes, my present boss at The Johns Hopkins University, have been enormously supportive of my intellectual and professional explorations. They have also provided me with wonderful role models of executive wisdom in action. My long-term writing colleague, Nora Myers, has been a constant critical companion for nearly 20 years and has helped me in virtually every project I have undertaken since the mid-1980s. Kate Weaver, my colleague at Hopkins and a superb graphic artist, has consistently been able to take the most primitive hand-drawn illustrations and ideas and turn them into figures and tables that really do express what I was thinking. She has a rare gift and a great sense of humor. Susan Reynolds, Emily Leonard, Harriet Kaplan, Tiffany Klaff, and the rest of the editorial staff at the American Psychological Association are quietly superb in what they do for the membership and for their authors. I am truly and constantly amazed at their ability to question, point out where clarifications and changes are needed, and simultaneously let an author speak for him- or herself. Once again I am in their debt. Finally, I want to recognize my son, Ben; my brother, Jim; and my sisters, Amy Majetic and Jane Alcorn, whose constant love and consistent support have been a central part of my emotional life. Without such people in my life, this book would not have been possible.

Executive Wisdom

INTRODUCTION

Every book or intellectual project begins with a spark, a moment of inspiration, a penetrating insight that leads the author/protagonist/actor—could we say hero?—to an adventure in curiosity, a journey with many twists, turns, cul de sacs, breakthroughs, and a lot of work. This is particularly the case when the author possesses enough experience and sheer stubbornness to see the voyage through to a successful conclusion. As it often turns out, the end of the journey begins another story, which then leads to another story, and so on, in any sustained intellectual life. This book started at a dinner that I had with my colleague and friend, Catherine Fitzgerald, a psychologist, fellow executive coach, penetrating intellectual, voracious reader, and all-around wonderful person. Occasionally, we have a meal together and talk like kids do about their new toys, only in our case, the new toys are the books and articles we've been reading, the people we've been studying with, or the professional challenges we've encountered.

At this dinner, we spent a long time talking about executive cognition and the various approaches that we have explored. At one of our previous dinners, she had introduced me to Robert Kegan's work, and we were both interested in social constructionism as a methodology for coaching and as an intellectual tool. At some point in that discussion, we turned to the question of where cognitive development ultimately leads an executive. If I recall the exchange correctly, I said something like, "Well, the end state has to be something like becoming a wise person." She replied, "Have you seen Sternberg's book on that?" Of course I had not and, as often happens when I have dinner with Catherine, I ran up my Amazon bill when I got home.

Robert Sternberg's (1990) collection of papers on the subject of wisdom will stand as a sort of brilliant little gem in the history of psychological exploration of the topic, for it collected the best of the scholars who were working on the subject at that time. A small band of investigators had begun to raise questions about the good things that happen in late adult development instead of just documenting the declines. Holliday and Chandler (1986) did a marvelous job of succinctly documenting the early history of these studies in their research monograph that specifically demonstrated that human beings do carry around with them a rather consistent internal model of what constitutes a wise person. By the mid-1980s, the life span developmentalists had indeed begun to demonstrate that for human beings, old age is not just some place where society parks a person at the end of life devoid of virtue, energy, or the ability to contribute to society. Rather, old age is a destination, a specific stage of development in and of itself, and it possesses unique conflicts; challenges; and for those who successfully plumb its mysteries, untold treasures of human competence.

The study of wisdom also coincided with psychology's return to both its cognitive roots and its early foundations in the exploration of the foundations of morality and human character, as behaviorism finally gave up its choke hold on the science and a new generation of investigators created tools to penetrate the black boxes of the human brain and human mind. During the past 40 years, neuroscience, neurology, medicine, neuropsychology, and cognitive psychology have given humanity a more highly nuanced and greatly expanded understanding of what goes on in those most complex organs.

Reading Sternberg's collection of papers pushed me into these areas of research and practice and, paradoxically, right back to my own roots as a psychologist, for I had done both my master's and doctoral dissertation research projects using Piagetian concepts and methods under the supervision of Alex Siegel at the University of Pittsburgh (Kilburg & Siegel, 1973a, 1973b). Since that dinner with Catherine, the past 8 years or so of my intellectual voyaging have involved a delightful return to my youth and repeatedly reminded me of many of the conversations that Alex and I had in the early 1970s about where cognitive science would take psychology in the future.

I took the work of Sternberg and others and applied it liberally to my first book on executive coaching (Kilburg, 2000). Since then, I have continued to read, think, and practice on the basis of an increasingly wide and deep intellectual and philosophical foundation. For over the past 5 years,

I have found myself increasingly spending more and more time with the work of many of the finest human minds in history. In 2002, I was honored by the Society of Psychologists in Management with their Distinguished Psychologist in Management award. As is usual with awards, I was asked to give a talk to the attendees of their annual meeting, and it was on March 2 of that year that I gave my first presentation on what I called "Executive Wisdom." It represented an effort on my part to create a subset of the human wisdom literature that focused primarily on what it took to create wise leaders, because since I have read Sternberg's collection of papers, I have found myself looking at everything that I do and see in others through these concepts.

In my consulting work, in my personal life, in my efforts to provide leadership on human resource development initiatives at The Johns Hopkins University, and in my intellectual and spiritual explorations, I have been asking over and over and over, "What would be the wise thing to do?"; "What would a wise leader do?"; "Where does wisdom dwell in this situation?"; and "What is wisdom?" Repeatedly confronting these questions creates a rather daunting set of challenges, because they immediately force a different mind-set and emotional focus on anyone who asks them. They beg you to define *leadership wisdom* generally and specifically. They tease you to define its opposite, *leadership folly* or *stupidity*, and to avoid the foolishness and the catastrophes that it has created throughout human history. When asked repeatedly, these inquiries stimulate an aching human quest that turns out to be as old as the human ability to question itself systematically, for what I have found in my explorations is that humans— and indeed, the very best of humans—have pondered these issues truly and deeply for a very, very long time.

As just one brief example, Collins (1962), in a wonderful essay on wisdom, spent most of his time exploring what St. Thomas Aquinas and René Descartes had to say on the subject. Collins said in part,

> When Descartes opens the Discourse on Method with the famous remark that "good sense (bon sens) is mankind's most equitably divided endowment," he is not indulging in a fatuous optimism contradicted by every sober survey of human history. On the contrary, he is packing into a single phrase the result of his early reflections on wisdom or bona mens. To attribute good sense to mankind is to attribute to it the seed of wisdom, considered in an initial and minimal way as an intellectual impulse toward gaining a masterful understanding of ourselves and our destiny. Good sense is the basic germ of human intelligence which is dynamically ordered toward its proper perfection in moral wisdom. Thus good sense and bona mens are intrinsically and dynamically related as the initial and terminal moments in the human mind's quest of wisdom. (pp. 51–52)

These five, good, declarative sentences point us to the central challenge for our species and especially for our leaders. In the daily cacophony of executive life, how can leaders manage to create both *bon sens* and *bona mens* for themselves, for their organizations, and for all of humanity? When we humans invest our leaders with the power to determine our destiny, our very history as a species, simultaneously performing acts of profound faith and of an unconscious and biologically informed intraprimate compulsion to give power to someone who will lead us to safety, do we not hold our collective breath and silently pray that we are right? Do we not individually and, in our increasingly democratic times, often vocally, question the evidence that our leaders are demonstrating both good sense and wisdom? And in the sheer, brilliant, desperate hope of our democratic institutions, have we not reserved the right to change leaders when they show us that their thoughts, feelings, and actions are indeed stupid and taking us to the brink of some sort of destruction? Any cursory trip through human history shows that these issues are at the very heart of our collective journey and that both we and our ancestors have and continue to suffer from the foolishness of leaders and to benefit from their wisdom.

The next question then became how a passion for understanding human wisdom and applying it to the work of leadership can best be expressed. As I created my talk in early 2002, I knew that the answer was that if I were to write another book, it would focus on the subject of Executive Wisdom. And now, approximately 8 years after the dinner with Catherine Fitzgerald, years of reading, writing, speaking, thinking, consulting, coaching, leading, following, and feeling, I have tried to pour out what I have learned. In the middle of 2003, I approached Susan Reynolds, one of the acquisitions editors at the American Psychological Association (APA), to determine whether APA might be interested in publishing what could be thought of as a sequel to the book we did together on executive coaching in 2000. Much to my delight, I found her enthusiastic and supportive, and after the usual process of submitting a proposal for review, APA gave me the go-ahead for the project. For a full year, I pulled together what I had read, lectured on, and created in my own continuing search for wisdom. This book is the result.

It should be considered, as all books truly are, a report, a summary of my "work in progress." This is especially true of the quest for *bona mens*, for I have discovered that I stand at the very end of a truly long line of humans who have pondered these issues and questions. It is daunting to attempt to add to what people like Confucius, Socrates, Plato, Aristotle, Augustine, Cicero, St. Thomas Aquinas, and Descartes contributed, to say nothing of what the current generation of psychological scientists and management theorists and practitioners have been trying to do. In the end, it has been a special joy to simply assemble in my own way some ideas that I believe may assist both leaders and those who help develop them to understand that the supreme end to which they are pursuing their efforts is the creation and use of wisdom in the service of their organizations and their fellow humans.

I have tried to anchor this book simultaneously in human history, the trajectory of human thought on the subject of wisdom; in my own practice experience; and in the results of recent psychological science. Any such effort requires editorial judgment, for an author can never include everything that has been written, read, or thought in the work at hand. Thus, every book is a social construction that elevates some thoughts and promotes them for consideration while simultaneously excluding others with the judgment that they are less worthy. I have tried to be conscious in the act of this construction, explicit about my choices, and clear that I understand that the book is just that: my current best effort, within the page limit created for me, to select and report on what I think is important about this subject. I hope you as my readers will take the time to work through the material and then form your own judgment about the subject and how it might apply to you. In some of the chapters, you may find a little redundancy, a tendency to restate or re-present the work of a few people. This is especially true for Robert Sternberg, Paul Baltes, and Ursula Staudinger, perhaps the three preeminent psychological writers on wisdom, and Chris Argyris and Don Schön, those most intrepid organizational scholars and practitioners who first illuminated the issues of organizational defensiveness and the reflective methods that can counter it. I hope that the treatments of their concepts are specific to the material in each chapter, but I do want readers to understand that I believe that their ideas are almost universally applicable to the tasks of leadership and to the work of coaching and consulting.

This book tries to be both theoretical and practical. It summarizes ideas and research; tries to create some models that will help illuminate a very complex set of concepts; and provides some specific suggestions for what leaders and their coaches and consultants might do to improve the probability that they will perceive, decide, and act wisely. I hope that you will find the work both interesting and useful.

The remaining elements of this book are divided into two major sections. The first focuses on the foundations of Executive Wisdom and provides a set of concepts and illustrations that describe what I have come to understand about this subject. The second section focuses on *wisdom mapping*, what I now envision as a set of practices that individual leaders and executive groups can undertake to improve the probability that they will decide and act with more consistent long-term success.

Chapter 2 provides an explicit model of Executive Wisdom that focuses on three major components: discernment, decision making, and action. This model for the emergent function of Executive Wisdom is in turn embedded in a larger set of dimensions of individual, organizational, and environmental behavior that create the conditions for the occurrence of what I describe as wisdom, savvy, or stupidity in the performance of leaders. Chapter 3 focuses on the metacognitive and psychodynamic underpinnings of wise executive performance. A set of broad models is presented that help to explain the complexity that underlies the human capacity for wisdom.

Chapter 4 initiates the practical section of this book. I do not believe that an abstract discussion of Executive Wisdom contributes a lot to the art of leadership in action. A huge conceptual and research literature on leadership has emerged over the centuries, and yet repeatedly in my work with senior executives I find them struggling with the fundamental questions of what are the wisest things to do and ways to take action. It is a complete truism that leaders must act. As anyone with any experience knows, even their silences and refusals to take action are acts of leadership. Any book that proposes to help executives and those that help them lead must be practical and provide actual methods to improve their performance. So chapter 4 describes a complex set of barriers that can inhibit or prevent Executive Wisdom from occurring and an approach to overcoming those barriers that I call *wisdom mapping*. Chapters 5, 6, and 7 follow with explicit descriptions of a set of reflective methods that when applied by leaders, advisors, and their coaches, are more likely to promote wise decisions and actions. Chapter 5 focuses on gaining personal and family awareness to help improve executive function. This is the domain of emotional intelligence that has emerged over the past few years. Chapter 6 emphasizes the more traditional areas of organizational and executive group awareness that most texts, courses, articles, and consultation efforts tend to stress as the way that leaders can ensure their success. Chapter 7 completes the wisdom-mapping processes by covering methods to improve situational awareness, the application of moral and value compasses, and the operation of human wisdom itself.

Chapter 8 brings the conceptual and practical material together in an effort to demonstrate how leaders and their advisors can both see and walk the path to wisdom. It places special emphasis on the skills and processes of making decisions wisely and the various practices and pitfalls that every leader needs to know. I call this process *reflective engagement* and emphasize, along with a number of other modern authors, the need for leaders to be masters of taking stock of their situations and themselves and simultaneously being able to pursue vigorous and explicit action directed toward the goals that they set. Chapters 9 and 10 finish the book with an effort to address how leaders can act wisely in their executive groups. In many cases of executive derailment that have been reported in the literature, what has ultimately and most surely led to failure has not been leaders' ability to diagnose a situation accurately or even make a wise choice but their inability to implement their ideas and choices wisely in the context of their leadership teams. The chapters endeavor to explore a series of major issues that confront leaders as they actually try to execute their ideas with their colleagues.

I invite you to read these subsequent chapters and to walk this path with me for a while. On its completion, I guarantee that I will have made you think more deeply about what makes for the development and actual emergence of wisdom in leaders. I also guarantee that you will be exposed to some methods that may well help you to be wiser in your own personal and professional decisions and actions. I hope that you will come to agree with me that creating concepts and methods to enable executives to decide and behave wisely constitutes one of the major challenges of this or any other era in human history. Human culture and technology have finally handed the leaders of the species the means to protect and secure its future against most of the catastrophes that can befall it. Humans have simultaneously invented the means to virtually destroy life on the entire planet. *Homo sapiens* as a species now has the ability to be able to understand and to predict, if not yet totally control, what our ancestors repeatedly referred to and could only understand as acts of God. We now predict the path that hurricanes will take, the likelihood that tornados will strike, and that volcanoes will erupt. We can cure many forms of cancer and other formerly untreatable diseases. We are also in the process of destroying the coral reefs of our world's oceans, despoiling the coastlines of our nations, and extinguishing thousands and thousands of biological species from our planet. I have come to believe that as we humans take our first staggering steps into the 21st century, the fourth truly historical human millennium, that our collective fate remains in the hands of leaders deciding and acting either wisely or stupidly. We must collectively work toward wisdom and learn to systematically fear and work against leadership folly.

1

LEADERS AS IDIOTS AND GENIUSES IN HUMAN HISTORY

For the very true beginning of wisdom is the desire of discipline; and the care of discipline is love.

—*The Wisdom of Solomon*, 6:17

Pick up any textbook that focuses on human history and you will most probably begin to read a critical assessment of the leaders of the period under study. It is almost axiomatic that history is made by leaders, and in order for later generations to understand what happened to create the foundations for their social, psychological, and physical existence they must understand what the individuals charged with the responsibility for making choices on behalf of large segments of humanity did or did not do. In the past century, the study of leadership itself has taken many turns that have introduced new ways of understanding the phenomenon called *leading*.

When any scholar attempts to add substance to a well-established discipline like leadership, he or she is faced with a monumental task. How can one create a different way of seeing something that every other scholar in the field knows so well? How does one offer a perspective that will be seen as at least useful, if not establishing a wholly new paradigm? Potential readers are seasoned, critically thinking, and emotionally mature individuals who have themselves read, researched, practiced, and carefully considered the same material for years, if not decades. They will all open a new volume critically ready to administer judgment based on their own perspectives, their own experience, and their own values. You have opened this book in a similar fashion, perhaps hoping for something new, ready to be curious at least, if not ready to believe. How do I as an author, a colleague, a scholar, and a fellow traveler in the fields of leadership theory and practice capture your attention and, I hope, pieces of your mind and heart? It seems a daunting task. The purposes of this chapter are to provide a global introduction to the subject of Executive Wisdom through the exploration of five historical case studies and to provide the central thesis that has guided the creation of the extensive material that follows. The essence of that thesis is that leaders and those who try to help them develop do their best work when they are either creating or actually exercising wisdom in the service of their organizations.

Let us begin with a few questions. What makes a leader successful? Why do leaders fail? What can educators, mentors, coaches, and those others responsible for the development of leadership potential in humans do to increase the likelihood that those who are called to lead will do so well? How can those of us who help leaders become more sophisticated, more insightful, more caring, and much better at doing our jobs with them? Are there ways for us to better comprehend the complexities involved in assisting leaders with developing themselves and their organizations? As a practitioner of executive coaching, a leader of a fairly large group of human development professionals, a psychologist interested in these phenomena, and a human being struggling mightily to be as competent and helpful as possible in all of these complex roles, these questions and the pursuit of their answers haunt me every day. I regularly talk to, correspond with, or work alongside people who lead other humans and who often face tremendous stresses and strains in doing their work. This book is the result of my experiences, my journeys, my curiosity, and my values and beliefs. It represents an effort to add substance to the understanding and practice of leadership and to improve the ability of professional coaches of leaders to assess their clients and intervene with them in more efficient and effective ways. These, I realize, are large expectations. I hope that after they read this volume, my faithful readers will believe it was worth spending the time and effort on some complex and interesting ideas.

Where should we begin this effort to find answers to my questions? How can I capture your attention and your curiosity? Let me ask you another question. Have you ever had the personal experience of watching someone in a leadership position do or say something that made your eyes roll up into their sockets? That is, have you found yourself so profoundly disturbed by the event that you said to yourself, if only in the perpetual inner dialogues that constitute so much of our lives, "That has to be one of the stupidest things I've ever seen or heard"? Have you ever wanted in such a situation to stand up and fairly shout at the leader, "That's just plain idiotic, and you shouldn't do it!"? Have you ever tried to stop a leader from doing something reckless, inappropriately injurious, or downright criminal? If your answer is yes, then I think you will find some benefit in reading this book.

Simultaneously, have you ever had the experience of watching someone in a leadership position operate so skillfully, with such artistry, sensitivity, and nuanced long-term vision, spiced with an intuitive sense of what is needed immediately, and seen how the people around him or her respond with relief, certainty, security, determination, courage, and yes, even joy? Have you ever heard yourself think "God, that was a wise thing to say or do; I would never have thought of it"? Have you ever scratched your head trying to figure out just how a leader was able to move an organization of human beings to do something everyone else thought was impossible? Do you find yourself longing at times to have a client in whom you believe totally, or a boss whom you would want to follow in any endeavor at any time? If your answer to any of these questions is yes, then I think you will also find some benefit in reading this book.

Because in human history one can find endless examples of idiots and geniuses who have held positions of leadership, let us begin this journey together with a variety of case studies I have carved from various historical texts. Through the lens of human history, we can see more clearly the long-term effects of actions taken or not, ideas followed or not, plans that worked out well or did not. Through history, we can begin to explore the phenomenon that I call *Executive Wisdom*.

HANNIBAL'S CHOICE

One can imagine what he must have felt and dreamed; we know what he planned and did. In the year 219 B.C., Hannibal of Carthage took control of the western armies of that great historical competitor of Rome in the newly conquered and rising lands of what we now know as eastern Spain (Lancel, 1997). His father, the legendary Hamilcar Barca, had drowned 10 years earlier while leading a retreat of Carthaginian forces across the Jucar River, also in Spain. At that point, Rome and Hannibal's country had been locked in furious competition and war for the control of the western Mediterranean basin for well over 100 years. Neither empire had been strong enough to eliminate the other.

Carthage had survived by using its naval skills and relying on an extensive history of colonization and trade. Rome's larger empire, extensive alliances, and land-based legions gave it a continual competitive edge. Earlier that century, the extended war with Carthage for Sicily had finally driven Rome to develop its own effective naval forces. The Romans learned slowly, but they learned well.

Using their new naval expertise, the Romans had defeated the Carthaginians; eliminated their colonies in Sicily, Sardinia, and Corsica; and negotiated a treaty with them in 241 B.C. in which they imposed reparations and limitations on their expansion. Carthage responded by vigorously and secretly expanding its efforts in Iberia (Spain), then beyond the reach of Rome's navy and army. They used well-established trading colonies that they had established there as bases for their expansion. Those outposts had been loyal to them for hundreds of years. Hamilcar had already heroically defended and saved Carthage in 238 B.C. from its own mercenaries who had attacked the empire after the defeat in Sicily. He was put in charge of the western initiative by the leaders of Carthage in the hopes that his military and political skills would gain new sources of strength for their empire. Hannibal and Hasdrubal, his two young sons, were with him during these military and political campaigns. Sometime during the year 235 B.C., Hamilcar, about to begin the Iberian campaign, took his son Hannibal to the altar of Zeus and made him swear an oath before that most powerful god never to be a friend to the Romans (Lancel, 1997).

Sixteen years after taking that oath, Hannibal, inheritor of his father's looks, military and political genius, and fanatical hatred of the Romans, decided to invade the heartland of Rome in an effort to destroy its war-making capacity and force a lasting peace on that belligerent and expansive empire. His exploits in crossing the Alps and the military successes in the center of Roman territory, culminating in the crushing defeat of Rome's armies at Cannae in 216 B.C., have remained the stuff of human legend and military history for over 2 millennia. His decision to lead his forces into the heart of Rome was fully supported by the elders of Carthage. Unfortunately, it proved to be a lethal choice for their empire.

Over the next 10 years, as Hannibal's armies raged through their homeland, the Romans reorganized themselves and successfully attacked and eliminated the Carthaginian bases in Iberia. In 203 B.C., deprived of reinforcements, cut off at sea by a now much-superior Roman navy, and knowing that Carthage itself was under attack by large Roman armies led by Scipio Africanus, Hannibal made his way home. In 202 B.C., the elders asked him to protect their empire. Outside the city of Zama Regia, now known as Jama, Scipio and Hannibal, two legends in history, led their forces to a fateful battle that ended in the complete destruction of the Carthaginian army. After imposing a humiliating peace that restricted all expansion of their empire, required significant reparations, and forced them to request permission to undertake any acts of war, the Romans left a garrison and went home. From the moment they signed that agreement, Carthage became essentially an agricultural colony for more than 50 years.

The Romans also feared their competitors in the east, and after vanquishing Carthage, they turned their attention in that direction. When the Romans finally secured their eastern flank by defeating the Macedonians at Pydna of Perseus in 168 B.C., they started to conceive their own "final solution" to the Carthaginian problem. In 149 B.C., they delivered an ultimatum to the leaders of Carthage, demanding that they leave their city and resettle at least 15 kilometers from the Mediterranean. The Carthaginians, who were the inheritors of the Phoenician thrust to the west by the greatest sailors of that millennium, the leaders of a culture that had been founded in 814 B.C., 665 years earlier and much older than Rome itself, refused. In the spring of 146 B.C., Scipio Aemilianus, the adopted son of the general who had defeated Hannibal, sacked and burned Carthage after an 18-month siege. The empire that had challenged Rome for supremacy for more than 200 years simply ceased to exist.

Hannibal's decision in 219 to invade and defeat Rome via the Alps, supported by his advisors, by the leaders of the Empire, and by their Gallic and Iberian allies looked to all involved at the time as a brilliant military and political stroke. An initial success in its first 3 years, it then drained the Carthaginians of all of their best military resources for the next decade. As Hannibal occupied the center of Italy, the Romans cut off their colonies, crippled them economically, took away their sea lanes and sources of commerce, and ultimately brought the war to the gates of their capital city. Seventeen years after his initial decision, Hannibal, defeated and humiliated, fled to Antioch for his own survival, where, years later, he died in peace. Carthage itself ended in blood and flames for most inhabitants and slavery for those who surrendered to Scipio.

KING JOHN'S CHOICE

From 1199 to 1215 A.D., King John of England faced a nearly impossible set of conditions. He needed to raise money and men at arms for the third crusade to free the "Holy Lands." Richard I had been captured by Henry VI, the Holy Roman Emperor, and was being held for a huge ransom. John's hold on the throne, already shaky, was worsened by an attack on Normandy by the French. Ultimately, in 1204, he lost Normandy, Britain's foothold on the continent of Europe. His barons had been vigorously prodded to support him during those 16 years, but they had grown restless and rebellious. John also had a running fight with Pope Innocent III from 1208 through 1213, during which he levied heavy taxes against the English Catholic Church ("Magna Carta," 1986).

In 1215 A.D., Stephen Langton, the Archbishop of Canterbury, fearful of a devastating civil war developing between the king and his barons in the heart of England, organized and focused the dissatisfaction and rebellious motivation of the barons into a demand for a formal set of liberties to be granted by the king. After substantive negotiations, the parties reached a settlement. On June 15, 1215 A.D., at Runnymede, which is adjacent to the River Thames, King John signed the first version of the Magna Carta.

That charter of rights became the law of the land. It consisted of a preamble and 63 clauses dealing with everything from the freedom of the Church to the laws of landholding, the reform of law, and the execution of justice. Rewritten several times during subsequent decades, it was reissued by subsequent kings of England and came to form the foundation for what we now call *English common law*. It also laid down the first principles of a more democratic form of government.

At the time, it must have seemed to John to be a humiliating and overwhelming defeat. Weakened by wars, sitting precariously on the throne, facing extinction as a leader, he sued for peace. He succeeded in what must have been his major goal, namely, the tactical strategy of keeping his throne. More important, and probably without conscious intent, he and his contemporaries established an entirely new way for human beings with power to relate to each other and to those without such influence. Over time, the rule of law gradually replaced the rule of the throne and the rule of the church as the primary form of governance in human communities. Under the rule of law, average people eventually gained the freedom to participate directly in elections of leaders and thus a measure of control over their destinies. Governments began to protect both the weak and the strong in society, thus establishing a way for people to resolve conflicts without violence and to live more peacefully and justly together. Because many of its principles have been incorporated into laws and constitutions throughout the human world, the Magna Carta stands as one of the crowning human accomplishments of the last millennium. I think it is safe to say that if it had been solely up to John, as a traditional king in the full blossom of his powers, he would have never signed the original document. His weakness as a king and his short-term defeat ironically turned this act into one of the wisest choices made by any leader in human history.

WILSON'S CHOICE: THE TREATY OF VERSAILLES

In the autumn of 1918, parts of Europe lay in ruins as a result of the "war to end all wars." Germany, exhausted by 4 years of stalemated combat, asked Woodrow Wilson to arrange an armistice. They accepted his 14 Points, and negotiations for a treaty began. Eight months later, on June 28, 1919, the Germans, French, British, and Americans signed the treaty in the Hall of Mirrors at Versailles. During the deliberations, the Germans were excluded from every discussion except the signing ceremony. The "big four"—Woodrow Wilson for America, David Lloyd George for Britain, Georges Clemenceau for France, and Vittorio Orlando for Italy—negotiated the terms and conditions and forced them on Germany. The treaty stripped that country of substantial territory in Europe and colonies in other parts of the world, eliminated the high command of the German army, and limited its ability to manufacture munitions and armaments and the size of its army to 100,000 men-at-arms. The terms of the treaty also required the Germans to accept public guilt for the entire war. It established a bill for the destruction in France and Belgium of $33 billion and required ruinous payment schedules that contributed to the rise of hyperinflation in Germany during the 1920s. As a result, Germany's leadership and the entire population of the country were publicly humiliated. The German people were abandoned by the major powers of the time and left alone to cope with a destroyed economy and their own grief from a terribly costly war.

Woodrow Wilson, seriously ill and primarily motivated by his desire to establish the League of Nations, agreed to the terms of the treaty despite his reservations about the goals and the ultimate outcomes of the provisions. The treaty did establish the League of Nations, through which member nations guaranteed each other's sovereignty. Despite the fanfare of its establishment, it failed utterly to reach its goals.

The Treaty of Versailles was revised several times during the 1920s, but by the 1930s the allies had virtually ceased any efforts to enforce its provisions. As we know, the global depression of the 1930s and the economic ruin of the previous decade laid the foundation for the rise of Hitler's Third Reich; the Axis Powers; and the horrifying reign of terror they unleashed on Europe, Asia, and Africa. Designed to create a lasting peace and to ensure that Germany would never again be a war threat in the heart of Europe, the terms and conditions of the agreement led paradoxically to the very end that the negotiators feared the most: a new and even more devastating war with Germany (Boemeke, Feldman, & Glaser, 1998).

TRUMAN'S CHOICE

On April 26, 1947, less than 2 years after the end of World War II, Secretary of State George Marshall returned to the United States after extensive meetings with his counterpart, Molotov, in Moscow. He had also met with Stalin during that grueling trip. Marshall had concluded that the Russians were completely unwilling to act constructively on the future of western Europe. He had also seen with his own eyes the immense deprivation and desperation of the people in Berlin and Paris. On April 28, in a radio broadcast, Marshall stated that "the patient is sinking while the doctors deliberate" (McCullough, 1992, p. 562). The next day, he asked George Kennan to pull a staff together and craft a plan to save Europe. On May 14, Churchill said Europe had become "a rubble heap, a charnel house, a breeding ground of pestilence and hate" (McCullough, 1992, p. 562).

On May 25, Kennan delivered his report, entitled "Certain Aspects of the European Recovery Problem from the United States' Standpoint." After less than 2 weeks of intense deliberations within the Truman Administration, Marshall, with the approval of the President, delivered the commencement speech at Harvard on June 5. He said, in part,

> It would be neither fitting nor efficacious for this Government to undertake to draw up unilaterally a program designed to place Europe on its feet economically. That is the business of the Europeans. This initiative, I think, must come from Europe. The role of this country should consist of friendly aid in the drafting of a European program and of later support for such a program so far as it is practical for us to do so. The program should be a joint one, agreed to by a number [of], if not all, European nations. (McCullough, 1992, p. 563)

Truman proceeded to invite all of Europe to a conference. Even the Russians attended. Five days after the start of deliberations, Molotov left the meeting on instructions from Moscow. Seventeen nations eventually decided to join together in what became known as the "European Recovery Plan." Crafted by George Marshall, George Kennan, Dean Acheson, Paul Nitze, Arthur Vandenberg, Clark Clifford, Charles Bohlen, William Clayton, and others, the proposal was eventually put before Congress. Clark Clifford urged the president to call it the "Truman Plan." Characteristically, the president refused and insisted that Marshall be given full credit. He remained true to his often-repeated belief that "much could be accomplished if you didn't care who received the credit" (McCullough, 1992, p. 564).

Later that year, Congress approved the Marshall Plan and allocated $17 billion that eventually would be given to the Europeans to decide how they themselves would best reconstruct their countries. The idea of inter-European collaboration on economic and political issues was thus conceived and executed. A strong German state in the center of Europe and of European affairs remained a key concept of the plan. The ideas and actions were unprecedented in history. Winners of a war would not extract reparations and continue to punish, rape, and pillage the lands and people of the defeated nation; instead, Americans would use their own resources to rebuild the countries and economies of their former enemies. Even the nation that was distrusted the most, Russia, was invited to participate. It was a risk, a proposal, a vision as breathtaking in its farsightedness as it was in costs.

Nearly 60 years later, Germany stands reunited. Europe now has a single currency, and its countries act together in a common political structure on economic, political, and military affairs. Relations with Russia have become more cordial, and thousands of years of warfare, intra-European political conflict, and devastation have been halted, at least temporarily. The creators of the Marshall Plan were trying to prevent a nightmare from becoming a real and all-consuming monster. They were trying to contain the spread of a communist ideology and political system that were the antithesis of the hard-won gains of the representative democracies. They were also trying to stay in political office. The next year, Truman ran for president and, in a victory that surprised everyone, was elected to his own term of office. His strength of character and his willingness to delegate strongly and to support the actions of people of courage, integrity, and real wisdom proved crucial to saving humanity from an even more devastating conflict in Europe. In supporting the emergence and implementation of the Marshall Plan, he enabled the world to see what Europeans could accomplish by working together instead of waging war on each other. Collectively, 60 years have passed without overt acts of war between the major countries of Europe. It has been a monumental and transgenerational accomplishment. Events in Yugoslavia during the 1990s aside, we have seen at least a temporary end of nearly 3,000 years of more or less continuous competition and open conflict in that part of the world.

DARKNESS AND LIGHT: QUEEN ISABELLA AND THE STORMS OF SPAIN

Born in 1451, Isabella was the daughter of King John II of Castile. When her father died in 1454, she was 3 years old, and her brother, Henry IV, became the king. Her mother protected her for the next 10 years, raising her carefully in Arevalo. However, when Isabella turned 13, Henry brought her and her other brother, Alfonso, to court, ostensibly to educate and protect her but in reality to protect himself from plots and maneuvers from Spanish nobles who would have used the young family members for their own ends. As she became an adolescent in 1464, Isabella began her leadership and political careers.

In 1468, 4 years later, Isabella's brother Alfonso lay poisoned and dead. Henry declared her to be the heiress to the throne, shocking the entire country by choosing her over his own daughter, Joan, who was thought to be the illegitimate child of his second wife, Joan of Portugal, and a favorite noble and confidant, Beltran de la Cueva. Isabella, now 17, showed remarkable maturity by refusing both the throne and the title and declaring that while her other brother lived, she would never be queen. However, in a remarkable episode of executive stupidity, Henry made her his direct heir in the same year anyway. For the previous 8 years, he had repeatedly maneuvered to marry her to a variety of nobles from Spain and other countries. All of these unions would have benefited his crown, and yet Isabella managed to stalemate all of them. She wanted to marry Ferdinand of Aragon, and when her brother journeyed to Andalusia in 1869, she escaped from Henry's grasp and went to Valladolid with the aid of her friends and supporters. From there, she sent word to Ferdinand, who made his way to her, and they were married that same year. She was 18 years old.

A few years later, Henry died and Isabella became the Queen of Castile. It took her until 1480 to clear her title, when Henry's daughter, Joan, completely renounced all claim to it and entered a convent. Ferdinand also succeeded his father as the King of Aragon during the same time period and, through their marriage, the throne of Spain was unified. Over the next few years, Isabella and Ferdinand took a variety of measures to consolidate their power over the nobles of Spain, including rescinding land grants, eliminating the nobles' power to coin money, and establishing a civil court system and a central army. Once they created the army, they began the reconquest of the Moorish parts of Spain in 1482. About the same time, they petitioned Pope Sixtus IV of Rome to start the Inquisition as a way of protecting themselves from the influence of Spanish Jews. Isabella and Ferdinand waged war against the Moors for 10 years and finally defeated and expelled them at the battle for Granada in January of 1492. In March of that year, they ordered the approximately 170,000 Jewish inhabitants of Spain to leave the country, thereby eliminating what they viewed as the last major threat to their rule over all of Spain.

As Isabella and Ferdinand were completing their conquest of Granada, Padre Hernando Talavera, Isabella's confessor, and Cardinal Mendoza introduced her to Christopher Columbus. Despite their preoccupation with domestic security and the military and political integration of Spain, they listened carefully to the Italian sailor and then agreed to support financially his exploratory adventure. They provided the funds to outfit three ships, which were organized and launched on August 3, 1492. By October 12, 1492, Columbus made landfall in the Bahamas and ushered in a new age in human history, an era in which the European domination of culture, economics, politics—indeed, of history itself—would slowly make room for the rise of the United States of America; of Asian countries such as China, Japan, and India; and of radically different forms of government, technology, and culture.

Isabella supported all four of Columbus's trips to the Americas and the establishment of new colonies there despite the initial disappointments of not finding a route to the Indies or major discoveries of gold and silver. When she heard of the atrocities committed against the native tribes of the Caribbean Islands, she established the Secretariate of Indian Affairs, which proved a largely symbolic gesture and completely unable to prevent the exploitation and eradication of most of the native inhabitants of the new lands. Over the course of the next 12 years, she and her husband Ferdinand ruled a united Spain that slowly began to emerge and build a global empire. Isabella died on November 26, 1454, at the age of 53. She had a remarkable career as a leader during that time period. Somehow, in the middle of major domestic political crises and a war over the integration of her country, she managed to raise her sights and to see the possibility of a world that was round, not flat; expanded in opportunities, not hemmed in by history and ancient feuds; and without the traditional boundaries of the existing nation-states of the day. Her capacity to rise above her moment in history and to both envision and enable experiments of change on such an enormous stage place her squarely as one of the wisest rulers humanity has ever seen. Of course, the same acts of leadership and historical events when viewed through the eyes of the native Americans that the Spaniards conquered, enslaved, and decimated would produce quite the opposite opinion of her ability to see the world in a new way and to somehow find the funding to support changing it. For those native Americans; and the Jews, who were systematically persecuted during the Spanish Inquisition and then expelled from their homes; and the Moors, who had lived in the south of Spain for centuries—for all of them, Isabella could only be thought of as an oppressive and homicidal tyrant (Rubin, 1992).

CENTRAL THESIS

I have started this book with these examples because they illustrate my central thesis. Executives and leaders of organizations, including nation-states and human empires, are required by their offices, their roles, and their times to make and execute decisions that often have the most profound consequences for themselves, their enterprises, and human history. I believe that those who have such roles and responsibilities and those who support and help develop them should have an extensive and fundamental grasp of the challenges of these offices and an understanding of how difficult it is for leaders to make and implement wise choices even under the best of circumstances.

Hannibal, inheritor of his father's mantle and burning inside with a long-declared oath of hatred, wanted to end the threat to and humiliation of his people. He and the elders of his country surely did not foresee the end of Carthage in their decision to invade Rome. King John was dragged to the bargaining table and virtually forced to share the substantial powers of his throne. Undoubtedly, he would not have done so if he had felt that he had the ability to resist, and he would have been appalled at the idea that kings and kingdoms would become mostly a relic of history at least in part because of the agreement he reached. President Wilson, rightly convinced that it would take an international organization with enforcement powers to end the psychosis of international anarchy, agreed to a set of conditions that led Europe inevitably to what it, and he, feared most: a deeply humiliated and enraged Germany and major new devastation of the European continent. He did not live to see the result of the decisions made at Versailles. Truman, trying to hold onto office, resisting the Russian-led onslaught of communism, working hard to prevent widespread starvation in Europe, and leading a nation still healing after nearly 2 decades of economic privation and war-time suffering, decided to open up the all-too-limited treasury of his own country and give recent mortal enemies some control over the disposition of those resources. He could not have completely understood the monumental scope of what would happen in the future as a result of that generosity.

Queen Isabella, at the end of a decade-long war to consolidate the throne and nation of Spain, cared enough about the future of her subjects and of her country to create funding for a little-known dreamer named Christopher Columbus to sail into history. At the time, it probably seemed like a small thing to do compared with the other challenges that occupied her. However, her actions led Spain to the pinnacle of its greatest power and, even more important some 500 years later, completely shifted the focus of Western history away from its traditional foundation in Europe and toward a global village of nation-states. Three decisions by Truman, Isabella, and King John resulted in tremendously good results, if not for the individual leaders, then for their worlds or those that followed. Two others, by Hannibal and Wilson, ended in disaster. Although we cannot be certain, it is probably safe to say that all of these decision makers at the times of their leadership trials surely thought they were making the wisest, best, or at least cleverest of possible decisions. No leader I have met or read about deliberately chooses folly and foolishness. Nevertheless, history records and provides us with example after example of leaders who decide or act stupidly.

These few excerpts from ancient and modern history demonstrate that the wisdom of leaders, what I have called *Executive Wisdom* (Kilburg, 2000), is in fact an ephemeral entity. Every person in an executive role reaches toward wisdom, is expected to have wisdom, and wants to be wise. Unfortunately, as these cases also show, all too often senior leaders fail in this central and most important task of their offices. In the remainder of this book, I argue that Executive Wisdom is an emergent property of the incredibly complex set of structures; processes; and social, economic, political, and psychological contents in which every leader is immersed. I examine three principal questions. First, what is this thing I have labeled *Executive Wisdom*? Although I believe most of us know it when we see it, virtually all of the authors who have written about leadership since Plato and Aristotle have ignored the specific subject of wisdom in leadership. Second, how does Executive Wisdom develop or come to exist? Can one sufficiently delineate its properties so that organizations and executive-development specialists, such as coaches, could come to possess some practical ideas of what do to aid its creation in individual leaders? Finally, how can executives and their coaches practice wisdom in their work? Are there tools or skills that leaders can acquire that will enable them to be consistently wiser in the choices they make and the actions they take? The prospect that such methods and practices exist and could be used to help anyone with leadership authority improve performance in his or her core responsibilities presents a tantalizing prospect, one that should be pursued vigorously in a world with an exploding human population, seething and very often bloody ethnic tensions, looming environmental catastrophes, and major resource misalignments. These issues, along with the questions that opened this chapter, serve as the guiding framework for what is to follow.

2

FOUNDATIONS OF EXECUTIVE
WISDOM: A MODEL
OF EXECUTIVE WISDOM

... so that he may prudently know all things divine and human.
—Guillaume Budé

Human wisdom has been a subject of study for as long as humans have been aware of the necessity to make difficult choices. Metaphysically, the search for wisdom can be dated as early as the Book of Genesis and the story of Adam and Eve. The devil himself tempts the mother of all humans with the fruit of the knowledge of good and evil. The consumption of the fruit leads Eve to share it with Adam, and through that act they discover both that they are naked and that they need to hide from God. In short, knowledge of good and evil leads them to be self-aware, to know that they have gone against the command of God, and to feel shame and guilt. Within the Judeo–Christian–Islamic tradition, the progressive development of human culture can be traced to these mythological events and to the ability of humans to reason and decide for themselves what is right and wrong, what must be done and avoided, and what the fate of the species will be. In essence, first Eve and then Adam decide to substitute human wisdom and judgment for that of almighty God and thereby initiate the whole of what we have come to know as history. Leaders of the extraordinary organizations humans have created by the beginning of the 21st century are now endowed with godlike powers within the boundaries of those entities. What they say must be heeded. What they order must be obeyed. What they think and feel must be accommodated. The directions they set, particularly those chosen by leaders of human governments, often determine who lives, who dies, and why. In our collective dependency on the thoughts and actions of such leaders, we frequently find ourselves hoping and praying that what they have chosen for us in the end will be a wise, if not divine, intervention.

Wisdom and the processes for developing leaders who possessed it can be seen as central issues during the emergence of both the Eastern and Western philosophical traditions. Confucius was born in 552 B.C., preceding Socrates and Plato by a century. Core pieces of his pragmatic philosophy can be summarized in the following:

> The illustrious ancients, when they wished to make clear and to propagate the highest virtues in the world, put their states in proper order. Before putting their states in proper order, they regulated their families. Before regulating their families, they cultivated their own selves. Before cultivating their own selves, they perfected their souls. Before perfecting their souls, they tried to be sincere in their thoughts. Before trying to be sincere in their thoughts, they extended to the utmost their knowledge. Such investigation of knowledge lay in the investigation of things, and in seeing them as they really were. When things were thus investigated, knowledge became complete. When knowledge was complete, their thoughts became sincere. When their thoughts became sincere, their souls became perfect. When their souls were perfect, their own selves became cultivated. When their selves were cultivated, their families became regulated. When their families were regulated, their states came to be put into proper order. When their states were in proper order, then the whole world became peaceful and happy. (Little, 2002, p. 12)

To this Confucius added the following idea: "The greatest fortune of a people would be to keep ignorant persons from public office, and secure their wisest men to rule them" (Little, 2002, p. 12). Thus, from one of the earliest and best-known human philosophers, we see intimate connections made among the need to develop as individual human beings, the good of the state or human collectives, and the importance of finding wise people for positions of leadership. For more than 2,500 years, great thinkers have been writing and saying the same crucial things.

In the 4th century B.C., as reported in Plato's *Republic*, Socrates identified four cardinal virtues—wisdom, temperance, courage, and justice—as being at the heart of the truly great city and the truly best people. In Socrates' dialogue with Glaucon in Book 4 of that volume, he said "This city which we have described is, I think, really wise. For it is prudent in deliberation, is it not?"

"Yes," Glaucon replied.

"And this faculty of prudent deliberation is clearly a kind of knowledge. For obviously, it is by reason of knowledge and not of ignorance that their deliberations are prudent" (Plato, 1999, pp. 110–111).

From this foundation statement, Plato went on to distinguish wisdom, which he called *sophia*, from belief. Knowledge itself was a related concept called *episteme*. Robinson (1990) elaborated on the core Platonic ideas on wisdom, suggesting that Socrates distinguished three separable forms of the virtue: (a) *sophia*, which represents the wisdom in those who retreat from secular life to contemplate divine truths; (b) *phronesis*, the form of wisdom held by senior statesmen and leaders of nations; and (c) *episteme*, which evolves in those who accrue scientific knowledge through intensive study.

The truly wise leaders are those who love *sophia* and *episteme* and who pursue and practice them with temperance and courage. By doing so, they produce justice for people and for the city itself and thus become *phronesis* artists. For Plato, these truly wise practitioners were philosopher kings who, after extensive education, he believed should be given their roles by a grateful population that would look to them for continued leadership and guidance. He also stated explicitly that leaders must leave their positions from time to time for periods of reflection and continued study if they are to continue to develop their virtues and capacity to govern.

Many of the greatest minds of antiquity, the Middle Ages, the Renaissance, and modern times have continued to be preoccupied with the idea of wisdom: how it can be defined; studied; and, most important for the fate of humankind, obtained by those in positions of leadership. E. F. Rice (1958) provided a tremendously valuable summary of ancient and Renaissance ideas about wisdom. He traced the obsession of Western thinkers with *sapientia*, the Latin term for the wisdom or knowledge of the divine, and with *scientia*, or the knowledge or wisdom of that which is human. The dialogues and debates about the roots and practices of wisdom have raged for millennia. For the ancients, the medievalists, the Renaissance explorers, and the pre-industrialists, the fundamental distinctions made by Aristotle and Plato formed the foundation of virtually all of the discussions. On the one hand, there is the knowledge of things divine and absolute, what we have traditionally understood as in the realm of God, of religion and metaphysics. On the other hand, there is the knowledge of the universe, of what humans can discover and comprehend through their own efforts. The dialectic between God knowledge and the human hand reaching for such knowledge as it can possess continues to inform, if not enrage, philosophical, political, religious, and scientific discussions to this day.

Speaking about the transcendent nature of wisdom and its relationship to the divine, Nicholas of Cusa stated in 1450,

That is highest which cannot be higher. Only infinity is so high. Of wisdom, therefore, which all men by nature desire to know and seek with such mental application, one can know only that it is higher than all knowledge and thus unknowable, unutterable in any words, unintelligible to any intellect, unmeasurable by any measure, unlimitable by any limit, unterminable by any term, unproportionable by any proportion, incomparable by any comparison, unfigurable by any figuration, unformable by any formation, unmovable by any motion, unimaginable by any imagination, insensible to any sense, unattractable by any attraction, untasteable by any taste, inaudible to any ear, invisible to any eye, unapprehendable by any apprehension, unaffirmable in any affirmation, undeniable by any negation, indubitable by any doubt, and no opinion can be held about it. And since it is inexpressible in words, one can imagine an infinite number of such expressions, for no conception can conceive the wisdom through which, in which and of which all things are. (De Cusa, quoted in E. F. Rice, 1958, pp. 9–10)

Cusan logic and advocacy about wisdom, along with that of St. Thomas Aquinas (1981) in his *Summa Theologica*, formed much of the foundation for the Christian philosophical and theological explorations of wisdom in the Middle Ages. As we can see in de Cusa's words above, he left no doubt about humans' inability to attain what he saw as the divine virtue of wisdom, while simultaneously acknowledging the universal human desire to stretch to and obtain it (E. F. Rice, 1958).

Similarly, Collins (1962) in his insightful essay discussed the work of St. Thomas Aquinas and Descartes on wisdom in the context of Plato and Aristotle. He quoted St. Thomas's summary of Aristotle's definition of the wise man as follows: "The wise man is described as one who knows all, even difficult matters, with certitude and through their cause; who seeks this knowledge for its own sake; and who directs others and induces them to act" (Collins, 1962, p. 132). He also pointed out how easy it is for a subject to fall out of focus in the halls of academic study despite its universal applicability, appeal, and importance. He went on to say,

> Natural philosophical wisdom and religious wisdom are threatened by the specializing demands made upon our intelligence and by the manipulative attitude taken toward all values in nature and society. It is difficult to be wise in the unrestricted sense in a world where only the limited and instrumental significance of men and things is permitted to attract our minds. (Collins, 1962, p. 138)

His words were prophetic, for where in business journals and the seemingly endless series of books written about various aspects of leadership in the past 40 years does the specific subject of the necessity for leaders to pursue and practice wisdom even arise? The short answer is rarely, because each journal article as well as each book tends to be earnestly focused on what is narrow and differentiable from the work of others. Efforts to integrate ideas and work across generations of authors, practitioners, and scholars tend to be limited to books published by small academic presses and to be read by small bands of what one could think of as radical intellectual explorers.

In this vein, modernism and the postmodern challenge to logical positivism and scientific method (Gergen, 1999) have forced virtually every field of academic inquiry to incorporate new ideas about cherished truths and beliefs. In this recent intellectual tradition, humans are forced to confront their assumptions; to try to provide such data as are available to defend their suppositions; and most recently, to recognize that every argument, whether supported by data or infallible logic, is in the end a construction of human thought. Such constructions are always open to challenge with postmodern methods on the basis of the essential fact that anyone making an argument chooses some words, ideas, representations, and data to support his or her view. Through such choices, those views or arguments are automatically granted power and privilege over those views that are not present in the words, ideas, and data. In the worst cases, what can be shown as an irrefutable proposition made by a scholar, a politician, or a leader of one religion or another turns out to be merely a very good job of editing in information and logic that supports his or her thesis and eliminating that which supports the antithesis.

Thus, from some of the foundational philosophical concepts of both the Eastern and Western worlds, we come to see wisdom as a process of careful consideration in the creation of human decisions and actions that produce goodness for society and for individuals in the form of justice. *The Oxford English Dictionary* (Simpson & Weiner, 1998) confirms this emphasis, stating that *wisdom* is "the capacity of judging rightly in matters relating to life and conduct; soundness of judgment in the choice between means and ends; sometimes, less strictly, sound sense esp. in practical affairs; opposite to folly" (p. 2325). We see here in this more modern definition a confirmation of the combination of judgment, decisions, and actions. The wise person reasons and acts with practical prudence and presumably thus avoids folly.

The literatures of philosophy, metaphysics, theology, history, religion, economics, political science, and even the hard sciences are replete with efforts to understand, engage, and teach others about wisdom. Any effort to understand the subject thoroughly, let alone to offer comprehensive ideas on its development and use, is thus a daunting undertaking and is well beyond the purposes of this book. However, one does not need to conduct a complete survey of human thought about wisdom to reach an agreement that in general terms, all of humanity would be better off in the long run if those individuals chosen or otherwise selected to lead others possessed wisdom and applied it generously in their daily work.

Counter to the trend of the study of wisdom falling out of academic focus in many disciplines, scientific psychology has in recent decades turned to studies of wisdom to further refine its long-held fascination with human intelligence and as a way of determining how humans come to live good and just lives. So now the discipline of psychology is hot on the trail of this most ancient and rare characteristic of human behavior. Recent reviews of the modern scientific literature are available in Sternberg (1990, 1999, 2003, 2005), Brown (2000), and Baltes and Staudinger (2000). A search of the PsycLIT database on the topic of wisdom for this book yielded more than 1,300 entries.

Two major conceptual approaches appear to have evolved in the literature of scientific psychology: Sternberg's (1990, 1999, 2003, 2005) balance theory of wisdom and Baltes and Staudinger's (2000) Berlin wisdom model (Baltes, Gluck, & Kunzmann, 2002). Sternberg sees wisdom as the application of tacit knowledge in pursuing the goal of a common good. First and foremost, it requires a balance of intra-, inter-, and extrapersonal interests and a balance of responses to the environmental context through the choice of shaping, selection, or adaptation strategies over short and longer periods of time. The application of successful intelligence and important human values are key parts of the exercise of wisdom. Sternberg (2003) stated,

> Wisdom is not just about maximizing one's own or someone else's self-interest, but about balancing various self-interests (intrapersonal) with the interests of others (interpersonal), and of other aspects of the context in which one lives (extrapersonal), such as one's city or country or environment or even God. Wisdom also involves creativity, in that the wise solution to a problem may be far from obvious. ... when one applies successful intelligence and creativity, one may deliberately seek outcomes that are good for oneself and bad for others. In wisdom, one certainly may seek good ends for oneself, but one also seeks common good outcomes for others. If one's motivations are to maximize certain people's interests and minimize other people's, wisdom is not involved. In wisdom, one seeks a common good, realizing that this common good may be better for some that for others. (pp. 152–153)

In a recent article, Sternberg (2005) crystallized his approach to applying his model to the work of leadership by using the acronym WICS, which stands for wisdom, intelligence, and creativity synthesized. He stated that

> effective leadership is, in large part, a function of creativity in generating ideas, analytical intelligence in evaluating the quality of these ideas, practical intelligence in implementing the ideas, and convincing others to value and follow the ideas, and wisdom to ensure that the decisions and their implementation are for the common good of all stakeholders. (Sternberg, 2005, p. 29)

In this article, he made a special point of emphasizing five forms of stereotyped fallacies in thinking in which he believes leaders often engage:

1. The *unrealistic-optimism fallacy*—believing only good things will result from one's ideas and actions.
2. The *egocentrism fallacy*—believing that one's opinions are the only ones that matter.
3. The *omniscience fallacy*—believing one knows everything.
4. The *omnipotence fallacy*—believing one can do what one wants.
5. The *invulnerability fallacy*—believing one can get away with anything.

Through the remainder of this book, I will further elaborate the theoretical and practical foundations and the real consequences of these fallacies in the thinking of leaders in greater detail.

Baltes and Staudinger (2000) defined *wisdom* as an "expert system . . . of the fundamental pragmatics of life" (p. 124). They and their colleagues have constructed what is probably the most comprehensive model of human wisdom currently available, which they call the *Berlin wisdom paradigm* (because they were working at a Berlin institution when they created the model). I spend more time on this model a little later in this chapter.

Can we distinguish between what we can think of as normal human wisdom, as described and defined by Sternberg and Baltes and Staudinger, and Executive Wisdom, which is implied by Plato and Confucius and made explicit in the five cases presented in chapter 1? I have come to believe that Executive Wisdom is human wisdom that is displayed by individuals and groups when they work on behalf of others in positions of leadership as opposed to that which is exercised on behalf of themselves as individuals. I have also come to see it as an ephemeral property of an extraordinary complex set of interacting systems. Human beings have the sense that they know wisdom when they see it exercised. Indeed, Baltes and Staudinger (2000) reported on explicit research studies that used structured evaluation models to help "objective" judges determine whether the responses of research participants to probe problems could be defined as wise. Holliday and Chandler (1986) suggested, on the basis of their own research, that people reliably assign to others whom they judge as possessing wisdom such characteristics as superior understanding; social adeptness; exceptional decision making; proper behavior; the ability to see essences and understand contexts, be in touch with themselves, and be intuitive, diplomatic, and empathic; judgment and communication skills; awareness, astuteness, and comprehension; ability to weigh consequences and consider points of view; being a source of good advice, worth listening to, alert, intelligent, curious, and creative; thinking a great deal; and being well read, articulate, educated and knowledgeable, kind, unselfish, quiet, unobtrusive, and nonjudgmental.

Holliday and Chandler agreed with Socrates that wisdom consists of "realizing its own ignorance, by knowing what it does not know" (p. 91).

A small group of theorists and practitioners in management science have also begun to apply these wisdom models to the challenges of leadership and knowledge management in organizations. Bierly, Kessler, and Christensen (2000) advocated for a reassessment of the knowledge transfer models of organizational learning. They stated clearly that the research in this area lacks sophistication, and they described their preference for a four-level paradigm that began with data that were integrated into information and then into knowledge for the people in an organization. They also suggested that knowledge itself is insufficient unless it is applied with wisdom, thus adding an action component to how organizations learn. They further advocated that wisdom must be disseminated throughout enterprises via transformational leadership, learning cultures, and systematic knowledge transfer. San Segundo (2002) echoed their call in her own assessment of the inadequacy of the knowledge transfer literature. She too advocated for the addition of the meaning making functions of wisdom to the rigorous analytic practices that are based on modern information systems. Dimitrov (2003) argued that significant advances must be made in the fuzziness of how humans know things and live in the world. His article demonstrated significant connections between modern software algorithms and ancient Socratic maxims. He too argued that "knowledge can be transferred, borrowed from books and experts, imparted and taught; wisdom is non-transferable, it is a unique individual treasure accumulated while riding on the tides and ebbs of life" (p 499). And in a recent article, Küpers (2005) used phenomenology to advocate for a revised understanding of management that centers on the emergence and practice of wisdom that arises in and from the relational dialogues conducted by groups of senior leaders in organizations.

These conceptual papers were matched by a call from Darwin (1996a, 1996b) for an approach to management that explicitly incorporates what he called the "wisdom paradigm," which he suggested moves leadership practice away from the predictability of Cartesian and Newtonian models and toward the uncertainty of extremely complex, multidimensional, chaos theory. Similarly, Small (2004) called for the introduction of the study of some of the philosophical classics and the recent findings of scientific psychology on the development and expression of human wisdom into modern programs of business education. This small but steadily growing body of wisdom-centered thinking in the organizational and managerial practice literatures thus strongly supports the central thesis of this book and the conceptual and research efforts of Sternberg (2005), Baltes and Staudinger (2000), and others in the scientific psychology community.

I now believe that assessing the exercise of executive wisdom may be impossible by conventional psychological measures primarily because of the scope of time against which leaders' judgments, decisions, and actions must be evaluated. Immediate, external assessments of Hannibal's actions from 219 through 216 B.C. would have made him out to be quite the wise leader. Seventy years later, he looked like an extraordinarily able fool. Similarly, King John's acquiescence to the pressures of his barons to him must have looked and felt like an insulting defeat. Nearly 900 years later, the flexibility and pragmatism that led to the development of many of the foundations of modern democracy make him look like one of the all-time political geniuses in leadership history. Therefore, how can we come to better understand this complex mystery I call *Executive Wisdom* when it seems to appear and disappear like a wraith on the wind?

THE CORE ELEMENTS OF EXECUTIVE WISDOM

Figure 2.1 presents a model that describes some of the major domains that contribute to the emergence or inhibition of Executive Wisdom. It is

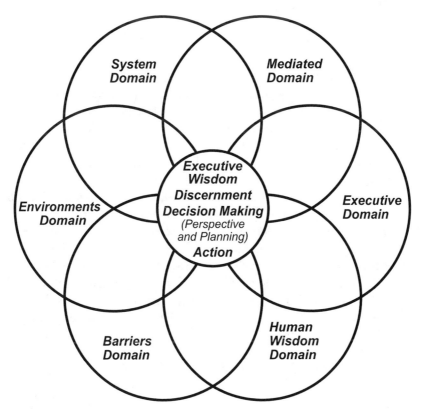

Figure 2.1. Six domains contributing to Executive Wisdom.

based on the model I initially presented for the integration of systems and psychodynamics in organization development (Kilburg, 1995) and further elaborated as the foundation of my conceptual approach to executive coaching (Kilburg, 1996b, 2000). Figure 2.1 contains six major domains that can be seen operating in the typical senior executive's working world: Domain 1, the system of the organization; Domain 2, the mediated system of behavior and relationships; Domain 3, the executive him- or herself; Domain 4, the operation of human wisdom itself; Domain 5, explicit and implicit barriers to the emergence of wisdom that may be present in or absent from the other domains; and Domain 6, the environments domain. Executive Wisdom is depicted in the center circle of the figure to show that it arises out of the complexity and organization of all six of these active domains. Executive Wisdom in this model comprises three key interacting components: (a) discernment, (b) decision making in the context of perspective development and planning, and (c) action. In constructing this model, I have incorporated as many of the historical, philosophical, religious, and modern research notions of wisdom as possible. In the following sections I briefly examine each of the contributing domains and how they may be related to wisdom as practiced by executive leaders.

The System Domain

Figure 2.2 presents the major elements of the system domain. Described more fully in Kilburg (1995, 1996b, 2000), it combines the classic elements of structure, process, content, input, throughput, and output that make up any organizational system. Every executive lives within such an organizational system. The size and complexity vary greatly, from small, entrepreneurial businesses to the largest governments of the modern nation-states. On a daily basis, the average executive leader is consumed with and by the operating details of the primary organization in which he or she lives and works. Trying to ensure that this organized entity operates with reasonable efficiency and effectiveness usually overwhelms the attention and physical energies of the leader. However, seeing to the long-term adaptation and survival of the organization remains the most important aspect of the job of leadership. Most leaders chronically complain of the lack of time and energy they have to actually think about the long-term consequences of their actions and the real futures of their organizations. However, if an organization's systems function effectively, an executive can more or less be assured that some time might be available for contemplating issues of longer term importance, if and only if the individual leader makes constructive and creative use of that most precious resource.

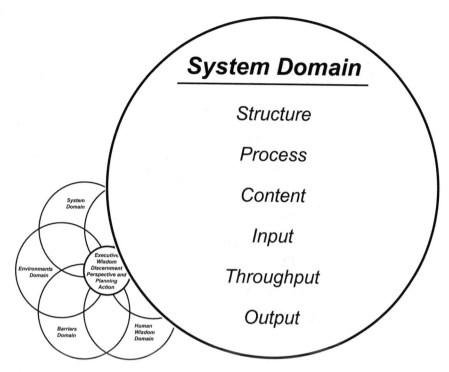

Figure 2.2. Major elements of the system domain.

The Mediated Domain

Domain 2, depicted in Figure 2.3, consists of the mediated interfaces the individual has with the organization. All executives work primarily with and through a core foundation of past, present, and future relationships. All activities of an enterprise are guided by the group of people the executive gathers together to perform the work of leadership. Previous relationships, in the form of mentors, parents, enemies, and supporters, are always in the room when executives meet with others. Future relationships must be anticipated and pursued by a leader to secure his or her success and the survival of the organization. Figure 2.3 also identifies various behavioral settings in which the leader operates, from dyads through groups and on to whole organizations. An executive must constantly shift the focus of his or her attention and action through these domains to conduct the business of the enterprise. Dozens and often hundreds of such contacts and interactions occur daily. The truly great leaders master the members, rules, resources, and expectations of each of the settings and use them to create individual and organizational advantage.

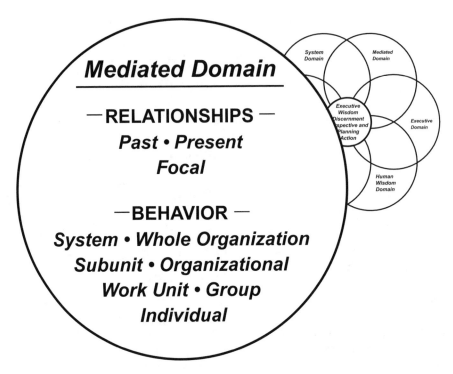

Figure 2.3. Mediated interfaces between the executive and the system.

The Executive Domain

In the third domain, presented in Figure 2.4, one finds the individual executive as he or she dwells and operates in the specifically defined leadership role within the organization. Discussed at length in Kilburg (2000), this domain consists of the psychological structures and personal and professional history, knowledge, skills, and abilities of the individual. The internal psychodynamic processes, forces, and motivations that engage, nurture, and sometimes torture the executive often play major roles in how he or she makes judgments and acts as a leader. This domain also includes the thoughts, emotions, defenses, and conflicts of the individual. These intricate and powerful elements can exert tremendous influence on the executive. The tasks, jobs, roles, responsibilities, and authorities of the person in the position also occupy this domain. Of special importance are the functions and duties the person in the role has as a leader. Whether the executive heads his or her own small business, a global industrial conglomerate, a nation-state, or a transnational service organization such as a church or educational institution, the tasks and responsibilities of office reside in the executive domain. It is on this domain that most of the leadership literature has focused in

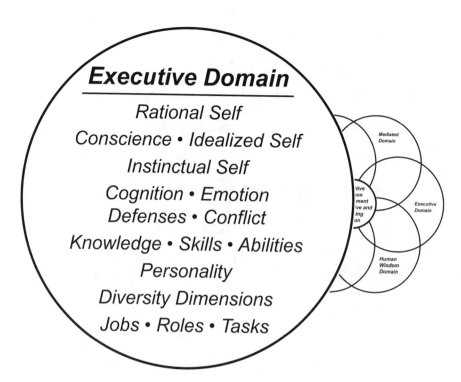

Executive Domain

Rational Self

Conscience • Idealized Self

Instinctual Self

Cognition • Emotion
Defenses • Conflict

Knowledge • Skills • Abilities

Personality

Diversity Dimensions

Jobs • Roles • Tasks

Figure 2.4. Domain of the individual executive.

an attempt to find answers for what constitutes a good leader and for what goes wrong when leaders fail in their jobs. When searching for a leader to fill a position, most organizations will emphasize this individual domain in trying to determine whether there is a good match between the needs of the enterprise and the capacities and accomplishments of the person being considered. The success of everyone involved depends on the quality of the match, for it is in the mind of the individual leader that wisdom forms, and it is through the mind and behavior of the individual leader that wise decisions are made and wise actions are taken. This brings us to the fourth domain, the human wisdom domain.

The Human Wisdom Domain

In Domain 4, depicted in Figure 2.5, I have placed the schematic of the Berlin wisdom paradigm summarized by Baltes and Staudinger (2000). I believe this is currently the most comprehensive model of the major elements of human wisdom available and, as they described, it has begun to yield systematic research results. In their paradigm, three general components contribute to what can be thought of as the *wisdom system* of the individual.

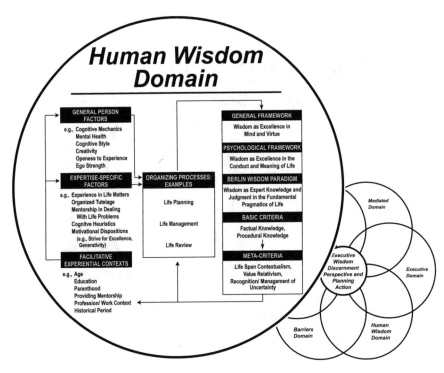

Figure 2.5. The Berlin wisdom paradigm.

First, there are general person factors, such as cognitive mechanics, mental health, cognitive style, creativity, ego strength, and openness to experience. Second, there are expertise-specific factors, such as experience in life, organized tutelage, mentorship in dealing with life problems, cognitive heuristics, and motivational dispositions. These first two sets of factors are largely components of the second and third domains of my model. Third, Baltes and Staudinger described what they called *facilitative experiential contexts.* These include age, level and types of formal and informal education, nature of the parenting he or she has received or is giving to his or her own children, experience in providing mentorship to others, professional and work context in which the person operates, and the historical period in which the person lives. These components overlap into Domains 1 and 2 in Figure 2.1.

The Berlin paradigm, then, suggests a series of organizing processes through which the wisdom system is often exercised. These include the major tasks of life planning, life management, and life review. All of these tasks are critically important to the long-term well-being of any individual. Extraordinary flexibility and complexity are required in trying to determine the best possible solution to the variety of problems and challenges anyone faces in an average lifetime in such things as life planning or life management.

In my view, the heart of the Berlin paradigm is seen in the series of boxes at the right-hand side of the flow chart depicted in Figure 2.5. In the Berlin framework, human wisdom is conceived of as excellence in mind and virtue. The interaction of the operations of mind with influences of highly developed virtues, such as Plato's temperance, courage, and justice, constitutes the essential condition from which wisdom can emerge. The psychological framework consists of performance excellence in the conduct and meaning of life.

Ericsson (1996) and others have demonstrated that it takes a minimum of 10 years for any individual to rise to a level of recognized excellence in any focused area of human activity. His comprehensive review of the human performance and effectiveness literature suggests strongly that two of the major variables accounting for the emergence of excellence in human behavior are (a) focused and structured practice and (b) the presence of and interaction with expert mentorship or coaching during the period of development. Baltes and Staudinger (2000) hypothesized that wisdom usually follows the dictum of performance excellence in the conduct and meaning of life, tying their paradigm in a most interesting way to what is known in general about human effectiveness. Their research also suggests that although young people can behave—or at least, think and respond wisely—Baltes and Staudinger reported other studies demonstrating that there is some additional benefit to age provided by experience in the world. In any case, it is clear that older people are likely to have had more opportunities to practice within their own wisdom system and to have gotten a better feel for how they work in the face of life's uncertainties and complexities.

Staudinger (1999) suggested that there seems to be a complex set of interacting variables that determine when wisdom can arise in individuals. She demonstrated that the cognitive declines associated with normal aging processes can directly interfere with the creation of wise responses to the tasks she set for her experimental subjects. Nevertheless, she also stated that "when selecting older adults who demonstrate performance in cognitive processing comparable to that of young adults, those older individuals show higher wisdom-related performances than young adults of the same performance levels" (p. 659). Baltes, Gluck, and Kunzmann (2002) also reported the results of at least one study that suggest that wisdom as Baltes et al. defined it seems to peak in humans between the ages of 55 and 65, but they offered no real explanation of this finding other that the obvious one that age and experience in life seem to improve the likelihood that individuals will develop this virtue.

As defined above, the specific focus of the Berlin wisdom paradigm consists of wisdom as an expert system of knowledge and judgment in what Baltes and Staudinger (2000) called the *fundamental pragmatics* of life. They also identified two basic and three metacriteria to operationalize the paradigm. The basic criteria are that the person has rich factual and procedural knowledge about life. In essence, he or she has lived a lot, seen a lot, and done a lot that enables him or her to have a wide and deep pool of experience, patterns of experienced and imagined behavior, and information to draw on in any situation that may arise. The metacriteria are life span contextualism, relativism of values and life priorities, and the recognition and management of uncertainty. In essence, these components of the paradigm act in such a way as to help the individual orient him- or herself in space, time, ideologies, emotional and social forces, the tasks of life, and the requirements of living. The wise person sees life spread out in multiple dimensions along lengthy timelines; understands that values and life priorities can change because of circumstance, culture, desire, or even fate; and recognizes and is capable of managing the uncertainties that come with and as a result of life itself. These criteria and the wisdom system are shown in Figure 2.5 as flowing back to the processes of life planning, life management, and life review and as having an influence back to the basic conditions or foundations for the operation of wisdom.

By extension back to Figure 2.1, the wisdom system of the individual executive is and should be available to the person in the exercise of his or her duties and responsibilities as a leader in a particular organization at any given time in that enterprise's life span. Our attention should be drawn to the fact that individual human wisdom is one major component contributing to the rise of Executive Wisdom, which in turn should be seen more as a feature of how a leader executes his or her role inside the organization at a given time in that organization's history. Indeed, executive and human wisdom sometimes may even conflict with each other, such as when decisions about what is good for an organization conflict with what is good for the individual executive, his or her family, or for humanity in general. Such conflicts are often the most profound and difficult situations with which leaders must cope.

Human wisdom thus can be used by the leader to address personal challenges as well as to provide one of the major foundations for the effective execution of the organizational tasks and responsibilities required. Although Sternberg's (1990, 1999, 2003, 2005) balance theory of wisdom can help one understand that leaders enmeshed in such conflicts can work simultaneously on goals and activities that can benefit both his or her personal well-being and the common good, there are inherent challenges when this criterion is specifically applied to the complexities of guiding an organization. In the end, the human wisdom component of an individual executive may dictate one course of action because it results in better outcomes for all involved, but his or her fiduciary responsibilities on behalf of an enterprise may well dictate a different choice. The components of the Berlin paradigm, such as life span contextualism, managing uncertainty, and the relativity of values, can help a leader evaluate and reconcile a decision like this, but they will not reduce the difficulty, stress, or intense emotional responses involved in such circumstances. Indeed, both in the past and in the present, leaders often have had to make decisions that put the lives of their loved ones explicitly in danger despite their desire to protect them.

Baltes and Staudinger (2000, p. 135) also provided a set of general criteria that outline the nature of wisdom:

- Wisdom addresses important and difficult questions and strategies about the conduct and meaning of life.
- Wisdom includes knowledge about the limits of knowledge and the uncertainties of the world.
- Wisdom represents a truly superior level of knowledge, judgment, and advice.
- Wisdom constitutes knowledge with extraordinary scope, depth, measure, and balance.
- Wisdom involves a perfect synergy of mind and character, that is, an orchestration of knowledge and virtues.
- Wisdom represents knowledge used for the good or well-being of oneself and that of others.
- Wisdom is easily recognized when manifested, although it is difficult to achieve and to specify.

Thus, this intricate and complex model of individual human wisdom surely contains relevant elements that incorporate the system in which an effective and mature executive works, the relationships and behavioral settings that mediate his or her behavior, and the internal workings of the person. The Berlin wisdom paradigm incorporates the key features of Sternberg's (2003) model by suggesting that balancing the field of forces in any situation and searching for solutions that produce a common good are central criteria for the practice of wisdom. The only specific aspect of Sternberg's (2003) model that the Berlin paradigm does not appear to address is the three major types of strategies individuals can use to balance their responses to organizational contexts. To recap the previous brief description in this chapter, they include "adaptation of oneself or others to existing environments; shaping of environments in order to render them more compatible with oneself or others; and selection of new environments" (Sternberg, 2003, p. 154). This additional dimension is essentially a reformulation of the Piagetian concept of accommodation and assimilation processes in human learning (Piaget, 1971).

The first three domains of my model—the individual executive, the organizational system, and the mediated interface—are necessary components for the emergence of Executive Wisdom but are insufficient by themselves to yield consistently wise leadership behavior on the part of any individual under consideration. I believe that without an advanced and well-developed capacity for individual wisdom, it is doubtful that any leader can consistently deploy what I identify as Executive Wisdom, and thus this fourth domain is an absolutely necessary addition to help one understand this ephemeral property of leadership. I also believe that the Berlin paradigm provides the best current way to understand the vast complexity involved in the development and creative use of individual human wisdom.

The Barriers Domain

Figure 2.6 presents an explicit summary of many of the barriers that can prevent an executive from thinking or acting wisely. The list is not all inclusive; instead, it tries to demonstrate that characteristics and components of the other domains can arise specifically, spontaneously, or chronically to inhibit or block the exercise of wisdom by a leader. For example, an individual might conceivably have certain developmental deficits that might inhibit his or her generation or use of wisdom. In the case example of the Treaty of Versailles, we know from the historical record that Woodrow Wilson was quite ill during some, if not all, of the negotiations of that peace

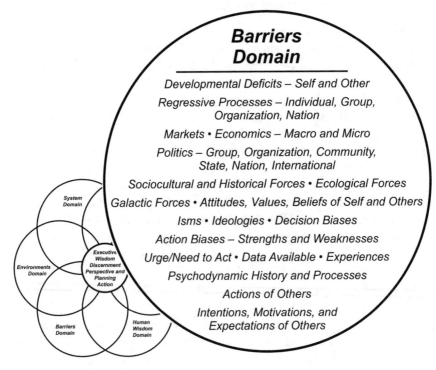

Figure 2.6. Barriers to Executive Wisdom.

agreement. Such a physical regression can greatly affect a leader's capacity to think clearly and to act with prudence. In the case of Hannibal, the centuries-long war with Rome for the domination of the western Mediterranean basin no doubt was the most prominent feature of his cognitive and emotional landscape. Such internal preoccupations can both focus attention and cloud judgment, thus impairing the exercise of wisdom by leaders.

Similarly, global markets; national, local, or organizational politics; economic forces; and the influences of social and historical trends can present barriers to development or the emergence and use of Executive Wisdom. If we looked at the years of Lincoln's presidency before he signed the Emancipation Proclamation as a third example, we could see clearly the power such trends and forces had in sustaining the status quo of slavery despite his values and clear desire to do the right thing. Racism, sexism, ageism, and other systems of prejudicial thought and feelings can prevent wisdom from emerging in individuals. The executive tendency to prefer action over deliberation, the usual insufficiency of data on which to operate safely, the individual's psychodynamic history and internal processes, and the actions of others can also block executives from doing what they believe they should do over the long run. In short, when one examines what can get in the way of wise thinking and action, it becomes clear what a tricky, fickle, and ephemeral phenomenon Executive Wisdom is in the real, daily lives of leaders in organizations. At any given moment in the hugely complex and interactive web of forces the average leader faces, any of these barriers can block the capacity for wise and effective long-term executive action. I address these barriers more specifically in the next and subsequent chapters.

The Environments Domain

Figure 2.7 provides components of the environments domain that contribute to the rise of Executive Wisdom. As can be seen, first and foremost, the past, present, and future are all operating constantly in the world of the average leader. Past decisions and actions are carried as general features of history and may serve as guides to the present and the future either about what to do or think or about what not to do or think. In particular, the presence of extreme experiences in the past can affect executive thought, feeling, and action. Patterns of great success in decisions and implementation as well as incidents of traumatic failure or injury are often influential in shaping what a leader will intuitively believe is the right strategy. The present always looms as the largest feature of the leader's mental, emotional, and professional landscape. It weighs on the mind of the executive like layer after layer of sedimentary stone in the earth's crust. The present presses for thought and action every minute of every day. With the constant call for such immediate and intimate involvement, the future

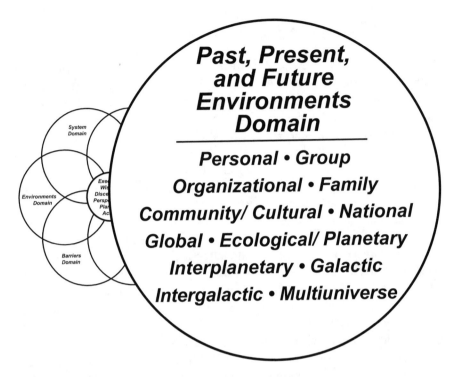

Figure 2.7. Environments domain.

often disappears from a leader's mind like water in a grasping fist. The future is wispy, hard to see, even harder to hold. The pressure the executive experiences to deal with the real and present troubles of the organization tends to squeeze most detailed consideration of the future out of his or her mind. Leaders are thus often left with the emotionally stressful sensation that the future is something important to consider but that they have no substantial time or energy to devote to the task. The most visible manifestation of this consists of the frequent complaints made by leaders concerning their lack of time for thinking, for planning, for anticipating. This problem focuses on the leader's central role of seeing and planning the way forward for the organization. There is no doubt that each organization has a future and that it will unfold with or without individual anticipation and action by a leader. However, most leaders would agree that they themselves are both responsible for, and would feel more comfortable with, charting the possible destinies of their own enterprises.

This domain also includes personal, group, organizational, community, cultural, national, and global environments as objects of consideration and as potentially having an impact on the emergence of Executive Wisdom. Ideas, plans, and actions taken by an individual leader within an executive team of a particular organization can look savvy inside the boundaries of that entity, but when they are executed in real time in external environments that are in all probability at least partly both hostile and competitive, they can look and be profoundly foolish. History abounds with examples of the environmental influences on executive action. Failed mergers, unanticipated competitive responses from other enterprises, governmental actions, aggressive actions by enemies, and the responses of global markets are just some of these types of environmental effects.

This domain also includes ecological, planetary, interplanetary, galactic, intergalactic, and multiuniverse environment effects. With the development of space technologies and remote sensing abilities, humanity has begun to have a whole new set of technological, conceptual, and operational ways of viewing itself and the consequences of its actions. Satellites now help predict the weather, measure the temperatures of oceans, chart the rise or fall of ozone, record the effects of massive erosion caused by human activity, demonstrate the poisoning of the Gulf of Mexico by U.S. agricultural and industrial runoff via the Mississippi basin, track hurricanes, predict where tornadoes might hit, and chart the heavens. Humans have given themselves senses that enable them to ask and get answers to questions they only dreamed of answering in the past. The Hubble telescope has now answered questions that have been sources of profound human debate for centuries. Other stars in our galaxy do have planets. Comets and meteors do collide with the earth and have wiped out virtually everything alive in the past. Supernova of nearby stars could kill life on this planet. Our sun will surely die in the far future, leaving the earth uninhabitable by virtually every form of living creature that we know. Human leaders now have a great many new things to consider and much longer time frames against which to gauge the success of their actions. Recent developments in theoretical physics and cosmology (Hawking, 2001) now provide fascinating and tantalizing glimpses into how this universe may have been formed and what its long-term prospects might be. It may well be that ours is not the only universe and that time, space, matter, and energy are truly infinite, interlinked processes and structures. Leaders in some human organizations have begun to speculate on the meanings of such ideas and the possibilities they might well have for the future of our planet and our species.

All of these environments can influence the emergence and execution of Executive Wisdom. Some are easy to see and work with, whereas others remain sheer intuitive speculation. What is clear is that past, present, and future environments do and should directly affect any leader's thoughts, plans, and actions. They must be incorporated into the theories executives create to guide their activities. The savvier, more sophisticated, and saner such environmental understandings become, the wiser the executive's ideas and actions are likely to be.

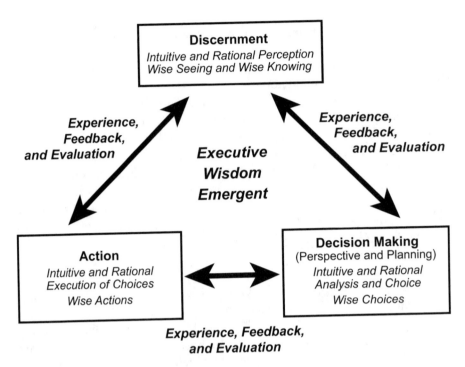

Figure 2.8. The core of Executive Wisdom.

THE STRUCTURES AND PROCESSES OF EXECUTIVE WISDOM

Now we come to the heart of the proposed model. In the center of the six domains, I have placed the structure and processes that I refer to as *Executive Wisdom*. The preceding discussion identifies the complexity of the domains that form the foundation for wisdom and interact in an impossibly rich and varied way in the mind, body, and spirit of the individual leader. He or she attempts to incorporate some of these influences analytically and intuitively and then is pressured by the reality of executive life to decide and to act. I believe Executive Wisdom results when the forces interact and are shaped by the leader to produce long-term, positive results for the organized entity for which he or she is responsible. In the examples I have discussed, the Marshall Plan, the voyages of Columbus, and the Magna Carta are three such wise outcomes. The Treaty of Versailles and Hannibal's attack on the Roman Empire represent the opposite, executive folly.

As I have thought through what the components of Executive Wisdom might be and, even more important, how a leader develops and can exercise it with some degree of predictability, I have experimented and tossed away a variety of ideas and schemes. Figure 2.8 represents the best of my current thinking about this. Executive Wisdom seems to follow much of what is understood to be normal human wisdom. The contributions of Baltes and Staudinger (2000), Holliday and Chandler (1986), Sternberg (1990, 1999, 2003, 2005), and others are most instructive here. However, in general their models do not address the enormous complexity and strains that come with leadership responsibility. As we have seen, these researchers have defined *human wisdom* very broadly. I now believe that Executive Wisdom can be seen as a component of human behavior that transcends normal wisdom because of the requirement of scope and the inclusion of the notion of the well-being of the organization with which a leader is entrusted. In Baltes and Staudinger's (2000) definition, human wisdom is an expert system in the fundamental pragmatics of life. By extension, I define Executive Wisdom as an *expert system in the fundamental pragmatics of organized human life.* This concept of Executive Wisdom incorporates Baltes and Staudinger's definition and the Berlin paradigm, but it also transcends them because of the necessity for the decisions and actions of a leader to create profound positive outcomes for large sections of humanity over long periods of time. Simultaneously, it incorporates Sternberg's (2003) notions of adaptation by extension to the organization for which the executive is responsible. Leaders can shape their enterprises to meet the environmental demands and pressures that they face. They can attempt to change their environments to make them more hospitable for their institutions. Finally, they can attempt to move their organizations from an environment that has become hostile and uninhabitable to one that they believe will be more supportive. The current business and political headlines of any major newspaper can be read through this lens, and the strategies of leaders become absolutely transparent with careful examination.

Figure 2.8 shows that Executive Wisdom consists of *discernment, decision making* (perspective and planning), and *action.* For leaders, being able to discover or create the right thing to do is never enough; they also need to do the right thing in the right way and against the right time frame. It is the unique combination of thinking, deciding, and acting wisely through time on behalf of groups of humans, and sometimes on behalf of every human, that separates Executive Wisdom from normal human wisdom. In human organizations, people invest leaders with the power and authority to think and act rightly on behalf of those inside the boundaries of the entity and often for those with whom that bounded organization interacts. Leadership is fundamentally and above all else an art that must be practiced. Executives who take no action are still leading, whether they decide actively not to intervene in a situation or simply sit by idly, if not ineptly, as a challenge or problem manifests itself in front of them.

In this model, discernment is viewed as a combination of rational and intuitive perception (Klein, 1999, 2003). Wise leaders see and know what is going on in the complex domains I have identified. They are able to use their perceptions to discern what is truly crucial and what must be done as a result. Perspective, planning, and decision making occur in an interaction with discernment. The time frame against which strategies are formed and evaluated and decisions are made is a central component of perspective. Central questions that leaders constantly face include the following: Is this a decision meant to stand for a day, a week, a year, 10 years, 100 years, or forever? How does the decision shift when a different perspective or a different timeline is adopted? When must this decision be made—immediately, today, tomorrow, next week, next year? Although time horizon is a key component, perspective also includes such issues as the effects of possible actions on affected individuals and groups; possible unintended consequences; and the nature of the motives, biases, beliefs, feelings, and attitudes of the decision maker. Planning is what is now recognized as either structured or unstructured strategy work (Mintzberg, Ahlstrand, & Lampel, 1998). Perspective and planning are intuitive and rational analyses and choice-making (Klein, 1999, 2003), which I explore in more depth in the next chapter. The third component of the tripartite model consists of wise actions, the rational and intuitive execution of choices. We know from history and from various studies that a wise choice is not always implemented wisely and can lead to true folly in action, if not in thought (Dotlich & Cairo, 2003; Finkelstein, 2003; Picken & Dess, 1997).

Figure 2.8 also demonstrates that the three elements of Executive Wisdom are linked dynamically and interactively with each other through experience, feedback, and evaluation. In a sense, wisdom-in-action is an exercise in continuous reflective learning. Each component must feed the other. Additional experience, feedback, and evaluation dramatically affect discernment and decision making (perspective and planning). Executive action, then, must be a flexible and adaptive process guided by the other components and is embedded in the complexity of the interacting domains. I explore the processes of executive action more thoroughly in chapter 8. This combination of richness, connectivity, constant change, and adjustment make it easy to understand why Executive Wisdom is extraordinarily difficult to both obtain and sustain by leaders.

CASE VIGNETTE

A simple illustration of wisdom-in-action can be seen in one of my coaching cases. A senior leader in a nonprofit organization that I have worked with for some time was talking to me about the severely changed fund-raising climate in the United States. The executive noted the conservative and religious shift in the national political scene and that traditional sources of finance for their organization were beginning to erode severely.

The organization remained completely dependent on external financing and could ill afford a sustained decline. He went on to discuss the liberal and sectarian values of the majority of the staff in their organization and that although these continued to power the programs and work efforts of the enterprise, they also potentially represented a major barrier to the changes that the organization would probably need to make if it were going to continue to thrive.

At some point in the conversation, I asked this leader if there were any members of the organization's staff whose values and religious beliefs were more aligned with those that were emerging on the national scene. The executive affirmed that this was the case and that these individuals tended to keep their views to themselves. They shared the commitment to the core programs and services of the agency, but they tended to work in somewhat different areas than other staff members. I then asked if the leadership team had ever tried to pull staff together to discuss the role of religion and ethical principles in the work that they did. The individual replied that they had never done so in any formal sense. Finally, I asked him what would happen if they were to try to create a meeting in which they could have a discussion like that. We then spent a period of time discussing the pros, cons, and approaches that might work to structure such a meeting.

On my next visit to the organization, I met with this leader and heard a detailed report of the new initiatives that the leadership team had started to conceptualize to create new partnerships with the many religiously affiliated nongovernmental organizations that shared parts of the mission and many of the core values of their own agency. These efforts were being powered by the staff members we had discussed in our previous session. In the time between our meetings, a small seminar had been held to discuss the issues of religion and moral principles in the work of the agency. The attendees came from a variety of religious traditions but shared a core commitment to spiritual practice in their lives and to the power of these beliefs to change human lives positively. No new staff or financial resources had been required to undertake these new program thrusts. The capacity of the people in the organization to change direction and to adapt to its changed world was latent in the motivation of their staff and the spiritually suppressed culture of their agency. Tapping these resources unleashed a new source of creativity and energy that the leadership team had been unable to see before the discussion that this client conducted with some of the staff.

This vignette demonstrates the enactment of all three of the components of the model of executive wisdom discussed above. The discussion with that senior leader enabled a change in perspective. The religious and conservative shift in political and cultural landscapes was no longer seen merely as a threat to the continued survival of the organization. The changed perception then led to the hypothesis that there might well be major opportunities and synergies for the organization if effective alliances could be built with a new group of partnering organizations. That discernment allowed the leadership group's decision to tap into their organization's previously unseen reservoir of staff motivation and energy. The relatively simple action of allowing their colleagues to have a structured conversation about some of the issues unleashed new streams of creativity and provided hope that they would be able to remain afloat in the new fund-raising environment that they faced. This demonstrates the process in which shifts in discernment can lead to effective decisions and the creation of wisdom in executive and organizational action. Of course, there is much more to this case example than this simple summary presents, but the general outline illustrates the model of Executive Wisdom precisely because it takes in all six domains as well as the core components described above.

THE INNER LANDSCAPE OF LEADERS

The models of wisdom described above consistently suggest that people who develop and express this virtue have created extremely rich internal worlds that they use to construct responses to the problems and events they encounter in the world. Consequently, it seems consistent that one of the most significant challenges for leaders and those who help to develop them involves the evolution and emergence of complexity in the inner mental and emotional landscape that the experience of being an executive creates for individuals. A better understanding of this world can unleash many, many new ideas; potential pathways for growth; and an understanding of barriers to change for coaches and leaders themselves.

Figure 2.9 attempts to go inside the world of the individual executive in a more detailed way. It depicts what I call the *behavioral geography* and the *psychological geology* of the cognized—that is, the mental and emotional—environment of the individual executive. It follows on models presented in Kilburg (2000). In the behavioral geography we see the operating environments of the executive: Domains 1, 2, and 6 in the current model of Executive Wisdom. Data and experience are accumulated from the operating environments, the organization, and the mediated interfaces in the executive's world and penetrate into the leader both consciously and unconsciously. The individual engages in monitoring activity to track what happens in these external and internal worlds and uses control behaviors and actions to respond. The result in the organizational world is what is called *leadership*, which is usually seen and experienced as management, including excellent interpersonal, inclusive, and transforming behaviors when the executive performs well. Inside the executive, we observe the psychogeological world,

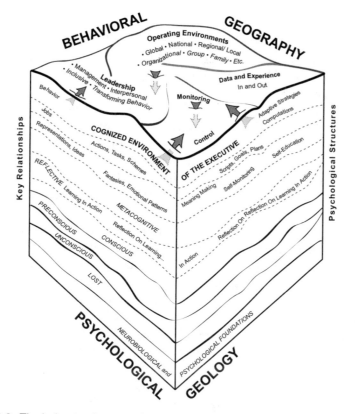

Figure 2.9. The behavioral geography and the psychological geology of the cognized environment of the executive.

which in this figure comprises six levels. The lost level is at the bottom and consists of knowledge, skill, and experience that may well have been developed in the past but are currently unavailable in any recognized or usable form by the leader. This level allows for the potential of current influences of such lost experience in the executive's life while simultaneously recognizing that it is virtually impossible to describe or uncover what those influences could be.

In the next level, we recognize the conventional unconscious described by Freud, Jung, and many others. This consists of experiences, thoughts, feelings, fantasies, conflicts, defenses, complexes, archetypes, and compromise formations arrayed in incredibly rich and delicately interacting layers (Kilburg, 2000). The unconscious is accessible to individuals through dreams, slips, jokes, acting-out behavior, visible patterns of defensive operations and compromise formations, and various forms of reflective experience. The unconscious presses on consciousness through the *preconscious level*, which consists of such things as dreams, images, feelings, and fantasies that usually symbolically incorporate components of these unconscious elements. The conscious mind and experience is that which is readily accessible on a moment-to-moment basis. Thoughts, feelings, sensations, perceptions, memories, and real world exchanges are constantly experienced in a never-ending dance.

The model also suggests that in the executive's inner world, consciousness can be further differentiated into states of reflective mind. Following Schön (1987) and Argyris (1993), we see learning-in-action, reflection on learning-in-action, and reflection on reflection on learning-in-action. Using this structure in the context of the wisdom model presented in this chapter, at the first level of reflection an executive is able to act wisely while examining the action in progress; at the second level, he or she can critically evaluate the entire wisdom sequence of discernment, decision making (perspective and planning), and action after it has taken place; and at the third level, he or she can assess how well that second-level reflective evaluation of a wisdom process was executed and what should be incorporated into future strategies and actions and reflective processes on the basis of the experience (I revisit this model in chaps. 8 and 9). In this way, wise executives can in fact systematically enrich their virtuous behavior. Finally, we see the metacognitive level, which consists of a complex representation of the internal and external realities of the leader. This metacognitive map or complex theory is used to guide the thinking and the actions taken by the leader. Leaders make meaning of and for themselves as they build these representations. Fantasies, emotional patterns, ideas, scripts, goals, plans, motives, self-monitoring activity, self-education actions, tasks, and schemas are all organized through the jobs, behaviors, and adaptive strategies and responses of leaders. These are used to interact with and create impacts in the worlds of the executive. In addition, Figure 2.9 shows the levels of mind also interacting through key relationships in time and through the major psychological structures of conscience, rational self, idealized self, and instinct, following Kegan (1982, 1994) and Kilburg (2000). I further explore the issues in the metacognitive foundations of Executive Wisdom in chapter 3.

Figure 2.10 provides an enriched version of the executive's cognized environment using Klein's (1999, 2003) complex model of expert, intuitive cognition. In this elaborated version of Figure 2.9, the geographic world is filtered into the cognized layer through the experienced culture, society, history, language, dimensions of diversity and national and tribal–familial structures of the leader. The individual experiences him- or herself as a complex, saturated, polyvocal, multifaceted self, following Gergen's (1991, 1999) ideas that the complexity of global civilization and modern technology have profound impacts on the organization and functioning of individual human psychology. Embedded in this complex self-system is a cognitive

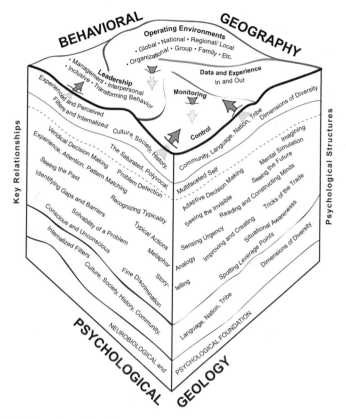

Figure 2.10. The extended cognized environment of the executive.

apparatus that Klein (1999, 2003), Goldberg (2001), and many others are beginning to delineate in ever-increasing detail. In this cognized world, we see the operation of the executive brain and mind. Humans perform two basic forms of cognitive activity that Goldberg called *adaptive decision making* and *veridical decision making* and that Klein (1999, 2003) elaborated as *intuitive decision making* and *analytic decision making*. According to Goldberg, adaptive work involves learning new things and constructing creative adaptations to complex and novel situations, usually in real time and often against pressing time demands. Veridical work involves rapidly and efficiently resolving routine and well-known challenges, even if they are complex. Adaptive decisions are usually slower and involve trial and error as the new situation is mastered. Learning a new piece of music, finding one's way around a new city, and writing an original piece of fiction or poetry are examples of adaptive decisions and learning. Driving a car in traffic, presiding over a routine staff meeting, and dancing a well-rehearsed routine are examples of veridical processes that can be complex but nonetheless managed with extreme efficiency and effectiveness.

Following both Klein and Goldberg, on the adaptive side of Figure 2.10 we see activities such as imagining, mental simulations, seeing the future, seeing the invisible, situational awareness, reading and constructing minds, sensing urgency, spotting leverage points, applying tricks of the trade, improvising, and creating solutions. On the veridical side, we see pattern-matching, intuition, experience, seeing the past, problem detection, identifying gaps and barriers, recognizing typicality, recognizing the solvability of the problem, rational analysis, typical actions, and fine discriminations. These two types of cognitive processing occur in the mind of the leader both simultaneously and sequentially, usually in a seamless way. Often, they are most directly experienced in the forms of metaphors, analogies, and storytelling by a leader who reports them as the narrative products or results of these extremely complex internal processes. At the bottom of this cognized layer we see that these processes can be both conscious and unconscious and that the unconscious mind is filtered through to the cognized layer by the same internalized structures that buffer the person from the external world. Thus language, dimensions of diversity, culture, nation, tribe or family, history, and so on, can shape what enters into the unconscious, which then can seep back into and create impacts on the cognitive functions of the leader. In other words, Figures 2.9 and 2.10 illuminate all of complex levels of interior processes and structures and exterior interactions that interact as an executive tries to make sense out of the chaotic worlds in which he or she functions and to use that sense-making to guide his or her leadership assessments, choices, and actions on behalf of whatever organized entity he or she is managing.

A BRIEF EXAMPLE

In my work with leaders, I frequently encounter situations in which an individual can become virtually paralyzed in his or her relationships with colleagues, particularly at the chief (often called "C") level in organizations. In particular, CEOs can be completely unaware of patterns of behavior that they display that can demoralize and undercut their most trusted and important subordinates. In one such case, I was working with a senior vice president (SVP) of a company who, over time, found himself increasingly anxious, uncomfortable, and almost unable to speak in front of his CEO. The SVP could lead and act wisely on a moment-to-moment and day-to-day basis with virtually everyone else in the company, but in the presence of his boss, he became unhinged. As any reader can imagine, this was not only extremely distressing to the individual, but it also had become a job- and career-threatening pattern of behavior, because the CEO had both observed this behavior and criticized his colleague for his inability to be assertive in senior meetings and his difficulty in working closely with him.

After several sessions of exploring the nature of the behavior and making any number of suggestions for this individual to try to improve his performance in this arena, I finally decided that something besides knowledge or skill deficits were powering this continued pattern of ineffective performance. At one point in one of our discussions, I simply asked this client if the CEO reminded him of anyone whom he had experienced in his life prior to joining the company. In response to the question, the individual went quiet for what seemed to be a long time. I listened to his silence and waited as respectfully as I could. After his withdrawal, he finally murmured in a voice that was quite different in quality from that in which he usually expressed himself, "My father."

A series of short follow-up questions quickly revealed that this competent and highly successful leader had grown up in an executive family (i.e., a family in which one or both parents hold executive role[s] in organization[s]) led by a father who was rarely home because of his business responsibilities and who, when he was at home, was often both drunk and verbally abusive to everyone in the family. My client was the oldest of four children, and he told me several stories of maneuvering himself between his father and his mother and siblings in order to protect them from the waves of rage and hypercritical verbal filth that would erupt any time his dad consumed more than three drinks at home. The SVP had never really made any connections among his own career path, his experiences of his working relationship with his boss, and the patterns of behavior in his family of origin.

Our conversation then moved in two intersecting loops in which we explored the kinds of behavior he witnessed and experienced with his CEO and his deeply rooted, psychological responses to his father's drinking and verbal abuse. Needless to say, his CEO had a quick temper; criticized members of his management team whenever he perceived any problems; and possessed a keen intelligence, quick wit, and sharp tongue. It became apparent to me that the pattern into which they had fallen involved the SVP going to the CEO to discuss business problems in his areas of responsibility and then having the CEO begin to pick apart both the performance problems in the SVP's organization and his colleague's approach to managing the issues. We finished the work of that session with an exploration of what he could do to change the pattern of his exchanges with his boss and a discussion of the possibility of his pursuing some psychotherapy to work through the long-standing family-of-origin issues he had been holding for his entire adult life.

Initially, the SVP simply stopped reporting business problems to his boss until he thought he had gotten on top of both the causative factors

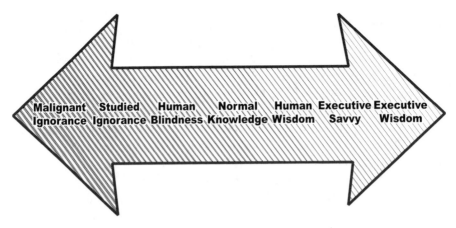

Figure 2.11. A continuum of Executive Wisdom and stupidity.

in the situations and had undertaken at least some initial action to resolve the difficulties. He found that taking his solutions to the CEO yielded less critical feedback and, as a result, he started to feel more confident and less reluctant to speak out in executive meetings or any other time in the boss' presence. Over time, he also reported that the psychotherapeutic experience he had undertaken had yielded significant gains in his relationships with his wife and children. He was also able to help mobilize his siblings to help to confront their father, whose drinking had accelerated in his retirement years. Together, they were able to help him enter a recovery program and to begin to heal the long-standing damage to the relationships in the family.

This vignette illustrates the importance of understanding the complexity of the inner landscape of senior executives, their organizational worlds, and the potential for extraordinarily delicate and often unconscious interactions between them. Inhibitions of wisdom and poor performance over time should alert leaders and coaches to the possibility that these kinds of disordered patterns of interaction and behavior might have roots in the sometimes mysterious and nearly always interesting and complex inner worlds of executives.

Figure 2.11 presents a simplified way of understanding the problem that confronts executives, leadership groups, and their coaches. In essence, it depicts a continuum that is anchored on one end by what I call *malignant ignorance* and on the other end by Executive Wisdom. There are five other anchor points along the continuum as well. I have already defined Executive Wisdom as the ability of a leadership group to do the right thing in the right way against the right time frame within an organizational framework. *Executive savvy*, the point next to Executive Wisdom, refers to individuals who in their discernment, decision making, or action steps achieve suboptimal but nonetheless significant results. Most often, one sees examples of executive savvy when leaders and their teams make and execute decisions that make really good short-term sense for their organizations but have less than stellar long-term implications. A careful examination of the merger-and-acquisition literature suggests that the vast majority of these kinds of transactions fall into the category of executive savvy because they rarely produce the results they are supposed to. Normal human wisdom can appear within an individual executive or leadership group as executive savvy (i.e., the organizational expression, short of Executive Wisdom, of doing the right things in the right way) is expressed, but unless it is applied to the operation of the organization itself, it often falls short of being maximally helpful to the enterprise. I spend a little more time on the group implications of this in chapter 9.

Similarly, *normal knowledge* (at the center of Figure 2.11) in a leader or his or her team can be extremely useful and is always needed if not always readily available. However, driving the long-term future of an organization with the knowledge and skill base derived from such foundations will not necessarily enable the enterprise to do well. Next on the continuum is ordinary *human blindness*. The best way to think of this is that an executive or leadership group might have no real knowledge of certain aspects of the competitive situation they face because the norms that have evolved for themselves or their group around competition or compensation may inhibit their ability to see certain aspects of reality. Blinded in these ways, it becomes difficult if not impossible for such an individual or leadership group to discern reality accurately let alone make wise choices or execute well.

At the next anchor point, *studied ignorance* can be readily seen in individuals or leadership groups who have organized themselves around a set of attitudes, beliefs, values, technologies, markets, norms, relationships, or sources of data that they cherish greatly. These frameworks then can become a form of lens or filter through which all information must pass and against which every decision and action must be weighed. Such lenses and filters can become forms of systematic bias that can dramatically decrease the ability of an executive team to function (Bazerman, 1998). Cherished beliefs in products, services, business plans, distribution networks, technologies, people, financial models, or methods and size of compensation are all examples of belief systems that can become so firmly entrenched that leaders and their management teams cannot really see or understand their implications. I have seen this operate most clearly in meetings of executive groups in which they find themselves discussing difficult and complex organizational situations while they literally cling to spreadsheets that they somehow believe define the complete reality of what they face. I have found it challenging in these circumstances to push the members of the group to put their spreadsheets aside and conduct an examination of the difficulty that is informed but not controlled by the numbers that appear in the columns. These have been both amazing and trying experiences.

Finally, we come to *malignant ignorance*, on the pole opposite from Executive Wisdom. We see malignant ignorance in executives and leadership groups who persist in beliefs that lead to destructive or ineffective action despite the ready availability of evidence to correct the beliefs. The worst cases of malignant ignorance we can seen in organizations such as the Third Reich, Mao's Cultural Revolution, or Stalin's Soviet government, in which the mind-sets of the leaders led not only to wholesale human carnage but also, in some cases, to the utter destruction of the leadership groups themselves.

I hope these models demonstrate the complexity and richness of the world of the average leader and why it may be difficult for individuals in these influential positions to perform in a consistently wise fashion. Executive Wisdom, defined in this framework as doing the right thing, in the right way, and against the right time frame, can be seen as more than a bit of a crapshoot in which the individual does his or her level best to discern what is happening to and in the organization, apply appropriate perspective and planning to decide what to do, and then to act in an appropriate and determined way. History and experience are the ultimate judges of the quality of such deliberations and actions on the parts of leaders. My introductory examples demonstrate clearly that these decisions and actions often involve life and death and, for the leaders of organizations and nation-states, the very fates of all of the people for whom they are responsible rests on their shoulders. In the worst cases of human folly, destruction on nearly unimaginable scales has occurred. Thus, I believe it is critically important to try to improve the ways in which leaders function in order to improve the chances that they will produce wise results rather than foolishness and human tragedy. What then can be recommended that leaders do to increase the probability that they will think and act wisely?

CREATING EXECUTIVE WISDOM

Exhibit 2.1 presents eight elements that if used consistently can support the emergence of Executive Wisdom. First and foremost, executives must create reflective space and time within which to consider their worlds, their decisions, and their actions (Mezirow & Associates, 1990; Schön, 1983, 1987; Siebert & Daudelin, 1999). In many, if not most, modern organizations the average leader's time is completely absorbed by activity. There is little if any routine time made for carefully considering key issues and major decisions. Unless leaders plan and protect reflective time, for most of them there is no routine space in the schedule to undertake such reflective activity.

EXHIBIT 2.1
Elements Supporting the Emergence of Executive Wisdom

1. Reflective space and time
2. Emotional and behavioral containment
3. Reflective processes: Deconstructive, polyvocal discourse with others
4. Reflective structures: Levels, types, and foci for reflection
5. Personal, group, and organizational preparation; self, group, unit, and organizational development
6. Necessary and sufficient information
7. Necessary and sufficient knowledge
8. Necessary and sufficient individual and group wisdom

Even suggesting retreats, coaching meetings, brainstorming sessions, and other times for it can yield a barrage of complaints from leaders about the work that will not be done as a result of engaging in reflection. Nevertheless, establishing reflective time and space opens the gateway to Executive Wisdom. I spend more time on this issue in chapter 8. Second, executives must become experts at emotional and behavioral containment (Stacey, 1992, 1996). The stresses and emotional demands of leadership are often overwhelming. Anxiety; shame; sadness; anger; joy; frustration; guilt; greed; lust; the need for power, achievement, affiliation, and transcendence; and many other complex human motives and feelings enrich and complicate the decisions and actions executives must undertake. Being able to contain the emotions and prevent acting-out behaviors in themselves and their colleagues while appropriate deliberations occur and informed actions unfold against the best possible time frame are some of the key elements in thinking and acting wisely.

Third and fourth, leaders must learn how to establish reflective processes and structures in which many voices and points of view are encouraged and even demanded. Choosing with whom to discuss issues, making sure that alternative points of view are considered, and deliberately challenging prevailing ideas and beliefs must be standard practices in organizations and led by their senior executives. Much of the rest of this book is devoted to how to create and use such reflective processes. Fifth, individual executives must develop themselves and then work hard to develop their teams and their organizations to ensure that they have the appropriate knowledge, skills, and abilities necessary and sufficient for the exercise of wisdom. Again, it means investing time and energy to ensure that people are as ready as they can be as individuals and that the groups are well prepared to function as groups. Working with people who have well-developed self-awareness, individual knowledge and skill, and high levels of savvy about how to work in groups and organizations can make it much easier to overcome barriers to wisdom on a routine basis. Finally, the leader must have necessary and sufficient knowledge, information, and individual and group wisdom at his or her disposal. If executives do not create such a foundation, then the emergence of Executive Wisdom becomes a random or chance occurrence. In chapters 5 through 9, I spend more time on these issues of wisdom implementation and practices.

Finally, Exhibit 2.2 presents a list of 13 questions that leaders can ask themselves before, during, and after making a decision or implementing an executive action. I have found these questions to be personally helpful, and some of my clients have also found them extremely useful. All of the questions try to promote improved states of reflection, not only about the issue or challenge under consideration but also about the process of reflective decision making itself. Asking oneself and one's colleagues about negative consequences; relevant time frames; who benefits or is suppressed by decisions and actions under consideration; validity of information; whether other voices have been expressed, heard, and incorporated; how truth is determined and tested; and whether and how the process itself has been reflected on can create crucial ways of uncovering barriers, biases, and blindness and generating innovative and long-lasting strategies before it is too late. Making assumptions without such tests of inquiry invites the worst forms of abuse and folly.

Both history and the daily practice of leadership demonstrate how difficult it is for executives consistently to discern, decide, and act wisely. All too often, what looked good on Monday looks far less appetizing on Friday. Decisions and actions that are thought to bring both immediate and long-term relief and prosperity to an organization and its people too often create misery and abject failure a year or two later (Hartley, 2003). In a human world increasingly interconnected and incredibly accelerated by technology that contains (a) huge numbers of organizations and nations led by executives without the time, structures, training, or inclination to be reflective professionally and (b) technologies whose use threatens the continued existence of much of what we know and value as life on this planet, it is increasingly important that we individually and collectively work to improve the likelihood that leaders will more routinely exercise Executive Wisdom. Not to do so invites catastrophic effects for organizations and the people who inhabit them and for the world that provides them a home.

MODELS IN MOTION: ACTIVITIES TO IMPROVE LEADERSHIP AND COACHING

1. Take a moment and allow yourself to relax. Now, ask yourself the following questions:
   a. What is the stupidest thing you have ever done as a person or as a professional?

Questions Supporting the Emergence of Executive Wisdom

1. Will the decision, action, plan, or strategy you are considering or have implemented increase or decrease your status, power, prestige, and effectiveness as a leader in the long run?
2. What are the risks for you, your organization, family, community, nation, or the world if the decision, action, plan, or strategy you are considering or have implemented doesn't work?
3. Who or what does the decision, action, plan, or strategy you are considering or have implemented benefit?
4. Who, if anyone, does the decision, action, plan, or strategy you are considering or have implemented suppress, denigrate, disadvantage, or oppress? What are the long-term risks for you, your organization, family, community, nation, or the world of doing so?
5. What attitudes; values; beliefs; biases; urges to action; issues; psychodynamics; group and organizational dynamics; politics; economics; metaphors; analogies; narratives; and historical, social, and cultural forces and connections can you detect operating in your thinking, decision making, or implementing actions?
6. Have you sought anyone else's opinion about the decision, action, plan, or strategy you are considering or have implemented? Have you listened to anyone who objects or opposes the decision, action, plan, or strategy you are considering or have implemented? Have you invited the critical thinking of others on this matter?
7. What sources of data and information support the decision, action, plan, or strategy you are considering or have implemented?
8. What other sources of data and information are being ignored or were ignored or not considered as you constructed the decision, action, plan, or strategy you are considering or have implemented?
9. Against what time frame are you making this decision: 1 hour, day, week, month, or year, or 5, 10, 20, 50, 100, 500, 1,000 years? Is the time frame of sufficient duration to reflect the importance of the matter under consideration?
10. Do you need to be directly involved with the execution of the decision, action, plan, or strategy you are considering or have implemented? If yes, when, where, with whom, why, how often, with what means and to what ends?
11. What are the effects of your chosen methods of discourse, decision making, and implementation on this and other situations? What have you gained or lost? What are the chosen methods' potentials and shortcomings?
12. What means are you using to test the truth of how you are or have made meaning in coming to the decision, action, plan, or strategy you are considering or have implemented?
13. Have you, with whom, and how have you reflected in coming to the decision, action, plan, or strategy you are considering or have implemented? Have you reflected on how you performed the reflection?

---

b. If you are a leader in an organization, what is the stupidest decision or action you have ever taken?
c. What made the decision or action stupid? When and how did you know it was stupid? What criteria did you use to judge its merits?

2. Now, ask yourself,
   a. What is the wisest thing you have ever done as a person or as a professional?
   b. If you are a leader in an organization, what is the wisest decision or action you have ever taken?
   c. What made the decision or action wise? When and how did you know it was wise? What criteria did you use to judge its merits?
3. Can you develop any internal sense of how you created, accessed, and used a sense of rightness in the situations in which you believe you acted wisely as opposed to stupidly? If so, jot down and reflect on what you think and feel went into the emergence of that sense of rightness.
4. Take a few minutes to talk to someone out loud about what you have explored or, if you are reluctant to share it with another person, dictate some notes into a tape recorder and then listen to yourself afterward. The experience of giving voice to inner work can often provide additional insight and learning. If that feels like something you do not want to do, first try to create a written record of the exploration and then read it back to yourself or to someone else. Try to notice in the reading what you emphasized and perhaps what you may have undervalued or omitted.

3

THE METACOGNITIVE AND PSYCHODYNAMIC ROOTS OF EXECUTIVE WISDOM

A wise man's question contains half the answer.
—Solomon Ibn Gabirol, *The Choice of Pearls*

By this time in my career, I have sat in literally thousands of meetings of leadership groups in a wide variety of organizations. If you have gotten this far in this book, you know as well as I do that these spaces for collective reflection and action can be soul-numbingly boring for long periods of time. Individuals drone on and on about what seems important to them, but the entire room falls into a kind of stupor as other attendees busy themselves with doodling; reading material they have brought along; or, in this new Wi-Fi era, they are hunched over with their arms on their thighs and thumbs madly typing away as they answer e-mails on their BlackBerry, Palm Trio, or other wireless devices people now carry to keep them plugged into the World Wide Web.

On rare occasions, a meeting bursts into conflict. The participants can then look like the triple-tag teams in the ring of a World Wrestling Federation show. It becomes difficult to keep track of the furious action as alliances that were unseen before a divisive issue ignites the group suddenly spring to life and individuals who were soundless, motionless, and seemingly brainless jump into articulate action, alternately attacking their opposition or defending their positions. The room becomes electrifyingly alive, hyper-adrenalized, and often dangerous for individual careers or for cherished programs or initiatives that come under attack.

Even more rarely, a leadership meeting elicits from the participants a form of fully engaged, creative thinking in which seemingly impossible problems suddenly become illuminated in a comprehensive way that leads the group inevitably to learn how to solve what had been so troubling. The individuals in the room lean forward, PDAs turned off; their pupils dilate and nostrils flare, their faces contort with the effort of learning, and wisps of joy mingle with furious curiosity. No one fights, although there can be many significant disagreements. The meeting becomes a living entity as minds mingle in this impossibly creative and exhilarating dance.

Such experiences lead logically to questions about what goes on in the minds of the executives who participate. How do they construct and understand the events that they themselves create? What are the cognitive foundations of executive thought and group and organizational behavior? How do individual leaders develop their own minds and those of their subordinates? How can coaches and consultants constructively enter into and intervene in these decision-making spaces in organizations? How can they understand what constitutes excellence in an executive mind and simultaneously what is dangerously primitive? How can wisdom be created and stupidity avoided?

In this chapter, I explore the metacognitive foundations of Executive Wisdom. I start with two case studies that illuminate the stark differences between equally intelligent leaders who think about and function in their jobs in incredibly divergent ways. We will take a short and narrowly focused trip through the past 35 years of research findings on the human mind, I will discuss how underlying psychodynamic descriptions of the structure of the mind and patterns of conflict and defensive operations can influence the ways in which leaders think and act, and I will apply concepts of human consciousness to the mental lives of leaders. Finally, I will explore some methods that I have found useful to help me coach and develop these cognitive capacities in individual leaders. As I have explored these literatures, I have discovered with glee that many questions I had as a graduate student about the functioning of the human mind have been answered even as other more complex and difficult problems have been uncovered. Of most importance for the work that I do with executives, the application of the research findings to coaching and consulting practice appears to help individuals and groups make significant improvements in their ability to think and act with more wisdom. Let us now dive into some real life cases to try to understand the challenges of executive cognition.

THE BIRTH OF COMPLEXITY: TWO EXECUTIVES IN CRISIS

Tom Lehrman was the chief financial officer in a mid-sized financial management company. He had served in that capacity in a smaller company with some distinction and was recruited to his present position with the great hope that he would continue their tradition of sound financial performance and technical excellence as a company. In the 18 months he had served in his position, he had developed a reputation for being extremely competent from a technical perspective and an excellent collaborator and colleague by his peers in the company. However, he had also become known for often being vocally and publicly critical of his subordinates.

The CEO of the company, Henry O'Shay, had risen to his position from financial operations and had previously held Tom's position. Tom was his hand-picked successor for that unit. Henry maintained excellent working relationships with everyone in financial operations and consistently supported Tom's leadership of that function despite a continuous parade of his previous subordinates coming to his office to complain about their new boss. Henry provided consistent advice and steady support to these people and always returned them to Tom for direction. He had had several discussions with Tom about the succession process and his progress in the company, and both of them agreed that the unit's performance remained quite good despite the complaints.

The situation changed significantly however, when, partly on the basis of Tom's advice, the senior executive team decided to purchase and install a new enterprise-wide information system and asked Tom to lead the change effort. Within months of the start of this initiative, Henry began hearing a steady drumbeat of complaints about Tom's high-handed approach and his inability to listen to his subordinates and that the installation of the new system was in trouble because of the intensity of the conflicts that the process was creating.

Henry decided to act when he heard directly from some of the other vice presidents in the company that they too were hearing complaints and had major concerns. He contacted me, provided a briefing on the situation, and asked if I would be willing to coach Tom. I agreed, assuming that Tom was willing and a contract could be negotiated successfully.

Henry invited Tom to a meeting with me. He reviewed the history of the succession process, expressed his ongoing support, described the problems he had been hearing about, and invited Tom to work with me as his coach to see if improvements could be made. Despite some defensiveness that took the form of an elaborate description of all of the challenges he had faced since taking on the job, Tom agreed to begin coaching. We successfully negotiated an agreement for me to collect some information from his key subordinates and to have regular coaching meetings, and we began to work.

On the basis of my initial feedback of data and discussions with him, Tom immediately undertook some vigorous steps to assess the situation in his department and with the information initiative. He appointed two diagnostic task forces, put them on aggressive timelines, evaluated their findings in public meetings, and began to implement many of their suggestions. These actions seemed to quell the initial dissatisfaction with Tom's leadership. However, in a coaching session that occurred approximately 3 months after we began, we started to address his ongoing complaints about his subordinates. He described some of them as "crazy," and he believed that others needed to move on in their careers because they seemed to be so dissatisfied working for him. He suggested that he was constantly needing to help them with their work and that they were always bringing problems in for him to solve. He took great pride in his diagnostic acumen and ability to come to a rapid and decisive answer given a minimally appropriate amount of information. He told me that he believed he was firmly in command of his department and, indeed, felt like he was running every aspect of it. Our conversation then continued in the following way.

"Tom, do you think your key subordinates are capable of running their own units?" I asked.

"Well, mostly. But they are always in here asking for help. So I guess I'm not really sure."

"Do you enjoy telling them what to do and taking on all of their responsibilities in addition to yours?"

"No, I think they ought to lead their own units."

"Do you believe that your work with them is teaching them how to lead their units or how to follow your orders?"

Tom paused for a moment or two. "I know that I need them to be leaders, but they are not."

"Do you see it as your job to do their work or to enable them to become leaders of their units so that they can get their work done?"

"Well, I have to make sure their work is done well, don't I?"

"Of course you do, but just how are you doing this?" I prodded some more.

"I listen to them and give them great solutions to their problems," he answered.

I paused for a moment, searching for a way into the challenge that I now saw more clearly as a classic case of overusing some of his strengths. Tom's abilities as a financial technician and problem solver and the relative absence of any capacity to see himself as someone who was developing leaders seemed to be at least partially responsible for the difficulties that had arisen. In essence, his mental and emotional maps of the situation he faced seemed all too limited to me. I needed a way to illustrate the problem to him, and a story he had recently told me came to mind.

"You have an adolescent daughter, don't you?" I asked him.

"Boy, do I."

"You told me she was learning to drive. How is it going?"

"As a matter of fact, she just passed her test. My wife and I are very proud of her, but we're scared to death now that she can drive on her own."

"So, are you still letting her drive, despite your fear?"

"Oh, yeah; how else can she learn?"

"And when you were out driving with her and she made a mistake, what did you do?"

"Mostly held on tight and tried to point out what she could do to improve."

"You didn't grab the wheel and push her out of the seat?"

"No, of course not. She'd have never passed her test that way. What does this have to do with my subordinates?"

"Well, your description of some of your interactions with them suggests to me that you may be pushing them out of their seats and taking over control of their jobs and their units. If that is happening, you could be shaping them quite unintentionally to be dependent on your knowledge and skill rather than their own. Instead of developing leaders who can do their jobs, by using your excellent diagnostic, financial, and problem-solving skills, you may be doing their jobs for them. How would you feel if Henry was taking such an approach with you?"

Tom paused again. "I guess I'd be pretty frustrated and pretty mad."

"What would you do about it?"

"I'd complain about it and then probably leave."

"What would happen to your unit if most of your direct reports left?"

"In the short run, it would be a disaster. In the long run, some of them have to leave to move up in their careers."

"Of course, but do you want them to go because they feel your leadership approach pushed them out, or do you want them to go to positions they really want?"

"That's obvious."

"Are you ever aware that you are pushing them out of their chairs and grabbing the steering wheels of their units when you are with them?"

"I'm aware that we are solving problems, but no, I don't think I see myself as pushing them out of their chairs."

"Well, one thing you could try as a homework assignment is simply trying to be aware when you are answering their questions for them and telling them what to do."

"Then what?"

"Then, try to determine if that's the right thing to do at that time or whether you want to experiment with another approach."

"Like what?"

"Like asking them what they think, or suggesting they get some more information, or going back to their office and creating a plan to deal with the problems that they bring to you."

We spent several more minutes talking about how he could try to change this behavior with his subordinates. I subsequently sent him an e-mail to remind him about the homework assignment. He replied that he had been trying but that it was very hard for him to be aware, when he was doing it, to try to think of something else to do that was better than just giving the answer or directions and to say something that wouldn't make people defensive. His note was full of frustration and conflict; he clearly was trying to follow through on the suggestion but was struggling with the knowledge, skill, and ability that were required. I encouraged him to continue the experiment.

In several subsequent sessions, I continued to explore this with Tom. He was trying to delegate more, refrain from providing set answers, use his diagnostic skill to help his subordinates learn how to become better diagnosticians themselves, and not express the anger and frustration that he sometimes felt with them. I watched his efforts to develop as a leader and to expand his knowledge and skill base. I gave him several reading assignments in addition to our sessions. We continued to work well together, but his progress in what were for him new areas of proficiency continued to be slow.

Henry reported to me that Tom's unit seemed to have moved back from the precipice but that he was still getting complaints that Tom was having a hard time listening. Henry also told me that he was reluctantly starting to think that he would have to ask Tom to leave. I pushed Tom to go meet with Henry soon for a progress report and feedback session and, despite his reluctance, he agreed to do so.

Now let's turn to an entirely new case to illustrate some major alternatives to how different leaders can approach similar situations. We will return to the situation Henry faced with Tom shortly.

The Case of a Reflective Leader

Nancy Walker was the senior director of operations in a mid-sized distribution company who had approached me for coaching as a way of improving her performance in complex situations with major subordinates. She was known in her company as a highly competent senior manager who often provided assistance to her peers when they experienced various forms of trouble. Our sessions typically focused on her working relationships with key people in her unit and how she could help improve their performance. In one session, we were discussing her ability to reflect on the situation she confronted and create a good solution inside the moments of reflection. As I described the various levels of reflection that an executive can use in these situations, she smiled and nodded.

"I know exactly what you mean when you describe that," she said.

"How do you experience it?" I asked.

"Well, I often tell my subordinates that when they are having trouble with someone they are working with, they should imagine that they are a little bird on their own shoulder that watches the face of the other person to assess how he or she is dealing with the situation. I know that the people who I have on my team who can do this are much more likely to identify and solve problems than those who look at me like I don't have my head glued on when I try to talk to them about this. I know that I can see whether someone is reacting badly to what I'm saying as I'm saying it. When I notice something like that, I often ask a question that tries to get at whether the person knows that they are having a reaction."

"What usually happens?"

"Well, that all depends on the person. The people who have this reflective ability you just described are easy to approach. I know that I can talk to them with a greater degree of flexibility and in more depth than those who don't have it."

"It sounds like you are coaching them to develop the skill as well."

"Well, I didn't know that I was doing it. But now that you describe it to me, I think that's exactly what I've been trying to do without knowing exactly what or why I was attempting to accomplish. This conversation will really help me better coach them in the future."

Lessons Learned From Coaching Tom and Nancy

These two case studies illustrate both the importance of metacognitive ability to executives and the fact that individuals with similar knowledge, skills, abilities, achievements, and intelligence levels can vary widely in the degree to which they have developed this capacity. In its most general terms, *metacognition* refers to people's ability to think about how they think. In other words, they can create moments in which they actually see their minds at work sensing situations, perceiving patterns in what they sense, and asking questions about the patterns they discern. I find it far easier to coach individuals who have already developed this ability, and I have learned that to help clients who are not metacognitively advanced, it is necessary to help them create this skill and capacity for themselves before truly significant progress can be made.

I believe that human beings know when they are in the presence of a leader who can think and behave from a reflective mindset. When people work with such leaders, they are likely to feel more secure, more like taking risks, and more like their true selves. When they are working for people who are blind to themselves and to others, the reverse is true: Individuals tend to walk around on pins and needles waiting for something bad to happen. People take fewer risks and, most often, leave their true selves at home. The capacity for reflective action and the ability to process information metacognitively are central to the development and use of Executive Wisdom, and without them, leaders are far less likely to decide and act wisely.

In these two cases, it is clear that Tom possessed little capacity for metacognitive thinking and reflective discernment. He rarely thought about the effects he had on people; did not perceive accurately the reactions of his key subordinates to his words or deeds; and seemed shocked, anxious, and defensive when I suggested that we explore what might be happening in his relationships. He had to force himself to think in this way, and he nearly always lost his concentration when we started to discuss these issues. He would frequently change the subject and try to take me into a conversation in which he was an expert and could inform me about what was happening in a situation in juicy detail. It was only with great effort on both of our parts that we could return to the issues of how he was thinking about his subordinates and organization.

Nancy, on the other hand, not only had a well-developed ability to think about her thinking, but she also was curious about this area and eager to become more skilled in it. She practiced between our coaching sessions, created her own metaphors and explanations for her experiences, and had begun to try to teach her subordinates how to use these same tools. Nancy's career was on track, and she was due for promotion in the near future. Tom, on the other hand, faced extinction in his organization if his behavior and performance did not improve. Let's dig a little deeper into these ideas through a quick tour of some relevant literature.

METACOGNITION AND SELF-REGULATION
IN HUMAN BEHAVIOR

Flavell (1977, 1979) first introduced the concept of metacognition as a way of initiating research on the long-recognized ability of the human mind to report on itself and its functions. Indeed, the very beginnings of experimental psychology were rooted in the methodology of introspection (Boring, 1950; Watson, 1963), which continued as the main tool for studying human behavior until criticism of its fundamental subjectivity led to the beginnings of the behaviorist paradigm. Behaviorism then dominated the field through most of the middle part of the 20th century. However, in the 1960s, revised methods and concepts led to the reestablishment of psychology's long-standing interest in the life of the mind, and the second cognitive revolution took off, at least in part because of the ground-breaking studies of Piaget (1971), Vygotsky (1962), Luria (1976), and many others (e.g., Neisser, 1967). The elucidation of the sequence of stages of cognitive development in humans and the concurrent evolutions of computer science,

EXHIBIT 3.1
Definitions of Metacognition

- "Knowing about one's cognitions" (Shimamura, 1994)
- Thinking about thinking
- Feeling of knowing
- Judgment of knowing
- A mind imagining and symbolizing itself
- The experience of the mind
- The mind watching and striving to regulate itself
- Internalization of externally guided inquiry and the advanced evolution of the ability to ask questions for oneself

neuropsychological testing, neuroimaging, and neuroscience have led to an enormous blossoming of research on how the brain works and how the activities of the human mind evolve out of their biological foundations.

Exhibit 3.1 presents several succinct definitions of the concept of metacognition. Shimamura (1994) stated simply that metacognition involves "knowing about one's cognitions" (p. 253). Another way of understanding the basic premise is that metacognitive processes focus on thinking about how one thinks. Research methodologies have sprung from the fundamental human experience that everyone has when they feel or sense that they know something (Miner & Reder, 1994) and the subsequent and more empirically derived notion of judgment based on the experience that one has learned something. In other words, metacognition involves how accurate and assured a person's perceptions of the feeling that he or she knows something end up being in reality (Herrmann, 1990; Nelson & Narens, 1994).

Understanding metacognition requires a leap of imagination that strives to conceptualize that an individual human mind can and does symbolize both its own existence and its methods of functioning. Virtually every person has had the experience of watching him- or herself try to learn, remember, think, feel, or regulate behavior in some way. We have these moments of clarity in which we see ourselves having experiences, recognize that we are having them, and are able to think and feel about the experience of those acts of recognition instead of merely having the experience of living them. Perhaps the most common variant of this metacognitive activity is trying to recall the name of a person that one is walking up to at a party or meeting or a fact to which one was previously exposed as one takes a test. This feeling of knowing someone or something and the active effort to retrieve the information while watching and feeling yourself try to pull it out of seemingly empty space describes the essence of the metacognitive functioning of the human mind.

The two case studies that began this chapter point out the difference between Nancy, who readily and spontaneously witnessed herself deliberately and strategically interacting with others, and Tom, who had great difficulty doing so. The ability of each to modify their behavior, talk about what was happening in their relationships with others, and conceptualize the changes that they would need to make to increase their leadership effectiveness was, I believe, based significantly on their metacognitive capacity.

Exhibit 3.1 also shows that metacognitive development, as practiced largely by educators, involves efforts to have students internalize externally guided processes of inquiry or instruction and thereby create an increased ability to ask questions for themselves to regulate the pace and success of their own learning (Fogarty, 1994). In other words, people can be taught to improve their metacognitive abilities by learning how to ask their own questions and find answers about how they learn and how they experience learning. I have come to believe that we must extend this kind of education to leaders in organizations.

Borkowski, Chan, and Muthukrishna (2000) presented a process-oriented model of metacognition in which they discussed the links among motivation, cognition, and executive function in the human mind. What follows is a listing of the 10 criteria they used to define a child who is a good information processor:

1. Knows a large number of useful learning strategies.
2. Understands when, where, and why these strategies are important.
3. Selects and monitors strategies wisely and is extremely reflective and planful.
4. Adheres to an incremental view regarding the growth of mind.
5. Believes in carefully deployed effort.
6. Is intrinsically motivated, task oriented, and has mastery goals.
7. Does not fear failure—in fact, realizes that failure is essential for success—and hence, is not anxious about tests but rather sees them as learning opportunities.
8. Has concrete, multiple images of both hoped-for and feared "possible-selves" in the near and distant future.
9. Knows a great deal about many topics and has rapid access to that knowledge.
10. Has a history of being supported in all of the above by parents, schools, and society at large. (Borkowski et al., 2000, p. 4)

If one applies these criteria to the two executives in the opening case studies, one can clearly see that, in all probability, Nancy met these criteria as a child and Tom, despite his many professional accomplishments, intrinsic leadership ability, and native intelligence, was probably lacking in a number of them. Indeed, Borkowski et al.'s (2000) model of a child as a good information-processor is a decent foundation on which to build a wise person. The similarities between Borkowski et al.'s research-based examinations of the cognitive and interpersonal functioning of children and the studies underpinning Baltes and Staudinger's (2000) Berlin wisdom paradigm and Sternberg's (2003) balance theory of human wisdom appear unmistakable. The research foundations on metacognition suggest that it can be taught to students in elementary and secondary schools, and individuals who do develop these abilities either early or later on in their lives become far more able to engage in the extremely complex and delicate activities called *leadership*.

Butterfield, Albertson, and Johnston's (1995) model of executive function in the human mind was effectively summarized by Borkowski et al. (2000) as consisting of three components: (a) task analysis, (b) strategy control (selection and revision), and (c) strategy monitoring. Individuals using their executive mental functions assess the tasks required of them; select, implement, and revise their strategies for accomplishing the activities involved in the tasks; and then monitor the effectiveness of the strategies they have systematically implemented.

For Butterfield et al. (1995), cognition, metacognition, and executive functioning constitute the three major components of a human mind at work. The cognitive level consists of all of the knowledge, skills, and strategies present in an individual's long-term memory. The metacognitive level consists of the "awareness of the cognitive level and contains 'models' of the various cognitive processes as well as an understanding of how knowledge and strategies interconnect" (Butterfield et al., 1995, p. 15). They further suggested that the metacognitive level is trainable: "Executive functioning coordinates the two levels—cognitive and metacognitive—by monitoring and controlling the use of the knowledge and strategies in concordance with the 'mental model building'" (Butterfield et al., 1995, p. 15). Thus, Butterfield et al. suggested that children can build models of their own minds in operation and use these models actively to regulate their performance on any given task as well as to develop and extend the ways in which they are learning at any chosen moment.

Again, the case examples illustrate two bright, experienced, and successful executives: Nancy, with good levels of metacognition and executive functioning, and Tom, with poor levels of them. Is it any wonder that Nancy was on the rise in her organization and that Tom had reached a plateau and was in danger of derailing? Coaching activities with Nancy focused on the elaboration of her previously developed metacognitive foundations in the leadership setting. With Tom, the coaching sessions tended to focus more on building basic capacities for the executive functions of his mind. Under the best of circumstances, this is difficult work. In the pressure-packed, hothouse environment of a senior leadership team, and with intense and public scrutiny of his performance on a daily basis, Tom had limited time to practice; limited room to fail; and, as a result, a limited executive future in that company.

The lessons here for leaders and those who coach them are challenging. Some leaders, like Nancy, have highly developed metacognitive and executive function capacities. They demonstrate their abilities to reflect on themselves, on how they think about their problems and experiences as leaders, and about the challenges they have with their organizations. However, in my experience, many, many others are, like Tom, nearly blind to themselves and have developed little reflective or metacognitive capacity. These individuals often have significant difficulties in their positions and with their organizations. I would also suggest that the same assessment could probably be applied to coaches themselves.

Major reviews of metacognition and research on metacognitive processes are available in several collected sets of articles, summaries, and essays (Bogdan, 2000; Cavanaugh & Green, 1990; Cavanaugh & Perlmutter, 1982; Gupta, 1992; Herrmann, 1990; Hertzog, Hultsch, & Dixon, 1989; Lovelace, 1990; Metcalfe & Shimamura, 1996; Schraw & Impara, 2000; Yzerbyt, Lories, & Dardenne, 1998). A search of PsycLIT for this book yielded more than 1,200 references to the terms *metacognition* or *metacognitive*. This conceptual and scientific literature is much too broad and deep to review here except to say that the core phenomenon of teaching people, even young children, to watch their minds in action can actually be done, and it improves their performance at all sorts of mental and behavioral tasks. That is, researchers have discovered that through systematic education, the human mind can learn how it learns, how to change how it learns, and to watch itself go through those experiences with an evaluative intent to improve over time (Kegan, 1982, 1994; King & Kitchener, 1994; Perry, 1999; Schön, 1983, 1987).

Similar bodies of literature have developed more broadly regarding the application of self-regulatory concepts to a wide variety of human behaviors (Bronson, 2000; Carver & Scheier, 1998; Schore, 1994), including emotional expression and social behavior. Carver and Scheier (1998) described it in this way:

> Human behavior is a continual process of moving toward, and away from, various kinds of mental goal representations, and . . . . this movement occurs by a process of feedback control. This view treats behavior as the consequence of an internal guidance system inherent in the way living beings are organized. The guidance system regulates a quality of experience that's important to it. For that reason, we refer to the guidance process as a system of self-regulation. (p. 2)

Bandura (1977, 1982, 1997) and his many colleagues have thoroughly demonstrated the impact that self-efficacy and related self-regulatory behaviors have on improving people's life circumstances and coping capacities. These self-regulatory paradigms all incorporate descriptions of processes and methods through which people can come to understand that they typically behave in one way and that if they want to behave differently they must determine the form that other behavior patterns should take and the mechanisms through which they can learn how to comfortably and reliably perform any new behavior. One can see this clearly in the performing arts when professional actors begin to learn a new role or professional musicians first play a new piece. With practice and coaching, both of which help individuals see and understand what they are doing and how they are doing it, those initial bumbling attempts to learn lines and notes are transformed by the performer's learning into polished performances in which audiences often transcendentally experience the character as enacted by the actor or the music as played by the musician and conceived by the composer. In the best cases of such artistry, audiences do not even see the professional as a person separate from the performance. Actors or musicians in such transformations seem to become their music or their roles. One can see similar transformations in the behavior of world-class athletes in competition, chess masters at their games, and effective leaders as they work with their colleagues.

Thus, the cognitive, metacognitive, and self-regulatory literatures all strongly demonstrate that human behavior in a wide variety of domains can be positively influenced by a variety of techniques and methods that teach humans to monitor and control various types of behavior and their accompanying mental states. The evidence now is all but irrefutable, but it has not been systematically applied across most domains of human behavior. Specifically, I could find no studies or references that explored metacognition in executives or leaders. There is a long and deep literature on executive and managerial decision making and problem solving (Bazerman, 1998; Gerten, 2001) but, case studies (Kilburg, 1996a, 1996b, 2000, 2004, 2005) and anecdotal evidence aside, I could find no established scientific facts that improvements in the metacognitive skills of executives help them be better leaders or that organizational performance increases if they improve these abilities. In a tangential set of studies, Siebert and Daudelin (1999) did demonstrate that as part of leadership development activities, managers who engaged in specific forms of reflection on their experiences were able to systematically identify many more things that they learned than those who were simply asked what they thought they learned a few months after their assignments. I spend more time on these and related findings and methods in chapter 8. The application of the theories of reflective learning and metacognitive teaching to the tasks of management and leadership thus seems to be in an early but nonetheless useful and highly directive state.

On the basis of my own experience in coaching leaders, I have come to believe firmly that those who have such metacognitive and reflective abilities and who work to improve them are able to do a better job and that their organizations perform more effectively than those whose leaders seem blind to such capacities and skills. The two case examples illustrate this point admirably. In the first scenario, Tom came close to destroying himself in his organization because he could not see his performance, did not hear the feedback being provided by everyone around him—including, most importantly, his boss—and he seemed to have no real idea of the impact he was having on people or why he was creating such an impact. Nancy, on the other hand, knew exactly what she was doing for herself and what she was trying to develop in her subordinates. Although her performance as a leader was not perfect by any means, her subordinates liked working for her, she had a good reputation as a manager in her company, and her boss thought her unit was performing well. I believe that by looking for the presence or absence of these metacognitive capacities in leaders and their subordinates, we can devise realistic and effective ways to help these clients improve what they do, how they do it, and their satisfaction with their overall working experience.

Psychodynamic and Human Performance Contributions to an Understanding of Metacognition

Two other streams of literature are relevant to the ideas presented later in this chapter. First, within the psychoanalytic literature, Erikson (1963), Freud (1910/1964, 1923/1964), Greenspan (1989), Greenspan and Benderly (1997), Hartmann (1958, 1964), Stern (1985), and Valliant (1993) have all described and discussed in significant detail the initiation, growth, and differentiation of the human ego. In psychodynamic theory, the *ego* is generally understood as a term that describes a structure within the human mind that strives to integrate the demands of the inner realities of physical, emotional, and mental pressures with the external demands of reality. This stands in contradiction to the more popular notion of ego as an inflated sense of self-importance, better known and described as *human narcissism*. Extensive studies have shown that humans develop ego capacity from infancy through childhood and continue to do so all the way through adulthood. Some of the capacities of the ego correspond to the development of the cognitive and self-regulatory capacities described above and to the overall subject of this book. Still more of the functions of ego concentrate on the management of intrapsychic, interpersonal, and social conflict and human emotion. The ego operates on both the inner and outer worlds in extensive efforts to transform them and make them safe for the individual. It is constantly engaged in evaluating experience, gauging levels of threat, making decisions, and performing both defensive routines and creative adaptations. Levinson (1981) and Czander (1993), among others, have explored the nature of the adult ego in work settings and have discussed some of the psychodynamic aspects of leadership and "followership" in organizations. Baltes, Staudinger, and Lindenberger (1999) provided a stellar review of the life span psychology literature and its relationship to the concepts and research in cognition and intelligence. Srivastva (1983) extensively explored a related set of ideas and concepts pertaining to the definition and description of *executive mind*.

In addition to the general concept of ego, psychoanalytic scholars have further differentiated two identifiable states within which this psychic structure appears to operate. These have been identified as the *experiencing ego* and the *observing ego*. The concept of observing ego was first introduced by Freud (1932/1964), who described the capacity as follows: "The ego can take itself as an object, can treat itself as an object like other objects, can observe itself, criticize itself, and do Heavens knows what with itself" (p. 58). Many other analysts have described the evolution of this capacity in their patients through the course of analytic treatment, which uses the introspective method of free association as its fundamental tool. In a relatively recent article, Glickauf-Hughes, Wells, and Chance (1996) described many different techniques that can be used to develop and strengthen the observing ego in the therapeutic process. It is most interesting that these suggestions and the descriptions of the results of the emergence of an observing ego appear to closely parallel those found in the literature on metacognitive states in cognitive functioning.

The experiencing ego, on the other hand, is described as the part of the mental apparatus that actually dwells in life; copes with its challenges; has the feelings; and enacts the defensive operations or the creative behaviors that people are most likely to see in themselves, family members, friends, and work colleagues. The experiencing ego is what most humans understand as "my self," that differentiated being who is separate from others and has his or her own thoughts, feelings, beliefs, and ways of being in the world. The experiencing ego tries; succeeds; fails; sweats; sleeps; gets angry; feels sad; acts seductively, foolishly, or with courage; gets exhausted; has relationships, ideas, and fantasies; carries the burdens of life's traumas; and lives the true joy of transcendent moments. The experiencing ego cannot help but rejoice and die each and every moment of each and every day. The extent of the joy, challenges, and particularly the suffering of these moments determines how each human being's character is formed.

Effective teaching, mentoring, coaching, and therapy are all methods that have been developed through human history that can help people observe their experiencing egos, their very selves, as they go about the business of learning and living. The ability to move gracefully and artfully back and forth between these two states of observing ego and experiencing ego is one of the major goals of these various forms of psychological and educational interventions. I hope that as you read deeper into this book, you will come to agree with me about the importance of helping executives better perform this skill as they lead their organizations.

The literature on ego and metacognition strongly suggests that the development of leaders requires and involves the differentiation of the adult ego into an identifiable subcomponent, what Jung might have called the *leadership elements* of the persona and the true self—the King and Queen archetypes (Campbell, 1971). Phenomenologically, the leader-differentiated ego consists of all of the normal components of the adult ego that provide its foundation. In addition, it possesses an array of knowledge, skills, abilities, and experiences that have been created through the course of the leader's organizational and educational careers. Depending on the extent of those experiences, the capacity of the individual, and the opportunities provided or obtained during life, the leader emerges progressively as a novice, journey-person, and expert. Effective organizations can and do track the progress of their executives through these stages via their succession management and leadership development programs (Conger & Benjamin, 1999).

Finally, the ideas presented below are informed by the research on the development of human expertise or exceptional performance that I briefly referenced in chapter 2. Ericsson and Lehmann (1996) provided a tremendously rich introduction to this area of long-standing interest in the psychological literature. Beginning with Galton's work in 1869 (see Surowiecki, 2004), psychologists have explored how and why some individuals seem to be able to reach the pinnacle of performance in various domains of human activity. Chase and Simon (1973) created a theory of expertise based on their interest in the evolution of chess masters. In their review, Ericsson and Lehmann suggested several major findings from this literature. First, it appears that it takes at least 10 years for human performance to rise to the level of recognized international mastery, regardless of which domain of human activity is involved. Second, the emergence of such levels of mastery is directly related to deliberate practice over a long period of time. Third, the importance of time and deliberate practice is independent of domain and human capacity. Fourth, what emerges after this long period of gestation is a complex mental landscape that experts use to guide their diagnostic pattern recognition, strategy formation, and execution of tactical behaviors. Finally, even genius appears to take this long to flower fully, and it does so only when native ability is steadily honed through years of activity dedicated to learning and improvement.

The implications of these various streams of literature for the fields of executive education and coaching are profound. All too often, programs of coaching, development, and training are short-term, hit-or-miss affairs. In exploring these different areas of research and clinical practice, I have come to see that we are only slowly beginning to understand how a mature, wise, and fully integrated human comes into being. It takes a long time and specific, dedicated practice. Formal and informal education, learning on the job, mentoring, and coaching can all make important contributions to executive excellence. The combination of the concepts in these various streams of intellectual, clinical, and scientific work have led me to the following conclusion. I now believe that with at least 10 years of consistent developmental work, expert leaders can emerge within organizations. These become executives who can make wise decisions based on a well-developed and differentiated adult ego that has an extensive capacity for self-reflection, metacognition, and virtuous behavior. In the rest of this chapter, I describe some concepts to enable leaders to help their subordinates and coaches to assist their clients in making this most arduous and glorious journey.

Metacognition and the Executive Mind

Studies of managerial decision making and other processes have exploded over the past 30 years, and a great deal has been learned (Klein, 1999, 2003). In the following sections, I attempt to apply some of what is known about metacognition to the challenges of what is known about how executives adapt and try to create wise approaches to the complex realities that they face.

Figure 3.1 presents a simplified and basic model of metacognitive functioning described by Nelson and Narens (1994). In essence, metacognitive and self-regulatory theories and research suggest that the cognitive realm of human activity can be best understood by applying the models developed in the fields of cybernetics and systems theory (von Bertalanffy, 1968). In the figure, the external environment presents an object, an event, a situation, or an interaction of some sort that a person is challenged to understand and master. The individual detects this object or situation by means of monitoring behavior, and information flows into the mind, where the person creates a mental model of the experience. This internal representation of the object is held in memory, and efforts to further understand or change the model by the person are conducted through control behaviors that interact with the object or situation in the environment. Thus, at its most basic level, a metacognitive system can be seen as a feedback loop between an internally perceived and experienced external object, person, activity, experience, or event and the mental model an individual constructs of it.

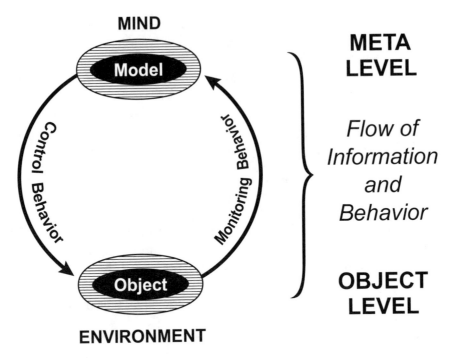

Figure 3.1. Basic model of metacognition.

In the model of Executive Wisdom presented in chapter 2, the emphasis is on discernment, decision making, and action: Information flows to the mind to create the model via monitoring efforts and, after processing, information and control behavior flow back to the object to create interactions with and modifications of it. This simple system has three components: (a) the external object, person, situation, or event itself; (b) the inner experience, cognitive processing, and constructed mental model of it; and (c) a two-way exchange of information and behavior between the internal representation and the external object. This process and system can be seen clearly operating in leaders or executive teams as they perform due diligence on a merger or acquisition target. As they begin the process, they have an idea about what the target company is like. As they collect more and more information about the organization, their inner model is selectively modified to more fully represent the real and substantive nature of the company.

Bruner (1986), Gergen (1999), Gupta (1992), Shimamura (1994), and many others have suggested that the learning and adaptation function of human beings is based on the processes of social and cognitive construction. Figure 3.2 presents a simplified illustration of these ideas that elaborates on the model described above. The figure shows the two-level system of the external world and the mental model developed to understand and interact

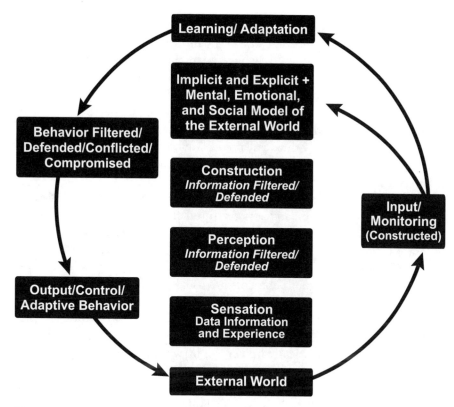

Figure 3.2. Rudimentary model of human learning and adaptation.

with it along with the dual-level feedback loop of input or monitoring and the output or control behavior designed to interact with and adapt to the external environment. However, the illustration adds several elements that increase the complexity of the system. The input or monitoring information is further broken down into other components. Human sensory systems initially collect data on the environmental situation and move it on to perceptual processes. Perceptual processes in the human brain begin the tasks of filtration and defense. Raw information is translated into objects and situations that can be identified and understood by the individual. A wide variety of studies have illustrated the human ability to construct different perceptions from the same data elements and even to deny that the external reality, or pieces of it, exists (Valliant, 1993). External objects and situations are rapidly classified as potentially threatening, rewarding, interesting, or boring.

Figure 3.2 also illustrates that the perceptions lead to internal mental, emotional, and social constructions of external reality. When a construction takes on sufficient and recognizable shape, an internal model of the external situation can be said to have been created. That model will have both implicit and explicit features because of the filtration and defensive processes that went into its creation. What have been called the *defensive operations* of the human ego are always involved in the definition of these models (Valliant, 1993). These mental, emotional, and behavioral patterns are designed to keep distress to a minimum, especially in the short term. In most human beings, these defensive systems of behavior operate out of conscious awareness and thus can present major challenges to any leader or group of subordinates facing a significantly threatening external or internal organizational environment (Argyris, 1993).

To learn and adapt, the person then uses the internal model itself to guide assessments, choices, and actions. Interaction with the external world occurs when the person behaves in some fashion. Most often, this interactive behavior is filtered and defended in different ways that reflect various conflicts and compromises reached in the internal processing (Gray, 1994; Kilburg, 2000). The output behaviors are usually directed at efforts to cope with and exercise control over the external world and are usually seen as adaptive but can also be destructive to both the person and to others. Thus, in the development and exercise of Executive Wisdom, one can clearly see that the process is dramatically influenced by what occurs in the individual executive's construction of the model from which he or she will try to lead in the organization. The more accurate the process of discernment, which includes perception and internal model building of the external object or situation, the more likely the leader will be able to operate on and with that model to take perspective, plan interventions, make decisions, and take appropriate action. The less accurate the process of discernment and model building is, the more likely it is that the leader will make less effective decisions and thus that there will be problems in executive action.

For example, if an individual executive is trying to decide whether to make an acquisition or to execute a merger, the more data the leader collects, the more likely it is that he or she will create an accurate model of that target company. However, the desire of the individual to make a deal, the political or market pressure on the leader to decide, or the economic motivations of the people involved can all significantly color the perceptions and interpretations of the data collected and can thus change the quality of any decision that will be made. Leaders who are aware of how their minds operate to form these models are much less likely to make evaluative and strategic mistakes in their decision making.

Following the theoretical description of Nelson and Narens (1994), Figure 3.3 presents an illustration of a more complex two-level, executive metacognitive system. The bottom of the figure shows the basic metacognitive system presented in Figure 3.1. However, the basic system is replicated four times to demonstrate a more differentiated environment that an execu-

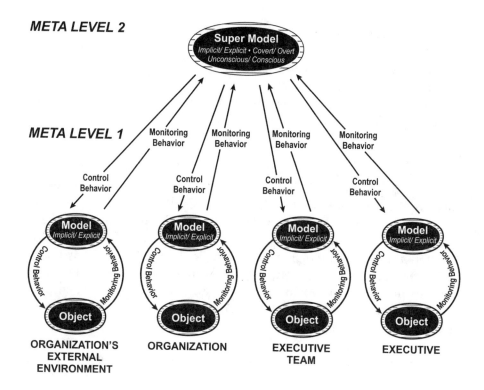

Figure 3.3. Elementary two-level executive metacognitive model.

tive typically faces: in the external world of his or her organization, the world of the home organization itself, the team with which he or she works, and his or her own internal system. Each of these subsystems is dynamic, constantly changing and interacting with the executive, and each of them leads to the creation and continuous refinement of the internal models that are used for monitoring and control purposes. The figure also illustrates that a second "super model" is created that the executive attempts to use to integrate the data and experience obtained from the four first-level metacognitive subsystems. Efforts are made to understand information obtained from the first-level interactions and models and integrate it into the implicit and explicit elements of the higher level model. This higher level model is shown as having overt and covert components as well as conscious and unconscious components. Efforts to interact adaptively with the first-level models and, through them, to interact with the actual environmental objects, are shown as control arrows or behaviors in the flow chart. Nelson and Narens suggested that human metacognitive systems can comprise many different interacting levels and that these levels naturally tend to subordinate to and interact with each other. Again, the implications for the use of the model of Executive Wisdom are pretty obvious. The better a leader is at the processes of discernment and metacognitive model construction, the more likely it is that he or she will truly understand the nature of the realities that his or her organization and executive team face. Effective executive action in the first instance again depends on these diagnostic processes.

Figure 3.3 allows one to understand how a leader who is evaluating a merger or acquisition candidate can progressively add data and models of various aspects of that business to his or her overall conceptualization of the company. Systematically acquired information about the finances, markets, leadership, human resources, history, and culture of any organization that elaborate the overall internal models that a leader would ultimately use to decide to acquire or merge can be built up in a progressive fashion. The way in which those micromodels interact with the existing mental map that the leader has of his or her own organization leads, it is hoped, to a more finely grained appreciation of the overall effects that such a merger or acquisition would have on the executive's enterprise. The systematic refinement of this complex model-building process is what happens during most of these kinds of strategic decision-making processes in business organizations

THE BEHAVIORAL GEOGRAPHY AND PSYCHODYNAMIC GEOLOGY OF EXECUTIVE MIND

Figure 3.4 follows the model of environmental geography and internal geology introduced in chapter 2 and pushes additional complexity into our understanding of the adaptive and self-regulatory behavior of leaders. On the top surface of the cube, the external world of the individual leader is presented as a chaotic landscape. Following Kilburg (2000), virtuous and vicious attractors and repulsors are represented by the whirlpools that populate the landscape. *Attractors* are regions of behavior or the environment that exert a strong influence on the individual and tend to pull him or her into a response or interaction pattern that may be difficult to escape. Conversely, *repulsors* are regions of behavior or the environment that exert a strong influence on the individual but tend to push him or her away from a particular response, person, or interaction pattern. Attractors and repulsors in action can most clearly be seen in human behavior in the form of good and bad habits, what are often thought of as strengths and weaknesses (Buckingham & Clifton, 2001; Clifton & Nelson, 1992). An executive who tends to lose his or her temper in times of increasing interpersonal tension,

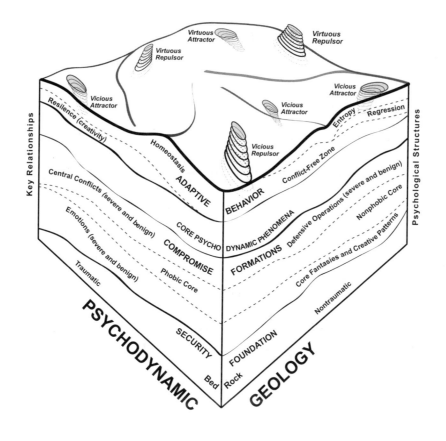

Figure 3.4. Chaos and behavioral geography and geology.

leading to the emotional wounding of and continuous fighting with colleagues, can be said to fall repeatedly into a vicious attractor. This same executive might struggle constantly with an inability to inhibit aggression in these situations and can be said to have difficulty with such inhibition because it represents a virtuous repulsor for him or her.

The reverse of this pattern can also be illustrated. In this situation, the executive is constantly pulled into a virtuous attractor in which aggression is initially inhibited when organizational tension is high. This individual might well experience the expression of anger or temper tantrums as a region of behavior that acts as a vicious repulsor for him or her. Such an executive might well get into trouble when situations in his or her organization call for an appropriate and aggressive response. As Figure 3.4 illustrates, this area can be seen as the observable aspect of the executive's behavior and world, which I described metaphorically in chapter 2 as the behavioral geography of the individual.

As I also described initially in chapter 2, Figure 3.4 illustrates that the world below the surface geography is complex and cannot be ignored. Metaphorically speaking, this inner subsurface world is best identified as the psychodynamic geology of the individual. Because it lies below the surface, it is difficult to see or experience directly. Executives themselves are not always familiar with this shadow domain and its often far-reaching influence on behavior. As in the real world relationship between geography and geology, they interact with each other in complex ways. Thus, geological features of the world such as mountains, oceans, and tectonic plates often have major impacts on geographic features of environments such as the rise and directional flow of rivers, the presence of lakes, the populations of flora and fauna that inhabit a region, and the aspects of human civilization that are possible to attain.

In the world of behavioral geography and geology, most of these interactions can be seen in the adaptive behavior initiated by an individual. Following Kilburg (2000), such adaptive efforts usually fall into creative efforts to become more resilient, homeostatic patterns that maintain the status quo, or regressive episodes that lead the person to more primitive and usually less effective behaviors. In Sternberg's (2003) balance theory of human wisdom, these efforts involve activities through which an individual adapts to the situations the world presents and shapes the external world in a way that best meets his or her needs or decides to select a different environment that is thought to present a better set of opportunities. Leaders are creating these responses for both themselves and their organizations. Most of these adaptive efforts are the result of complex exchanges that result from inner, psychological compromises, which themselves can sometimes represent the resolutions of trauma-based conflicts experienced by the individual (Wurmser, 2000), and from outer, psychosocial experiences a leader may have had in the past or be having in the real time present. Past psychological trauma can involve physical or mental injuries incurred early in life as a result of inadequate or abusive parenting, toxic interpersonal and social environments, or relationships that have left an executive with individual psychological or physical scars. Trauma can also be current, such as troubling relationships at work or in a person's private life. The area of adaptation also identifies a region in which behavior can be seen as conflict free or independent of such compromising traumatic processes.

The inner world of an individual's psychodynamic geology is extremely complex. It rests on the bedrock of what is labeled here as the *security foundation*. Humans begin their lives as helpless and relatively powerless beings (Bowlby, 1988). For many people, their initial months are secure and nontraumatic. Caretakers, parents, and others ensure that the infant's physical and emotional needs are met. The baby can concentrate his or her energy and attention on the tasks of development. However, many other people have traumatizing early experiences, including episodes or long periods of physical or emotional abuse or neglect. For these individuals, substantial psychological and physical resources are most often diverted from the tasks of normal mental, emotional, physical, and social development into efforts to identify and manage threats and injuries from the external world and the extreme emotional and physical responses that arise from them. As described by Erikson (1963), the security foundation for humans defines whether they approach the world in a fundamentally trustful versus a mistrustful fashion. In human organizations, a leader's ability to create and use trusting relationships represents the cornerstone of both emotional intelligence and the entire base of psychosocial capital on which an organization depends and through which the enterprise does its business. Flaws or problems in the ability to assess, create, or express trust in human affairs often leads to difficult performance at best and catastrophic tragedy at worst.

Following Wurmser's (2000) formulations, Figure 3.4 further identifies phobic and nonphobic cores of an individual's behavior. In areas of traumatized experience, most people develop strong emotional and often defensive responses, and these are often laced with intense fear that sometimes rises to the level of an explicit phobia (Wurmser, 2000). Cognitive responses and core fantasies, often primitive, are associated with these emotional reactions. Such responses need not be extreme or lead to phobic reactions. In a secure environment, infants learn curiosity, joy, and exploration (Greenspan, 1989). These bedrock structures and experiences can often influence the behavior of an executive in his or her daily efforts to lead in an organization. They can determine whether the challenges in these complex social roles are experienced primarily from a psychological foundation of fear, mistrust, and their associated defensive reactions or from a foundation of curiosity, trust, excitement, and their associated resilient responses of creative, competitive, and collaborative exchanges with colleagues and business partners.

Figure 3.4 also illustrates that the emotions and primitive cognitive responses that arise out of traumatic experience lead to efforts at self-protection or psychological defense and to core psychological conflicts. The interaction of emotion, cognition, defense, and conflict most often produces compromise formations that themselves are efforts at adaptive behavior. The figure further suggests that such compromise formations underlie and support the core psychodynamic phenomena that are most often seen in the world by others as features of human character and the complex behavior patterns that are manifested in human relationships and in work. Each side of Figure 3.4 shows key relationships and psychological structures, both of which mediate the geological world of psychodynamics and the geographic world of behavior (Kilburg, 2000; Wurmser, 2000). Key relationships include those in the past and present, such as parents, siblings, and other family members; spouses; children; teachers; clergy; subordinates; peers; bosses; customers; and so on. The psychological structures include the rational self; the ego, previously described in this chapter, which is responsible for adapting to reality; the *conscience*, a structure that manages morals and values and helps to determine what is right and wrong in behavior, about which I have more to say in chapter 7; the *instinctual self*, which responds to reality in a way that maximizes both pleasure and survival; and, finally, the *idealized self*, which serves as an internal model and helps manage self-esteem.

This material is introduced here to clarify that the metacognitive processes and structures identified in Figures 3.1, 3.2, and 3.3 are, as has been suggested, strongly influenced by complex inner and external experiences. Often, these experiences can only be hinted at or hypothesized about by the executive or by a coach or consultant working with him or her. Figure 3.5 illustrates this well. Following Gupta's (1992) formulation of cognition and metacognition in an ecological framework, one can see that the executive formulates what can be identified as a cognized environment through which he or she both experiences and mediates all interactions with the outer world of behavioral geography and the inner world of psychodynamic geology. This cognized environment is complex and for most people is only partially metacognitive in capacity and structure.

The merger and acquisition example that I have been using to illustrate the leadership applications of metacognitive concepts will help understanding of these complex models. Let us hypothesize a case of three different CEOs, all of whom are considering a major strategic move for their companies. The first leader had a fairly traumatized childhood with a difficult family background, troubled parents, and impoverished economic circumstances. This background left this individual determined to rise out of this situation at all costs with an intense drive to succeed, excellent analytic skills developed in an entrepreneurial career, and a degree of self-confidence and self-centeredness that bordered at times on arrogant megalomania. Once this leader decided to do something, he would let nothing stand in the way of his accomplishing the task. In our merger and acquisition scenario, such a leader would tend to face such a strategic choice out of an internal psychological structure that might well push him to ignore many sources of important data about the downsides of the deal once he felt internally that he wanted to drive to completion. Subordinates, colleagues, even financial backers might well have extreme difficulty in dissuading such an individual from making the deal and might even risk forms of antagonistic retaliation with this kind of internally structured executive. They might find that decision-making processes are shortened because of the urgency with which

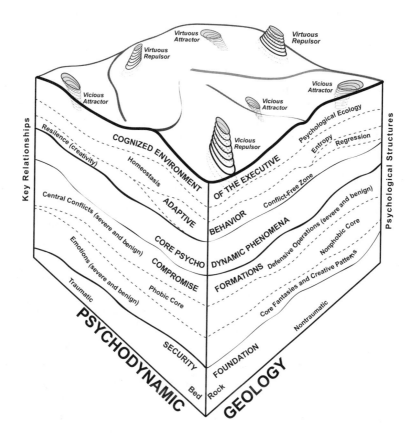

Figure 3.5. Cognized world of the executive.

such a leader wanted to complete the transaction and might be quite anxious about the long-term consequences of an inadequately considered choice.

A second person with a similar background and experience set also has risen to the top of a corporation through hard work and high energy. This leader, however, responds to inner insecurity with a defensive and adaptive psychological base that emphasizes caution in major choices, attention to the finest details in data sets, and making sure to check out all of the potential downside risks in a merger and acquisition deal before proceeding. Such an executive might lead a due diligence process that would exhaust everyone with endless and paralyzing analyses; repeated meetings to go over and over the details; and constant requests for fact checking, cost–benefit determinations, and alternative-scenario construction. These kinds of business partners tend to wear everyone out as they work through problems and issues because their internal insecurity and defensive organizations can never truly be satisfied. They will usually be able to avoid the big mistake with such an approach, but they will also tend not to make the brilliant stroke that will redefine a business or remake an industry.

A third person who comes at the same business problem with her internal landscape based on secure foundations and a defensive and adaptive psychological foundation that emphasizes reality-based competition and strongly supportive relationships might well organize the due diligence and model-building processes of an acquisition determination in a different way than the first two leaders I described. Using the talents and skills of colleagues and business partners to collect data, build strategic and tactical understanding of the acquisition and merger target company, and create realistic post-decision-making and implementation alternatives, such a leader might well be appropriately anxious about the ultimate impact of a major deal on her company, her leadership team, and her career, but she would be more likely to use the resources around her and the network of relationships she has constructed to surface these concerns in a timely fashion. Rather than ignoring downside consequences in a hell-bent drive to make the deal or engage in analysis paralysis and endless quibbling with partners, such a secure leader would tend to construct business deals with as many reality-based checks and balances as possible. This kind of executive would also tend to lead the implementation process in ways that emphasized realistic problem solving rather than either blaming others for problems or the extremely cautious approaches that might be taken by our first two leaders.

Figure 3.6 attempts to pull the previous illustrations together to demonstrate the complexity of the inner and outer worlds of the executive. The external, chaotic landscape of the executive's geography consists largely of the operating environments in which he or she functions. These can be seen to be the family, group, organizational, regional and local, national, and global arenas. One also sees the leadership exerted by the individual in terms of management, interpersonal relationships, and efforts at inclusive and transforming behavior. Keep in mind that although the chaotic attractors and repulsors are not presented in this figure, they are still operating. The data and experience that the individual accumulates when interacting with the external world are brought into the inner world via the monitoring processes described in Figures 3.1, 3.2, and 3.3, depicted by the arrows labeled *Monitoring*, which penetrate into the psychological world of the executive.

Also keep in mind that this monitoring behavior is socially and cognitively constructed and therefore active and interactive. The data and experience accumulated are not simply internalized as experienced; they are operated on in a dynamic, often-defensive, and multileveled fashion as they come into the cognized layer of the executive. In these acts of construction, a leader builds complex maps of him- or herself, the world of the organization

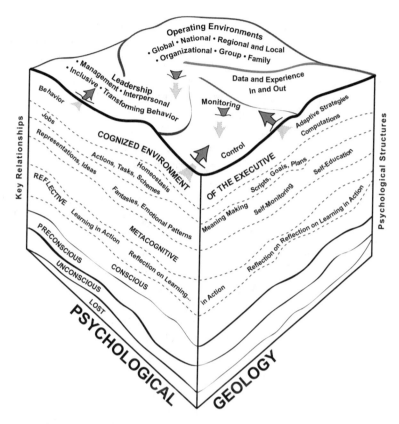

Figure 3.6. Complex metacognitive view of the world of the executive.

in which he or she works, and the environments with which the enterprise interacts. In a true sense, an executive simply invents the internal model of the world that he or she experiences. In these inner cognized maps, executives operate mentally and emotionally to determine the correct steps to take in leading their businesses. Problems in constructing accurate maps, interpreting the maps in terms of deciding what is the correct action to take, or using the maps to guide the daily execution of decisions made will move a leader away from wisdom and toward folly. The number of variables in play at any point in time in a leader's internal and external worlds highlighted in these figures demonstrates just how difficult it is for an individual to be consistently wise in the execution of his or her duties.

Figure 3.6 follows Figures 3.5, 3.4, and 2.9 in form but presents the psychodynamic world somewhat differently to emphasize several other important elements. What can be seen here are six levels of executive mind. The lost areas of the mind are at the lowest level. These components consist of memories of experiences and events that are completely unavailable to an individual. For example, most people cannot remember what happened on the 2nd day of the 3rd year of their lives unless it was truly significant in a positive or negative way. The organization and operation of short-term memory systems in the central nervous system virtually guarantees that events and experiences in life, although sequentially encountered and initially recorded for potential use, are edited, culled, and stored for their long-term, adaptive implications (VanLehn, 1996). Although some of these historical experiences may be relevant for executives, the lost level of mind illustrates that these data will not be normally accessible.

The next level of mind consists of what is known as the *unconscious*. Events, experiences, reactions, emotions, fantasies, and thoughts—some extremely relevant to daily life and patterns of personality and coping, and some completely inconsequential—are stored in long-term memory and for the most part remain consciously unavailable to individuals. We get hints, glimpses, illustrations, and sometimes full recollection of parts or all of our unconscious minds in dreams, fantasies, slips of the tongue, jokes, writing, and external behavior, especially conflicted and compromised behavior. Unconscious material is often relevant to executive performance but not usually accessible to the client or to a coach or consultant (Kilburg, 2000). The influence of the unconscious on the other levels of the human mind cannot be overemphasized.

The *preconscious* is the next level of mind seen in the figure. One can think of this level of mind as the doorway between the unconscious and conscious levels of mind. Fantasies, wishes, desires, emotions, ideas, and all types of behaviors that one sees in people on a daily basis are significantly informed and influenced by this doorway. Because coaches and their clients usually do not have direct access to their unconscious worlds, they most often work together on conscious or preconscious material. When working at this level of mind, the unconscious usually can only be inferred as being present.

For example, an executive may be angry and frustrated dealing with a group of colleagues at work on a specific project. A coach or someone else observing the behavior may hear the person say something like "I'd like to drop them all off in the woods and leave them permanently," or "I really need a break from them." On the conscious level, these comments express the frustration, anger, and perhaps some potential anxiety on the part of a leader. This material is accessible and fairly easy to address at this level. However, the comments hint at what may be unconscious desires or wishes to hurt the collegial group by abandoning them or, in the second comment, the wish to simply avoid or escape from the conflict explicit in the passage the group is making. In either scenario, the comment could also depict deeper, more permanent patterns of adaptation learned earlier in life when the individual did in fact experience authority figures who abandoned people during troubled times or an avoidant approach to conflict management that reflects how his or her family of origin managed these situations. It may be difficult or even impossible for an executive to see these connections or for a coach to interpret these wishes to a client directly without additional information, but the material of the preconscious level can really help a coach discuss with a client what may be happening at the deeper levels of mind and what can be done with it constructively. An executive's inner awareness can also lead him or her to constructively question motives, emotional responses, and coping patterns for him- or herself.

Obviously, the *conscious* level of mind operates above the preconscious. This layer contains the material available to all of us on a moment-to-moment basis and is a reflection of the existential and phenomenological experience of each person. For the most part, it is easy to access and report on, if a person desires to do so. Thoughts, feelings, daydreams, fantasies, plans, goals, and so on, float in and out of focus in what William James referred to as the *stream of consciousness* (James, 1890/1950). Coaching work with clients takes place most often at this level of mind, and interventions are usually based on what is presented out of the stream of consciousness of the client. Once a coach negotiates an agreement, this level of mind in clients is usually available for reporting on experience and for developing both increased knowledge and skills. Most leadership work is also conducted out of the conscious layer of the mind and at any given moment provides an executive with the raw material with which he or she crafts responses to the organizational and environmental demands of the enterprise.

The fifth level of mind illustrated in Figure 3.6 is labeled *reflective*. This layer represents what Argyris (1993) and Schön (1987) described in their ground-breaking work in which they identified three levels of reflection usually available to people: (a) learning-in-action, (b) reflection on learning-in-action, and (c) reflection on reflection on learning-in-action (see chap. 8 for more extensive treatment of this material). I have used these concepts extensively to describe the basic processes involved in coaching clients (Kilburg, 2000). As described previously in this chapter, Siebert and Daudelin (1999), as well as Mezirow and Associates (1990), among others, have extended this notion of reflective mind. When intervening with a client, coaches are usually trying to elicit at least one level, if not two levels, of reflection. Listening to a client tell a story almost always involves hearing how the individual was learning his or her way through a particular problem or situation. This is the level of learning-in-action. When coaches ask clients questions about what has been reported, make observations, provide feedback, or ask clients to consider making some sort of change, they automatically take the client to the next level of reflecting on learning-in-action. Similarly, when coaches ask clients to examine what they experience in these interventions, with questions such as "How did you think this session went?" or "Was this suggestion helpful to you?" they are taking clients to the third level of reflection on reflection on learning-in-action. Such interactions in coaching sessions are often seamless, and both individuals may not realize the extent to which reflective mind is in use. However, a coach must be using his or her reflective mind continuously in any direct interactions with clients.

Similarly, executives themselves, completely independent of interactions with coaches or others, can create these multileveled reflective experiences. If they simply watch themselves, their organizations, and their subordinates doing work and try to modify it in the process, they engage in learning-in-action. When they call staff meetings, planning retreats, brainstorming sessions, or quality circles, they use second-level reflective practices of reflecting on learning-in-action. And when they investigate how effective such reflective experiences have been, they use the third-level interventions, or reflection on reflection on learning-in-action.

The sixth and final level of the model presented in Figure 3.6 is the metacognitive level. It is included as a separate structure because I believe that once reflective processes are well established in a particular area in a person's life, they take on a different form. In essence, they become self-regulatory subsystems that are nearly autonomous in their levels of sophistication and complexity. The metacognitive layer also incoporates the two levels shown to be immediately on top of it. The layer includes representation, mental models, scripts, and so forth that individual leaders use to cognitively organize and integrate their external worlds and internal experiences. Following the descriptions provided above regarding Figures 3.1 through 3.3, the metacognitive mind of an effective executive consists of sophisticated models of environmental, organizational, team, and individual functioning. Monitoring operations are continuous, and high-functioning individuals repeatedly scan the most relevant aspects of the environmental object(s) being followed. These operations are represented in Figure 3.6 by the bidirectional arrows exiting from the top of the figure and penetrating from the top into the subsurface. Monitoring functions are seen in the arrows descending through the surface, and control functions are seen in the arrows that ascend and exit into the top of the figure. Thus, data are continuously obtained and presented from the complex, chaotically functioning external world via monitoring behavior. The vicious and virtuous attractors and repulsors illustrated in Figure 3.5 are presumed to be operating here but are not pictured because of the existing complexity of the drawing. The attractors and repulsors and unconscious components of experience, cognition, and emotion act consistently as challenges to Executive Wisdom because of the degree to which they exercise either seen or unseen power and influence on the leader's ability to discern correct direction; make correct decisions; and execute choice in the right way and against the right time frame for the individual, the executive group, and the organization.

Slywotzky, Morrison, Moser, Mundt, and Quella (1999), in their book on profit patterns, described a set of 30 approaches that business leaders can take to adjust the strategies of their enterprises to take advantage of the constant, chaotic shifting that characterizes the global economy. They explored megapatterns, such as when leaders lack strategic imagination and profits disappear, when the rules by which a business has been competing change radically, and when new technology completely shifts the name of the game an enterprise plays. In these and a variety of other detailed cases, they also provided some interesting and worthwhile suggestions about how leaders can recognize that such patterns are rising and how they can adapt themselves and their organizations to take advantage of them. In the framework of this chapter, it becomes clear that Slywotzky et al.'s approach to understanding and using profit patterns to help executives manage the futures of their organizations involves the processes I have described in this chapter through which they develop and use their metacognitive models to do their work.

The two case examples framing the opening of this chapter can be used to understand this six-level model of executive mind. The two executives who were discussed both clearly had lost, unconscious, preconscious, and conscious levels operating in themselves on a daily basis. However, there were major differences regarding the degree to which their reflective and metacognitive layers of mind were active. In Tom's case, I could push and encourage him to create reflective states during our coaching sessions, and he found these experiences useful, but he struggled with the process of putting the reflective practices into his leadership repertoire on a daily basis. He had developed metacognitive models of his colleagues, subordinates, organization, and competitive environment, but there were major gaps in his constructions, and his ideas tended to be both inflexible and difficult to modify. Adding nuanced meanings to his ways of thinking about and responding to situations was an arduous experience at best for both him and me. In the end, coaching for Tom did not have an extremely positive outcome. Although we were able to stabilize the situation in the short run, he did not improve to the extent that his boss, Henry, desired. He faced an uncertain future in his organization.

On the other hand, Nancy had evolved to be able to create her own reflective states of executive awareness on a routine basis. She was well along in helping her subordinates develop the same skill. Her metacognitive models were rich, deep, flexible, and easy to engage. She readily added information and perspective to her models to change them and make them more useful to her and the others with whom she worked. In our sessions, she was not only able to report on how she functioned at these levels of mind, but she also quickly engaged with my abilities to work with her on this material and used the exchanges to strengthen her concepts and skills. She also reported routinely on her efforts to put her new ideas and abilities into practice following our sessions. The descriptions she provided gave me a great deal of confidence that she was growing steadily and that coaching was having a significant positive effect.

HUMAN CONSCIOUSNESS AND EXECUTIVE WISDOM

Damasio (1999) provided a succinct framework for understanding human consciousness in general terms that I believe provides an additional and somewhat larger perspective within which one can understand these metacognitive roots of Executive Wisdom. His work was based on the study of the clinical neurology of brain-damaged patients as well as experimental studies of human cognition and neuroanatomy. Damasio proposed three levels of human consciousness. The lowest level, which he described as *proto consciousness*, consists of the neurological and psychophysiological elements, particularly in the brain stem, that go into the core human functions of basic wakefulness; low-level attention; background emotions, such as the ability to feel pleasure and pain; and the capacity for specific behaviors. At an intermediate level, he suggested another differentiated set of neurological and psychophysiological components that provide the infrastructure for what he called *core consciousness*. This level of human cognition comprises the abilities for focused attention; specific emotions, such as fear, anger, shame, sadness, and joy; specific actions or behaviors under both conscious and unconscious control; and the capacity for language and thus verbal reports of both internal and external experience. He provided an extensive discussion of core consciousness because of its central importance in human behavior.

Damasio (1999, pp. 124–125) suggested that core consciousness has a variety of attributes, which he described in the following ways:

- It has significant impact on other cognitive processes, focusing and enhancing basic attention and the capacity for working memory.
- It supports the creation of memories that are central to human identity and to complex cognitive operations. Without good memory of the images and objects one creates in the cognized environment, a human is incapable of higher level mental processes, including those I have been discussing as wisdom and Executive Wisdom.

- It provides essential support for the operation of language functions.
- It expands the capacity for planning, problem solving, and creativity, which are all core components of the models of wisdom I have discussed here.
- It is central to the human ability to sense individuality and to the basic functions of metacognition (i.e., the human ability to both sense and use the fact that they are in the act of knowing about themselves and their environments).
- It provides the foundation for all of the higher level operations of consciousness.
- It rests on the human being's inner sense of the images created with his or her mental and emotional infrastructures, including the images created of feeling experiences.
- It creates tremendously influential nonverbal experiences of relationships to objects in the external environment.

Damasio (1999) went on to state that

> core consciousness is generated in a pulselike fashion, for each content of which we are to be conscious. It is the knowledge that materializes when you confront an object, construct a neural pattern for it, and discover automatically that the now-salient image of the object is formed in your perspective, belongs to you, and that you can even act on it. You come by this knowledge, this discovery as I prefer to call it, instantly: there is no noticeable process of inference, no out-in-the daylight logical process that leads you there, and no words at all—there is the image of the thing and, right next to it, is the sensing of its possession by you. (p. 126)

This is a terrific description of the sensation of the "feeling of knowing" that has been a central component of the development of metacognitive theory and science. Leaders and their coaches often have these experiences of the feeling of knowing as they construct or recognize patterns of behavior in themselves, executive teams, organizations as a whole, or external competitive environments.

For Damasio (1999), the highest levels of cognition are seen in what he called states of *extended consciousness*. Based largely in the neurology and psychophysiology of the forebrain or prefrontal cortex, its complex connections to the centers of emotion in the midbrain immediately behind it, and the foundations of attention and information processing in the brain stem, extended consciousness consists of the executive functions of mind described by Goldberg (2001) and covered in chapter 2 of this book. Such functions include planning, including hypothesis generation and scenario construction; problem solving; and decision making. Within Damasio's conceptualization of human consciousness, human wisdom is an emergent state of extended, metacognitive consciousness possessing the properties he attributed to the feeling of knowing that arises in core consciousness. When wise human beings confront a difficult situation in their own lives or the lives of others, pathways or solutions occur to them in the same kind of spontaneous way of "knowing" or awareness of the object being imaged that Damasio described as happening when people just know they know something. In a parallel sense, wise humans or humans expressing wisdom know the way or the path to address a challenge, problem, or opportunity that usually turns out to be correct.

This spontaneous yet extraordinarily complex and mysterious ability to discern, decide, and act rightly—in other words, the capacity to create, access, and use the knowing of "rightness"—is what scientists, philosophers, religious sages, and normal humans have come to describe as *human wisdom*. The application of this capacity to the functions and future well-being of organizations, including those most complex organizations that humans have yet constructed, nation-states, is in essence what I am labeling *Executive Wisdom*. In Damasio's (1999) scheme, one can thus see Executive Wisdom as what could be called a subset or superform of extended consciousness resting on all of the neurological, psychophysiological, and cognitive building blocks he and others have described and that I have tried to summarize thus far.

The metacognitive level depicted in Figure 3.6 thus represents a highly evolved form of extended consciousness in Damasio's (1999) framework, and it provides the functional infrastructure for the emergence of those superstates of consciousness or "sense of knowing organizational rightness" that I am calling Executive Wisdom. In the figure, control functions or efforts to interact with and regulate the various external environments of the executive are illustrated by the arrows flowing from the metacognitive layer into the external environment. Verbal, nonverbal, and all other types of behavior can be used by the executive to construct control strategies and initiatives. Leadership-influencing behaviors aimed at strategy, human resources management, organizational operations, inclusion, interpersonal relationships, and transforming organizations are among the control strategies used by executives.

Figure 3.6 also illustrates some of the complexity of the metacognitive layer of the executive mind. After my initial discussion of Executive Wisdom in chapter 2, I have once again referred to it here as arising out of the elaborated version of the cognized layer of the inner environment of the executive, following Gupta's (1992) description. The figure labels some of what takes place in humans when they systematically build complex internal image and pattern structures based on their interactions with people and other aspects of a particular slice of their worlds. In the cognized layer one can see such elements as behavior, jobs, tasks, activities that are inordinately complex translations of images or representations, actions, schemes, scripts, goals, plans, adaptive strategies, computations, ideas, fantasies, emotional patterns, meaning-making, self-monitoring, and self-education. All of these elements are terms of art that have arisen in the cognitive literature to describe ways in which the human mind organizes, internally represents and structures, and then uses experience.

Gupta's (1992) monograph contains an excellent summary of the metacognitive literature and concepts. The reflective, metacognitive processes can be simply described as involving the ability of humans to identify objects, experiences, people, and events either externally or internally; then to create complex images of them that are held in their neural structures; and finally to develop and be aware of the ability to see these images as cognitive creations and to be able to operate on them consciously as such. The awareness of the processes involved in the creation of these images then enables a person to operate on them both mentally and emotionally with more or less rationality, complexity, and effectiveness. Past and present experience can be compared against the internal representations and experiments in projecting future changes that can be conducted by individuals (Damasio, 1999; Goldberg, 2001; Klein, 2003).

We can see versions of this activity very simply when any one of us plays a game like chess, checkers, Go, or Scrabble. As the pieces are laid down on the board, we form images in our mind. We can then perform mental experiments on those images and project changes forward in time in a series of if–then conjectures. Each time we conduct one of these projections, we then need to change the configuration of the board in our minds and anticipate what our playing partners or opponents will do in response. Expert chess players are able to project seven or more moves ahead in a game. Supercomputers and their chess software simulations can now literally assess the potential of thousands and thousands of possible moves forward and their associated risks in a matter of seconds, duplicating the feats of true genius of chess masters with brute computing power. Leaders of major organizations face much more complex situations than a chess board every day and perform similar operations in their personal, cognized environments. They then have the responsibility to make choices for their enterprises and exercise the authority to act on them. It is my contention that coaches and consultants seeking to help such senior executives must have similar capacities mentally and emotionally.

Figure 3.6 also illustrates that the boundaries between these layers of mind are permeable and open to influencing each other. As I described above, unconscious material can and does interact with and shape the conscious, reflective, and metacognitive components of mind and thus how monitoring and control activities are undertaken. Similarly, the interactions with the external world can and do provide hugely complex sets of information and experience that shape the inner, unconscious levels of the human mind. In addition, the figure demonstrates that the various forms of psychological structures, such as the rational self, the instinctual self, the conscience, and the idealized self that I have described in earlier work (Kilburg, 2000) interact with these layers of mind, as do key relationships with family members, friends, and colleagues. These inner psychological structures and social relationships thus mediate all of the cognitive processes and executive actions undertaken by leaders.

A FRAMEWORK FOR UNDERSTANDING THE METACOGNITIVE EVOLUTION OF THE EXECUTIVE MIND

Table 3.1 presents a framework for understanding the cognitive development of adults as they strive to create themselves as professionals in various fields of endeavor and in particular as executives. As described above and summarized by Ericsson (1996), Ericsson and Lehmann (1996), and Ericsson and Smith (1991), it currently seems clear that humans take approximately 10 years to achieve true expertise in any field of complex activity. Similarly, Jaques and Clement (1991), Kegan (1982, 1994), Piaget (1971), Perry (1999), and many others have described how the cognitive operations and capacities of humans take decades to develop. The questions that

TABLE 3.1
The Executive Mind in Development

Stage	Levels of mind (Kegan, 1992)	Levels of complexity (Jaques & Clement, 1991)
Novice	Levels 2 and 3 Categorical thinking	I → III
	Cross-categorical thinking	B-1 → B-3
	Conscious	
Journeyperson	Levels 3 and 4 Cross-categorical thinking	IV → V
	Systemic thinking	B-4 → C-1
	Reflective	
Expert	Levels 4 and 5 Systemic thinking	VI → VII
	Postmodern deconstructive thinking	C-2 → C-4
	Metacognitive	

naturally arise are how a person becomes an expert executive and how long it takes. The structure of the Table 3.1 suggests a way of understanding this process.

At the novice level of functioning in an executive position—say, during the first 3 years or so—the literature and current concepts would suggest that a person struggles to organize and understand the incredibly complex organizational world he or she has entered. Although the individual may well have risen to an expert level of functioning in another field of accomplishment and even have an international reputation for achievement and professionalism as an executive leader, he or she still can function as a novice who tries to organize basic understandings of the external organizational world; create appropriate categories for the experiences had and efforts undertaken; and conceive, execute, and evaluate the impact of his or her managerial decisions. As the table indicates, I believe the cognitive skills and levels of mind capable of being applied by executive apprentices correspond to Kegan's (1982) levels of categorical and, eventually, cross-categorical thinking and to Jaques and Clement's (1991) levels B-1 to B-3 of information processing. Most interactions with these individuals as leaders will be through their conscious minds and the lower unconscious levels presented in Figure 3.6 and described earlier in this chapter.

When using categorical and cross-categorical thinking, leaders are usually able to differentiate people, organizations, situations, strategies, tactics, challenges, and problems and to see them both objectively and from a diagnostic perspective. They are able to identify whether the issue being confronted goes into one category of problem versus another, such as finance or marketing. They may be able to see the financial aspects of a marketing plan and even go into the details of such a project with savvy and competence. Leaders who function primarily at this level and in this way can be marvelous at setting clear expectations, discerning major diagnostic problems, exploring what constitutes a particular issue, and pursuing how it might relate to other issues in the organization. They typically operate within the normal, 1-year budget cycles of their organizations, but as they continue to grow, they begin to see and use implications of their data sets and models to project action 2 or 3 years into the future.

As the person continues to grow through a minimum of 2 to 5 years of additional experience, and for some as many as 10 to 20 years, in a leadership position, he or she can evolve from a novice into a journeyperson. The basics of leadership and management are mastered, and the individual begins to create understanding, meaning, and effective operations at higher and more complex levels. For at least a significant number of normally intelligent people, this transition is partly experienced as a shift from cross-categorical to "systemic cognition" in Kegan's (1982) terms and to levels B-4 to C-1 information processing in Jaques and Clement's (1991) terminology.

At the journeyperson level, the individual properly identifies what is happening in an entire organizational system and in him- or herself and operates on sophisticated understandings of categories of problems and issues. Such executives also increasingly observe refined and complicated connections between categories and create strategies and approaches that can take advantage of this complex knowledge. They are able to create new ways of seeing and operating in enterprises based on their cognitive capacities. They can see the structures of the whole organization and its various subparts, the processes that go on between and among the components and the external environments of the organization, and how to modify them. In Jaques and Clement's (1991) framework, the journeyperson is able to work in time frames stretching 5 years or more into the future. In human terms, these executives come to understand that the metaphorical ankles and necks of organizations are indeed richly and subtly connected and that the actions of leaders can have consequences that radiate out much farther in enterprises and into the future than might be initially intended.

These cognitive abilities inform and enable their interpersonal and intraindividual behaviors as well. It is in the here and now of how individuals relate to others and enable them to work most effectively that one most often sees the capacity for reflective activity emerge in systematic ways that can be defined as leadership, and the work of coaches and consultants can help leaders discover and stimulate the improvement of these abilities. The individuals who develop to this level of cognitive and related interpersonal skill almost automatically rise within organizations to greater levels of responsibility and authority and are often frequently seen in upper mid-level management and senior level executive positions. As journeypersons, they typically have internal, metacognitive models and maps for how to accomplish various levels of organizational and leadership tasks and requirements and use the maps to operate in increasingly successful and complex ways. Following the models I have described above, they can also use their experience to refine and deepen their models by means of their monitoring and control efforts.

Table 3.1 indicates that if individuals continue to develop, and few leaders do, they rise to a level of expert functioning. These individuals become cognitively capable of "postmodern, trans-systemic, deconstructive thinking" in Kegan's (1982) terms and levels C-2 to C-4 information processing in Jaques and Clement's (1991) system. It is in these individuals that coaches and consultants will find sometimes extraordinary levels of creative leadership thought and activity. These people not only can see what is present in systems, environments, and all of the richness of the connections, but they also often see what is not there and how to take advantage of that knowledge. They are also able, within Jaques and Clement's framework, to operate against longer time horizons; Jaques and Clement suggested that some rare individuals may be able to see the need for, create strategies around, and take actions to execute tactics that have major implications for organizations, governments, and societies 50 or even 100 years after they are initially implemented.

These individuals are among the most challenging and rewarding of clients, and their abilities represent the kind of long-term developmental objective toward which coaches and those responsible for executive development efforts should strive with each person in their caseloads or programs. These individuals routinely use all three levels of reflective processes to create complex metacognitive models of themselves, their environments, their relationships, and their organizations. Only after substantial experience and development does one see these capacities arise, and it is extremely rare to see these levels of leadership expertise in individuals with less than 10 years of managerial experience. The literature on human wisdom reviewed in chapter 2 suggests that the emergence of such extraordinarily high levels of executive functioning is most likely to be seen in individuals 50 or more years of age, although someone who is younger can develop a postmodern mind; in fact, postmodern thinking can and should be taught to leaders as early as possible in their careers. However, it is the complex interaction of the ability to operate cognitively in this way, along with the accumulation of decades' worth of experience, that eventually lead someone to be able to demonstrate what I am describing as Executive Wisdom.

The storage of pattern upon pattern upon pattern of human and organizational responses experienced over those years when combined with emotional maturity, truly reflective mental states, and the cognitive complexity of a postmodern mind creates the best set of conditions for Executive Wisdom to emerge. Leaders who have the capacity for Executive Wisdom will be able to at least occasionally access the internal "sense of rightness" I described earlier in this chapter as they perform their duties. Interacting with individuals who are tapping into and using Executive Wisdom can be a disconcerting experience for many people, because a leader in such a state will often have levels of understanding, models of the world, and the capacity to internally and rapidly operate on and with these components of their awareness and experience in ways that are unavailable to anyone else in the immediate environment.

DEVELOPING METACOGNITIVE AND SELF-REGULATORY CAPACITY IN LEADERS: PRINCIPLES FOR COACHES AND EXECUTIVES

The implications of this literature and these concepts for the practices of executive development and coaching are extensive. Although they are not all clear to me at the present time, several major ideas are, and I believe they can form a coherent set of 10 principles to inform leadership development efforts:

1. Leadership development involves the differentiation of the adult personality and mind into a revised set of structures, processes, and contents using the prior mental, emotional, social, and personality foundations of the individual. When this development works effectively, a "true leader" is apparent when encountered.

2. Leadership development begins with the enhancement of the experiencing ego of the person by providing an individual with exposure to supervisory, managerial, and leadership knowledge, skills, activities, and roles. It then extends to the strengthening of the observing ego of the leader in development as he or she acquires increasing amounts of mentored experience; more sophisticated mental models of human, group, organizational, and environmental function; the capacity for postmodern and systemic thinking; and emotional maturity.

3. Leadership development advances progressively, from novice to expert levels, following the principle of *vertical declage*— one stage or level that then builds up another and then additional successive levels (Gupta, 1992; Piaget, 1971)— and creates the capacities of the experiencing and observing egos of the individual to operate in managerial and leadership positions. Vertical declage involves constructing interrelated capacities that require each other for the fully competent expert leader to emerge. In this context, cognitive development from categorical to trans-systemic thinking and social and emotional development from childlike dependence to full adult, interdependent maturity are required for the creation of a wise executive.

4. Individuals may have developed the capacity to think and operate metacognitively in other domains of activity before they start the process of becoming formal leaders. These experiences will inform their growth as leaders and may be tapped routinely by themselves and coaches to help them evolve their capacities and abilities. However, the presence of true, world-class expertise in other domains does not necessarily transfer into performing as a wise leader.

5. Leaders operating metacognitively as experts across a wide variety of organizational, interpersonal, economic, political,

and social domains will tend to make better decisions and create more refined and sophisticated interventions in their enterprises and lives. Therefore, they will be more likely to succeed, especially in complex, turbulent, and chaotic organizational and market conditions. Metacognitively developed wise leaders have minds that are able to symbolize themselves as executives with Damasio's (1999) sense of extended consciousness in the realm of organizations. They can reflect with sensitivity, critical analysis, and objective awareness on their performance and on how they analyze and think about how they perform. The best of the best of these individuals create, access, and use the internal "sense of rightness" I have described as Executive Wisdom.

6. Some of the core functions of coaches and other development professionals are to assess the capacity for and scope of the metacognitive operations in their executive and management clients and to promote the further development and broader applications of these abilities.

7. Coaches and coaching activities assist leaders in creating metacognitive fields or structures within which they use monitoring, control, and reflective processes to guide their experiences and improve their ability to address the challenges of leading their enterprises.

8. Coaching, other leadership development activities, and experience stimulate and facilitate the healthy differentiation of the leader's adult observing and experiencing egos into what can be called the *leader* or *executive self*. At the most advanced levels, these activities promote the emergence of Executive Wisdom.

9. Coaches and coaching can provide psychosocial, emotional, and physical support for the client—in other words, a living containment or structured interpersonal relationship (Kilburg, 2000)—during the emergent process that can lead to the creation of virtuous leader selves.

10. The coach's or other development professional's metacognitive capacity and adult, differentiated observing and experiencing egos will significantly influence how successful he or she can be in providing assistance to clients in developing themselves. This is not to say that coaches and other development professionals must have had senior executive experience themselves in order to help people develop these capacities (although it cannot hurt to have such experience) but that a coach or professional who does not have the capacity

to think trans-systemically and behave in a mature fashion is unlikely to be able to help a leader develop his or her full potential. Coaches who are incapable of recognizing states of human wisdom and Executive Wisdom or who struggle with the creation, access, or use of their own capacities for wisdom are unlikely to provide a great deal of assistance to leaders struggling to develop or use such abilities.

METHODS TO STIMULATE METACOGNITIVE PROCESSING IN LEADERS

Given these 10 principles, what specific kinds of activities, methods, and techniques can coaches use to promote the process of differentiation and the evolution of the expert metacognitive, wise leadership mind? Suggestions of coaching methods, inquiries, and probes to improve metacognition and self-regulation in clients are provided in Exhibits 3.2 and 3.3.

Space limits the degree to which these complex items can be explained and explored, and additional suggestions for practice are covered in more depth in chapters 4 through 10. The questions and probes provided in Exhibit 3.3 are straightforward and can be used by any coach or development professional without further explanation. For example, asking a client what he or she wants to be different typically stimulates a high-level review of the current situation being faced and furthermore requires the individual to think and emote regarding what might actually improve the situation. Similarly, asking people how they know how they know something calls on them to review their sources of data (read: monitoring activities) and their mental models of the situations in which they find themselves. The other questions and probes provided can and do encourage both the client and the coach to explore the situation; the process of monitoring it; the model(s) being created and used; and the control or intervention efforts and their effects on the person, organization, group, or inner life of the executive.

The methods and techniques listed require much more elaborate explanations, and many of them are already described elsewhere in the literature (Fogarty, 1994; Hargrove, 1995; Kilburg, 2000). It is especially useful and important early in a coaching assignment to explicitly talk with the client about the issues of levels of mind, cognitive development, and the need to become a more reflective person and leader. Instructions, illustrations, and reading material on the topic can provide important methods for beginning or furthering the processes of ego differentiation into the leader self and

EXHIBIT 3.2
Coaching Methods to Promote Metacognition and
Self-Regulation in Leaders

Self-monitoring instructions, education, and homework assignments (thoughts, emotions, physical status, interpersonal issues, knowledge acquisition of management and leadership, knowledge retrieval, conflicts, psychodynamics, images, cognitive distortions, fantasies, free association, introspection).

Reflection instructions and cues (Schön, 1987).

Brainstorming.

Strategy development processes and exercises.

Evaluation processes and exercises.

Case studies with and without debriefing and deconstruction:
- Seeing impacts on self, others, group, organization, family, community, and so on.
- Examining how impacts on others are created.
- Examining injuries to self and others and how they are created.
- Examining performance-enhancing components for self and others and how they are created.
- Examining what is working and what is not.
- Examining what is "between the lines" or what is inferred in the situation, behavior, verbal or nonverbal exchanges, images, and symbols.

Objectification, categorization, cross-categorization, systematization, and deconstructive examination of emotional, cognitive, interpersonal, group, organizational, community, political, economic, social, and other complex material.

Models for description, understanding, and prediction.

Debriefing and deconstructing of coaching sessions.

Thought experiments, what-if exercises, scenarios, fantasies, and creative inventing.

Deconstructing of planning, strategy formation, and evaluation exercises on personal, interpersonal, business, or organizational topics.

Self-control or regulation exercises (emotional, cognitive, behavioral inhibition or expression, skill practice, behavioral rehearsal).

Deliberate alteration of perspective or role (empathic identification, role reversal, role playing, gestalt empty-chair technique, empty-chair with a mediator technique).

Psychodynamic behavioral sequence analysis.

Thinking out loud with and without feedback and deconstruction.

Self- and other inquiries (360-degree evaluations, personality and other assessments, dialogues, feedback processes, deconstructive feedback; Kegan & Lahey, 2001).

Listening experiences and exercises.

Reflective journaling (written reflections on journal entries).

Dreaming, fantasies, dream and fantasy logs.

Self-talk, talking out loud.

Metaphors, similes, symbols.

Stories, fables, novels, movies, poems, songs.

Socratic inquiry and other Socratic methods.

Videotaping or audiotaping of feedback on behavior.

Guided readings.

Role modeling new behavior (reflection, metacognitive skills, observing ego).

Teaching new skills, models, ideas.

(continued)

EXHIBIT 3.2   *(Continued)*

Deliberate refocusing of attention on elements of situations, behaviors, present or
   past moments or relationships.
Reality testing (seeking additional data outside client's experience; encouraging
   consultations; validating and invalidating client reactions, perceptions, thoughts,
   ideas, emotions, inferences, and attention to facts).
Self-soothing.
Limit-setting, boundary maintenance, countering, confronting, exploring, and
   managing client's defensive operations.
Clarifications, confrontations, interpretations, reconstructions.
Behavioral contracting.
Humor, jokes.
Self-disclosure.
Framing and reframing.
Left-hand column exercise (Argyris, 1993).
Ruts exercise (Hargrove, 1995).
Envisioning, imagining futures.

---

the enhancement of reflective activity and, eventually, metacognitive capacity. The other techniques can and do come into play during various sessions and at different points during a coaching engagement with a client.

Figure 3.7 provides an overview of the process of a typical coaching session. This process was reviewed in Kilburg (2000) and suggests that the coach and the client establish the containment for the work and then proceed with an initial exploration of the potential material of importance. Usually by the middle of a session, they are engaged in multiple rounds of disclosure, feedback, inquiry, and exposition that constitute the bulk of the effort that they both make. Viewed through the lenses of the development of metacognitive capacity and pushing toward the emergence of executive wisdom in the client, the figure demonstrates that the interactive dynamics of the coach and the client almost automatically promote states of reflection that often lead to metacognitive activity. Use of the methods, inquiries, and probes suggested in Exhibits 3.2 and 3.3 during this inherently reflective process can strengthen, deepen, and increase the rapidity with which metacognitive structures and processes can emerge or strengthen within executives and thus improve the likelihood that the individual leader will be able to discern, decide, and act rightly on behalf of an organization.

Finally, some suggestions for evidence of the emergence of enhanced metacognitive functioning in executives are presented in Exhibit 3.4. I look for stories provided by the client or people who know the client or observable examples during coaching sessions in which executives can better think, behave, change, or feel in themselves or in and through their leadership roles. Although the list itself is self-explanatory, it is particularly relevant

EXHIBIT 3.3
Inquiries and Probes to Stimulate Metacognition and
Self-Regulation in Leaders

What do you want to be different in this situation?

If you had a magic wand and could change anything that you wanted, what would you do?

If you had a secret wish, what would it be?

What do you want from this situation, person?

What do you need from this situation, person?

If this were happening to your friend, daughter, son, mother, dad, spouse, and so on, what would you think, feel, say, or do? How would you say or do it?

What do you know about this?

How do you know what you know about this?

Do you often know how you know something?

Do you often ask yourself how you know this person, problem, organization, group?

How do you know this knowledge?

How extensive is this knowledge?

What are the limits of this knowledge?

What is missing, or what are the inconsistencies in this knowledge?

From whom and when did you obtain this knowledge?

Why is it important for you to know, obtain, clarify, use, or change this knowledge?

Do you know the difference between *knowing* and *guessing*?

What knowledge do you need to complete this picture, solve this problem, fill this gap? From whom or what sources can you get it?

How can you operate cognitively on this picture, problem, issue, challenge, conflict (objectification, categorization, cross-categorization, systematization, deconstruction, paradoxes, polarities, creative troubleshooting)?

Can you observe your mind performing these operations? How good are they? Can they be improved? How? What is missing from them?

How do you feel about this problem, issue, challenge, person, family, group, organization, conflict? Are there gaps in the feelings?

How do you feel about this knowledge of feelings about problems and issues?

How do you feel about the operations you have completed? What is your evaluation of the process, success, failure, impacts, outcomes?

What have you learned from this experience?

How would you describe your model of leadership? What are its components? How do you apply it in your group or organization? How effective is it for you? What is missing from it? When it succeeds or fails, why does it do so?

What do you need to help you grow and develop as a leader?

What are the three best examples or lessons in leadership that you can remember? Why were they good? Do you use them when you lead today? Why? Why are they useful today?

What are the three worst examples or lessons in leadership that you can remember? Why were they bad? Do you use them when you lead today? Why? Why are they useful today?

What do you "resonate to" as a leader (balance sheets, financial reports, market analyses and data, business strategies, human resources issues, power dynamics, political situations, rumors, gossip, investor community pressure, legal and regulatory issues, interpersonal relationships and conflict, values, virtues, vices, board of directors relationships and decisions, new ideas, feelings)?

(continued)

EXHIBIT 3.3   *(Continued)*

Why are you tuned into these issues?

What do you typically tune out? Why?

How could you change what you typically resonate to?

How do you try to create meaning with and for the people in your organization and the people it serves?

What works in your meaning-making activities? What doesn't work? Why?

How would you describe your model of your mind? What are the lenses, filters, preferences, biases, methods, assumptions, beliefs, attitudes, values, virtues, vices, emotions, patterns of thought, conflicts, and patterns of compromise that your mind applies in organizationally relevant, interpersonally relevant, and intrapersonally relevant situations?

What are the key factors, preferences, and biases that affect your judgment?

What are the key factors, preferences, and biases that affect the accuracy of your judgment?

How would you characterize these biases, preferences, or distortions? Do your patterns have patterns?

What can you do to decrease these patterns, preferences, or distortions?

How you use these preferences, biases, and distortions to transform or influence your behavior, group, family, organization, community, and systems?

Can you see yourself applying these preferences, distortions, and biases?

Do your preferences, distortions, and biases need to be modified? If yes, how? How can you do so? What effect or outcomes do you hope to achieve?

Can you think and talk out loud while responding to any of the above questions?

Does this remind you of someone or something that you have experienced or know already?

Why is this a good or bad idea?

How might you use this?

When have you used this before?

Can you describe a new application of this knowledge?

Why are you learning this?

How is this idea relevant?

Is this idea a fact, opinion, belief, bias, feeling, or memory?

Is this reaction objective or subjective?

Is this information observable, reliable, and valid?

How decisive are you?

How flexible are you? Do you change your mind easily? Why? How?

What went well? Poorly?

What is the "big idea" here?

How does this connect to other big ideas?

How can I use this big idea? How can I generalize this idea?

when reports are provided that show that the individual's circumstances or his or her organization demonstrate significant shifts from where situations, enterprises, or people started. Because these ideas, principles, and methods are truly exercised in the direction and on the behalf of improving clients as leaders and thereby improving their organizations, using them increases the likelihood of succeeding as a coach who is promoting the emergence of Executive Wisdom.

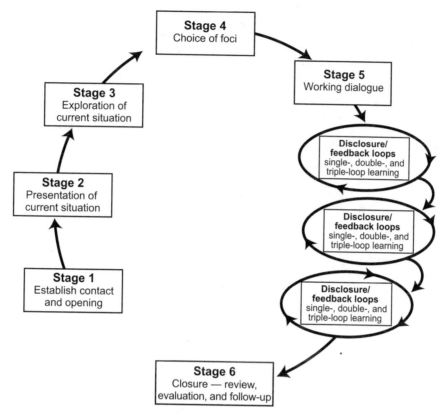

Figure 3.7. Stages and flow of a coaching session.

EXERCISE TO EXPERIENCE AND PROMOTE METACOGNITIVE PROCESSING

Take a few minutes to examine Exhibit 3.1 carefully. Think about how much experience you have had as a leader or as a coach who works with leaders. Now, try to answer the following questions for yourself.

1. What project, activity, program, or task that you have accomplished in your lifetime has taken the longest amount of time, and how much time did it take? Did your experience and levels of understanding about what you were trying to do change during the activity or project? If so, how?
2. In regard to your answer to the first question, did the activity or project take longer than 5 years to accomplish? If not, have you ever tried to conceive of something that would take that long to do?

EXHIBIT 3.4
**Behavioral Evidence of the Emergence of Metacognitive Functioning
in Executive Coaching Clients**

1. Reports, stories, and examples given by clients of improved ability to perform
   the following:
   a. Think and strategize about their own behavior, other individuals, groups,
      their organizations, business, government, and so forth.
   b. Problem-solve or troubleshoot complex, difficult, long-standing situations
      and challenges and create clearer and increasingly real understandings of
      them and propose and execute solutions to them.
   c. Deliberately create or modify a verbal, emotional, or behavioral approach
      to a person, group, or situation.
   d. Deliberately change a position, preference, behavior pattern, or emotional
      response or approach taken or used repeatedly in the past.
   e. Demonstrate accurate empathy and genuine regard for people.
   f. Identify biases, preferences, distortions in patterns of thought, emotion, or
      behavior in self, others, and groups.
   g. Identify and modify patterns of resonance in interpersonal, group, or
      organizational situations.
   h. Engage in explorations, challenges, and exchanges with diverse or
      different people.
   i. Negotiate mutually on the basis identified interests and needs.
   j. Voluntarily use creativity, curiosity, objectification, and systemic and
      deconstructive approaches to solve problems.
   k. Deliberately create reflective spaces and holding environments for
      themselves and others.
   l. Demonstrate management of complex emotional responses such as
      shame; anxiety; anger; sadness; lust; frustration; greed; impulsiveness;
      withholding; sadism; masochism; the desire to hide, avoid, or cover up;
      and so on.
   m. Demonstrate the application of virtues in leadership situations—
      temperance, prudence, justice, fortitude.
   n. Describe mental maps or models they use to understand themselves,
      others, and their organizations and guide their leadership behavior in the
      organization.
   o. Execute rapid and accurate responses to complex intrapsychic,
      interpersonal, group, family, or organizational challenges.
   p. Execute rapid repairs to damage done, problems uncovered, and models
      discovered as weak, defective, or ineffective.
2. Reports and stories of a–p above provided by superiors, peers, subordinates,
   and other stakeholders.
3. Emergence of clear and perhaps revised values, attitudes, emotional patterns,
   ideas, and behaviors that guide leadership action and activity on a sustained
   basis.
4. Deliberate, conscious shifts in the allocation of time and other resources
   toward clearly established and articulated goals.
5. Deliberate efforts to evaluate outcomes of strategies, investments, projects,
   and behaviors.
6. Intrapsychic, interpersonal, personal, and career changes that the client
   identifies as pushing him or her to be more authentic and more in touch with
   what he or she describes as his or her true self.

(continued)

EXHIBIT 3.4   *(Continued)*

7. Changes in external demeanor and behavior for the better over the long term—client is happier, more confident, and more successful; demonstrates more fortitude, prudence, temperance, and justice; has higher self-esteem; and is less anxious, defensive, angry, sad, shamed, conflicted, and so on.
8. Deliberate efforts to teach and develop others.
9. Significant positive and observable changes in organizational, group, or individual performance attributable directly to the actions or changed activities of the executive—the amelioration or prevention of regressed states and the emergence of creativity in individual, group, and organizational behavior.
10. Significant positive changes in relationships with colleagues, subordinates, customers, investors, spouses, significant others, children, and friends.
11. Evidence of creative activity, new ideas, adventures and explorations, fantasies, dreams, knowledge, attitudes, emotions, and behaviors.

3. As an example of such thinking, take a few minutes and consider what life will be like for you personally and professionally when and if you reach 70 years of age. What do you think life will be like, or should be like, when you get there? In what kinds of activities will you like to engage? What have you done in the past 3 to 5 years to prepare for such activities? What are you doing this year to get ready? Have you considered what you should be doing in the next 5 to 10 years to prepare? If you have not, can you set some time aside to do so? If you have, take a careful look at what you have considered and ask yourself what might be missing from the plans.

4. Now, ask yourself a similar question about what your organization could or should be like in 10 years. Take yourself through a similar process of considering how you need to get ready personally and how you get the organization moving in the directions you think it needs to move. Ask yourself to prepare a map to guide these considerations. Finally, test your ideas against the internal "sense of rightness" that was explored in this chapter. Do they seem like abstractions, possibilities, what one could consider as tabletop exercises? Or does the formulation you have evolved seem to have an inherent sense of validity, a well-rounded, carefully considered, but nonetheless spontaneously "known" internal sense of "yes, that is the right future for the enterprise"? If it is the latter, even though such projected images are always conditioned on what the future really holds, it is much more likely to be based in the operations of Kegan's (1982) fifth-order mind and Executive Wisdom.

If your responses to this exercise are in the vein of "of course I've done that, and it's all laid out," then you are most likely functioning at an expert level of executive metacognition and to have demonstrated at least periodically this ephemeral capacity for Executive Wisdom. If the questions seem intimidating, strange, or make you want to simply put this book down, you most likely are still functioning at a novice or perhaps at best journeyperson level of executive metacognition, and you have some additional work to do before you have the ability to either spontaneously or routinely tap into the capacity for the inner "knowing of rightness" as a leader.

4

BARRIERS TO LEADING WISELY

History is the ultimate judge of judgment.

In the first three chapters of this book, I have attempted to provide both a conceptual and a practical description of the phenomenon I call Executive Wisdom. The material thus far has been rooted in philosophical studies and traditions, psychological science, history, and real life experience. In this chapter, I turn toward deepening our understanding of how wisdom does or does not work in the daily lives of leaders and of how executives and development specialists such as coaches can move more systematically toward the creation and use of wisdom. The focus here is on the barriers domain of the core model of wisdom introduced in chapter 2. In other words, what can and does get in the way of executives developing and using the ultimate in human virtue as they work on behalf of their enterprises?

It has become clear to me that there are an enormous number of barriers that can impede or prevent an individual leader from accessing or using wisdom at work. In this chapter, I present a detailed discussion of some of these roadblocks along with a description of a pathway that can be used to help individuals activate this virtue in themselves. I want to emphasize at the outset that the pathway that will be described is only one way to create and access wisdom. As I have discussed in the previous chapters, there are many others. Let's begin with a brief case study of Andrew Carnegie, one of the leading figures in the entrepreneurial history of the United States. The material presented describes some of the general history of this "business genius" and focuses on a critical and difficult decision that he made early in his career, which led to his success. The choice and the reasons for it will be contrasted with the path chosen by Carnegie's closest professional colleague during that period of his life, Thomas A. Scott, as a way of illuminating some of the issues underpinning how barriers to wisdom are created and what it takes to overcome them.

RETAINING WISDOM IN THE FACE OF FOLLY: THE CASE OF ANDREW CARNEGIE AND THOMAS A. SCOTT

Andrew Carnegie, full grown at 5 feet, 3 inches tall, met Thomas A. Scott at the age of 17 while working at O'Reilly's Telegraph Shop (Tedlow, 2001). Scott had taken over the management of the western district of the Pennsylvania Railroad, which was based out of Pittsburgh. Scott decided early on that he needed his own telegraph office and recruited the talented and energetic Andrew from O'Reilly.

On February 1, 1853, Carnegie became Scott's clerk and telegraph manager. They soon became friends, management colleagues, and business partners. A short time after he started to work for Scott, his boss gave Carnegie his first investment opportunity. With the support of his mother and of Scott, for $610, Carnegie bought 10 shares of the Adams Express Company, a business Scott and others had started, and began learning that his money could make a lot more money. In 1859, Scott, a very able and ambitious manager and entrepreneur, was promoted to vice president of the railroad. He proceeded to persuade J. Edgar Thomson, the president of the railroad, that he should also promote the 24-year-old Carnegie to become the superintendent of the western division of the company at the then-amazing salary of $1,500 per year. At about the same time, Carnegie purchased a one-eighth interest in the Woodruff Sleeping Car Company and began to accumulate significant amounts of money. Scott took Carnegie to Washington, DC, with him at the start of the Civil War, but Carnegie soon returned to Pittsburgh.

By 1863, Carnegie had become a very wealthy man by the standards of the time. He earned $42,260.67 that year, despite making a salary of $2,400.00 working for the railroad. At the age of 30, Andrew had already established himself as an independent businessman and investor. Five years later, in 1868, he sat down and created a list of his investments. After 10 years of hard work and wise choices, his initial $610 investment had grown to $400,000 in net worth. In that year, he made $56,100 from investments and was one of the richest people in the United States. By 1873, Carnegie had determined that his financial and personal future would be based in the still-nascent but blossoming steel industry. The railroads were exploding westward, and they would need thousands of miles of steel rails. He marshaled his finances and plunged into the project head first.

In the meantime, his long-time friend and mentor, Tom Scott, had decided that his own future lay in building a new railroad from the Louisiana–Texas border to the Pacific Ocean. He enlisted Carnegie for a $250,000 initial investment, and a number of others joined the effort, but he launched his project without a firm, long-term financial foundation. In mid-September of 1873, the Jay Cooke and Company banking house failed, setting off a major financial panic in the country. By the end of that month, Scott's shaky southwest railroad adventure faced the renewal of several major loans. Scott called Carnegie to a meeting in Philadelphia, and telegraphed him that "a large loan for Texas Pacific had fallen due in London and its renewal was agreed to by Morgan & Co., provided [Carnegie] would join the other parties to the loan" (Tedlow, 2001, p. 42). No one knows exactly who attended the meeting. It is clear that Scott and Thomson, giants of the Pennsylvania Railroad, and the men most clearly responsible for Carnegie's early success, were in deep trouble and were counting on him to help save their fortunes and their entrepreneurial futures.

One can only imagine the pressures Carnegie faced at that meeting. At some point early on, Scott or someone else must have called the question of who would be supporting the loan from the Morgan organization. Tedlow (2001) reported that Carnegie recorded his answer as

> I declined . . . . I was then asked if I would bring them all to ruin by refusing to stand by my friends . . . . It was one of the most trying moments of my whole life . . . . Yet I was not tempted for a moment to entertain the idea of involving myself . . . . The question of what was my duty came first and prevented that. All my capital was in manufacturing and every dollar of it was required. I was the capitalist (then a modest one, indeed) of our concern. All depended upon me. My brother with his wife and family, Mr. Phipps and his family, Mr. Kloman and his family, all rose up before me and claimed protection.
>
> I told Mr. Scott that I had done my best to prevent him from beginning to construct a great railway before he had secured the necessary capital. I had insisted that thousands of miles of rail lines could not be constructed by means of temporary loans. Besides, I had paid two hundred and fifty thousand dollars cash for an interest in it, which he told me upon my return from Europe he had reserved for me, although I had never approved the scheme. But nothing in the world would ever induce me to be guilty of endorsing the paper of that construction company or of any concern other than our own firm. (pp. 44–45)

The aftermath of that meeting quickly arrived. By November of the same year, another short-term note came due, and when Scott and his investors could not pay, they slipped into bankruptcy. Scott offered to resign his executive position at the Pennsylvania Railroad, but the board, led by Thomson, refused to accept his resignation. Scott succeeded Thomson as the president of the railroad in June 1874. He held that position until his retirement on June 1, 1880. He rose from bankruptcy, and led the railroad through a difficult time, but he never achieved the prominence of his "Andy." He died in 1881, at age 57.

After the meeting, Carnegie returned to Pittsburgh to meet with his bankers. They had expected him to support his friend and accordingly were prepared to withdraw funding from his steel venture. Carnegie surprised and pleased them when he reported that he had declined to get involved in the second round of railway financing. From that point forward, Carnegie established his own completely independent reputation as a businessman, and he never had significant trouble raising money after those events. Eighteen years later, after building the steel industry in and around Pittsburgh, Carnegie and his partners sold the Carnegie Steel Company to J. P. Morgan for $480 million. Carnegie's share was $300 million. Thus, by the beginning of the 20th century, Carnegie had become the richest man in the country. He lived another 18 years, during which he devoted his time and a significant portion of his wealth to the dissemination of knowledge. His legacy lives on today, 100 years later, in the form of the Carnegie Endowment, which is still devoted to the vision of its founder.

This case tells the story of two men who rose to power and wealth in the tumultuous times of the mid- and late 1800s. The first, Tom Scott, plunged enthusiastically into a visionary enterprise to open the southwestern U.S. to further development via a new railway line. The second, Andrew Carnegie, a reluctant initial investor, declined to join the second and crucial stage of the project. As a result of his choices, Scott eventually went into bankruptcy and, although he continued his executive career, never rose above that social and economic position. Carnegie, on the strength of his conviction and the decision to go his own way, became the richest man in the country, and eventually his name became synonymous with philanthropy and bringing knowledge to the world.

LESSONS LEARNED

One man's vision and executive action led to folly and company ruin. The second man's vision and executive action led to the most successful capitalistic enterprise of its time and to a reputation still widely known and enjoyed more than 100 years later. One can reasonably ask, what differentiated these two obviously able men? Why did one choose so wisely and the other so foolishly? What can we learn from this case about the ephemeral nature of Executive Wisdom and how leaders can reasonably protect themselves from the potential folly that lurks in many of the decisions that they are routinely challenged to make?

Evaluating the exercise of Executive Wisdom may be impossible by normal measures of cognition, such as those provided by intelligence tests; other cognitive abilities, such as complex reasoning; or the more recent examples of instruments designed to assess emotional intelligence, primarily because of the scope of time against which a leader's judgments, decisions, and actions must be assessed. Similarly, garden variety approaches to performance management used by organizations, including the various forms of 360-degree reviews, are unlikely to yield good data about wisdom, because most of them are not designed to ask questions about performance through time or how the organization for which an individual has been responsible has fared over the years of the person's tenure and beyond (Luthans & Peterson, 2003). Preliminary external evaluations of Scott's southwestern railway vision of opening up the new territories after the Civil War were sufficiently optimistic to generate an initial round of funding. Scott's and Thomson's reputations for running the Pennsylvania Railroad no doubt played into the confidence they generated in the investment community. To them and their partners, it looked like they could not lose, and yet they did lose, in a catastrophically short period of time. Similar tales abound in the history and lore of the venture capital industry of the late 20th and early 21st centuries (Hartley, 2003).

However, Carnegie was able to see the likelihood of failure when his partners and others could not. He was also able to envision the development and consolidation of the steel industry over a 20-year period and positioned himself perfectly to take advantage of a market opportunity that would yield unimaginable wealth for his time. He had enough courage to say no to his long-term colleagues and friends. In doing so, he succeeded where they failed. He became a business legend and internationally recognized philanthropist; they became historical footnotes in the life story of Andrew Carnegie. They lifted him out of obscurity and poverty and gave him an opportunity. He exploited the opportunity and used it to climb farther than they could.

So, how can we come to better understand this complex mystery called Executive Wisdom when it seems to appear and disappear like a wraith on the wind? And how can we help executives understand this phenomenon and avoid the many barriers that prevent them from routinely exercising the wisdom that they may be capable of achieving? In this chapter, I provide a succinct summary of many of the factors that have been identified that contribute to executive and organizational failure. I present many of the barriers that can inhibit leaders from displaying wisdom in their roles, more thoroughly examine a model to understand these barriers, and introduce some specific methods that may help them and their coaches to more routinely act in wise ways that I cover in even more depth in chapters 5 through 8.

DERAILING LEADERS AND CRASHING ORGANIZATIONS

The story of Tom Scott is one that has played out repeatedly on the rather extensive stage of human history. Indeed, reading history texts and biographies of individual leaders can leave one with a pretty dismal view of the overall impact of leadership on the welfare of humanity. In many, if not most, corners of the world the decisions and actions of executives with the responsibility for the safekeeping of organizations and their most treasured resources, their people, demonstrate clearly that many of them were and are ill suited for the positions that they held. In fact, many of them have created nothing except vast and wanton destruction. Hitler, Stalin, Pol Pot, Saddam Hussein, Ken Lay, Bernie Ebbers, and others like them worked assiduously and successfully to rise to the positions of eminence from which they all fell precipitously and with catastrophic results for those around them. To be sure, corporate executives who lead their companies into bankruptcy and failure cannot be compared with the butchers of human history with the single exception that they ended their careers in disgrace with their organizations in shreds, irreparably harmed, or completely destroyed. These stories are well chronicled, and in many cases one need only mention a name to elicit nods of understanding from people gathered from the far corners of the earth. Sitting in a meeting with mid-level managers who are complaining about a CEO and hearing the person compared with Hitler or Stalin creates an unmistakable metaphorical image and a type of understanding that need not be explained in words. Unfortunately, I have had this experience often.

PATTERNS OF BEHAVIOR THAT DERAIL LEADERS AND DESTROY ORGANIZATIONS

The literature on leadership has followed these concerns and produced many books and articles focused on the causes and prevention of executive derailment and organizational catastrophes. Hogan, Raskin, and Fazzini (1990); Hogan and Hogan (2001); and Hogan, Curphy, and Hogan (1994) have summarized most of the empirical literature available on the subject of derailment and leadership performance and have arrived at a variety of conclusions about the patterns of behavior and personality that often lead executives astray. Hogan et al. suggested in their 1990 chapter that the base rate for managerial incompetence in America is between 60% and 75%. Of particular concern in their research was a bipolar pattern of supervision and management, with the extremes being described as individuals who ended up leaving their enterprises because they had what could be called either a *micromanaging* or an *abandoning* supervision style, both of which were perceived by subordinates as abusive leadership. Either of these approaches, compulsively applied, often ends with the leader being pushed out of the organization. In essence, these studies appear to reinforce the long-standing model of *situational leadership* advocated by Fiedler (1967) and Hersey and Blanchard (1977), in which managers are encouraged to assess the level of developmental maturity of their subordinates and the situations that are being faced and then adjust the level and type of their personality, style, and engagement accordingly.

Recent in-depth reviews and assessments of these problems have been provided by Dotlich and Cairo (2003), Finkelstein (2003), and Picken and Dess (1997). Dotlich and Cairo focused on the patterns of behavior individual leaders enact that most often get them into trouble. They identified 11 different habits or approaches that lead to trouble if consistently used by an executive:

1. Arrogance—insisting that one is right and everyone else is wrong.
2. Melodrama—always trying to be the center of attention.
3. Volatility—sudden and unpredictable mood shifts.
4. Excessive caution—having real difficulty making a decision.
5. Habitual distrust—focusing on the negatives.
6. Aloofness—disengaging and disconnecting from the organization.
7. Mischievousness—constantly bending and breaking the rules.
8. Eccentricity—trying to be different despite the impact on others.
9. Passive resistance—silence and inaction, interpreted as agreement by others.
10. Perfectionism—concentrating on the little things while the organization runs amok.
11. Eagerness to please—enacting leadership as a popularity contest.

Dotlich and Cairo (2003) provided a host of advice and specific steps that leaders can take to avoid falling into these traps, including hiring a coach; learning about the stressors that are likely to initiate these derailing behavior patterns; conducting an adversity analysis; assessing the strengths and weaknesses of the organization and subordinates; evaluating one's own capacities, including carefully reviewing one's failure experiences; finding a mentor; being open and honest about one's own leadership challenges; and providing developmental support and coaching to the rest of a management team. Their focus was on the leader as an individual person and on what he or she could do to self-manage the risks of falling into a derailing pattern of behavior. Other scholars and practitioners have taken a somewhat different approach to this subject.

Finkelstein (2003) broadened the view of what can cause leadership failure by focusing on the organization and the challenges it faces, and the strategies that leaders use, as well as the behaviors of individual executives. In a study of 51 major business failures, he and his colleagues identified four major passages in organizational life and four destructive patterns of executive behavior that significantly contributed to these disasters, including, as Dotlich and Cairo (2003) did, specific kinds of personality and actions that create major risks for derailment. Finkelstein thus departed significantly from Dotlich and Cairo's approach by including the developmental and environmental problems of the organization itself as major causes of executive catastrophe.

In Finkelstein's (2003) study, the four passages that created such major risks included (a) creating new ventures, (b) dealing with innovation and change, (c) managing mergers and acquisitions, and (d) addressing new competitive pressures. The four behavior syndromes contributing to failure were (a) error-prone mindsets that distort the perception of reality, (b) delusional attitudes that keep the distortions in place, (c) communication problems that inhibit the management of urgent information, and (d) leadership qualities that reduce the likelihood that executives will take corrective action once problems are uncovered (Finkelstein, 2003, pp. 16–17). Like Dotlich and Cairo, he also provided a list of what he called the "seven habits of spectacularly unsuccessful people." His nominations included the following:

1. They see themselves and their companies as dominating their environments, not simply responding to developments in those environments.
2. They identify so completely with the company that there is no clear boundary between their personal interests and corporate interests.
3. They seem to have all the answers, often dazzling people with the speed and decisiveness with which they can deal with challenging issues.
4. They make sure that everyone is 100 percent behind them, ruthlessly eliminating anyone who might undermine their efforts.

5. They are consummate company spokespersons, often devoting the largest portions of their efforts to managing and developing the company image.
6. They treat intimidatingly difficult obstacles as temporary impediments to be removed or overcome.
7. They never hesitate to return to the strategies and tactics that made them and their companies successful in the first place. (p. 238)

Finkelstein (2003) also provided some significant advice to leaders about what to do to avoid making these major mistakes. He focused on looking for five major early warning signs: (a) unnecessary complexity, (b) speeding out of control, (c) distracted leadership, (d) excessive hype, and (e) questions of character in senior executives. He also emphasized the need to create organizational climates and cultures that anticipate that errors and problems will occur and to build systems of inquiry and learning that ensure that the people in the whole organization remain open minded even in the face of the often-messy world of business. Several organizations that spread information about both best practices and spectacular failures were described as he focused on the ability of leaders to learn from mistakes as individuals and to build infrastructures in their organization that ensure that the rest of the members of the leadership community will pressure themselves to learn as well.

Picken and Dess (1997) took on the same topic of derailing companies, but they chose to focus less on the behavior patterns of individual leaders or executive teams. Instead, they identified seven *strategic traps*, as they termed them, that often trip organizations:

1. Blind spots: Misreading the environmental tea leaves.
2. Flawed assumptions: Right strategy and wrong problem.
3. Creating competitive disadvantage.
4. Subtracting value by adding businesses.
5. Tripping over organizational processes, functions, and boundaries.
6. Arbitrary goals and unbalanced controls.
7. Leadership failures. (pp. 5–6)

Like Finkelstein (2003) and Dotlich and Cairo (2003), Picken and Dess (1997) provided conceptual models to understand each of the seven traps and then went on to encourage leaders to conduct systematic forms of inquiry to determine whether they have an adequate grasp of the essentials of environmental scanning, strategy formation, organizational structuring, effective implementation, and senior leadership. They emphasized developing a sound strategy and then implementing that strategy in as error-free a fashion as possible. They mirrored part of the definition of Executive Wisdom introduced in chapter 2 by basing their approach on Warren Bennis's clarification of the difference between *leaders* and *managers*, with leaders being those who do the right things and managers being those who do things right. In essence, they tried to focus leaders on the fact that what they do is extraordinarily complex and that they can get most of their jobs right and yet still fail in a significant way by ignoring, underemphasizing, or misassessing only one of the crucial areas of responsibility with which they are charged. Along with Finkelstein, Picken and Dess pointed to the need to consider both the organizational challenges as well as the personal characteristics of leaders to understand what causes them to fail.

Neustadt and May (1986) broadened the horizons for us in their careful consideration of the need for executives to understand the historical context in which they are leading their organizations. They provided a variety of examples, from the ancient Greeks through to some of the more recent challenges faced by American presidents, including President Kennedy and the Cuban missile crisis, President Reagan and the challenges of recrafting the financing of the Social Security System, and President Johnson and the Vietnam War. According to Neustadt and May, leaders often create significant errors in their decisions and actions simply because they do not properly explore the historical roots of the situations that they face and the traditions, values, and mindsets that the histories of themselves as individuals and those of their organizations often impose unconsciously on the decisions that must be made. They suggested a variety of methods and techniques that, if implemented properly, will improve the likelihood that a leader will both understand his or her historical context and will create strategy and actions that take those into account. I explore their recommendations further in chapter 7.

CAN ORGANIZATIONAL CATASTROPHE AND EXECUTIVE DERAILMENT BE PREVENTED?

When we then look at these four relatively recent and fairly comprehensive examinations of why leaders and organizations fail, we see mirrored in their findings and recommendations rather similar considerations of the issues of executive and organizational development and environmental adaptation that have been studied and widely disseminated by scholars and practitioners coming at the same challenges from the perspective of how to lead organizations correctly. The literature on individual derailment closely parallels the extensive material available on executive development represented in the work of Howard and Bray (1988), Fitzgerald and Kirby

(1997), Jaques and Clement (1991), Levinson (1981), Rothwell and Kazanas (1999), Yukl (1994), and Zaccaro (2001), among legions of other authors. Any individual or organization wanting to do the job of developing themselves or creating programs to nurture whole generations of leaders has an enormous body of research and practice on which to draw. Virtually all of the authors previously cited have addressed many of the problems and issues that have been identified in the derailment literature. Indeed, as I reviewed in chapter 2, the essentials of successful leadership programs have been known since the times of Confucius and Socrates. So, it appears that human organizations and human beings continuously confront a set of common leadership problems and have the ongoing, transgenerational need to address them from the simultaneous vantage points of trying to prevent as many disasters as possible from happening; trying to limit the damage from those that do occur despite the best efforts of the people involved in them; and, it is hoped, managing the evolution of executive leadership talent that will be less likely to create such chaos because they actually have the knowledge, skills, and abilities that their organizations need them to have.

Similarly, the literature on organization development has very clearly outlined the normal challenges that face evolving enterprises. Greiner (1972) described in his classic article a core set of issues that arise as institutions increase in size and age, suggesting that they go through five phases of development, each creating a specific crisis that executives need to address. These include the crises of leadership, autonomy, control, red tape, and vision or mission renewal. He also suggested strategies for addressing these crises, such as emphasizing creativity, direction, delegation, coordination, and collaboration, depending on the specific nature of the problems being encountered.

Adizes (1988), in a classic book on the subject of organization development, provided a formal typology of the 10 stages through which corporations typically evolve. He identified these as (a) courtship, (b) infancy, (c) go-go, (d) adolescence, (e) prime, (f) maturity, (g) aristocracy, (h) early bureaucracy, (i) bureaucracy, and (j) death. He stated that each stage requires different management approaches if leaders are to successfully steer their enterprises through them. Indeed, the literature on organization development, leadership, and managerial strategy are in uniform agreement that the most important job of senior executives is to ensure the continued evolution and survival of the institution for which they are responsible. Kilburg, Stokes, and Kuruvilla (1998) came at the same issue from the opposite perspective by creating a conceptual model of organizational regression. They described many of the forces driving organizations toward reduced performance and states of failure as well as those that enable enterprises to maintain their resiliency in the face of the pressures of internal integration and external adaptation. Even more important, they provided a substantial set of recommendations on what to do to maintain world class performance. Levinson (2002), in his recent summary of how consultants should conduct an organizational assessment, also emphasized the need for practitioners and leaders alike to understand the evolutionary and developmental histories and challenges facing any enterprise in which they work.

The third major source of what we can think of as the proactive or preventative literature dealing with leadership and organizational derailment focuses on the strategic problems emphasized by Picken and Dess (1997). Again, the literature and methods that have been developed to help individual leaders and executive teams formulate organizational or business strategy—really another name for how to shape the environmental adaptation of the enterprise—have become quite extensive. Mintzberg, Ahlstrand, and Lampel (1998) provided a comprehensive review of what they called the *10 schools of organizational strategy formation*. They provided a common framework to examine these approaches to strategy, which they defined as including (a) design, (b) planning, (c) positioning, (d) entrepreneurial, (e) cognitive, (f) learning, (g) power, (h) culture, (i) environment, and (j) configuration schools. They suggested that the early days of strategy work, in the 1960s and 1970s, tended to focus on matters of organization design. That was followed by an intensive interest in planning through the 1970s and 1980s. Planning was slowly supplanted by the positioning school in the 1980s and early to mid-1990s. They also pointed out that there has been a recent growing interest in organizational learning as a fundamental approach to strategy-making. Left with a breathtaking array of ideas and methodological recommendations to contemplate, it is little wonder that leaders often find themselves in a state of confusion and high anxiety. Mintzberg et al. did little to relieve these tensions because they explicitly stated that these developments, which have occurred over the last 60 years or so, have only served to educate leaders about the complexities of the process of organizational adaptation and the decision-making and execution responsibilities that they acquire with their positions. They urged executives and consultants alike to tolerate the ambiguity that comes with this complexity and to use their improved understandings to explore their situations in depth even as they must make real and sometimes personally and organizationally threatening decisions about the future of their enterprises.

Mintzberg et al. (1998) also provided a wonderful gateway to the extensive literature on strategy formation and execution. In-depth considerations of various well-known advocates of some of these approaches can be found in Hamel and Prahalad (1994); Moore, Johnson, and Kippola (1998); Porter (1980); Senge (1990); and Slywotzky, Morrison, Moser, Mundt, and Quella (1999), among others. Pearce and Robinson (1997) and a number of other academics have gone on to provide rich textbooks that summarize most of these ideas and give many valuable suggestions for the practice of strategy formation. These concepts and methods, when combined with the core notions of external assessment introduced by Neustadt and May (1986), clearly point to the need for leaders to be able to orient to the present and future environmental challenges that they face while simultaneously comprehending the historical forces with which they are contending inside their organizations and inside those other enterprises with which they find themselves competing. These are very deep and textured challenges indeed, especially when combined with the need for the individual executive to master the nuances of his or her own ways of thinking, feeling, and behaving.

I believe that if and when a person can step back from the derailment, development, assessment, and strategy literatures and try to gain some in-depth perspective on the large subsets of issues with which leaders and leadership groups must contend, it becomes clear why the emergence of Executive Wisdom is so difficult to predict and control. As Finkelstein (2003) suggested, leaders who fail spectacularly usually have had long track records of success before they manage to come unglued. We must come to understand that executives at senior levels of organizations face enormous difficulties and many barriers as they strive to become and act wisely. We must also appreciate deeply that the concepts, strategies, and behaviors that enable a leader to succeed in and with an organization at one point in time can, at another point in time, create disaster.

In the case example that introduced this chapter, Andrew Carnegie's choice not to join in the second round of financing for the Southwest-to-Pacific railway project and to focus on the development of a steel manufacturing industry that supported the continued expansion of the American railroad system represents Executive Wisdom in action. Scott's initial decision to build a railway without permanent financial arrangements and lack of a fallback plan in the face of an economic reversal represents the opposite, executive folly. Somehow, Carnegie was able to see through the tremendous thicket of personal, group, financial, environmental, and organizational variables and dynamics and properly discern the right course of action. He was able to make the right decision at the right time despite what must have been enormous personal pressure on him to do otherwise. Finally, he was able to execute that decision in a way that resulted in the preservation of his own capital position, his relationships with his bankers and financial backers, and his overall organizational and economic strategy. Despite the obvious tensions reported in his diary entries, he managed to hold to his own view of "rightness." And because history eventually does decide whether such decisions and actions were correct, we are now able to bear witness to the wisdom of his choices compared with those of his friend and mentor, Thomas Scott.

I hope the models presented in chapters 2 and 3 demonstrate the complexity and richness of the inner world of the average leader and why it may be difficult for individuals in these positions of such influence to demonstrate the ability to perform in a consistently wise fashion. Executive Wisdom in this framework can be seen as more than a bit of a game of chance in which the individual does his or her level best to discern what is happening to the organization as well as in and to him- or herself, apply appropriate perspective and planning to decide what to do, and then to act in an appropriate way against the correct time frame. This chapter's introductory example demonstrates clearly that these decisions and actions often involve the creation of individual and organizational failure and success. In the worst cases of human folly, destruction on nearly unimaginable scales has occurred. Thus, I believe it is critically important to try to improve the ways in which leaders function to better increase the chances that they will produce wise results rather than foolishness. So, what can we recommend that leaders do to increase the probability that they will think and act wisely? One of the most important tasks for coaches and other development professionals is to understand more clearly the barriers that they often encounter on the road to wisdom and what we can do to help leaders overcome them.

BARRIERS TO WISDOM

Figure 4.1 reintroduces a more detailed look at some of the major barriers that executives may encounter that in turn can inhibit their ability to think and act wisely. As you will recall, I introduced this domain in chapter 2 as part of the overall set of factors influencing the emergence of Executive Wisdom. The figure suggests that in very human terms, almost anything an executive confronts can turn into such a barrier. The personal history of a leader, his or her psychodynamics, issues in a person's family of origin, and the structures and processes of the executive's core group of colleagues or home organization can significantly inhibit executive functioning. In addition, market forces; micro- and macroeconomic trends; and politics at local, regional, national, or global levels can create dramatic and often-unforeseen shifts for leaders to ponder and incorporate into their implementation efforts. The existence of racism, sexism, ageism, other ideologies and beliefs, and the values of the leader and those with whom the executive interacts can provide fertile ground for the derailment of wisdom. If an executive does not have the appropriate information, is faced with an urgent need to act, or carries unrecognized decision-making biases, it will also be difficult for him or her to discern situations accurately, create effective strategies, or act with any degree of long-term effectiveness. As one can see from the short list of elements contained in this figure, a broad array of

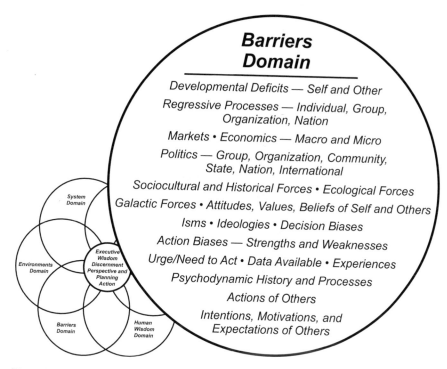

Barriers Domain

Developmental Deficits — Self and Other

Regressive Processes — Individual, Group, Organization, Nation

Markets • Economics — Macro and Micro

Politics — Group, Organization, Community, State, Nation, International

Sociocultural and Historical Forces • Ecological Forces

Galactic Forces • Attitudes, Values, Beliefs of Self and Others

Isms • Ideologies • Decision Biases

Action Biases — Strengths and Weaknesses

Urge/Need to Act • Data Available • Experiences

Psychodynamic History and Processes

Actions of Others

Intentions, Motivations, and Expectations of Others

Figure 4.1. Barriers to Executive Wisdom.

things can nullify the determined efforts of even the most dedicated of leaders.

THE IMPORTANCE OF DECISION BIASES FOR LEADERS

Out of the enormous range of things that can adversely affect the emergence of Executive Wisdom, there are several specific kinds of barriers to which coaches and leaders must attend as they do their work. The first of these involves the presence and operation of unseen and unknown biases that may influence the judgment of a leader. Bazerman (1998) did a brilliant job of describing and addressing the issue of the heuristics, or rules of thumb, that leaders often use to guide their decision making. It is important to keep in mind that any executive may or not be conscious of the rules of thumb that are in use in a particular situation. Bazerman suggested that these heuristics often operate as unstated or unknown biases that influence the way decisions get made. He identified three general rules of thumb that are most often pushing judgment processes: (a) availability, (b) representativeness, and (c) anchoring and adjustment. In that context, he went on to explore 13 interconnected biases that can dramatically affect what someone thinks and therefore what he or she might discern and decide in any situation.

Availability biases include the following:

1. Ease of recall—leaders judge both positive and negative events that are easily and vividly recalled as occurring more frequently than they really do happen.
2. Retrievability—leaders have biases based on how their memories search and retrieve information. Research on memory processes suggests that people do engage different approaches to memory retrieval.
3. Presumed associations—leaders can overestimate the probability of two events co-occurring on the basis of the ease with which they recall and correlate their relationship. If they do not retrieve or associate other critical correlated events, their decisions can be extremely flawed.

Representative biases include the following:

4. Insensitivity to base rates—leaders ignore base rates with which certain events occur when any other information is present. For example, it is easy to ignore the recessionary history of economies during a boom time.
5. Insensitivity to sample size—leaders underappreciate the role of sample size as they consider the reliability of information. For example, data from a few focus groups do not necessarily generalize to national populations.
6. Misconceptions of chance—leaders see randomness in randomly generated data sequences that are really too short to assess statistical validation. In other words, without data from longer term studies of trends, it is easy to dismiss real patterns of performance or influence as temporary or simply chance.
7. Regressions to the mean—leaders fail to see that extreme events tend eventually to regress to the mean when repeated. A market leading product that is not updated or revised in the face of competitor pressure can rapidly become "average" and lose significant market share as a result.
8. The conjunction fallacy—leaders tend to see co-occurring events as more probable rather than as a small subset of a larger set of nonoccurring events. In the absence of a broader perspective, local or recent trends or events can be assessed incorrectly.

Anchoring and adjustment biases include the following:

9. Insufficient anchor adjustment—leaders tend to start into strategy, negotiation, or conflict management processes with initial estimates based on past experience and often do not make appropriate adjustments for the unique situation being faced. This often happens in negotiations in which initial price or cost estimates incorrectly distort the entire process of putting the right numbers on the deal.

10. Conjunctive and disjunctive events bias—leaders overestimate the probability that events will co-occur and underestimate the probability that they will not. They do not make a proper assessment of the likelihood that two or more events will or will not co-occur in the future.

11. Overconfidence—leaders tend to be overconfident in their judgments regarding difficult questions and situations. Trusting their own experience and intuition, they do not undertake the necessary due diligence and miss critical information, patterns, or options that may critically affect a decision.

Additional biases include the following:

12. The confirmation trap—leaders try to find information that reaffirms their choices and tend to discount information that undercuts them.

13. Hindsight and the curse of knowledge—leaders tend to see themselves as smarter after the fact when an event happens than they really were before it occurred, and they often do not see the influence of information that they have that others do not when they predict the behavior of others. (Bazerman, pp. 39–40)

The operation of any one of these biases or any combination of them in a given adaptive situation faced by a leader clearly can introduce potentially fatal consequences to an individual executive, his or her organization, or both. Yet, in all of my years of working in organizations as a manager and with leaders as a coach and consultant, I can truthfully state that it is exceptionally rare that I see or hear anyone even ask a question about whether biases are operating to influence a particular decision or process. Klein (2003) directly addressed this problem in his book on intuition in managerial decision making by suggesting that leaders introduce and conduct what he called a "PreMortem Exercise." In this process, he has the members of project or leadership teams meet before the beginning of any project or initiative and try to imagine that their collective effort has failed in a humiliating and obvious fashion. Then he asks them "What could have caused the failure?" and to generate lists of reasons why it could have occurred. This is a process in which Bazerman's (1998) judgment biases can be easily introduced ahead of time as potentially affecting the ways in which a team of people were able to see themselves and their situation operate. The lists of the individuals participating in the exercise are then consolidated and the major risks to a project are identified by the group and used to help guide the planning and execution processes. Klein (2003) also suggested periodically revisiting the PreMortem lists during a project to see whether anything should be added and whether the team is appropriately attending to the issues. But how often do you see any executive team or even individual executives try to examine their own biases or anticipate that their efforts would fail in an embarrassing way? For me, the answer is "not very often," and I submit that the willingness and ability to engage in such examinations reflects a degree of humility and understanding of the fragility of human executive action that must be present for wisdom to emerge.

CORE PSYCHOLOGICAL CONFLICTS IN LEADERS AS BARRIERS TO EXECUTIVE WISDOM

In my recent book (Kilburg, 2000), I carefully examined the issues of the ways in which conflict and defensive operations can directly affect the degree to which a coach can work effectively with any client, and these processes represent the second specific set of barriers that affect the operation of wisdom in leaders. Following Wurmser's (2000) descriptions of core issues around which psychodynamic strife often emerges, the following major categories of conflict, operating frequently in individual leaders, their management teams, and entire organizations, can be noted:

- Security concerns—trust, suspicion, paranoia, paranoiagenic situations, diversity dynamics.
- Attachment and separation concerns—involvement, belonging, boundaries, connectedness, enmeshment, rejection, abandonment, dependency, independence, differentiation, integration, professional and personal identity, downsizings, rightsizings, mergers, acquisitions, diversity dynamics.
- Power and control concerns—helplessness; hopelessness; omnipotence; narcissistic processes; promotions; demotions; conformity; deviance; creativity; independence; authority; independence; dependence; taking and giving orders; obedience; rebellion; mutiny; professional, personal, and group identity; boundaries; diversity dynamics.

- Competition, rivalry, and achievement—dominance, submission, pride, humiliation, recognition and credit, taking and giving orders, obedience, rebellion, mutiny, professional and personal identity, promotion, demotion, boundaries, diversity dynamics.
- Standards of performance—pride, shame, guilt, professional and personal identity, promotion, demotion, success and failure, norms, goals, expectations, values, beliefs, attitudes.
- Conflicts of loyalty—family versus organization, boss versus subordinates, right thing to do versus the adaptive or expedient thing to do, friends versus organizational roles, organizational policies and procedures versus what will work, ethics and moral principles versus what a leader wants or what reality demands.

It is impossible for humans to live and work together without eventually confronting most, if not all, of these types of conflict in their relationships. In organizations, we have seen the rise of many formal human resources processes, such as performance management systems; equity assessment processes; mediation services; employee relations counseling; employee assistance programs; organization development services; and yes, even executive coaching, as methods designed at least in part to help an enterprise keep these altogether normal but extremely powerful conflicting processes under control. Yet, as Argyris (1993), I (Kilburg, 2000), and many others have documented, executives and their collegial groups frequently prove incapable of identifying and managing their conflicts, often with horrendous prices being paid by everyone involved.

As is known from the extensive literature on individual and organizational defensive operations (Argyris, 1990, 1993; Kilburg, 2000), conflict on any one or combination of such issues is likely to induce self-protective behavior that usually is effective in the short term in warding off the depressive, anxious, often humiliating, and most frequently hostile emotions generated by people in these situations. The array of behaviors that can defend against looking at and solving the real problems underlying or contributing to conflict is stunning. Most often, these operations simply shift the attention of the person or group involved in a conflict away from what is truly generating the problem and its subsequent pain onto other issues that serve most often as short-term, fantasy substitutes for managing reality. In its simplest and most devastating forms, defensive operations lead individuals and leadership teams to deny that conflict or problems are present. In such situations, humans find it impossible to anticipate what might happen because they consciously cannot and unconsciously will not see the challenges in front of them. The agendas for meetings of executive teams in such denial do not have the issues and problems that are most threatening even present, and so no real time is spent considering what must be done to address the difficulties involved.

From such devastatingly simple defensive operations one can go to the opposite end of the continuum and see rituals and sequences of behaviors, often obsessive and compulsive in their elaborate detail, used to similar self-protective ends. When faced by anxiety-arousing novel situations, it is all too easy for individuals and groups to rely on precedent, policy, procedure, planning processes, and decision-making structures to manage both the emotions involved and to limit consideration of what changes in routine operations, attitudes, beliefs, behaviors, technologies, or strategies that might be necessitated by the nature of the conflict. I have repeatedly witnessed management teams in meetings steadfastly focusing on the fantasies projected into PowerPoint and spreadsheet presentations instead of discussing very real organizational, group, personal, market, or leadership problems that are the causes of their troubles.

Heifetz (1994) and Heifetz and Linsky (2002) have discussed the difficulty—and, indeed, the dangerousness—to executives when they try to focus the attention of organizations and nations of humans on the real problems that they face. They presented a number of historical cases in which leaders were actually murdered for courageously trying to confront what they called the *real adaptive learning challenges* that the executives were responsible for managing. These kinds of conflict-based, defensively structured situations can ignite the most primitive forms of behavior imaginable in individuals or groups of humans. Thus, conflict and its associated defensive processes can present as tremendous barriers for leaders trying to discern, decide, and act wisely and can serve as major roadblocks to the deployment of wisdom.

ENVIRONMENTAL BARRIERS TO THE EMERGENCE OF EXECUTIVE WISDOM

A third and final major source of barriers can be found in the environments in which organizations exist and struggle for survival. As we know all too well, and as virtually every book on organizational strategy, leadership, politics, economics, and management attests, the worlds in which leaders work present them with enormous challenges because of their perpetually fluid competitive pressure. Perhaps the best treatment of this subject is available in the evolving work on complexity theory summarized by Stacey (1992, 1996) and Butz (1997). As professionals who work in and with organizations, leaders and consultants know them as metastatic systems that appear stable on their surface because of their structures, processes, resource flows, roles, relationships, products, services, and people. In reality, the organizations themselves are constantly changing as people move in and out of them to find employment and personal satisfaction and as competitors, goals, technology, demographics, and global economics force agonizing reappraisal after agonizing reappraisal of just how things are going.

The public investment community in America now insists on empirically measuring the performance of companies every 3 months. Investor and analyst conferences require business leaders to provide accurate projections of revenues and expenditures on an annual and quarterly basis. Large companies literally face dozens if not hundreds of very knowledgeable critics, skeptics, and investors as they conduct these quarterly reviews of their results and watch their fates shift, sometimes violently, as the large, public ownership community known as the stock markets react to the very latest news about how they are doing and about their future prospects for making money. A good quarter can lead to a 5% gain in stock price, but if it is followed by one in which forecast earnings are missed by as little as a penny per share, those gains can not only be given back, the stock can often be punished in what, to me, seem ridiculous shifts of opinion based on some of Bazerman's (1998) decision biases. Indeed, there are now hundreds of empirical methods for assessing organizational performance. Return on investment, return on net investment, EBITDA (i.e., earnings before interest, taxes, depreciation, and amortization), employee turnover, capitalization, cash reserves, free cash flow—the variables go on and on, often requiring very large companies to employ economists and applied mathematicians to help them do their own assessments of what is happening in defensive anticipation of what the Wall Street analytic community will be saying or asking. All of these efforts in measurement have as their fundamental purpose answering the following question: How is the leadership of this organization doing at the job of enabling the enterprise to adapt to the ceaseless changes that the global economy produces?

When one then throws in the extreme unpredictability of geopolitical, socioeconomic, and ecological forces that large companies are forced to take into account, the array of issues senior leadership teams face is extraordinary. Weather patterns in the Pacific or Atlantic basins can dramatically alter shipping schedules; in cases of extreme weather, plants can be destroyed, inventory lost, and people displaced or even killed, creating traumatic challenges for leaders. In the past year, we have seen whole cities destroyed by the power of ocean waves generated either by wind or by earthquakes. The internal politics of countries in and with which an organization does business can swing wildly. In the worst cases, coups, assassinations, crime sprees, revolutions, and local labor and environmental concerns can force agonizing appraisals of whether to continue operations, shift them to other countries, or even revise corporate strategies. In the face of these extraordinarily complex and seemingly unpredictable circumstances, how can leaders stretch themselves and create that sense of wise rightness that we have been exploring?

WISDOM MAPPING

With this broad sweep of barriers and challenges that can impede any leader's efforts to perceive, think, and act wisely, we must address the issue of whether there is anything that an executive can do to increase the likelihood that he or she will not fall prey to any of these impediments. Figure 4.2 presents an overview of at least one global approach that I have come to believe can increase the probability for Executive Wisdom to emerge more routinely for and in an individual and can be used by coaches who work systematically to help executives with this evolution. I think the core methodology can best be called *wisdom mapping*. In Figure 4.2, the emergence of Executive Wisdom and its component parts rest on a foundation consisting of six integrated areas of awareness. Through decades of work as a leader,

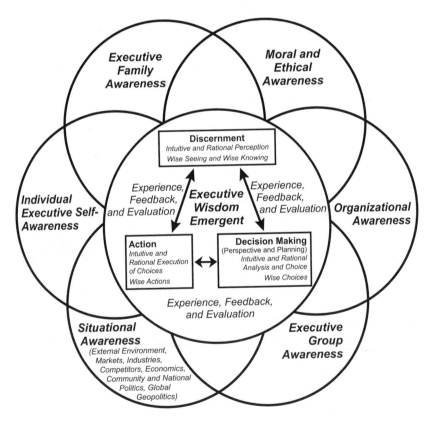

Figure 4.2. Wisdom-mapping components.

consultant, and coach, I have become increasingly convinced that individuals who are able to engage higher level cognitive and emotional processes in an effort to improve their awareness of what is going on inside of and around them are much more likely to demonstrate the capacity for and ability to use Executive Wisdom. We can see wise executives repeatedly use the ability to be reflectively and intuitively mindful in these six areas and then to engage this extensive awareness to act in equally reflective and intuitive ways as they go about their daily work. As Figure 4.2 illustrates, the six areas of awareness include (a) the individual executive; (b) the person's nuclear and families of origin; (c) the group with whom he or she works most closely; (d) the organization(s) that the executive leads; (e) the complex situation that the leader faces at any moment in time; and, last but not least, (f) the moral and value lenses that often unconsciously influence the behavior of a leader.

Figure 4.2 places the processes of emergent discernment, decision making, and action in the center or heart of these six forms of awareness, and, I hope, this reflects the challenge that initially faces any leader in a difficult situation. He or she must determine what is going on in present and historical terms, who the key people involved are and what their motivations, politics, and patterns of behavior have been and currently are, and the nature of the time frame and behavioral ecology in which an accurate assessment must be made. The leader must be aware of his or her own developmental legacies, patterns of family and individual dynamics that may influence decision-making biases and preferences, patterns of emotional responses, diversity dynamics, and internal conflicts and defenses that can result in distorted views of data and decision alternatives. I have worked with leaders who create wisdom maps using these six components of awareness to guide them in their decisions and actions. I believe that their assessments, decisions, and actions will be much more accurate and therefore provide better guidance to them for the creation and execution of strategy if they become much more systematic in how they construct and use their maps and that coaching based on these models will provide them with both the opportunity to develop and practice better skills in these areas and to explore the reasons why they may be more or less blind in one or more of these types of awareness.

THE WISDOM-MAPPING PROCESS AND BARRIER REDUCTION

Figure 4.3 depicts what I think of as the wisdom-mapping process. Each of the six areas of awareness is laid out as a necessary but not sufficient step in creating wisdom. At the start of any particular problem, challenge, trauma, or even just normal activity, a coach working with an executive or the leader him- or herself will find what one can think of as the initial

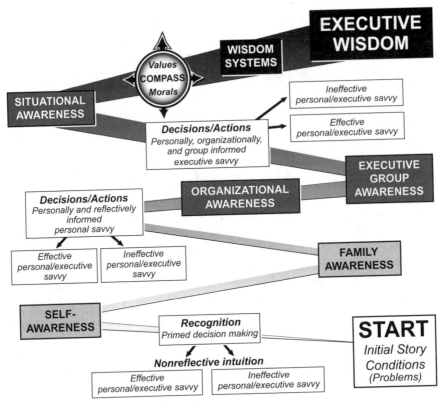

Figure 4.3. The wisdom-mapping process.

story and conditions. As I explained in chapters 2 and 3, this is a socially constructed reality on the part of the people involved. An individual leader will build an inner model of the circumstances, images, and variables involved. He or she will most often use what Klein (2003) termed *recognition-primed decision making*, in what could be called a *nonreflective intuition mode*, and then use that model to discern, decide, and act within that initial understanding. As the figure depicts, this usually leads to what I call *effective* or *ineffective personal or executive savvy*. If the outcome is the effective form of savvy, what usually happens is that the decisions made and actions pursued usually work, at least in the short term, and the individual then moves on to make an unconscious and more or less uncritically examined assumption that the judgments exercised and actions undertaken were the right things to do.

During the average day of an average leader who is pretty effective at his or her job, this is usually how one sees them in action. They more or less intuitively move through a long list of situations and problems, making their decisions and executing actions without a great deal of energy being expended on any one challenge. However, one will also witness leaders using the same operations, making assessments and decisions, and then implementing them in ways that lead to the opposite, namely, ineffective savvy. Depending on the rapidity of feedback available from the environment, and their ability and willingness to process that information with all of its complexity, executives either will or will not quickly detect errors and problems that have arisen. Their subsequent actions will reflect their maturity, experience, internal psychological sophistication, and the operating capacity of their executive teams and organizations. Effective leaders move quickly to incorporate error messages, modify their models, and implement (it is hoped) corrective changes. Less effective executives are subject to the whims of their defensive operations; knowledge, skill, and experience deficits; or the problems within their teams and organizations, and they may or may not attempt to fix their problems quickly.

Mapping Self- and Family Awareness

Figure 4.3 then illustrates that the proposed pathway to Executive Wisdom can be initiated by an individual leader with or without the assistance of a coach. This begins, of course, with self- and family awareness. Given our knowledge of executive derailment and leadership competence as summarized earlier, it should be no surprise that Hogan et al. (1994) suggested that between 60% and 75% of leaders were sometimes ineffective at their jobs and that, as often as not, the key factors in their poor performance were combinations of personality traits and supervision patterns. On the other hand, Luthans and Peterson (2003) demonstrated that the combination of 360-degree feedback followed up by individual, developmentally oriented coaching increased leadership effectiveness and thus decreased the likelihood of derailment. Thus, it seems clear to me that unless individual executives know themselves, their family backgrounds, and the key components that feed their managerial and leadership behavior preferences, they will be far less likely to be able to consistently execute their jobs wisely. The figure illustrates that if an individual leader is able to be more or less consistently aware of self and family variables that influence behavior, the likely results are executive performance that will be characterized by effective or ineffective personal executive savvy. The available studies suggest that increasing self-awareness does improve managerial performance. However, I can also attest to many experiences with individual leaders who know very well what aspects of their preferences and family histories are most likely to get them into trouble and yet persist in behaving in ineffective or downright dangerous ways. One is most likely to see examples of ineffective personal executive savvy in these latter situations.

Mapping Organizational and Executive Group Awareness

Further along in the mapping process, we see leaders engaging in organizational awareness. In my experience, it is this area to which most individual executives turn their initial attention to manage any problem that they face. They are usually very comfortable talking about their enterprises in great detail. Coaches often need to be careful not to let their clients overwhelm them with the sheer volume of their knowledge and experience with their businesses. To be sure, leaders can be securely confident in and blindly ignorant of the biased views that they hold of their institutions, and in these situations coaches and consultants may need to prod them to expand or challenge what they know or how they know it. Indeed, consultants are most often hired to help executives increase their knowledge of what is going on inside their businesses.

Figure 4.3 also illustrates that this stage of drawing a wisdom map involves learning about and knowing the group with which an executive works most closely. I find that many executives are quite good at assessing the leadership and management performance of their direct reports even though they may not provide routine and effective feedback to them. However, most leaders whom I have known have very little formal training and low levels of intellectual understanding of group dynamics. Although they are very experienced in working with and through groups, they most often do so with only a rudimentary understanding of what makes them perform well or fail. Again, the average individual can usually talk in great detail about what is going on inside of his or her team and what he or she is trying to do about it as a leader. However, he or she is often unable to articulate what is happening with any degree of group sophistication. Expanding awareness in the areas of organization and group operations and dynamics lead to discernment, decisions, and actions that are significantly informed with more information. Again, this model of mapping indicates that one sees effective or ineffective savvy resulting from adding these additional types of awareness.

The model of the wisdom-mapping process formally illustrates what I have come to believe, namely, that self-, family, organizational, and group awareness are necessary elements in the development of the capacity for Executive Wisdom but, by themselves, are insufficient. Discernment, decisions, and actions based on these types of awareness alone can result in highly effective performance at times, yet it will often leave much to be desired, especially when viewed through the lens of history.

Mapping Situational and Moral Awareness

For longer term effectiveness and increased likeliness of the emergence of wise leadership, one must add *situational* and what can be called *moral* awareness. As I described earlier in this chapter, many biographers, historians, and students of leadership have focused their attention repeatedly on the ability of individuals to either accurately assess their situations, historical times, allies and adversaries, and alternative pathways, and thus make choices and execute them well, or not to understand what they face and create chaos and disasters. Furthermore, one often sees examples of leaders who do understand their times, opportunities, and environments correctly but, because of the values that they hold and their particular preferences for certain forms of moral reasoning, they make choices and execute them in ways that reflect fundamental orientations that can get them into profound trouble.

A most recent and glaring example of this involves the complete collapse of the Enron Corporation, which by most accounts was due primarily to significant lapses in attending to moral issues (McLean & Elkind, 2003). The incredibly rapid descent and bankruptcy of one of America's most admired companies led to the suicide of Cliff Baxter, a member of the inner executive circle, the criminal indictment of virtually all of the senior leaders of the enterprise, and a series of huge financial settlements with legal plaintiffs who sued the organizational partners of Enron for their complicit participation in a massive fraud organized and operated against the global marketplace. In essence, the leaders and those who enabled them lied to the public, to the government, to most of their employees, and to their owners. Only greed and the fear of having their mistakes discovered drove their moral reasoning, and the cost of that absence of sophistication in morals and values was astronomical for everyone involved.

We have seen example after example of such moral and ethical lapses in for-profit, nonprofit, and governmental organizations throughout history. When the leaders of an institution lose clarity about the moral and value implications of how they are seeing situations, what they are deciding to do, and how they are acting, the worst catastrophes in human history occur. Wars, famines, genocides, plagues, bankruptcies, and failures of all imaginable kinds are the direct result of human consciences gone to sleep or malfunctioning. Thus, the final step in wisdom mapping consists of trying to ensure that questions of moral propriety and the underlying values involved in choices are carefully considered. When all six of these types of awareness illuminate the daily performance of a leader, he or she has the highest probability of exercising Executive Wisdom. The absence or dimming of one or more of the types of awareness in a given challenge or problem will dramatically reduce the likelihood that wisdom will be present in the processes and outcomes of executive work.

BARRIER REDUCTION AND WISDOM MAPPING: REEXAMINING THE CASE STUDY

If one briefly reexamines the case study of Andrew Carnegie's decision not to support the second round of financing of Scott's railroad venture, one will see that Carnegie's own words speak to his level of self-awareness. He stated that he knew and understood his priorities and commitments and that he would not be deterred from meeting those obligations. This knowledge enabled him to resist what must have been considerable interpersonal, economic, and social pressure to support his long-time mentors and fellow investors. Self-awareness can enable such firmness in the face of environmental turbulence and provide substantial emotional stability when others are losing theirs.

The case example can also illustrate the organizational and group components of wisdom mapping. At the time of the meeting in Philadelphia, Carnegie had continued to be involved with his first group of colleagues. He let himself be enrolled in the railway initiative despite his better judgment. He did not withdraw and paid the quarter of a million dollars, probably knowing that he would lose it. Simultaneously, he created his own executive group, headquartered in Pittsburgh. He knew the financial and executive capacities of that group and fully understood that its success depended on his full and complete engagement in the steel enterprise. His calculations of the consequences of his decision not to support further the railway project were based at least in part on his knowledge of the capacities and relationships with and between the people involved in the two groups. Awareness of the team of people with whom a leader works most closely is a necessary feature for supporting the emergence of Executive Wisdom.

When one applies the situational-awareness component to this case, one can see that Scott had a brilliant idea. With the end of the Civil War and the vast migration to the West underway, it was entirely logical to want to extend the railway infrastructure of the country. He had the necessary knowledge and skill to build and operate a new railroad. However, when seen from the vantage point of history, he did not truly understand the importance of long-term financing for such an undertaking. So, he built his organization rapidly following the principle of speed to market and on the strength of his initial borrowing. Scott took at least one of his key partners, Carnegie, for granted. He assumed that Carnegie would continue to support an enterprise in which Carnegie himself had no initial role in formulating its basic strategy. Apparently, Scott did not carefully and sufficiently examine the possibility of major turbulence in financial markets. In short, he built his organization on a foundation of financial sand, and in the first stiff wind from an environmental challenge, the business completely collapsed. On the other hand, Carnegie did understand these fundamentals and practiced situational awareness seemingly religiously. He knew what his bankers wanted and would tolerate and what his partners in the new enterprise could and could not accomplish. He knew the central role that he played, and he held to a vision and strategy that he had carefully constructed on the basis of the best information he could get. His situational awareness helped him succeed where Scott failed miserably. This type of awareness is absolutely essential in helping executives make wise decisions and execute them effectively.

Finally, one sees clear evidence in Carnegie's diary entry of the moral reasoning he used to work through the decision not to invest further in Scott's railroad. He experienced a significant conflict in loyalty between the men whose early support led to his financial and professional success and those he had recruited to his own steel enterprise. He stated that he believed his larger duty was to the men and families who had agreed to join him. He knew that this would have both costs and consequences, and he persisted in what he knew was the right decision for him. With well over a century of history standing between us and Carnegie's decisions and actions, one may safely state that the motives underlying his choice in that situation were not purely moral. Wisdom mapping does not suggest that questions of moral propriety should or can be the sole determining factor in how leaders decide or act, although in most cases they should provide excellent guidance. Instead, the mapping approach, if exercised vigorously, guarantees that these moral and value implications will be examined by executives as they lead their organizations.

Walking through such a mapping exercise perhaps would have enabled Tom Scott to spot his unwarranted assumptions about the security of short-term loans to start a huge capital infrastructure project and perhaps notice the weaknesses in his executive team. It was possible to do such an analysis even in the 1870s, because Carnegie did, and Carnegie based his own investment decisions on a more clear-eyed, sober, and ethical assessment of what might go wrong. We do not necessarily know the details of the information available to him or the inner, metacognitive approach that Carnegie took, but it is clear from the personal accounts reported by Tedlow (2001) that Carnegie did know who was involved, what their capabilities were, the similarities and differences between the railway and steel investment opportunities, and the general thinking in the investment community of the time. His accurate discernment and perspective-taking ensured the possibility of his future success. However, Scott's inaccurate wisdom map led him and his colleagues into a financial catastrophe.

FROM CONCEPTS TO PRACTICE: A BRIEF PREVIEW
OF THE NEXT CHAPTERS

Now that I have introduced a considerable body of conceptual information, I turn to more practical matters. In the next section of the book, I explore what leaders and their coaches can do to conduct the wisdom mapping process and how to use that process in both the day-to-day management of an enterprise and in the strategic considerations of environmental adaptation and organizational learning. I conclude the book with a consideration of the issues involved with the emergence of wisdom in executive groups. This latter issue is crucial, because virtually all senior executives in modern organizations need and use such groups to multiply their impact and to exert their influence on the complex daily activities of the entities they lead.

EXERCISE TO IMPROVE YOUR UNDERSTANDING
OF BARRIERS TO EXECUTIVE WISDOM

Take a few minutes to consider the leaders whom you know who have left their positions with their heads hanging low. Some of them simply left quietly, without anyone knowing. Others may have had police officers escorting them out. Think about the feelings that these events generated for you. Were you curious, sad, or angry, or have a sense of resignation? Once you have a general sense of how you felt about the individual(s), ask yourself the following questions:

1. Did the person leave after failing to lead an organization's efforts to manage one of the developmental or environmental challenges identified by Finkelstein (2003; merger or acquisition, market change, etc.)?
2. To your knowledge, did the person display any of the personal characteristics described in this chapter? If so, what were they and how did you respond to them?
3. What advice would you give the person on the basis of what you have read so far in this book?

5

WISDOM MAPPING I:
SELF- AND FAMILY AWARENESS

My self-analysis remains interrupted. I have realized why I can analyze myself only with the help of knowledge obtained objectively (like an outsider). True self-analysis is impossible; otherwise there would be no neurotic illness.

—Sigmund Freud (as quoted by Barron, 1993, p. xx)

Any reading of philosophy, theology, psychology, and the various social sciences makes it clear that one of the central tasks of human existence focuses on the attempt to become self-aware. For thousands of years, substantial efforts have been undertaken to create pathways to such understanding. All such journeys result in increased pattern recognition and the evolution of metacognitive models of the self, of the nature of human existence, and of the nature and substance of life. In the first four chapters of this book, I presented a complex set of concepts attempting to explain how this happens and applied them to the challenges that leaders have in forging this kind of understanding of themselves, their organizations, and their environments.

In this chapter, I turn away from the conceptual and toward the practical. I offer a case study demonstrating how increased self- and family awareness can help to improve leadership performance. I then move into a more specific consideration of the nature of self-awareness, forms of inquiry, and other activities that executives and development professionals can undertake to extend this kind of knowledge in leaders. Improving such awareness in executives is one of the crucial steps along the path to both developing and creatively using wisdom in their working lives.

THE CASE OF THE UNLEASHED PIT BULL

I sat in this office for a few hours before that meeting and systematically worked myself into a sort of frenzy. I knew that the only way I could get his attention was to get very, very angry with him, so I concentrated on what I knew I needed to do. After that, the meeting was difficult, but mostly a formality. Once it started, I tore into him. I was like a pit bull. I grabbed him by the throat and never let go. Anytime he fought back, I bit deeper and harder. There was no way he was going to leave that room without acknowledging that he was wrong and that he had to do what I told him to do. There was simply no other choice.

I listened to this report by Cal Norton with a complex set of feelings and thoughts. Cal was a senior executive in an information services firm with which I had been working in a variety of ways for several years. On the surface, I had found Cal to be easy to approach and work with in coaching and consulting. He was an astonishingly bright, self-motivated learner. On his own time, he had laid out a reading curriculum on leadership, politics, organizational behavior, and change management and proceeded with dogged determination to plow through it. Indeed, like some of my other senior clients, he had introduced me to authors and ideas that my own explorations had yet to uncover. In an earlier meeting, he had shown me the typed list of books he had read in the previous 18 months. Although I knew most of them and over the years had at least skimmed through them, he had read them, all of them, from cover to cover, and done so critically. He had a reputation in his company for being a brilliant individual information systems analyst and had been tapped to provide senior leadership of a major section of his company.

I had been working on a consulting engagement in the company for some time and had come to know Cal as a valued member of the leadership team. I had also received reports from others that he could be a real problem for some people because he had a tendency to become extremely angry and suffered from bouts of "losing his temper." I had agreed to coach him as part of the overall service plan in the company, and the two of us had met on a number of occasions to discuss the challenges he was facing operationally, interpersonally, and politically. All in all, we had spent probably 4 or 5 days together over the course of a couple of years either in one-on-one discussions or in group meetings with his fellow leaders in the company.

"I think I need to get better at self-awareness," Cal continued in our coaching session.

After hearing the metaphoric description of his meeting with his colleague, I found it easy to agree with him, and simultaneously, I was curious about how he had come to that conclusion.

"What makes you say that?" I asked.

"Two things. First, I just finished reading the book you recommended, *Primal Leadership* (Goleman, Boyatzis, & McKee, 2002). The authors talked a lot about self-awareness in it, and I must confess that I just don't get it. I mean, I can understand what they are arguing for intellectually, and I certainly get the case examples that they used, but at some level, I just don't comprehend how to do it. The second thing is that one of my colleagues, Nancy Arendale, pointed out to me that I seem to need to use anger when I really want to make a point in the organization. As I've thought about what she said, I've come to believe she's right."

"Well, that's a pretty good example of the exercise of self-awareness right there," I replied.

"What do you mean?"

"Look at it this way. Someone provides you with feedback about yourself or an aspect of your behavior, and you take it in, consider it carefully, and end up agreeing with it."

"Yeah, but what do I do with it? I agree I do it. I know that I use anger deliberately and that it is very effective. When I decide to do something like that, I just tear into someone's throat and I don't let go until and unless he or she cries 'uncle.' If they do that, then I let them up."

"And if they don't?"

"I keep going. I escalate. I attack them personally. I don't let them reply. I'll do anything to win, to make them submit."

"Do you want to explore this a little further?" I asked.

He smiled and nodded in reply. We had worked enough together for him to know that he had just committed himself to further exploration. He also recognized that I had used that motivation to push him farther along the path that he himself had initiated.

"When you do attack a colleague or subordinate in the way you just described, what do you think the effects are on you and your reputation?"

"I win the arguments and fights I get into. I don't know about the effects on my reputation."

"Do you think the pattern has any effect at all on your reputation or on how others are likely to relate to you?"

Again Cal smiled and nodded. Over the years of our work together, I had learned that his smile meant that he was closely tracking our conversation, learning from it, and simultaneously that he was enjoying the process. Cal really liked to be challenged.

"How do you think more self-awareness could help you in this situation?" I asked him, obviously curious about whether he would be willing to explore this behavior more thoroughly.

"That's my problem; I don't know how it could help. I want to go back now and reread Goleman's two other books. I think I'll have a better chance of understanding them in more depth."

"Are you curious about this pattern of using anger?"

"What do you mean?"

"Do you believe it could help you to understand a little more about where it might come from, where it started?"

"Sure."

"OK, then let me ask you a few questions, if I might."

"Shoot," he said, still smiling.

"Very frequently, I find it's quite useful to have a little more background on the history of a particular pattern of behavior. So, growing up in your family, how was anger handled?"

"Well, if I got out of line, my dad used to kick the crap out of me. Mom never said much at all."

I found this answer, so candidly and freely given, simply breathtaking. I followed up with several additional questions and discovered that Cal was the oldest of four children in his family, two boys and two girls. The girls were 2 and 4 years younger than him. His brother was 16 years younger. His mom was a homemaker, and his father was a professional man who worked as a manager in a company. He described his father as a "big guy, over 200 pounds," who would fly off the handle when he got angry and slap Cal around. When he got angry with his wife or daughters, he would simply leave the house in a rage that was obvious to everyone, but he did not physically attack the women in the home.

"What do you think you learned from these experiences within your family?" I asked him.

"I learned to keep my mouth shut very early."

"And what happened to your anger, your response to these situations?"

"What do you mean?"

"Well, clearly, you must have had some pretty strong reactions to your father's physical treatment of you."

"Yeah, you can say that again. When I was 16, I was 5 foot 2 and weighed 77 pounds. I was a little guy until I turned 21. Dad was always a big guy."

I found myself cringing at the image of a 200-pound man physically punishing a frail little boy. Clearly, there was evidence that Cal had experienced some significant trauma while growing up, yet in virtually every aspect of his life he had created enormous success for himself.

With this additional background information, I decided to shift our attention back to the workplace rather than push further into the family and personal history. Coaches routinely face this kind of decision in their work as they explore the relationships among the person and his or her personal history, emotional reactions, and thoughts and the role that he or she plays in the organization. The deeper one travels into the interior responses of the client, the closer coaching comes to becoming psychotherapy. It is a fluid boundary that must be constantly monitored and strategically examined to ensure that a coaching engagement does not inadvertently become a formal counseling relationship. In Cal's case, I was virtually certain that we could make this shift readily, because there was no other evidence of psychological dysfunction.

"So, if we come back to your use of anger in the workplace, what are the situations in which you are most likely to use this 'pit bull' kind of behavior?"

Cal paused for a second and then said, without hesitation, "It's mostly in situations in which I think I'm not being heard."

"What do you mean by that?"

"Well, at times, I feel invisible around here. No one pays attention to what I am saying. When that happens, sometimes I need to trot out the pit bull. That gets people's attention."

"So you use the anger strategically to make yourself heard?"

"Definitely. In the situation I described to you, I had to sit here for a couple of hours psyching myself up for that interaction. It's not something that I do easily."

"And yet, you seem to have a reputation as someone who gets angry easily and around whom people have to be careful."

"Yeah, I guess so," he answered with another smile on his face.

"What's it like to be invisible at work?" I asked.

"It's terrible. I feel powerless, like I can't get anything accomplished, like no one cares about what I say."

"And yet, in the situation in which you are working right now, it seems clear that you have been enormously influential and mostly without losing your temper," I said.

This reminded Cal of his leadership of a complex major project that his boss had given him. He had pushed that initiative forward in major ways in a short period of time through a series of savvy independent actions and well-conducted meetings.

"Do you feel you've been invisible in that project?"

"Well, no. But I don't feel like I'm in control of it, either. It's really very political, and it could fall apart at any second. I'm not sure what the politics are, where I'm going, what I'm supposed to do from here."

"Do you think losing your temper will help you lead this project?"

"Oh, definitely not. I'm working with many of the major players in the company. I can't afford to attack them."

"So who are you likely to attack?"

"Mostly peers who won't agree with me or are wrong or subordinates who screw up and won't admit that they have blown something."

"Who did you attack in your family?" I asked pushing him back toward his family history, trying to both understand more about his history and to deepen his awareness.

"No one. I pretty much kept my mouth shut."

"Did you feel invisible there, too?"

Cal hesitated with his answer. His smile disappeared, and his face flushed a little more than usual for him. "Yeah, I did a lot of the time. I had two older male cousins that I used to hang out with. The only way they'd let me tag along was if I made myself invisible."

"And if you didn't let yourself be invisible?"

"They'd either dump me or beat me up."

"Did you ever feel like you got even with them or were able to express your anger with them?" I asked.

"Well, I couldn't beat them up, if that's what you mean. They were always bigger and stronger. But I was very good at games. As far back as I remember, I was always good at games. I started to play chess with them when I was 3 years old and I never lost. I mean never."

The image of a 3-year-old learning the basics of the game of chess and then using that knowledge in a determined way to gain a sense of parity and power with his older cousins made intuitive sense to me. Cal was known for being a brilliant technician in the company. The evidence of the pervasiveness of his curiosity and motivation to learn was evident in how he was going at the job of self-education on leadership and change management. I could easily see him practicing his chess skills, learning to read at an early age, and honing his ability to concentrate for long periods of time. Simultaneously anxious about his cousins either abandoning or beating him, he had found a way to level the playing field between them and so preserve his own sense of pride, self-efficacy, and power.

"What do you think was the effect of your victories on your cousins?" I asked.

"I have no idea, but there was this one incident with a friend of mine. We used to play games a lot together, and one day it turned out that he won. Well, much to my surprise, he leaped up in the air and started to dance around the room. He was screaming over and over again, 'I won, I won!' He got up on the couch and just kept jumping up and down yelling like that for a long time."

"How did you feel about that?"

"I thought it was kind of stupid. It was only a game."

"Do you think he felt diminished by all of the losses he suffered at your hands?"

Cal paused for a moment and then said, "I don't know."

"Losing constantly can make you feel small, almost invisible," I said.

Cal was visibly touched. We went on from there to discuss the kind of leader he had been and the kind he wanted to be. As a result of this relatively brief examination of a few crucial aspects of his personal history, he could now readily see that he had developed a reputation for his temper and the positive and negative implications that involved. I further pointed out that on the one hand, he was not manipulated or taken for granted much, but on the other hand, many of his colleagues had trouble trusting him at an emotional level. He absorbed the feedback with curiosity during the early part of that coaching session. However, he was far more interested in and motivated to discuss the politics of his major project. So, as we turned our attention to those issues in the rest of the time that I had with him that day, I made a mental note to return to the themes of invisibility, powerlessness, and the use of anger in future meetings with him.

THE CHALLENGE OF EXECUTIVE CONSCIOUSNESS

The ephemeral yet glorious nature of human consciousness has fascinated and troubled many of the major thinkers in the history of philosophy and science. Confucius, Socrates, Plato, Aristotle, Descartes, Locke, Burke, James, Freud, Jung, and even Skinner (by his chronic denials and endlessly clever explanations of reinforcement schemes and situational variables) focused on the magnetic pull of the subject. It is safe to say that with the modern technologies of neurology, neuroimaging, neuropsychology, and cognitive assessments, human beings are even more interested in exploring these phenomena and slowly but surely are unraveling their secrets. In particular, the ravages of brain diseases such as Parkinson's, dementia, schizophrenia, stroke, and Alzheimer's are driving major pharmaceutical companies and government-funded basic research programs relentlessly deeper into the problems that the loss of consciousness creates for humanity. In truth, as much as most of us fear death by accident, heart attack, or cancer, it is the loss of one's mind that creates the greatest sense of anxiety as we age. William James (1890/1950), in defining what he called the *spiritual self*, said,

> A man's inner sense of subjective being, his psychic faculties or dispositions . . . are the most enduring and intimate part of the self, that which we most verily seem to be. We take a purer self-satisfaction when we think of our ability to argue and discriminate, of our moral sensibility and conscience, of our indomitable will, than when we survey any of our other possessions. Only when these are altered is a man said to be *alienatus a se*. (p. 296)

Natsoulas (1991) suggested that self-awareness was a special form of self-conscious judgment that he described as follows:

I newly learn or remind myself, on a firsthand basis (not from hearsay), about the kind of person I am in one or another specific respect . . . . I newly learn or remind myself of this, from having witnessed relevant actions I performed or experiences I had, and by now bringing this evidence to bear on how I conceive of myself, in terms of a trait or ability I therefore consider myself to possess, on perhaps other grounds as well. (p. 344)

In a wonderful chapter on the general subject of self-awareness, Natsoulas (1998) wrote that several specific components of the phenomenon must be present for anyone to state accurately that he or she is having such an experience. These include the following:

- Witnessing evidence of oneself in the world.
- Experiencing that witnessing truly as oneself and not in some other altered state of consciousness, such as dissociation, denial, delusion, and the like.
- *Retroawareness*, or having a sense of one's inner self as an object of observation in the stream of time.
- *Inner awareness*, or possessing the ability to remember specific things about the self in the process of remembering the self— how one perceived, thought, felt, planned, remembered, acted, or expected in specific situations.
- Self-thoughts and self-judgments in which one uses the witnessing and awareness as "evidence regarding the kind of person that one is with respect to the spiritual sphere as [William] James broadly defined it." (Natsoulas, 1998, p. 28)

The research literature on managerial self-awareness is currently anchored in studies of the use and effectiveness of 360-degree review approaches to performance assessment and leadership development. In a study using a method that assessed managerial self-awareness as a function of the congruence between self- and direct reports' behavioral ratings, Church (1997) found that high-performing managers had significantly more managerial self-awareness than average-performing managers, providing additional confirmation for the central thesis of this chapter that effective leaders should and do possess increased capacity for self-awareness. Yammarino and Atwater (1993) also demonstrated that non-self-ratings of managerial performance increased as the gap between a leader's ratings of his or her own behavior and the ratings of subordinates of the same behavior narrowed significantly. These findings coincide with the summaries of Goleman et al. (2002), who made it clear that self-awareness is one of the key features of emotional intelligence and that both are directly and positively related to effective management performance. Thus, there is a small but growing empirical literature supporting the thesis that as an executive's capacity for self-awareness improves, others are likely to rate his or her managerial performance as more effective.

REVISITING THE CASE STUDY: CAL'S SELF-AWARENESS

I have spent most of this book so far exploring how executives create, use, and misuse their own special brand of consciousness. The case study opening this chapter illustrates in depth that Cal had the ability to be self-aware; had received external feedback that caused him to reflect in precisely the ways that James (1890/1950), Natsoulas (1998), and many others have described as characteristic of the processes involved; and was motivated enough to raise the issue with me in a coaching session and to disclose some extremely interesting, relevant, and useful historical material regarding the developmental origins of the behaviors about which he had questions. In the case vignette, we can see my efforts to probe into the area with, I hope, some tact and sensitivity as a coach and as a person. Both Cal and I were richly rewarded by these efforts. I could understand him much better as a leader and as a person on the basis of the new information, and he improved his knowledge of the historical and emotional foundations of some of his behavior and how that behavior might prove troubling to some of his colleagues.

The case study stops short of illustrating what I subsequently did with the critical information that session yielded. In keeping with the approach I recommended in my recent book (Kilburg, 2000), that work has progressively pushed Cal in the direction of simultaneously deepening his understanding of his underlying motivations, his behavioral preferences and strengths, and his propensity to act in predictable and sometimes ineffective ways in using aggressively expressed anger instead of other behaviors more deeply infused with emotions in addition to his readily accessed aggression. We have also discussed at length alternative approaches that he can take when he has experiences of becoming invisible, powerless, and anxious in leadership environments. Through this work, he has become much more strategic in his use of himself; is less likely to resort inappropriately to the pit bull behavior pattern; and has improved his ability to operate in a sophisticated, political fashion in his organization. All of these improvements, though, are driven first and foremost by his ability to be self-aware as an individual and as a leader. His ability to see himself as an objective entity, a person whom he can operate with, on, and through, as well as to experience subjectively, has improved significantly.

I believe that this ability for self-observation provides the foundation for significant growth for any human trying to improve his or her performance. So, how then can one deliberately go to work on and improve an individual leader's ability to become more self-aware and to use that capacity to become a higher functioning and more conscious executive? How can leaders like Cal, when they sense that they are not fully self-conscious, become more so? And how can coaches assist their clients in becoming more conscious of themselves as leaders even in those cases in which individuals resist such knowledge and learning?

FOUNDATIONS FOR SELF-AWARENESS: A BRIEF REVIEW

For experienced coaches, the material in this chapter may well seem rudimentary—all coaches are, at a minimum, trying to improve self-awareness. On the other hand, the material may seem less obvious to executive readers, because many leaders view the application of psychological knowledge to the challenges of leadership and work in organizations as "soft stuff." "Soft skills," although seen by many executives as having a role in their enterprises, are often spoken about with a disparaging tone. Indeed, the categorization of the language of development and education into "hard" and "soft" classifications sometimes impedes the effort to resolve crucial problems in organizations. For literally thousands of years, many of the human species' most brilliant minds have struggled long and hard to help us see ourselves; our lives; and indeed, our very minds, with more clarity. As I indicated in the beginning of this chapter, Confucius, Socrates, Plato, Aristotle, Cicero, Augustine, Jesus Christ, Mohammed, Moses, the Buddha, Kant, St. Thomas Aquinas, and on down to Freud, Jung, Skinner, and a host of modern philosophers and scientists have all labored hard—and in some cases, given their lives—in the effort to improve the ability of humanity to see and understand itself. So, as an author, practitioner, and thinker in this arena, I know full well that the literature on self-awareness is impossibly vast and deep—it covers, for example, most of philosophy, theology, history, psychology, sociology, and anthropology. It seems clear that the more tools and approaches that are available to explore the crucial areas of executive function in modern organizations, the more likely coaches will be able to help leaders do their work more effectively.

For the curious and discerning reader who wants to spend a little more time exploring in depth in the areas of research and writing on self-awareness, I recommend a variety of resources. Kilburg (2000), Kampa and White (2002), and Kampa-Kokesch and Anderson (2001) have provided excellent summaries of the literature on executive coaching and its effectiveness in changing leadership behavior. The available scientific literature has begun to make clear that improvement in the self-awareness of leaders through feedback from 360-degree reviews and coaching processes is significantly correlated with perceptions of improved managerial performance by colleagues, subordinates, and superiors (Church, 1997). Ferrari and Sternberg (1998) created an extensive edited volume of papers on the subject of human self-awareness that draws on the thinking and research of many of the finest psychological minds of the past 50 years. The authors represented in these papers are some of the best-known scientific psychologists of the last century, and they provide excellent summaries of the variety of scientific methodologies and conceptual schemes that have been developed to understand how humans come to form a self-identity and to see themselves as distinct from others. Similarly, Barron (1993) approached the same topic from the view of classical psychoanalysis, offering a series of extraordinarily insightful papers exploring that discipline's ongoing efforts to describe, understand, and use explicit self-reflective methodologies for improving a practitioner's ability to work with patients. This collection covers everything from Freud's initial speculations about self-analysis and the rise of his consistent practice of it to more modern ideas about countertransference in psychotherapy and how to manage it when it arises.

I have come see that the first step to improvement in almost any area of human performance is to increase the awareness of the person or persons involved. My examination of the psychological literature in self-awareness itself yielded well over 1,500 currently available articles and book chapters. However, this search included only a small number of articles that examined the subject largely from the psychotherapeutic and scientific perspectives. None apply the issues and concepts formally to people in leadership positions. When one considers that there are two millenia of historical, theological, and philosophical studies to add to the century of psychotherapy and scientific psychology literatures, it is easy to see that the knowledge foundation for our exploration is indeed huge.

Gottschalk (1989) followed in the footsteps of Karen Horney (1942) and provided a lucid and pragmatic review of a variety of approaches to actually doing self-analysis. Although such efforts are necessary, and I believe that self-awareness is the cornerstone upon which Executive Wisdom rests, I want to emphasize that the capacity for self-delusion in human beings, including in those who provide coaching services to leaders in organizations, is legendary. For an in-depth exploration of the darker side of the human capacity for self-delusion—yes, even self-aware self-delusion—see Ronell (2003), who explicitly explored the subject of stupidity using the tools of philosophical exposition, literary analysis, and postmodern thought.

PROMOTING SELF- AND FAMILY AWARENESS IN EXECUTIVES

As I have thought about just how I do this kind of work with leaders, I have had to come to grips with the fact that I most often work in an intuitive way in my sessions. In my work with Cal, for example, I had a general sense from what I knew about him that there was a significant untold part of his story, but I did not go into the session that I described above with any deliberate strategy to create this experience with him. Instead, I entered that coaching space with him as I do with every one of my clients—namely, mentally and emotionally prepared to discover what is relevant and then to consistently and systematically push, pull, prod, and encourage the individual toward what he or she considers to be a more effective level of performance. In examining the process that I use with clients, I have come to see that it has six major components that work together to promote this type of learning. All of them help to create a supportive, interpersonal relationship and a sense of time and place in which reflective learning is encouraged and often takes place. What follows are some specific processes and steps that I find useful in strengthening and deepening client self-awareness.

Promote Curiosity

The first component consists of efforts to stimulate, enlist, and try to get the leader to engage in a high degree of curiosity about how he or she is put together and functions as a human being and as a leader. The challenge is to structure an opportunity in which the executive client really wants to examine him- or herself. By so doing, he or she simultaneously creates an inner and outer experience in which the self can be seen, heard, and felt subjectively as the "me" of the person and objectively as a human entity to be mutually, carefully, and respectfully studied, with the goal of improving the person-as-leader's capacity to perform effectively.

Often, and as I did with Cal, I will deliberately ask a client if he or she is curious about why they did something or responded in a particular way. Another frequent question I use to approach individuals is "Do you mind if I push you a little?" A third general approach is to nonverbally communicate that I am interested in what happened and then to ask a specific question. In most cases, I find that if I am truly curious about the person and the situation being faced, the client is able to become interested as well. These specific techniques are nearly always successful in eliciting a higher state of active curiosity in a client and in signaling that we are going to explore together.

Provide Emotional Support

In the second component of the process, I try to provide emotional support to the client who is struggling to learn and grow. Harry Levinson, a long-time mentor and colleague and a world-renowned consultant, has a wonderful aphorism that he uses to describe what clients go through: "All change involves loss, and all loss must be grieved." I have found this to be universally true in my own consulting experience, but the ways in which the change process pushes individuals through various emotional states vary widely. For some people, the primary emotions they sense and express mostly focus on the anxiety of learning something new about themselves, their organizations, or their situations. For others, feelings of sadness accompany the recognition that they must let go of or reduce the frequency with which they use particular patterns of behavior. For many men, the most likely emotions to be experienced and displayed are forms of anger or frustration. For many individuals, learning is a joy to be shared, and self-awareness elicits feelings of happiness, humility, and humor.

As these affective states are encountered, I view my job as primarily trying to recognize them and helping the clients to realize that they are indeed having emotional responses. I tend to push for explicit labeling of the feelings and will often probe for past experiences of similar emotional responses as a way of educating myself and the individual client that this is something that has happened before and probably will again. In a sense, by encouraging such explorations and explicit expressions, one ensures that the processes of emotional adaptation, growth, and grieving are engaged. An absence of monitoring for such responses and an unwillingness to stimulate their expression can often lead to further defensiveness and an incomplete, unsatisfactory, or failed learning experience.

In all cases, I view my job as trying to be "good company" on the complex and interesting but frequently arduous journey of executive growth. I also try to use empathy, emotional resonance, mirroring, and my own history to help me understand the client's experience. As I build my own internalized model of the individual, I can frequently anticipate their responses and the places and issues that are likely to trouble them, and I will often try to use humor as a way of helping the person see his or her situation from a somewhat different perspective. When I am trying to be funny—a pretty difficult thing, really—I am careful not to use sarcasm or other approaches that are likely to make someone feel ashamed or guilty. If I need to engender some of those adverse feelings because of a lack of intervention adherence, disrespect being displayed toward me, or when I believe that there is danger for individuals in what they are doing or about to do, I move carefully to try to frame my confrontative comments in ways that can be heard as me trying to protect clients rather than deliberately direct, humiliate, or demean them as a way of gaining control or power over them. I have found that clients, when properly supported from an emotional perspective, are often willing to take stunning leaps toward increased self-awareness. The case study that opens this chapter illustrates this well, because one does not ordinarily expect senior male executives in major organizations to be willing to undertake such explorations.

Provide a Proper Frame of Reference

The third component of the process of increasing self- and family awareness is to try to provide a proper frame of reference for these kinds of explorations. Coaching processes borrow a lot from what has been learned from doing psychotherapy and education. Executive coaching is not therapy, but it can be therapeutic (Kilburg, 2000). It is not formal classroom-based education, but it contains many of the elements of that process as well. So, I often find it both useful and necessary to provide an explanation to a client for what we are doing in a particular session and why I believe it is important. I have found that reliance on traditional Socratic questioning or other therapeutically based interventions, in which a practitioner deliberately withholds orienting information or signals about what is happening and why in order to have the client learn in his or her own way, is of limited use when working with senior executives. They usually have little time for coaching and not much use or patience for simply waiting and watching for what they think and feel to direct their attention. Although I believe coaches must be extremely cautious about the ways in which they deliberately inject themselves into the inner lives of their clients, I have come to see the practical wisdom and true effectiveness of taking a more active stance in coaching than is the case for more traditional forms of psychotherapy or Socratic approaches to education.

In this context, then, it is pretty easy to say, again as I did with Cal, "I often find it useful to have more history." Or I might follow up on material with strong emotional content with an explanation of how I think emotions work, their physiological and neurological foundations, and the relevance for how they can influence behavior in work situations. If I recommend a book, provide a journal article, or give a homework assignment, I will try to help the person understand the "why" of the suggestion. At all times, I am trying to demystify myself, decrease the distance between the client and me, and open up wider channels of communication. I frequently conduct coaching sessions during a meal, and I usually answer the tactful and simply curious questions clients ask about my personal life. In fact, in an informal setting such as dinner, I will look for relevant ways to introduce myself as a fellow traveler, which I find further deepens the relationship, builds rapport, and cements the client into the frame of seeing human development as a lifelong process.

Systematic Inquiry

The fourth component of the process involves the systematic use of inquiry, what I think of as one of the most important skills that any coach, consultant, or leader possesses. As I have gained more experience (a nice way of saying I'm getting old), I have become a connoisseur of questions. I look for them in books and articles. I create them from the assertions and findings of colleagues. They are always on the tip of my tongue, and when I am stuck and cannot figure out what to say or do with a client, I nearly always resort to trying to ask questions to generate more information, stimulate the client's thinking and exploration, and buy time to think more deeply about why I am stuck and how to move forward in a session.

Exhibits 5.1 and 5.2 provide dozens of effective questions through which coaches or individual executives can substantively explore themselves and their family histories in ways that relate to how they are likely to develop, defend themselves, or lead in organizations. Although there is no one question that works better or worse to help executives extend their awareness of the psychosocial and cultural roots of the ways they behave and, consequently, lead, in their professional roles, I most often find that the mere encouragement of some contemplative reflection on those wellsprings brings nearly immediate recognition of motivational patterns and action preferences.

The case study that opened this chapter is a specific example of how this tends to happen in development work. My description of that session with Cal is extremely close to my notes and memory of the actual flow of the conversation that we had. His personal observations and lamentation about self-awareness and my simple question to him led to a literal flood of relevant information that surprised both of us. As we entered into the initial conversation, he had no conscious idea that we would take a fast but in-depth trip into his past to illuminate his present leadership challenges and concerns and his intellectual conundrum. I often find that opening up the conversation with simple questions such as "From whom do you think you learned the most about leading as you were growing up?" or "Who were your leadership models or heroes?" almost automatically directs individuals to powerful, life-shaping memories that illustrate current challenges in the most remarkable ways. One of the keys to effective coaching, then, rests in helping the individual stretch for something more than just having the memory.

The other questions in the exhibits can be used to strengthen and deepen the exploration, but some caution is warranted as this process is undertaken, because many powerful memories and historical episodes in the lives of leaders did have traumatizing effects (Levine, 1997; Rothschild,

EXHIBIT 5.1
Questions for Promoting Self-Awareness in Executives

1. What are your dimensions of diversity—age, gender, nationality, culture, race, physical condition, religion, sexual orientation, marital status, personality characteristics and preferences, and so on—and how do they contribute to or inhibit the ways in which you lead?
2. What is your teachable model of leadership and management, and how do you typically convey it to others?
3. From whom did you learn your major positive and negative lessons about leadership? Can you identify and define the most important lessons?
4. From whom did you learn your major lessons about morality? Can you identify and define the most important lessons?
5. What were your experiences of competition as you were growing up, and how do you believe they affect how you currently lead?
6. What were your experiences of human conflict as you were growing up, and how do you believe they affect how you currently lead?
7. What were your experiences of problem-solving and decision making as you were growing up, and how do you believe they affect how you currently lead?
8. Identify three to five historical or present-day leaders you most admire and describe why you feel that way.
9. Identify three to five historical or present-day leaders you least admire and describe why you feel that way.
10. How do you learn best? Give an example of learning something extremely well.
11. What most interferes with your learning something? Give an example of failing to learn something.
12. What "hot buttons" or "pressure points" are most likely to get to or disturb you in the following situations?
    a. At work in general
    b. When interacting with a superior
    c. When interacting with a subordinate
    d. When interacting with a peer
    e. At home in general
    f. When interacting with your spouse or significant other
    g. When interacting with your children
    h. When interacting with your parents
    i. When interacting with your sibling(s)
    j. When interacting with your friends
13. From whom did you learn the most about expressing your emotions? Describe some of the lessons. Give examples. Do you manage your emotions in the same way at work as you do at home or in private? Why? Why not?
14. What were the circumstances of the worst failure you have experienced in life? What lessons did you learn from that failure?
15. What were the circumstances of the biggest success you have experienced in life? What lessons did you learn from that success?
16. When you have tried to change something in your life or yourself and struggled or failed; what happened or got in the way?
17. When you look back at your life at the age of 70 or perhaps 80, what would you want to have accomplished?
18. What would you currently write for your epitaph? Why?
19. If you could change one thing about yourself, what would it be? Why? Why hasn't it happened yet?
20. What are the key values you use to guide your life? How would you prioritize them? Why?

(continued)

EXHIBIT 5.1 *(Continued)*

21. If you could change one thing in the world, what would it be? Why?
22. If you could change one thing in your organization, what would it be? Why?
23. If you could change one thing in your own family, what would it be? Why?
24. Who is the wisest person you have ever met that has had an impact on you? Why did he or she have that effect?
25. Have you experienced patterns of behavior in your life that seemed to get in the way of your success or satisfaction that seemed inexplicable or mysterious to you and to others close to you? If yes, describe these experiences; provide examples for yourself and speculate on what the origins and underlying motivations of the patterns might be.

2000). I want to emphasize again that although coaching is not specifically aimed at producing therapeutic effects in leaders, when it is done well it can often create significant emotional and behavioral gains similar to those experienced in effective psychotherapy or counseling. Cal greatly deepened his own awareness of the roots of his day-to-day behavior in this one session, and on the basis of subsequent work with him, he has seemed less and less likely to reach for the pit bull solution. Yet he has retained the ability to be determined, sometimes confrontational, and assertive, as all leaders need to be.

Encourage Pattern Recognition

As useful as strengthening and deepening the types and levels of inquiry are for the development of Executive Wisdom, they are insufficient unless they lead to the fifth and sixth components of the process, which push the individual to actually do something with the information. Mere recollections or memories of the past or sudden insights into tendencies in and of themselves must be tied to the encouragement of pattern recognition. As I explored in depth in chapters 2 and 3, much of the cognitive work in human learning is based on pattern recognition processes. Indeed, Klein's (1999, 2003) research and practices demonstrate clearly that the ability to take rapid, effective, and wise actions in dangerous, high-stress, time-pressured, life-threatening situations depends on this capacity.

In Cal's case, after he disclosed his historical information, we spent substantial time exploring how those early developmental experiences had contributed to the establishment of highly effective patterns of coping and adaptation for him in many areas of his life. Those patterns were significantly responsible for the professional and personal success that he had experienced and were related to highly valued skills. Neither Cal nor anyone else would be willing to change these methods and patterns simply on the basis of a few questions and recall of some important childhood events. It took deeper

EXHIBIT 5.2
Questions to Improve Family Awareness

1. What explicit or implicit agreement do you have with your spouse or significant other about your relationship concerning expectations, psychological and physical needs, and how problems are to be handled?
2. What expectations do you have of your spouse or significant other in relation to your career and the work that you are doing currently?
3. What expectations does your spouse or significant other have of you in relation to his or her career and the work he or she is doing currently?
4. In your relationship with your spouse or significant other, do you have consistent problems in such areas as communications, conflict management, unfulfilled emotional needs, sexual satisfaction, finances, in-laws, children, infidelity, chemical dependency, physical abuse, or trust?
5. If you have children, are they reaching their developmental milestones in appropriate ways? If any of them are having trouble, are you and your spouse working creatively and productively with the child to resolve the difficulties?
6. What were the major dimensions of diversity of your and your spouse's or significant other's family of origin?
7. What did you learn in your family of origin about the nature of relationships, relating to others, conflict, competition, decision making, crisis management, problem solving, diversity, finances, ambition, spiritual beliefs, authority, obedience, creativity, independence, attachment, and separation?
8. What did your spouse or significant other learn in his or her family of origin about the nature of relationships, relating to others, conflict, competition, decision making, crisis management, problem solving, diversity, finances, ambition, achievement, spiritual beliefs, authority, obedience, creativity, independence, attachment, separation?
9. Are there differences in your answers to Questions 7 and 8 and, if yes, how do you think they affect your family relationships?
10. What are your goals for your relationship with your spouse or significant other? Do they differ from his or her goals for the relationship?
11. Do you have plans for your family? Do they differ from your spouse's or significant other's plans for the family?
12. What are the major strengths in your relationship with your spouse or significant other? In your relationship with your family? In your relationship with your family of origin?
13. What kinds of support systems do you have in place for your family in regard to health, day care, education, activities, spiritual development, and so on? Are they adequate for the needs and goals that you have identified?
14. How are your parents and siblings doing in their lives (assuming they are still alive)?
15. How would you describe your current relationships with your parents and siblings?
16. Do you see or experience any similarities between the ways you learned to relate within your family of origin and the ways in which you relate to others at work?
17. How does it feel to live in your family right now? Are those feelings affecting your ability to work?
18. What did you learn about being in and managing triangular relationships in your family?
19. What were the "hot button" and "can of worms" issues in your family of origin?
20. What were the major values you learned in your family of origin?
21. Are there patterns of performance or behavior that have interfered with the performance or satisfaction of your family for which no good explanation has been forthcoming? If yes, describe these patterns; provide examples for yourself and speculate on what the origins and underlying motivations of the patterns might be.

probing and efforts on my part to help him understand that by virtue of his previous experiences, successes, and strengths, he was predisposed to choose to behave in certain ways regardless of the overall level of effectiveness that the behavior would have. For him, the pit bull behavior was a necessary and important negative part of his ability to manage his life. In our work together, I tried to help him understand that that pattern could create untoward side effects and consequences for him as he continued to progress in his career. I carefully encouraged him to be more discerning of the situations that truly called for such radical acts of aggression and those that could be more effectively handled though the use of other skills. Cal has taken to this notion of diagnostic acumen and leadership intervention pretty well, and much of our subsequent work has focused on developing additional skills such as negotiation, coaching, and diplomacy.

Uncover Assumptions and Create Experiments

The final step in the process that helps leaders improve self- and family awareness involves uncovering and challenging the assumptions underlying the patterns of behavior and creating experiments and new alternatives. As a result of more than 100 years of research and practice in psychotherapy, it is now axiomatic in that field that simple insight does not necessarily lead to the change of any behavior. More is required of anyone who is trying to modify a long-standing pattern or trying to develop a new skill or ability. So, executives and their coaches need to use the knowledge derived from exercises designed to increase their self-awareness to push forward the agenda for change and professional improvement. With regard to the development of Executive Wisdom, nearly any improvement in self-awareness can lead to modifications and gains in the ability to discern, decide, and act in leadership situations. Predispositions to perceive situations, challenges, and relationships in narrow, historically governed ways are among the most difficult problems that any leader or leadership group must overcome. Similarly, deeply held prejudices about the correct ways to plan and decide, especially those involving the operation of cognitive, emotional, or unconscious biases, often doom leaders to simply repeat their pasts rather than cope effectively with the present. Finally, it has been my persistent observation, over the course of many years of providing consultation and coaching services in a wide range of organizations and to all kinds of individuals, that leaders' extremely skilled action preferences and strengths most often present major obstacles to their continued professional growth and development.

In the case example, it was extremely clear that Cal had a reputation in his organization for intellectual and professional brilliance and for his ability to be tough to the point of severe intimidation. He enjoyed being seen in this way, but it was a surprise to him and raised deep concerns when he heard from a colleague that he was publicly perceived as having problems with his anger. The discovery of the roots of his pit bull pattern of relating in certain circumstances enabled him to see that although this had been a major strength for him throughout his life, at a high senior level of leadership in a modern organization he would need to exercise greater discretion over the circumstances in which he took that dog for a public walk. Experiments with other forms of strategy and behavior in circumstances in which he felt a strong need to be firm, set limits, or oppose the actions of others became an important part of his development plan. The closer he has gotten to being aware of who he is and where he has come from and to being able to choose what knowledge, skill, and ability to exercise in any situation he faces as a leader has enabled him to more routinely decide and act wisely in his role.

Develop an Adherence Plan

Finally, given what has been discovered in the intervention adherence literature (Marlatt & Gordon, 1985; Meichenbaum & Turk, 1987), I believe it is necessary to think about how executives maintain the gains that their development work creates for them. In an earlier work (Kilburg, 2001), I provided a conceptual model and some operating recommendations for how the hard-won changes that leaders make in their lives can be better maintained through the creation and implementation of an intervention-adherence protocol. Careful attention to how the improvements in self- and family awareness are integrated into the life and work of a leader must be part of any effective developmental work.

REVISITING WISDOM MAPPING

I now return briefly to the model of the mapping pathway to Executive Wisdom. Figure 5.1 displays where self- and family awareness come into play in the process of developing and using this virtuous ability. As I noted in chapter 4, in a typical situation, an executive, or an executive along with his or her coach, begins to confront the initial story and conditions related to a problem or challenge. Absent any formal mapping activity, following Klein's (1999, 2003) models and research findings, most often intuition-driven, recognition-primed decision-making processes are activated that lead either to effective or ineffective personal and executive savvy. In short time frames, these processes can often seem indistinguishable from the exercise of Executive Wisdom. Indeed, in many situations the intuition of leaders is creatively informed by all of the components of wisdom

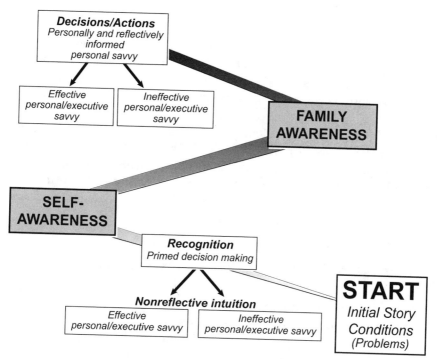

Figure 5.1. Mapping the executive self- and family awareness.

mapping, and the result yields wise discernment, decisions, and actions. However, to both explain and illustrate the models, I suggest strongly that one withhold final judgment on the quality of the outcomes of those initial efforts by leaders even in situations where it appears that they seem right on target.

As Figure 5.1 illustrates, the formal mapping of self- and family aware-ness onto any particular challenge or problem that a leader faces yields decisions and actions that are personally and reflectively informed. In turn, the action outcomes still tend to be either effective or ineffective executive savvy that is personally informed. Many leaders discern, decide, and act in the situations that they face with extensive knowledge of who they are as individuals and the potential contributions that their experiences in their families of origin might well be contributing to their work in a given situation. Such knowledge, although greatly informative and reassuring in most situations, does not necessarily lead to wise outcomes. In the end, I believe strongly that although self- and family awareness are necessary for the emergence and implementation of Executive Wisdom, executed by themselves they are insufficient unless the other components are also present. The model and Figure 5.1 suggest that the pathway and mapping process involves a linear, step-by-step process, but in many, if not most, cases such a sequential approach is probably not what happens. In intuition-driven, human executive deliberations and actions, all sources of data, evidence, and information appear to be considered in a complex, simultaneous, internal pattern recognition–matching–creation process that seems to magically yield its possible answers to questions or solutions to problems. The advantage of breaking out some of the components and suggesting that they can be linked to different outcomes along a pathway is that they can be examined and explored in greater detail. I hope that this more extensive and deliberate exploration leads to a better understanding of the phenomena that I propose go together to produce Executive Wisdom. In chapter 6, I continue my exploration of the wisdom mapping process by adding organizational and executive group awareness to the pathway.

AWARENESS EXERCISES FOR LEADERS AND THEIR COACHES

1. Executives themselves can begin to assess where they are in terms of their self- and family awareness by simply taking a little time to reflect on what activities they have engaged in either in the past or on an ongoing basis that may have pushed them to a greater level of knowledge and understanding of themselves and their individual history. There is no one true pathway to the development of this kind of awareness. Formal education; life experience; performance assessments; stresses; strains; problems; challenges; losses; victories; psychotherapy; growth groups; individual instruction in all sorts of activities; athletic coaching; corporate training programs; learning to play a musical instrument; performing in a play; family weddings, funerals, and other get-togethers; creating diaries and journals; intimate conversations with mature, insightful loved ones; spiritual development; meditation; going to church services; reading; and being an observing and discerning student of the nature of the human journey can all lead to experiences that strengthen and deepen the understanding of the self. In most cases, I believe executives simply need to be encouraged to give some consideration to the types of self-learning they have already done and to access it in terms that might creatively link past, present, or future leadership challenges with such knowledge.

2. In some situations, leaders can be encouraged to read biographies, novels, and histories and reflect on the similarities and differences they can discern between themselves as individuals and the people about whom they are reading. Similarly, some

leaders are in fact open to creating a diary or journal in which they write both factual expositions about what they are facing along with emotional narratives that reflect their inner experiences and how they may be linked to their personal histories.

3. Coaches may well want to provide copies of the questions in Exhibits 5.1 and 5.2 or subsets of those inquiries to their clients to encourage them to explore themselves and examine the relationship of this knowledge to how they are or are not leading or growing professionally.

4. In limited circumstances, when an individual leader or his or her coach determines that significant problems exist that are preventing a person from growing or performing productively, a discussion about the possible contribution that counseling, psychotherapy, some form of formal education, or another form of personal growth experience may be useful to further stimulate development.

6

WISDOM MAPPING II: ORGANIZATIONAL AND EXECUTIVE GROUP AWARENESS

In crowds, it is stupidity and not mother-wit that is accumulated.
—Gustave Le Bon, *The Crowd: A Study of the Popular Mind*

The extremely large, well-differentiated, smoothly effective, modern, bureaucratic organization can be thought of as one of humanity's greatest creations. In truth, without the modern bureaucracy, most of what we know and enjoy in life would disappear. Our capacities to overcome the cruelly chaotic and brutal aspects of nature are due entirely to this invention. Beginning with the agricultural village, thought to have arisen some 11 to 15 thousand years ago, our species has continuously learned how to make our enterprises more complex, more creative, and more productive. If we but open our eyes, the results bombard us. Humans fly over oceans at will, avoid hurricanes, laugh at blizzards in houses warmed to tropical temperatures, go to stores to buy anything they want to eat any time of day, travel thousands of miles safely at their whim, and communicate with family and friends all over the planet. These actions and many more are possible only because we have learned how to organize ourselves and work together. People are elected, chosen, hired, or promoted to lead groups of human beings in these enterprises, and most of what we call written history is merely about what those leaders cause to be done while they hold their offices.

If we expect executives to understand one thing, it is how organizations operate to produce their effects. Recruitment processes for leaders tend to focus on how they have demonstrated their previous abilities to create and manage in these kinds of enterprises. A sophisticated effort to evaluate leadership capacity also examines how an individual designs, develops, and works with a group of fellow executives to operate an organization. It is now a truism that our institutions are so large and complex that no one human being has all of the knowledge, skill, or ability to understand and manage them. As a result, what we look for most in leaders is their ability to be aware of what goes into building and running organizations and executive groups.

The issues of organizational and executive group awareness are addressed in this chapter in relation to the model of Executive Wisdom introduced in earlier chapters. I begin with a case study that demonstrates the complexity and importance of these forms of awareness in an organization that worked extremely hard to transform itself and learned the hard way that cherished aspects of its culture significantly contributed to the destruction of the change processes its executive team struggled mightily to lead. The chapter succinctly examines the case in the context of the literatures on organizational assessment and executive team structures and functions. In keeping with the emphasis on pathways to inquiry introduced in chapter 5, an extensive set of questions to create and extend these forms of awareness are presented and discussed. The chapter closes with some exercises to help extend these abilities in leaders and those who coach and develop them. Now, let's see what happened in an organization whose leaders really wanted to change it for the better.

A CASE OF ORGANIZATIONAL CULTURE GONE ASTRAY

"It's simply amazing," said Paul Michel, the silver-haired, long-term CEO of his medium-sized manufacturing company. We sat at the mahogany conference table in his office, where we were debriefing the status of his organization's attempt at changing its information systems infrastructure on a day during which I had interviewed a dozen of the key people in the company who were centrally involved in the project. He shook his head with an air of sadness and refined awareness as we mutually considered the complexities of the situation that he faced.

"I would have never believed that I would see something like this happen. We've spent nearly 2 years getting ready to do this conversion. We've spent millions of dollars and really tried to do everything right. We sat together in the room next door a month ago and went around the implementation and executive groups asking everyone whether they thought we were ready to do this. We had only one real dissenting voice. Everyone said 'Yes, we're ready to go live.' Now this unmitigated disaster, and the worst of it for me is to know that a lot of the reason for the failure is that when we got into trouble in those first couple of days, it was the very strength of our organization's history and culture that contributed most to our downfall."

Paul's company was a privately held firm with over 100 years of operating experience. They enjoyed a superb reputation in their industrial niche and had held off the competition, used successive generations of new technology, and maintained their own furious commitment to serving their customers decade after decade. The lore of the company contained story upon story of employees engaging their creativity and going to imaginative extremes to meet the needs and demands of those customers, who rewarded the company with their loyalty even when they could sometimes purchase something from a competitor at a lower price.

"It is hard to accept that everyone is doing their best, doing what they know how to do very well, and collectively producing a catastrophe, but that's my best summary of what I see has happened," I said quietly. After an exhausting day of talking to most of the key players in the organization, it had become clear to me that there had been several glaring errors in the final months of preparation for the implementation of the system. First, the integrating consulting firm and their principal staff had all but abandoned the company with a ruinously simplistic acquiescence to the internal assessments of the project staff. Second, key members of the internal implementing group had suppressed their grave reservations about the readiness of several of the units of the organization to actually implement the new processes because, after 2 years of extremely long hours and constant pressure, they just wanted the whole thing to be over. And finally, the CEO himself, with a major commitment to changing the leadership approach of the traditional, authority-centered, top-down approach that always had been used in the company, had delegated most of the work of the project to rising young executive stars whom he had recruited into the organization. As a result, he had less than an essential feel for whether his team was telling the truth or hiding from it when they conducted the final review. Nor did Paul have his own general sense of what the line managers in the organization thought about the new systems or their readiness.

"We lost it in that first week," Paul said, looking down at his hands. "When we got behind on order entry and the phones started to ring with complaints from long-term customers, all of our teams just swung into action. They called each other asking for favors to meet the needs of the customers. Data entry got way behind. The plants revised their manufacturing runs to meet the special needs of our larger customers based on pleas from key sales executives who had clout and relationships to use. The warehouse and distribution teams just pushed orders onto the trucks without scanning stuff into the system. Within a week, we were thousands of transactions behind in entry, and our credit and financial departments couldn't issue terms or even properly bill. Now, you're telling me that we only have a couple of people in the whole company who really understand how the whole information system works and that many of the folks we trained don't really know what they are doing." Once again, Paul just shook his head as he summarized my observations.

I answered, "Your strength has always been putting the customer first and doing everything possible, including spending extra time and money or violating your own policies, procedures, or operating norms, to help them. It's no wonder that when those people whom your associates know so well started to call in volume and howl with pain, your team just dropped the new ways they had learned to do things and went back to what they know and do best. No one, and I mean no one, really saw or trained or preached during the preparation or implementation phases of the project, 'We are going to serve our customers best by working with and through our new systems.' It seems to me that there is still no true understanding that what was needed in this project was a major shift in the culture of the organization. It appears obvious now that it went without saying it, but that seems to me to be one of the keys."

"You're right about that. The warehouse was just pushing stuff onto the trucks, and we have no idea of what went out of here. Drivers worked overtime, our managers haven't been home in weeks, everyone is exhausted, and the board has started to ask me when I'm going to go back to the old system. It's just like old times here. Everyone is standing around waiting for me to tell them what to do."

"Do you have any sense of what the impact is going to be on your numbers?"

Again, Paul shook his head. "There's no real way to know, because so much of what has happened was not entered into the system. It's going to be a big number, though."

"What do you see as your options?" I asked.

"Well, they're simple, really. Go back to our previous systems and try to clean up this mess as best as we can, or keep going forward and take our lumps on the way to a modern information infrastructure. If we go back, some of the members of my senior team have threatened to quit. If we keep going with the new system, we'll lose a lot of other people."

"Based on what you know now, could you make that decision today or even next week?"

Paul looked at me and said nothing for several moments. "I really can't. I mean, I don't know how much of the problem is that the software just can't work; how much of it is in the business processes we designed to use the software; how much of it is because we don't have enough of the right kind of people in the right places to use the system; how much of it is that we need better training; and finally, how much of it is that our middle management and line supervisors just can't operate with these kinds of tools and more responsibility. Our people are so accustomed to look up the pyramid for answers. Even with all the work that we have done with you over the past several years on leadership, delegation, and taking responsibility, at the first sign of a real crisis, nearly everyone stops just dead in the water unless I motivate them.

"If we don't get a new operating system in, we will never be able to really do proper financial statements and cost studies. Our inventory is way too large because we can't accurately forecast customer orders, and that costs us millions every year that we could drop to the bottom line or invest in the company. We really need to be able to have proper electronic interfaces with our key vendors and suppliers and eventually with our customers. In short, if we don't do something like this new system, and soon, we may be out of business.

"On the other hand, despite our solid balance sheet and the willingness of the banks to loan us all the money we need to get through this crisis, if the system doesn't work as promised and we have six more months of this craziness, we'll lose most of our key customers. I just don't know what to do."

After that opening discussion, Paul and I spent nearly 2 hours together at the end of that long day of consultation reviewing the situation in depth and considering his options. By the time we left the building in the early evening hours, he had crystallized his thinking along several major lines of action. First, he knew that he needed to get an independent assessment of the software configuration and whether the modifications that had been made and tested were really going to work for the company. No one on his team was qualified to do that evaluation, so he would reach out to a technical consulting company to help him. Second, he would talk to his management team and his board to put them on alert that he was getting outside help and that it might be possible that the company would have to go back to its previous software. Third, he would move extra staff into the distribution operation to pull them out of the mess that they were in. The company also would take the extraordinary step of taking no new orders for products for several days to help the front-end staff catch up and to take pressure off of the plants that were doing all of the crisis and custom manufacturing runs that customer demands had forced on them. He seemed relieved to have a specific plan going forward but no less traumatized and worried about what had happened and about the consequences for his highly successful company.

Over the next 6 weeks, Paul led simultaneous efforts to salvage the implementation effort and to assess whether the company should simply pull the plug on the project and go back to its old systems. The chairman and other key members of the board became fully involved with the decision making. I stayed in touch with Paul via e-mail and repeated phone conversations as he found an external consultant from another major firm to come in and help lead the review. He successfully mobilized his entire organization to try to serve the customers and determine the status of the business after those first disastrous weeks. All the while, they struggled to continue to revise the software and stabilize the processes. After nearly 2 full months of nonstop crisis management and a careful multidimensional review, including a review of the IT initiative by key members of his board of directors, Paul finally decided to turn off the new systems and resuscitate the old software and processes. Once again, they closed down their operations for several days to conduct an inventory in the warehouses, recalibrate their production lines, and reorient their customer service procedures.

Amazingly, the management team and company staff went back to their old technology and ways of operating with barely a whiff of complaint and no real problems that anyone could identify. Within 2 days of turning on the old software, the entire company seemed to be operating as though the 2-year nightmare of trying to convert to new systems and operating procedures was just a bad dream. Within 2 weeks, people were going home at their normal hours, although there were still huge problems to solve as a result of the carnage the failed conversion had left behind. After all of the reservations and anxieties expressed by the senior leadership team and members of the board about whether the organization could successfully return to the old way of doing business, everyone was absolutely shocked at the speed and ease with which virtually everyone in the company did what was necessary and got back to their normal operations.

In the months after those experiences, Paul repeatedly talked with a sense of profound amazement and respect for the culture of the company and its management team and a much deeper appreciation for how difficult it was going to be to bring about the kinds of significant changes in the organization's structure and operations that would be necessary if the enterprise were to survive going forward. He and the board were left trying to assess the performance of the executive team, the desirability and feasibility of restarting the information systems conversion, and his future as the CEO of the organization.

ORGANIZATIONAL AND EXECUTIVE GROUP AWARENESS: THE CORE CAPACITIES OF LEADERS

This case is but one illustration of any number of consulting and coaching experiences that I have had throughout my career that have taught me just how deeply rooted organizational culture and executive group dynamics are in most organizations. In situation after situation in which I have seen organizations fail to meet external challenges from competitors; fail to respond adequately to regulators; or fail because of demographic, technological, competitor, or market shifts, especially those that failed to respond to those challenges that involved the potential extermination of the organization, some of the major reasons for each downfall always resided in the essential elements of the organization's culture and the leadership dynamics in the senior team. Every classic work on the practice of leadership and management and textbook on the subject of change management emphasizes at some point that an executive must have an intimate working knowledge of his or her organization while simultaneously building a strong team of senior leaders through whom he or she really operates the enterprise (Conner & Lake, 1994; Hartley, 2003; Kotter, 1996; O'Toole, 1996).

Literature searches conducted in preparation for writing this book yielded literally thousands of entries on the subjects of organizational performance, executive team performance, and leadership in relationship to both. For example, theory and empirical work have pushed the knowledge base on organizational outcomes in multiple directions, and there are hundreds of measures of performance that leaders can apply. Bennis et al. (2002) provided a comprehensive review of many of the important financial formulas for assessing businesses, including their methods of calculation. Orlitzky, Schmidt, and Rynes (2003) demonstrated the depth and complexity of these studies with a comprehensive meta-analysis examining corporate social and financial performance and demonstrated consistent positive financial results in those companies pursuing socially responsible policies and practices. Michalisin, Karau, and Tanpong (2004) demonstrated that top management team cohesion is positively related to company financial performance. Wall et al. (2004) reported positive relationships between subjective and objective measures of organizational performance, and the empirical findings of Lee and Yu (2004) and Sambasivan and Johari (2003) suggested that organizational culture and commitment have significant impacts on organizational outcomes. Gelade and Ivery (2003) similarly found that human resource management practices and organizational climate are also directly related to the financial performance of organizations. And Morgan and Strong (2003), among many others, reported that organizational strategy is directly related to how well an enterprise performs. The scientific literature in organizational studies has exploded enormously over the past 30 years and validates the subjective impression of leaders and their coaches that there is a host of issues, elements, components, processes, structures, and so on, that go into ensuring that an organization operates well in a competitive environment.

Also during this 30-year time frame, a body of research, theory, and practice has emerged focusing on top management teams, their group dynamics, and their impacts on organizational performance. Zaccaro (2001) provided a succinct yet thorough review of this literature in his detailed examination of the research and concepts on executive leadership. Beginning with Cyert and March (1963), who discussed what they called the "dominant coalition" in organizations, and continuing with Hambrick and Mason's (1984) comprehensive review of what they labeled the "upper echelons," many researchers and practitioners have been exploring and explicating the impact and problems of senior leadership teams.

Pfeffer (1983) and O'Bannon and Gupta (1992), among the majority of researchers in this area, have explored the impact of the demography of the membership of these teams. Similarly, Hambrick (1994) examined such factors as age, tenure, and functional and educational backgrounds in members of executive groups, demonstrating that these variables can directly influence enterprise performance. Specific results, such as O'Bannon and Gupta's exploration, which suggested that increasing the cognitive diversity of these groups improved their perspectives, information, and decision-making processes; Wiersema and Bantel's (1992) research, which demonstrated that the demography of senior management teams affect the pace and shape of how change is managed in organizations; and Zenger and Lawrence's (1989) study, which suggested that social cohesion based on homogeneity in age, values, and cultural background leads to improved communication, greater acceptance, and faster implementation of decisions, are illustrative of the growing body of literature available on the subject.

In a recent and fairly comprehensive review of the past 50 years of work on organizational sociology, Scott (2004) provided a succinct summary of the six major conceptual approaches to the study of organizations that have emerged over that time frame. These avenues of exploration include (a) contingency theory, (b) transaction cost theory, (c) resource dependency theory, (d) network theory, (e) organizational ecology, and (f) institutional theory. He also focused on four major issues emerging in the study of organizations: (a) changing notions of the study of organizational boundaries, (b) the pervasive global trend toward externalization strategies in which enterprises decrease their own size while simultaneously focusing their performance on their core competencies and building a network of related organizations that assist them in competing in the economy, (c) shifts in uses and modes of power and control in organizations, (d) and significant moves away from considering organizational structures as things and toward an understanding of structure as involving relationships and processes.

The empirical foundations of the study of organizations and executive groups have readily translated into the practice literature of consulting by means of emphases on organizational assessment and team building. This body of work is readily available to any practitioner and extends to thousands of books written by professionals taking many of the perspectives supported by the scientific literature. This practical work is of importance to the development of Executive Wisdom because the emergence of organizational and executive group awareness are two of the areas of leadership function in which one could ordinarily expect senior executives to have reasonable competence.

Key examples of the practice literature can be found in Harrison (1994), Levinson (2002), and Weisbord (1978), all of whom provide excellent volumes that focus on the details of conducting an organizational assessment. Each of them takes a general systems perspective that encourages leaders and consultants to examine all of the major elements in, or interacting with, an enterprise and the nature of their exchanges, processes, and outcomes. The vast majority of experienced leaders in organizations can reasonably be expected to be broadly familiar with these concepts and with methods designed to provide them with information about how their institutions are functioning.

In another recent example of systems-oriented approaches, Becker, Huselid, and Ulrich (2001) took the issues of performance measurement and systems assessment and focused specifically on methods to examine the human resources functions of enterprises. They offered an extensive array of models and assessment measures for executives and consultants who are interested in bringing a more empirical approach to these traditionally fuzzy areas of organizational evaluation.

Organizational assessments often lead to large-scale system interventions such as reshaping the culture of an enterprise, reorganizing its structures, blowing up and reinventing business processes, and completely repositioning how a business goes to market (Bedeian & Zammuto, 1991; Hammer & Champy, 1993; Marks & Mirvis, 1998; Tenner & DeToro, 1997; Trice & Beyer, 1993). All of these actions are aimed at improving how an organization competes and performs, and it can also be said that all of them are fraught with extreme peril (Hartley, 2003), even though leaders are frequently compelled by environmental circumstances to attempt these transformations.

Similarly, extensive literatures now are available to practitioners who find themselves in consulting and coaching assignments with leadership groups, or what are frequently called *executive teams*. These structural units are key components of any enterprise because they constitute the major pathways through which a senior executive exercises direction and control over the strategy and performance of his or her organization. They are distinct from other forms of groups and teams that are usually constructed to perform an explicit project or focus on a specific kind of work such as quality circles, brainstorming teams, or problem-solving groups. The top leadership team of any organization develops its own subculture, set of roles, boundaries, communication processes, conflict-management methods, decision-making protocols, leadership and followership dynamics, politics, and defenses. These groups are self-sustaining, and when they are successful, they often become stable and productive over long periods of time. They can also be cauldrons of seething, destructive competition and conflict that ultimately erode, if not terminate, their organization's ability to grow and survive.

I spend significantly more time and space on the subject of coaching and developing wisdom in executive groups in the final two chapters of this book, but four relatively recent volumes provide extremely useful coverage of the issues involved in improving the functioning of these senior teams: Argyris (1993); Katzenbach (1998); Nadler, Spencer, and Associates (1998); and Sundstrom and Associates (1999). Each provides complex case material along with conceptual models for exploring how whole-group, subgroup, and individual dynamics influence organizational performance. Each also provides a wide variety of suggestions for intervening in the ways in which these groups operate to help them improve.

REVISITING EXECUTIVE WISDOM IN PRACTICE

In the model of Executive Wisdom proposed in this book, the importance of organizational and executive group awareness cannot be overemphasized. Although it is a reasonable assumption that most senior executives are familiar with these issues and the ways in which they can affect the performance of an organization, my experience suggests that there are no guarantees that they really are. In many organizations, individuals are often promoted to managerial positions solely because of their performance in the technical aspects of their businesses. Thus, one frequently sees the best sales representative, financial manager, engineer, lawyer, or physician promoted into a senior leadership position on the basis of the assumption that because they both understand and are good at doing the technical work of the enterprise, they will of course make good leaders of others who are doing the same work or executives of the entire enterprise. Although this assumption is safe in many cases, it is by no means universally true. In the best case, as these kinds of individuals gain experience, power, and visibility in their organizations, they often have additional opportunities to lead and thus rise in hierarchies. The most talented of them extend their knowledge and skill bases and emerge later as broadly experienced senior executives. However, many of them never learn what they must and stagnate by simply maintaining the abilities that got them promoted in the first place. Thus, coaching and development work must always ensure that these core areas of organizational and executive group awareness are probed and, where and when necessary, extended, especially with the members of senior leadership teams.

THE CASE STUDY IN CONTEXT

The case study that opened this chapter provides a realistic example of why organizational and group awareness are so important in the emergence of Executive Wisdom and why their absence can lead to executive stupidity and enterprise failure. Paul had worked for over a decade in the organization to rise to the position of CEO. He had served in long apprenticeships as the leader of the sales and marketing functions and then had been promoted to the position of executive vice president, which he had held for over 5 years. He was trusted deeply by the board of directors, the major stockholders, the previous two CEOs, and the entire organization. Once appointed CEO, and with the support of everyone, he had moved quickly, boldly, and yet with sensitivity to change the membership of the top leadership team and the ways in which they made decisions. He had pushed for considerable movement in the organization's human resources infrastructure and undertook major initiatives to strengthen the middle management team of the organization. He accomplished all of this without creating major, obvious strain in the enterprise, and he simultaneously raised the bar significantly on expectations for financial performance in the organization.

In addition, Paul had participated fully in the deliberations of his board and staff when they thought through the ways in which their information systems infrastructure supported the business, and he had strongly concurred in the commitment to change to new technology. In support of that initiative, he conducted a thorough review of the various technologies available, ran competitive bidding processes, and contracted with one of the most influential information systems integration consulting firms in the world to provide them with project management expertise and support. His performance through all of this over a prolonged period of time was nuanced, sensitive, and successful. Looking back at everything that had been done over a period of 10 years and in particular over the 2 years leading to the information systems implementation, it would have been difficult to criticize his performance. Indeed, with minor exceptions, the board of directors was pleased with him and had rewarded him generously and appropriately.

Paul had used consultation and coaching to push the members of his executive group and their subordinates away from the organization's traditional top-down command-and-control management culture. He consistently reinforced the need for more decentralization and delegation of decision-making authority. He recognized and rewarded those who took more risks, created successful initiatives, and were willing to work with him to try different ways to do things in the organization. He provided systematic approaches to executive and management development in the company for the first time. From his vantage point as CEO, and from mine as the major consultant to him and his leadership team, the management group as a whole had made considerable progress in a relatively short period of time.

I had been in the organization doing coaching work with the senior team members just a few short weeks before they made the collective decision to "go live" with the new systems and, at that time, found them collectively to be tired, eager to get moving on the initiative, confident that they were doing the right thing, and working reasonably well together to solve the complex technical and behavioral problems that such large-scale projects always produce. There was only the most minor hint that all was not well as they described their challenges to me and we worked on them together. I left the organization that day feeling both anxious for them about what they were trying to do and confident about how well they were working together to solve the problems they faced. Five weeks later, my first e-mail from Paul saying that they had gone ahead and were having major headaches was the first indication I had that their organizational train had derailed.

At Paul's request, I quickly returned to the organization, met with over a dozen people, and discovered a complete disaster. In conversation after conversation, I heard people with whom I had worked closely for several years tell me that they had had major reservations about what was going on; had not felt ready to actually execute in the new systems environment; and that the management team had become dysfunctional because of their fatigue, inability to handle disagreement and conflict, and the emergence of what could be described as the more traditional command-and-control kind of behavior by a number of key players. As a result of these dynamics, and despite their training, the individual coaching they had received, and the revised leadership and managerial culture that Paul had tried to instill, nearly half of the people who sat with Paul and publicly said they thought they were ready to go had withheld their true feelings about the project status and the behavior of leadership. Paul, however, had firmly believed that all of the participants in the team trusted him and each other enough to be honest in that meeting. He had clearly stated to them that he did not want to proceed unless they felt they were really ready as an organization. In the end, nearly half the members of the decision-making group looked directly at him and did not tell him the truth. Instead, they did what they had been socialized to do over a period of many decades: They listened closely to the messages of senior leadership, thought they understood that this project was moving forward regardless of the problems involved or their own professional and personal views, and simply acquiesced in what they believed Paul wanted.

When I talked with people one on one, to a person they could articulate the agony they had experienced in the meeting. They had felt extremely conflicted between the understanding that their responsibility to the leadership group and the organization was to be forthright and courageous even if it meant managing public disagreements. All of them stated their firm belief that Paul would not have punished them had they said "No, we're not ready." Yet, because of the way some dissent had been handled in the time leading up to the decision, none of them felt that they wanted to take the risk. They were also so exhausted from the continuous efforts required to do their jobs and to implement the new systems that they just wanted the whole project to be over. In short, instead of challenging, raising issues, putting data and their thoughts on the table, they simply threw in the towel and gave in to what they thought was inevitable. They engaged in their traditional dependent behavior—I'll do what I'm told and keep my mouth shut—and, as a result, the whole train derailed.

Interestingly enough, once we collectively reviewed what had happened and it became clear with the assistance of outside consulting expertise from a different information systems integration firm that it would take months of hard work to solve the problems of the new systems, Paul and the entire management team quietly and competently collected themselves together, made a decision to return to their old technology and processes, and made a virtually seamless transition backward in a matter of approximately 2 weeks. In subsequent conversations with the leadership group and team interventions, it became clear that once the green light was given to go back to what they knew, everyone simply reverted to form with few problems. Within a period of 6 weeks, the company went from hemorrhaging money to breaking even. Within 3 months, they were making profits again, and morale then returned to a semblance of normalcy. Once they were given a clear goal and were told what to do, the speed and confidence with which the management team executed the recovery was simply breathtaking.

As I talked to Paul, we concluded that the top-down, dependency-oriented, command-and-control core of the decision-making and relationship structures in the company had never disappeared; instead, the entire management organization seemed to have taken on the appearance of mastering the changes to a more decentralized, delegated, bottom-up form of management while continuing to expect unconsciously and nonverbally that the right way to behave would soon reassert itself. They were correct in the sense that their own more or less unconscious behavior as a group undermined what Paul and they were trying to do consciously. Collectively, they colluded in what became one of the largest management failures in the company's history.

EXHIBIT 6.1
Questions to Promote Organizational Awareness

1. What are the key values in your organization? Does your staff share them? Do they support the mission of your organization? Have they been publicly discussed and adopted?
2. What is the mission of your organization? Does the staff understand the mission?
3. What are the unit's goals for this year? Are there priorities within these goals?
4. How well is your organization performing financially in the marketplace compared with competitors?
5. Do your colleagues understand the nature of their roles in the organization?
6. Is the performance management system you are using yielding excellent results?
7. Are you satisfied with the quality, accuracy, and timeliness of the decision-making process in your organization?
8. Are the strategies and tactics you are pursuing in your organization aligned with the threats and opportunities and organizational strengths and weaknesses facing you?
9. Is the leadership team in your organization flexible in managing problems, barriers, changes, demands?
10. Does the leadership team manage well (vision, mission, external monitoring, delegation, discipline, crisis management, finances)?
11. Are the leadership and staff members of your organization working well together?
12. Are there problems that routinely get in the way of your staff members working together, such as deviance–conformity, diversity, norms and values, morale and cohesion, teamwork, followership, leadership, harassment and discrimination, negative affect, addition or loss of group members?
13. How effectively does your organization deal with change?
14. Is the diversity profile of your organization what you want it to be?
15. Is your approach to management-building an inclusive culture in which differences in gender, age, race, skills, ethnicity, and other dimensions of diversity are valued?
16. Are there major barriers that interfere with the effective performance of your organization?
17. If you could wave a magic wand, what would you change in your organization?
18. Are there patterns of performance or behavior that have interfered with the performance of the organization for which no good explanation has been forthcoming? If yes, describe these experiences, provide examples for yourself, and speculate on what the origins and underlying motivations of the patterns might be.

WISDOM MAPPING: CREATING ORGANIZATIONAL AND EXECUTIVE GROUP AWARENESS

In keeping with the models and methods outlined so far in this book, Exhibit 6.1 introduces a series of questions to help leaders and their coaches systematically probe just how much they know about their organizations, and Exhibit 6.2 provides another set of questions designed to examine various aspects of leadership teams. As the case example in this chapter and the models of executive mind introduced in chapters 2 and 3 illustrate, it is possible for leaders and consultants to work to change the culture and operating methods of an enterprise and executive group and also be completely blind to what is really going on below the surface. As I explored in chapter 2, my central understanding about Executive Wisdom is that it is an emergent property of complex systems. As such, it can rise and fall, come and go, appear and disappear, depending on a host of variables that are either loosely or closely coupled in a systemic sense. Thus, I firmly believe that for executives trying to lead in this chronic, chaotic uncertainty, wisdom most surely starts with the willingness and ability to make sensitive and sober-minded inquiries into the depths of themselves, their organizations, and their situations.

As you read through the lists of questions, three things will become pretty clear. First, the questions themselves form the foundation for a fairly comprehensive assessment of the overall status and operations of an organization and its leadership team. Any executive or coach who is provided with a data set comprising a range of diverse answers to these inquires from key people in an institution should be able to formulate a decent mental model of how the organization and its leadership team perform and where both strengths and problems may be present. The status of the organization, from its core values and mission to its competitive position, strategy, and financial performance, are the issues people know to examine most carefully. Indeed, if you read the reports of Wall Street analysts, they most often focus on these variables in determining what recommendations they will make to investors. Yet, the questions also point the way to a much more nuanced and sensitive examination of many of the other more subtle aspects of organizational and executive performance that contribute to just how well an enterprise will do against its competition.

Second, to be effective and to increase the possibility that wisdom will more consistently emerge, leaders and their coaches must push themselves to explore such other issues as how an organization manages change; what it is doing to address diversity in the complex and rapidly emerging global marketplace; and how the leadership team communicates, addresses conflict, makes decisions, defends itself against the emotional agonies associated with failure or threat, invites creativity, handles competition and collaboration, and deals with crises and catastrophes when they strike. Third, in my judgment, having an internal metacognitive model of the organization and its executive group that is complex, nuanced, and flexible enough to permit an open-minded investigation of what might be happening in any particular situation that a leader faces will permit him or her to perceive more

EXHIBIT 6.2
Questions to Promote Executive Group Awareness

1. Is the membership of the executive group clearly defined? What principles are used in making that definition? Do the members of the group understand those principles? Does the rest of the organization's leadership and management team understand those principles?
2. Are the goals, functions, structures, and processes of the executive group clearly defined? Do the members of the group know what they are? Do the rest of the organization's leadership and management team understand them? Are they relevant to the vision, mission, and strategies that the leadership has adopted?
3. Are the roles of the members of the group clearly defined?
4. Is the decision-making process of the group effective with regard to timeliness; adequate involvement of those affected; consideration of relevant information; openness to influence, challenge, or dispute; and correctability in the face of changing circumstances or new information? How is its overall effectiveness?
5. Do the members of the group effectively disclose information relevant to the performance of the group and the organization rather than deny, avoid, or distort disclosure efforts? Are group members honest and direct with each other?
6. Are the communication, conflict-management, and problem-solving skills of the members sufficient to address the routine challenges and major crises that the group faces?
7. Are the lines of communication within the group and between the group and the rest of the organization sufficient to address the routine challenges and major crises that the group faces?
8. Do group members manage their conflicts effectively, openly, honestly, and with positive results for themselves and the rest of the organization?
9. Do group members value and motivate each other, have a good sense of how their behaviors affect each other, have the ability to discuss their individual and group performance with each other in reasonably nondefensive terms, routinely reflect on how they function together as a team, and have good diagnostic skills and procedures related to group performance?
10. How does the group manage success and failure? Does the group take a learning stance when trouble is encountered, or do the group members look for someone to blame, punish, and publicly humiliate?
11. Do the members of the group collaborate with and help each other? Are they aware of how they depend on each other? Do they manage their interdependencies well? Do they share resources?
12. Are there explicit norms for group behavior? Are the norms public and revisited occasionally to determine how well they are working?
13. Does the group foster creativity, challenge the status quo or historical approach, take appropriate risks?
14. Is the membership of the group sufficiently diverse, and is it sufficient to address the needs, challenges, and requirements for knowledge, skill, and ability facing it? Do all of the members of the group feel included, recognized, supported?
15. Is the overall environment of the group sufficiently challenging and supportive for the members?
16. Is the atmosphere of group meetings comfortable for the members—sufficiently relaxed, stimulating, challenging? Are ideas exchanged freely? Do advice, information, criticism, and innovation flow freely? Are the meetings productive?

(continued)

EXHIBIT 6.2   *(Continued)*

17. Do the members of the group adequately balance the need for teamwork and collaborative effort with the pursuit of their own personal agendas and organizational initiatives?
18. Can the group easily change the way it works in response to external or internal demands when it needs to do so?
19. Is there evidence of subgroup, pairing, shame–blame, dependency, triangulation, fight–flight dynamics, or other forms of problematic behavior?
20. Do the group members adequately manage their individual and collective accountabilities?
21. Are there patterns of performance or behavior that have interfered with the performance or satisfaction of the executive group for which no good explanation has been forthcoming? If yes, describe these experiences, provide examples for yourself, and speculate on what the origins and underlying motivations of the patterns might be.

accurately, decide more intuitively and thus more quickly, and act with more precision and effectiveness. If a leader challenges him- or herself to know the darker, less effective, and even more pathological aspects of the behavior of the organization and team and not deny or otherwise defend against them, it seems reasonable to hypothesize that his or her performance is likely to be more effective through time.

Following the suggested process I introduced in chapter 5, this inquiry can also engage the six components of that process:

1. Push the leader to engage in a high degree of curiosity.
2. Provide emotional support to him or her in the process.
3. Establish a proper frame of reference for any investigation.
4. Systematically use inquiry to promote awareness and positive change.
5. Encourage pattern recognition.
6. Uncover and challenge assumptions underlying the patterns of behavior and create experiments and new alternatives.

I reiterate that following these steps and discovering the answers to core questions about how an enterprise and its executive team are functioning will not guarantee that a leader can consistently discern, decide, and act wisely. However, without such determined inquiry, an individual trying to make good choices will in essence be blindfolded to much of the reality that will influence the outcomes of those decisions.

REVISITING THE WISDOM-MAPPING PATHWAY

Figure 6.1 redirects attention to my previous discussion of the fact that the creation of Executive Wisdom in any given moment or situation involves

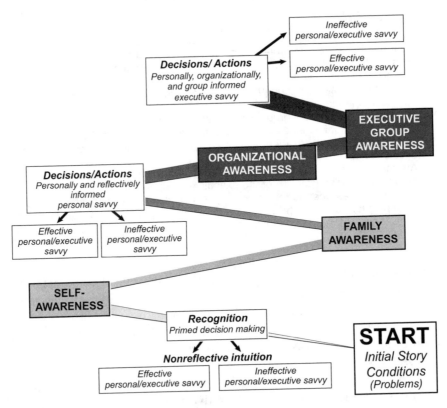

Figure 6.1. Wisdom mapping with organizational and executive group awareness.

a complex pathway. With the addition of organizational and executive group awareness, any leader's deliberations and actions would be informed much more extensively than if he or she were simply proceeding on the basis of self- and family knowledge. This turning of attention outward invites a more comprehensive view of reality and thus more thorough processes of thinking, feeling, problem solving, and action. The results are indicated as either effective or ineffective executive savvy.

Many day-to-day deliberations, decisions, and managerial operations rest merely on the foundations of self-, family, organizational, and group awareness. In fact, probably most of what goes on in medium- to large-scale organizations at a managerial level is best informed and influenced by the issues; challenges; strengths; and, yes, weaknesses in these four arenas. Adding organizational and executive group knowledge dramatically increases the chances that executives will be right in their choices and actions; however, although absolutely necessary, these levels of awareness by themselves are insufficient to support the more frequent emergence of Executive Wisdom. For that to happen, a leader must add situational awareness, have a values and moral compass, and be able to apply what research has demonstrated to be the structures of wisdom systems. I address these final components in the next chapter.

AWARENESS EXERCISES FOR LEADERS AND THEIR COACHES

1. The easiest homework assignment imaginable is for the reader to take an organization with which he or she is familiar and try to answer the questions provided in Exhibits 6.1 and 6.2 regarding how it and its executive group typically function. Keep in mind that your views are simply that: your own views. The data you have available will of course be limited; if you keep that in mind, you will understand one of the major problems that any executive faces. Knowledge, however it is obtained and no matter how extensive it becomes, always falls short of the complexity of the actual reality. To increase the sensitivity of your assessment, consider choosing an organization with which a friend or colleague may be familiar. Share the questions and together try to determine what you think of the organization. Do the colleague's views enrich yours, change your mind, or convince you that he or she is out of touch with reality?

2. Once you have formulated an understanding of the organization you have selected, try to practice what Klein (1999, 2003) has called the *art of mental simulation*. Pick one of the questions, perhaps one in regard to which you feel some significant degree of confidence in your knowledge, and conduct some thought experiments on that particular aspect of how you see the organization or group functioning. Imagine what would happen if a significant business reversal hit the organization, three key members of the executive group left within 1 year, the CEO retired, another organization tried a hostile takeover, a new product or service launch was an extreme hit, or the spouse or a child of a key member of the team became suddenly ill with a life-threatening disease. Let your mind drift then to the interplay of that element of organizational or group function, and try to imagine how the changes in one component of the enterprise would affect others. Select several others from the list of questions and let your mind gallop through the possibilities. If you have done Exercise 1 with a colleague or friend, do the simulations with him or her and see what you come up with.

In reality, most people who work in organizations probably find that they are repeating what happens whenever they get together with colleagues and discuss (I won't imply gossip about) what is going on in their enterprise. This goes on every day in workplaces. The key to the homework exercise is to use the framework of the questions to help guide a more systematic and, I hope, more useful form of mental simulation.

3. If you are coaching an executive or are in a leadership position yourself, use the questions with your client or with your own team to deepen your knowledge of your organization and group. Try to determine where there may be gaps in what you know. If and when they appear, pay attention to what they are and what sources of information may be available to close them that you are not examining. Also, ask yourself or your team how these "blind spots" might have originated. In other words, try to push yourself not only to examine the nature of the mental model of your organization and leadership group but also to inquire about how that model was constructed and is being maintained, perhaps to your and the organization's detriment.

7

WISDOM MAPPING III: SITUATION AWARENESS, VALUES AND MORAL COMPASSES, AND THE CHALLENGE OF CREATING VIRTUOUS LEADERS

A great part of the information obtained in War is contradictory, a still greater part is false, and by far the greatest part is of doubtful character. What is required of an officer is a certain power of discrimination, which only knowledge of men and things and good judgment can give.
—Carl von Clausewitz, *On War*

How can our conscience tell us whether or not we are renouncing things unless it first of all tells us that we know how to use them properly?
—Thomas Merton, *No Man Is an Island*

Give therefore thy servant an understanding heart to judge thy people, that I may discern between good and evil.
—Solomon's prayer to God, Kings 3:9

Character determines fate.

—Heraclitus

In Carl von Clausewitz's (1896/1986) classic book about the nature of war and leadership during warfare, he introduced a term that described the sociocognitive experience of generals during conflict. He called it *the fog of war*. It referred to the enormous difficulty that leaders have in getting accurate information about their armies (read: organizations) and the conditions that they faced once active hostilities commenced. It is easy to plan a war or a battle in the calm waters of peace that precede the first hostile salvos. It is incredibly difficult to prosecute either a war or a battle once it has begun, because the meta-stable conditions preceding action immediately dissolve into chaotically unpredictable situations. The response of the other parties to the war is the major cause of the instability. However, many other circumstances often arise that can negate any general's neatly drawn plans.

189

It has become clear that von Clausewitz's (1896/1986) description of the problems of generalship can be applied to virtually every other form of organizational endeavor. Leaders are expected to steer their enterprises toward success and long-term survival. They are expected to avoid or cope effectively with the problems they encounter along the way and to be able to figure out both what is happening to their institutions and to make the correct strategic and tactical decisions at each step. Yet, we know that the external environments that leaders and their organizations face are at best meta-stable, meaning that although they may have periods of predictability, they can destabilize extremely rapidly and in ways that even the most gifted executive could never have foreseen. The problem of coping with their external environments, then, is one of the most fundamental challenges that any leader faces. Failure in this arena not only threatens the career of individual executives but also can destroy the organizations for which they are responsible.

It is therefore axiomatic that the fundamental domains underpinning Executive Wisdom must include the ability for a leader to become sensitively attuned to his or her external world and that which faces the enterprise that he or she leads. For it is from this understanding that organizational strategy and tactics are created. The ability of leaders and their colleagues to effectively execute their strategies determines whether their institutions survive.

An additional challenge that leaders face in trying to become wise involves the complex task of determining what is morally correct. Virtually every decision a leader confronts contains implicit questions concerning what is just. The issue of corporate ethics, which really involves the moral judgment of the leaders of any enterprise, has moved front and center into the global public discourse. The massive corporate scandals and criminal frauds that have been exposed in the opening years of the 21st century have left most of the world at best uneasy about the capacities for moral reasoning of people at the top of some major institutions. Any conceptual or practical examination of Executive Wisdom in action therefore must address this perpetually challenging human issue.

In this chapter, then, I first explore the Arthur Anderson case, which will surely be seen in historical terms as one of the saddest and most instructive examples of ineffective situational and moral leadership in the early part of this century. I explore some of the concepts and research that describe how leaders can develop situational awareness. I also examine the moral reasoning issues and value systems that executives must deploy in their work. I am convinced that situational and moral awareness are critical competencies for leaders if they are to become truly wise. The chapter also ends with some practical suggestions for how leaders and their coaches can further explore these two domains.

THE CASE OF ARTHUR ANDERSON:
A LEGENDARY COMPANY LED ASTRAY

In 1913, Arthur Anderson, an accounting professor at Northwestern University, cofounded the firm that would bear his name and eventually become the largest and most successful professional services organization in the world. Led by the good professor, the company rapidly earned a reputation for both competence and ethical behavior. The more leaders of other organizations trusted the judgment of the members of the firm, the more it grew in importance and influence in the global economy.

In the mid 1950s, in conjunction with IBM, Anderson began to shift its portfolio of services by providing consultation to General Electric to help that company install a computerized payroll system. Thirty years later, Anderson's consulting arm was making more profit for the company than its traditional accounting business. However, by 1989, the organization's internal culture had become so divided and conflict ridden that a civil war between the consulting and accounting partners had become a permanent feature of its executive governance. The consultants initiated a decade-long battle to escape that eventually succeeded and, in 2000, led to the establishment of Accenture, now one of the largest consulting practices in the world.

Joe Beradino joined the New York office of the accounting practice of Anderson in 1972. With hard, successful work and savvy maneuvering in the intense political climate of the partnership, he rose to head the U.S. audit practice of the firm in 1998. Beradino demonstrated his crisis-management skills and political savvy in a major controversy that arose that year, when Arthur Levitt Jr., then the chairman of the Securities and Exchange Commission (SEC), urged new, tighter rules on the accounting industry out of the belief that the tensions between accounting companies' profit motives from their consulting practices and their public auditing responsibilities had gone way out of bounds in favor of approving virtually anything companies wanted to do by way of their financial reporting. At that time, Beradino was thrust into the middle of that public battle in his role as head of Anderson's U.S. audit practice. He successfully worked through those negotiations with the SEC and was publicly acclaimed for brokering an agreement that forced the accounting industry to disclose their fees from auditing and consulting but allowed the organizations to stay in the more lucrative consulting business.

During his tenure in that position, he also led an organization-wide effort to determine the "risk profile" of their 2,500 client firms. Their customers represented the who's who of the capitalist world. The list also included names that have become synonymous with the financial crimes of the closing years of the 20th century: WorldCom; Global Crossing; Sunbeam; Waste

Management; Qwest; and of course, the biggest disaster of all, Enron. Enron was deemed by Beradino's internal committee to constitute a "maximum risk" for Anderson. The deal with the SEC, his role in those negotiations, and his work in examining the risk profile of the company must have contributed significantly to the ultimate decision of the partners at Anderson to elect Beradino as their CEO. On January 10, 2001, Beradino was selected by 90% of the 1,700 partners to become CEO of Arthur Anderson. Over the course of his leadership, Enron imploded in the largest and most grievous accounting scandal in the history of American capitalism. On March 14, 2002, Arthur Anderson was indicted by the Federal Justice Department for obstruction of justice, and in what must be a world record in speed of prosecution, a jury found the firm guilty on June 15, 2002. This outcome proved to be a death sentence for this globally recognized leader in safeguarding the public trust (Byrne, 2002). In less than a year, the various pieces of the Anderson accounting practice either were sold, decamped en masse to join other organizations, or simply ceased to exist. Beradino, who had served the company and partners faithfully for 30 years and who had worked tirelessly and successfully to become its CEO, was reported to say,

> I paid the price . . . . I lost my job. I lost my firm. I've got less money today than I had as the newly elected CEO. I lost my partner capital. I lost my retirement. I don't have any stock options. I may never work again. (Byrne, p. 52)

Details of the Enron catastrophe have been provided by several extensive treatments of the events leading to the declaration of bankruptcy in 2001 (Swartz & Watkins, 2003; Smith & Emshwiller, 2003) and need not be repeated here. The central question in the tragic case of Arthur Anderson's related organizational suicide is, "How did it happen?" How did an organization with a global reputation for ethical practice in the complex and technical world of auditing the books of large, for-profit companies become capable of colluding with the manipulative and criminal executives of some of their client firms who were determined to do virtually anything to improve the stock prices of their organizations in the extremely heady days of the Wall Street market boom of the late 1990s? The answer, in a word, is "money."

Before 1980, Anderson got the lion's share of its revenue from its traditional accounting and auditing practice. With the rise of modern information systems and the merger-and-acquisition mania that rose to a fever pitch in the increasingly globalized corporate economy, it became clear to all of the major accounting firms that significant profits in the future would come from the much more lucrative consulting services that they could provide. In the space of a few short years, Anderson, and virtually all of its rivals in the accounting business, created internal stables of high-priced consulting staff through whom they could charge extremely large fees. In an internal economic and cultural revolution that took place in less than 10 years, the traditional auditing and accounting services arm of Anderson became little more than a less-than-lucrative way for the firm to introduce its rainmaking senior consulting partners to its large Fortune 500 companies. The profits derived from the consulting business soon began to drive the compensation and human resources practices of the company, especially those of the partners in the enterprise. The conflicts between the consultants and accountants over the identity, culture, and soul of the organization grew from being a simple annoyance to a life-threatening issue that ultimately was resolved by the divorce of the two branches of the firm.

With the loss of the consulting contracts and staff, Beradino campaigned for the leadership position by stating that his primary concern as CEO would be the restoration of revenue growth. On the basis of his discussions with staff members of Anderson, Byrne (2002) reported that once Beradino took over as the leader of the partnership, all he talked about was money. Keep clearly in mind that this was a company whose founding president, Arthur Anderson himself, faced a challenge similar to the Enron problem early in the history of the organization. When the president of a local railway client pressured him to approve an accounting change that would have artificially increased the company's earnings, Anderson responded by telling him that there was "not enough money in the city of Chicago" that would have motivated him to comply (Byrne, 2002).

When the consulting staff left Anderson to form Accenture, the parent company was stripped of much of its ability to generate profits. Weaker, desperate to regain consulting market share, and determined to retain a way of life based on the salaries and bonuses driven by consulting fees, the partners elected Beradino with the understanding that he would lead them back to profitability and prominence in that business. He took on the tasks of rebuilding the consulting practice with enthusiasm and drove with furious intensity to restore cash flow. Paul Volcker, who was hired by Beradino in a last-ditch effort to avoid federal prosecution from the Enron disaster, told *Newsweek*, "There is no question in my mind that Anderson took its eye off the ball. Their compensation practices were based on how much revenue you could generate" (Byrne, 2002, p. 52).

Enron was by no means Anderson's only accounting debacle. Along with Worldcom, Global Crossing, Waste Management, and Sunbeam, the company had been in the center of the economic and strategy choices of executive teams that collectively led to well over $200 billion in losses for investors. In retrospect, it seemed to many on the outside of the company that their organization had developed an executive mind-set that at best supported extremely aggressive accounting practices and at worst turned a blind eye to senior executives' efforts to create vast personal fortunes at the expense of the truth and the investing public. In case after case, Anderson was shown to have approved transactions that its founder probably never would have authorized. Anderson was successful at maintaining profits driven by the lucrative consulting and accounting contracts, but this was done largely at the expense of their hard-won and generations-old reputation for professional integrity.

The set of attitudes and behaviors that drove these organizational dynamics is best illustrated in the final actions that Beradino and his partners took in the Enron case. From Byrne's (2002) report, it is clear that the CEO and his key people understood very well that they had adopted an aggressive and risky accounting stance in their work with the energy giant. Nevertheless, Anderson was taking home over $50 million a year in revenue from Enron alone, and it was equally clear from reports about Beradino's statements and the conduct of internal organizational meetings that the most important yardstick by which professional performance was being measured was whether the staff was making money for the company.

Byrne (2002) reported that in December 1999, Carl A. Bass, a senior partner in the Houston office of Anderson and a member of the company's Professional Standards Group, documented in an internal e-mail that there was a significant conflict over how their client, Enron, should account for the sale of some options owned by one of several partnerships operated outside of the Enron Corporation by Andrew Fastow, the company CFO. Fastow, along with his wife, who was also an Enron financial executive, has since pled guilty to federal fraud charges. Bass argued for a method that would have led to a $30 million to $50 million charge to Enron's bottom line and would probably have adversely affected the company's stock price. He was overruled by the Anderson practice director in the Houston office.

Two years later, in February 2001, the senior managing partners at the Chicago headquarters were debating whether to keep the Enron account. Bass had been sent into Enron once again to monitor their audit and, true to his past form, he objected to some of the charges and methods that the accounting staff there wanted Anderson to approve. Aware of the growing disagreement in the Houston office and the risks to Anderson as a company, Beradino made a trip to Houston, during which he met with Enron's new CEO, Jeffrey Skilling, and Richard Causey, its chief accounting officer. Beradino said later that he did not meet with the Anderson audit team before the visit and claimed not to know of the conflicts in the local Anderson office. He also said that it was entirely a coincidence that Bass was removed from his oversight role at Enron a few weeks after his meeting with Skilling and Causey.

In the middle of August 2001, only a few months after meeting with Beradino, Skilling, Enron's high-flying CEO, resigned for personal reasons after slightly more than 6 months in that position. That announcement, along with the highly publicized power mess in California, in which Enron had played a major role, led to significant interest in the company by John Emshwiller and Rebecca Smith, reporters at the *Wall Street Journal* (Emshwiller & Smith, 2003). They spent the next 2 months trying to unravel Enron's complex, arcane, and nearly opaque financing structure. On October 16, they published a front-page story in the *Journal* detailing their findings and suggesting a colossal pattern of misbehavior. Twenty-four days later, Enron filed papers with the SEC that documented a multiyear history of off-the-book transactions, offshore companies, and fraudulent accounting practices. By December 2001, Enron, which had been the role model of the prototypical 21st-century global business for many on Wall Street, had filed for federal bankruptcy protection.

As the Enron scandal gained momentum in late 2001 and early 2002, Beradino shifted his crisis management skills into ever higher gears. He went to Capitol Hill and testified before Congress that Anderson had made serious mistakes in a number of companies, including Enron. In a flurry of flights, he personally met with the audit committees of most of Anderson's top revenue-generating client companies, trying to hold their business and retain their trust in the company. In February 2002, he hired Paul Volcker, the former chairman of the Federal Reserve Board, to create an external oversight board to recommend a new organizational structure that would lead a revamped Anderson to become a completely independent audit firm with a new management team. It was too little, too late.

Thus, on March 14, 2002, despite intense legal negotiations, came the Justice Department's indictment on obstruction-of-justice charges. On March 15, after a little more than 1 year as CEO, Beradino offered to resign in a last-ditch effort to save the company, but the 18 directors of Anderson refused to let him do it. Eleven days later, on March 26, he did resign. On June 15, Arthur Anderson as a company was found guilty in federal court of obstruction of justice because of actions taken in their Houston and Chicago headquarters offices to shred documents, delete e-mails, and otherwise get rid of potential evidence in the Enron case. By the end of 2002, Anderson had ceased to exist as a functional company.

In perhaps the greatest irony of this entire tragic case, on May 31, 2005, the U.S. Supreme Court overturned the Anderson conviction on appeal. In a 9-to-0 decision, the highest court in the country determined that the judge in the case had erred significantly in not providing careful instructions to the jury about how to determine culpability in the case. That is, he had more or less left it up to that group of people's own judgment rather than providing a refined set of guidelines about how to interpret the law and the evidence. In the minds of the jurors in the case, the company and its leaders were clearly guilty of breaking the law. In the minds of virtually every analyst and expert who wrote or commented on the case, the Supreme Court decision came far too late to provide any material benefit to the nonexistent future of the defunct Anderson organization.

SITUATIONAL AWARENESS: SEVERAL KEYS TO IMPROVED EXECUTIVE DISCERNMENT

The case of Joe Beradino and his handling of the Enron situation as CEO of Anderson illustrates some of the biggest impediments to the routine emergence of Executive Wisdom. It is clear that Beradino had worked hard, demonstrated his competence and dedication to the company, and created the understanding among his fellow partners at Anderson that he was capable of skillfully maneuvering in the complex world of modern capitalist companies and their governmental regulators. His handling of the SEC negotiations in 1998 was proof positive that he understood the risks of having the powerful agencies of the federal government as enemies and that the government was concerned about what was going on in the accounting industry.

Nevertheless, when it came to either doing the right thing in the right way in auditing the books at Enron or acquiescing to the desires of their executive team to approve what turned out to be fraudulent transactions, he largely made his decision on the basis of not wanting to risk losing the more than $50 million in annual revenue from that company. In the process, he and his executive group turned against their own colleague, Carl Bass, who, as history clearly shows, made the correct call and was trying to act wisely on behalf of Anderson. The choice on Beradino's part to remove Bass and support the Enron leaders instead of his own partner ultimately ended his executive career and led to the death of his company, because it clearly inspired the subsequent choices to shred documents, delete e-mails, and try to cover up what had transpired in Anderson's dealings with Enron. In short, Beradino's blind commitment to maintaining Anderson's profit margins so colored his discernment, decision making, and actions that he appears in retrospect to have been absolutely destined to lead the organization over the legal cliff.

One can only imagine the complex cognitive and emotional processes that Beradino must have gone through at the time. Applying the models of wisdom and metacognition, one must acknowledge that he surely understood that his actions as CEO and the choices of his company in the situation would eventually come under public scrutiny. After all, he had just authorized over $200 million in payments for penalties because of similar actions in other companies. He also understood the concerns of the SEC about role conflict in the industry, because he had brokered the deal that let his organization stay in the consulting business. However, he and his partners failed to anticipate that the profit-centered culture of Anderson had grown sufficiently influential that it came to dominate the original culture of public stewardship and fiduciary responsibility established by Arthur Anderson himself. It was Carl Bass, an audit partner in a fairly remote office of the company, who carried the burden of the founding father in his repeated efforts to force Enron executives to account publicly for the losses that their enterprise had incurred. As we now know, lawyers and senior partners in the Houston and Chicago offices of Anderson ordered and supervised the destruction of documents from their files when they were under orders from the Justice Department to produce that information. A jury found them guilty of knowing that they were trying to illegally destroy evidence. So one must ask if it was a moral lapse on the part of Beradino and his senior colleagues, sheer stupidity, blind panic, or something else that led them to make those choices.

On the basis of the complex, ephemeral nature of Executive Wisdom that I have been describing throughout this book, I do not think we can accuse Beradino or his colleagues of being simply stupid, in a blind panic, or completely without conscience. The decisions that they were making to protect the revenue of the company were rationally conceived and competently executed. They consciously chose to acquiesce to the desires of Jeffrey Skilling and Ken Lay, knowing that not to do so and to choose to back the judgment of Carl Bass was to jeopardize the contract and their long-term, lucrative business relationship. However, they did not fully appreciate, or failed to properly evaluate, the probability that the SEC and the Justice Department would initiate criminal investigations if the document shredding and destruction of electronic files were discovered. If their lawyers had properly informed the Anderson executive partners of those risks, those warnings went unheeded. They did not foresee that the profit-driven culture that Anderson had created and ridden to the heights was capable of ordering the wholesale destruction of evidence with the extremely flimsy rationalization that they were merely cleaning up their files. And until very late in the game, they seemed to have had no idea that their savvy maneuvering in the situation would lead to the criminal indictment of their entire company.

Standing outside of the crazed turmoil that must have consumed the Chicago headquarters during this whole mess, I find it impossible to believe that at some point in that process one of their senior attorneys did not tell Beradino and the rest of the executive leadership group at Anderson that one of the possibilities was that in any criminal proceeding they would have to produce evidence that would be damaging to their company. In retrospect, faced with a choice of how to best protect the organization, Beradino and his colleagues should have done the right thing at the right time and in the right way. When it became clear, in the fall of 2001, that Enron was dissolving, Anderson had a narrow window of opportunity to go to the agencies of the federal government and offer to completely open their files for what was most surely to be a public investigation. Just as surely, Anderson as a company would have been found culpable of the same patterns of behavior that they had followed at Sunbeam, Waste Management, World-Com, and other corporations. It is in fact likely that additional penalties and public embarrassment would have occurred and that perhaps some or even all of the leaders in the organization would have been forced out. However, if they had chosen the path of full disclosure, they would not have made the fatal choices that led to criminal prosecution.

Two features are readily observable in this high-profile and excruciatingly painful case. First, as Carl von Clausewitz (1896/1986) observed, wars and battles are fought by people who cope with the chronic, virtually insurmountable problem of not getting or having sufficient and clear information about what is truly happening. His term *fog of war* describes this terrible burden that leaders have that governs their every thought and action. In Plato's *Republic* (trans. 1999), Socrates used the metaphor of fire projecting shadows onto the wall of a cave to draw attention to the perpetual problem of finding the real truth behind what humans experience. Postmodern thought and the research on the social construction of reality that was discussed in chapters 2 and 3 provide a more detailed understanding of how people piece together their unique, internal representation of experience in the world and then use that to decide and act in, on, and through that understanding. The natural conclusion is that Beradino and his partners had so fundamentally altered their internal model of reality, they were so caught up in overinterpreting the importance of maintaining the Enron account and the revenues and profits that consulting brought into Anderson, they were so enamored of and invested in the shadow dance they were doing with the likes of Jeffrey Skilling and Ken Lay, that they simply did not correctly discern the danger that lay so clearly in their path.

Second, determinations of moral principle are only as correct and useful as the level of moral understanding and capacity for moral reasoning in the individuals making the choices. How does an executive or a lawyer working with an executive decide to purge files of interest to a federal agency when they know that a formal investigation is underway? The rationalization they provided, that they were merely in compliance with their own company record-retention policies, was as laughable as it was tragic. It bespoke a level of moral logic that had moved away from considerations of what was truly the correct thing to do and toward the simplistic; childlike; and, some would say, criminally minded attitude of "catch me if you can"—and the U.S. Department of Justice did just that. Independent of the decision of the Supreme Court in overturning the verdict of the jury in the case on the technicality of improper instructions by the judge, a group of people listened to the evidence and made a clear decision about what was right and what was wrong.

These considerations turn us, then, to situational and moral awareness, which I believe are the final two anchors of the phenomenon of Executive Wisdom. In the Enron–Anderson tragedy, it is clear that significant flaws in both of these types of awareness dramatically influenced Joe Beradino's ability to discern, decide, and act wisely.

Situational Awareness

The best and most nuanced discussion that I have found of the issue of situational awareness applied to leaders was provided by Neustadt and May (1986). Using a series of complex case studies drawn from their detailed knowledge of the challenges faced by American presidents in the post–World War II period, they accurately described the difficulties that any executive faces in getting the right information and making the right assessment of it to support his or her decisions. Drawing equally from successful and failed presidents, they pointed to a variety of issues that complicate the lives of choice makers. Even more important, they were able to abstract out of the literature, their experience, and the cases that they examined a number of methods that leaders can use to help them do a better job of both assessing the situations that they face and then making complex judgments and decisions based on the information they have. A succinct summary of these seven methodologies, which range from the simplest—how to frame useful questions—to the complex—how to place the people and organizations with which one is working, competing, or fighting historically and ecologically—is provided in Exhibit 7.1.

The foundation of Neustadt and May's (1986) approach rests on the "Goldberg rule"—get the story behind the facts.[1] They contended, and with considerable historic justification, that leaders—and, I would add, their coaches—tend to move rapidly into problem-definition and -solving activities before they often fully understand what they are facing. The Goldberg rule assumes that a leader does not necessarily have the proper perspective, and when the rule is applied early on, it pushes the executive to obtain a fuller version of the story behind the situation being faced. Getting the story correct does not guarantee that a leader or a coach will make the right choice or implement a decision well. It does ensure that he or she will have a better factual basis and richer context—read: less fog—from which to proceed further.

---

[1] Avram Goldberg, past CEO of Stop and Shop, responded to Neustadt and May (1986) during a presentation on issue histories with "his" rule.

EXHIBIT 7.1
Seven Methods to Produce Situational Awareness

1. Apply the Goldberg rule (see Neustadt & May, 1986): Don't ask, "What is the problem?" ask, "What is the story and what is the history of the story?"
2. Use situational mapping.
   - What is known, unclear, presumed, and advocated (KUPA) now and then (before) in the situation?
   - What are the similarities and differences (S & D) between the analogies and metaphors that underlie the facts, understandings, and approaches considered or taken in the precursor and current situations?
   - Define specifically what is the central concern, problem, issue, or challenge and the corresponding opportunity in the current situation.
   - Define the appropriate goal in the situation.
3. Create time maps for the situation: Precursors—when did the situation start? Sequence analysis—what were the key events and key players, and how have they related through time?
4. Use placement methodology for the people, organizations, nations, and alliances involved in the situation (describe and define their individual relevant timelines, the general contributing and relevant events, the special relevant events, and the relevant details for each).
5. Use methods of inquiry to create texture and context.
   - Reporters' questions—who, what, why, when, where, how, how much, with what effects?
   - Appreciative inquiry.
   - de Bono's (1999) six-hat thinking—current data, analytic, pessimistic, optimistic, creative, emotional, reflective overview approaches.
   - Deconstructive dialogue.
6. Ask for bets and odds.
   - What are participants willing to bet on their assumptions, analogies, definitions, goals, predictions, preferred courses of action?
   - What odds are participants willing to give on their predictions and preferred courses of actions coming true?
7. Ask Alexander's question: What fresh facts, if at hand or by when, would cause you to change your presumption (your direction, your position, the bets and odds, your decision)?[a]

[a]Russell Alexander, professor of public health at the University of Washington, asked this question at a meeting of an advisory committee convened in 1976 to recommend a policy on inoculating the population of the United States against the swine flu.

Once a leader gets the story, he or she can proceed to map the situation more completely by probing for what is actually known as fact in the particular circumstances being confronted; identifying what is unclear in the story that has been told; exploring what is presumed in what is discovered; and, finally, searching for positions or points of view being advocated by the people involved or by the storytellers themselves. Coaches can significantly aid in this process through careful listening and additional use of effective inquiry. In these circumstances, an executive does well to assume that there is a historical framework within which greater understanding can be reached, so he or she should ask what in the story happened in the past and what are the relevant facts at the moment the situation is being confronted. A leader or a coach then questions the similarities and differences between the analogies and metaphors that underlie the facts and positions being presented about the historical situation and any analogies or metaphors that are proposed for understanding the situation at the time of executive exploration. Once these sources of data and ideas are explored, then an executive can more safely proceed to a preliminary and specific definition of the problem and the goal(s) that might be useful.

To strengthen and deepen their understanding and diagnostic acumen, leaders can then create time maps by asking when the situation started and charting the sequence of actions taken by the people involved in the events. Furthermore, they can use placement methods to explore the relevant past and present lives of the people, competitor organizations, nations, or alliances that have been identified as being part of the story in which they are involved. They can then strengthen their understanding even further with traditional reporter's questions (who, what, why, when, where, how, how much), Cooperrider's (1996) appreciative-inquiry methods, de Bono's (1999) six-hat thinking approaches, and Kegan and Lahey's (2001) deconstructive dialogue. Use of these techniques can move leaders systematically to deep levels of discernment and perspective formation in the assessment of any situation they face. Again, coaches can help executives with this process through their own knowledge and use of various methods of inquiry.

Neustadt and May (1986) suggested that leaders then test the assumptions and formulations underlying their maps by forcing themselves to place bets and give odds about the probability that their views of the situation are correct. Engaging in this kind of testing encourages the people involved in decision making or action implementation to validate the degree of confidence they have in their views and in their information. The exercise pushes beyond the simple and conventional advocacy of a point of view that all too often permeates the thinking of individual leaders and the deliberations of executive groups and creates a different and more public degree of accountability for the thoughts and concepts that they will use to decide important matters. If a leader can then ask him or herself Alexander's question, "What fresh facts, if at hand or by when, would cause you to change your presumption?" then he or she creates the opportunity to look actively for information that would change the diagnostic picture created by the wisdom map.[2] Leaders should be extremely persistent in the pursuit of such disconfirming information because of the fluidity and turbulence that at present characterize the environments in which most organizations exist. Coaches often do their best work during this phase of situational

---

[2] Russell Alexander, professor of public health at the University of Washington, asked this question at a meeting of an advisory committee convened in 1976 to recommend a policy on inoculating the population of the United States against the swine flu.

exploration simply because leaders frequently do not take the time to challenge their own views. Also, the well-known aspects of group dynamics and defensive operations of executive teams, such as groupthink, will often preclude such challenges coming from key subordinates. Wisdom maps need to be updated frequently because business has grown significantly faster with the emergence and integration of electronic information-processing and telecommunications technologies.

The Goldberg rule, Alexander's question, and methods of inquiry are all examples of fairly simple approaches that any executive or coach can apply to help improve understanding of the situation that is being confronted. Situational mapping, time maps, placement methods, and using bets and odds (see Exhibit 7.1) are more complex approaches that when applied correctly can dramatically increase anyone's knowledge and help to refine the decisions that he or she makes. When coaching leaders, I often use the Goldberg rule to start our conversations. I always want to know the story behind the situation facing a client. Similarly, as a leader in an organization, I am constantly asking subordinates or superiors to provide a narrative that helps me put the principal parties; their behaviors; their histories, motivations, and values; and the complex history of the issues involved in a rich framework that helps me make up my mind about what is happening and about what I need to do or recommend. Depending on the time frame I am working against, I will often use aspects of the other six methods—particularly situational mapping, inquiry, and placement—to draw out more information from whoever is informing me. When making recommendations or decisions, I have also found that pushing myself to place bets or to speculate on odds helps me to shape and finalize choices. The method also helps me to be brutally realistic about what I believe will actually happen as a given action is undertaken.

Another useful set of concepts and methods to both understand and improve situational awareness comes largely from the research efforts of the U.S. Armed Forces, which are extremely concerned about how to improve combat performance (Endsley & Garland, 2000). Literally dealing with the fog of wartime conditions and trying to train pilots, tank commanders, and other soldiers to fight better in these life-threatening, impossibly stressful, and always confusing circumstances, the Armed Forces have made tremendous strides in constructing conceptual models and combat simulation training methods. SART is a "situational awareness rating tool" that asks respondents, often Air Force pilots, to rate 10 different elements of both the environment being faced and their responses to it. The constructs investigated include instability, variability, and complexity of the situation; the arousal, spare mental capacity, concentration, and division of attention of the individual soldier; the quality and quantity of the information available; and the degree of familiarity the individual soldier has with kinds of situations being experienced. The SART model aims to clarify the supply of and demands on attentional resources of pilots and the level of understanding that an individual can reach in any given set of circumstances.

In another example, described by Endsley and Garland (2000), the Situational Awareness Rating Scales (SARS) were developed to try to help pilots improve their air combat skills. The scales incorporate 31 identifiable elements in the following eight categories: (a) general traits, (b) tactical game plan, (c) communication, (d) tactical employment—general, (e) information interpretation, (f) system operation, (g) tactical employment—beyond visual range, and (h) tactical employment within visual range. This kind of complex modeling describes much more accurately the range of variables that affect a pilot's ability to figure out both what is going on and what to do in a combat situation. The perils are obvious, for if the individual does not discern, decide, and act wisely and rapidly, the result is loss of life for the pilot and perhaps even additional damage and death as air defenses are penetrated. Although the parallels to executive life and performance in most enterprises outside of military, paramilitary, or health care organizations are not perfect, particularly the requirements to make split-second decisions with life-and-death implications, the number of variables involved in the SARS assessment does by implication point to the thick and nuanced texture in executive environments and to the need for both leaders and their coaches to have an in-depth appreciation for all of the factors involved.

A third way of looking at and trying to help leaders and their coaches improve their situational awareness comes from what has emerged as the business discipline of competitor analysis. Porter (1980) provided perhaps the earliest and most comprehensive framework for the field of market assessment with his advanced work on competitive strategy. He framed his approach to competitor analysis around three deceptively simple questions: (a) What is the business doing now, (b) what is happening in the environment, and (c) what should the business be doing? In that context, he then explicitly directs the attention of leaders to their competitors' motivations, current capacities, and longer term abilities. If leaders understand the current goals of the management teams of the opposition at as many levels as possible, as well as the nature of their current competitive strategy, they are much better able to respond to both immediate challenges and long-term threats. Porter also encouraged executives to understand the assumptions and the organizational strengths and weaknesses of rivals as a way of clarifying the capacities that support their business strategies.

In the best cases, these forms of inquiry and data accumulation then help to create comprehensive frameworks that can lead to insights into the degree to which commercial foes are satisfied with their position and strategy; the kinds of shifts in strategy that they might reasonably make; areas and characteristics of their vulnerabilities; and the nature of possible attacks that if made will generate the most toxic or lethal responses from them. Similar to Neustadt and May's (1986) suggestions with regard to the governments of nation-states, Porter (1980) was clear about the need for business leaders to be keenly attuned to their external situations and just which rivals and other forces posed the greatest threat or provided the greatest opportunities for competitive success. Coaches themselves must also be intimately familiar with this imperative and how to help their clients gain such awareness.

Bennis et al. (2002) suggested a variety of cost-effective ways that leaders can collect information about competitors as they organize to address the threats that they represent. First and foremost, they pointed out the ease and importance of using the existing sales force of the enterprise to discern and discover just what rival organizations are doing in the marketplace. Customers are often willing to disclose the nature of offers being made by competing firms as a way of driving better deals for themselves. Industry newspapers and newsletters, the business pages of regular newspapers, advertising campaigns of competitors, the literature provided by rivals themselves, and the Internet can all be routinely scanned for critical data. Conventions and sales exhibitions, although occurring infrequently, can also provide critical opportunities to see actual products, hear sales approaches, and even obtain pricing information. Bennis et al. strongly cautioned against making decisions on the basis of incomplete information or that are subject to the biases I discussed in chapter 3. Porter (1980) as well as Bennis et al. have insisted that leaders ignore opponents at their peril. Coaches must also carry a fine-tuned sense of what opposing organizations can do to harm their client organizations. In a sense, such coaching awareness can provide effective strategic monitoring of the model-construction processes of their clients. Where gaps and insufficiencies are perceived, they can often be closed by simply asking a few good questions that can then drive executive action to improve situational awareness.

The Special Case of Political Awareness: Who Gets What, When, and How?

Finally, it seems clear that leaders also must have a superior ability to quickly size up the political landscape in any organization with or within which they work. Political awareness and insight are often central to an individual's ability to grow as a leader and to gain additional power and stature in an organization. The literature in this area is substantial and spans from the ancients to the events in today's modern global corporations and nation-states. From Cicero (Everitt, 2003) and Machiavelli (1514/1961), there are timeless lessons in the art of maneuver, thrust and parry, and conquest and domination. de Waal (2000) and Heifetz (1994) have suggested that the politics of modern human organizations are deeply rooted in their bioanthropological foundations as communities of primates and that they operate within most of the same parameters and behavior patterns as those of the other great apes: chimpanzees, gorillas, and bonobos. Pfeffer (1992) and Dubrin (1978) have provided realistic guides to navigating the political mazes in work-based enterprises. Neustadt (1970, 1990), Davis (2000), and Mearsheimer (2001) have provided deep and lasting insights into the interdependent political behavior of the governments of nations. Hariman (1995) developed and explored four identifiable political styles: (a) the realist, (b) the courtier, (c) the republican, and (d) the bureaucrat. Lustiger-Thaler and Salee (1994) and their contributors examined the politics of markets, communities, and families in the modern era as a way of trying to explore the different ways in which people are pursuing strategies of economic survival and their consequent political expression. Roy (2001) gave a succinct and devastating depiction of the complex relationships among politics, international diplomacy, the joint ventures of global corporations, public speech, and the spiritual questions embedded within the mega-projects of nation-states. No single book, let alone these cited references and these few small paragraphs, can ever do justice to the subject of politics in organizations and executive life. However, any effort to explore what gives rise to the phenomenon I call Executive Wisdom would be remiss if it did not at least draw attention to the tremendous importance of this most complex realm of human behavior.

Exhibit 7.2 provides an exercise that I hope might prove useful to readers in leadership positions or coaches who work with them. The questions are based on the methodology of deconstructive inquiry proposed by Gergen (1999) and founded in Laswell's (1936) formulation of politics as a determination of who gets what, when, and how. Within the framework of wisdom mapping, the exercise directs the attention of the executive or a coach to formal and informal structures and the ways in which they are overtly and covertly connected. It then suggests an examination of the sources of political influence available to the members of the organizational unit under consideration and an exploration of the history of the evolution of those sources of power. One must carefully examine the wins, losses, threats, promises, values, attitudes, beliefs, competition, cooperation, and formal and informal alliances to comprehend the motivational states and types of overt and covert behavior that are being encountered in any specific organizational environment.

Similarly, the exercise calls for complex model construction through the assessment of the structures, relationships, sources of power and influence, and so on, of the executive from the perspectives of various individuals, such as those who have knowledge, skill, and positions of formal authority in the enterprise and those who have less, or perhaps in the case of a nation-

EXHIBIT 7.2
Questions to Promote Political Deconstructive Inquiry

One must know before one can see. (Fleck, 1935/1979)

INSTRUCTIONS

Harold Laswell (1936) defined *politics* as a "social process determining who gets what, when and how" (de Waal, 2000, p. xiv). Leaders and their coaches would be wise to explore and understand the political landscape in an organization before finalizing a diagnosis and solution for any particular problem or challenge. With your client, or using your own knowledge of the situation you face, work through the following guide. Jot down your observations, responses, and hypotheses as you go along. Use the guide to help you see, but always, always, always challenge what you are seeing and the methods you have used to create your understanding.

1. Who are the formal leaders in this organization (unit)?
2. Who are the informal leaders in this organization (unit)?
3. How are they connected to each other—socially, psychologically, economically, through interests, shared time, shared history, similar backgrounds or educational histories, fraternities, sororities, shared values, geography, families, mutual friends?
4. What are their sources of political clout (formal position, talent, information, skill, past favors, special knowledge—blackmail—political bank accounts through dependencies, heroic action, achievements, mistakes, failures, fears, etc.)?
5. Who in the unit seems to know the local map best?
6. What are the bases of your assessments? How reliable and valid is the information you have obtained, the intuitions you have formed?
7. Place the people you have identified into a political hierarchy. Who is on top? Second? On the bottom? Why have you put them in this order?
8. Who currently has what by way of power and influence in the organization—resources, budgets, staff, buildings, equipment, decision-making responsibilities, information, strong relationships, ideas, knowledge and skill? Look at your answers to Question 4.
9. When and how did he or she get the power/influence?
10. Did anyone lose when he or she got it? Who, what, why, when, how much? Who had relationships with the loser(s)? Did anyone help the loser(s)? Who, what, why, when, how much? Are they still in the unit/organization? Did anyone help the winner? Who, what, why, when, how much? Who had relationships with the winner(s)? Are they still in the unit/organization?
11. Does anyone still around remember the events? Carry a grudge? Play to even the score? Redress the losses? Who? What has happened? With what impact? What are the information sources for your observations?
12. What are the ambitions, desires, wants, needs of the key players you've identified?
13. What approaches are they taking to get what they want?
14. Is there any overt or covert competition or conflict between these individuals or between groups of them? Do some of them want things others have? Who, what, why, how much?
15. Are they doing anything overt or covert to get what they want or need?
16. What is their personal history of competing?

(continued)

EXHIBIT 7.2 *(Continued)*

17. What is their personal style of competing? Of being in conflict?
18. Are there subgroups formally or informally organized and competing or in conflict?
19. What have been the outcomes, costs, benefits, consequences of the competition or conflict for the individuals, the unit, their careers, their families, their physical or emotional health?
20. What history, traditions, values, attitudes, beliefs, virtues, or vices have contributed to the development of the current landscape? For your client? For the other players? For you as a coach? How do you and your client define truth for yourselves? For others? How do the other actors in the situation define truth? For themselves? For others? What are the vocabularies of meaning being used by the actors—money, political power, status, ideas, relationships, programs, sex, love, hate, admiration, and devaluation? Are these also political currencies in actual circulation? Who keeps the books? What are people's balances with each other? What is the unit's balance with other units?
21. Are you, or is your client, prepared to suspend some or all of your or his or her current views of the situation? Which ones? If yes, why? If no, why not?
22. Is there anything missing from the picture drawn so far? Whom does the map privilege? Whom does the map oppress? What and whom does the map protect? Expose?
23. Can you examine the map from different perspectives—the privileged, the oppressed, the knowledgeable, the skilled, the ignorant, the haves, the have-nots?
24. Can you create a different picture, a new map of what the political and power landscape could be? What you would like or need it to be?
25. What steps could or should be undertaken to achieve such a vision? Do you, or does your client, have the required knowledge, skills, abilities, resources, and motivation to take those steps?
26. What barriers might be in the way of achieving the vision?
27. How might you address those barriers?
28. What new knowledge and skill will you or your client need to cope with the present landscape, create a new idea, identify or overcome barriers, and implement the actions necessary for change to occur?
29. How will you or your client know when you've changed the map?
30. How have you or has your client managed change in the past?
31. What typically gets in the way of you or your client making necessary changes personally or professionally?
32. What was the most difficult political situation you or your client has ever faced?
33. What happened?
34. What were the short- and long-term consequences for you (or your client)?
35. What made it difficult?
36. Is that history informing or influencing your current understanding and action in the present situation? How?
37. Have those patterns or dynamics repeated themselves for you or your client?
38. What was the best political situation you or your client ever faced?
39. Repeat Questions 33–37.
40. Can you detect any psychodynamic patterns or influences in the situation? Defenses, conflicts, emotions, cognitive distortions, trauma, repetition compulsion, sadomasochism, narcissism, dependency, or other character problems?

state, none. The exercise then turns toward interventions designed to do something besides just understand what exists in the organization. It pushes one to envision a different map and the barriers that might be encountered by anyone trying to pursue something different. The exercise ends with a series of questions that lead to a self-exploration of personally difficult political situations, their history, and their effects, including an effort to examine the unconscious or psychodynamic implications of the patterns and influences. When conducted either entirely or in part, the exercise will guarantee those who push themselves to do it a dramatically improved view of the politics in the organizations in which they are working or living.

It is easy to see the contribution that can be made to the ability of any executive to think and act wisely by improving his or her situational awareness. The concepts and methods provided here merely introduce the subject and explore a small set of approaches that can be used to improve awareness. As I explored in the Beradino case, failures in situational assessments can be fatal to organizations and careers. In the worlds of national and global politics, such failures can literally be personally lethal to individual leaders who misassess their situations and approaches to their environments (Heifetz & Linsky, 2002). Let us turn our attention now to the last two pieces of our wisdom-mapping process.

MORAL AND VALUE COMPASSES AND WISDOM SYSTEMS: THE FINAL COMPONENTS OF WISDOM MAPPING

As with most of the other topics in this book, the literature and human consideration of moral reasoning and the place of values in one's life are exceedingly complex. It is crystal clear from the retrospective examination of case after case of flawed executive judgment and leadership failure that the inability or unwillingness to determine how the values and moral inclinations of friends and foes are influencing their thoughts, feelings, and actions contributes significantly to many of these disasters. In the assessment of the Anderson case that introduced this chapter, we can ask ourselves whether or at what point the leaders of Enron and their accounting firm asked themselves what was the morally correct thing to do. A close reading of the detailed case studies of the Enron debacle and Anderson's contributions to it clearly reveals that the questions that those leaders asked themselves repeatedly were in the form of "what is strictly legal, what stretches the boundaries of conventional business and accounting practices and won't adversely affect the stock price, what will make us the most money, and what can we get away with?"

What is glaringly absent is the willingness on the part of anyone involved, with the exceptions of Carl Bass; Sherron Watkins, the accountant inside Enron who raised the risks of public disclosure of their business decisions; and perhaps a few unnamed and unrecognized others, to ask the moral questions. In a written internal memo to CEO Ken Lay on August 1, 2001, just after Jeffrey Skilling's resignation (Swartz & Watkins, 2003), Sherron Watkins raised the following issues, among others:

> One of the overriding basic principles of accounting is that if you explain the "accounting treatment" to a man on the street, would you influence his investing decisions? Would he buy or sell stock based on a thorough understanding of the facts? If so, you best present it correctly or change the accounting. (Swartz & Watkins, 2003, p. 364)

Although we do not know exactly what questions Carl Bass was asking on the two occasions that he came into open conflict with the executive leadership of Enron and his own firm, it is a reasonably safe assumption that he was raising the same basic issues. In essence, and in the best historical tradition of Arthur Anderson himself, both Bass and Watkins asked "What is the morally correct thing to do in this situation to properly inform the investing public about the risks this company is taking with their money?" Had that question been raised and addressed with determined leadership attention at any point in Enron's internal deliberations or during Anderson's partner reviews of the situation, it is extremely doubtful that the Anderson and Enron corporations would have fallen. They would have been severely hurt, but there would have been no criminal obstruction of justice because the books would already have been open to public scrutiny. The fact that Bass raised this issue at least twice inside both of the companies and was suppressed and marginalized by his bosses is a corporate tragedy. It is also a sad tribute to a values structure that had shifted significantly away from the emphasis placed on professional integrity and public accountability by the founder and first CEO of Arthur Anderson.

Psychological and Philosophical Contributions to Business Ethics

In the post-Enron era, as with past financial scandals at other major American corporations, there was a huge outcry of public indignation. Many people raised the issue of what students learn in today's schools of business. The conventional approach to addressing moral questions in organizations is through the examination and construction of systems of business ethics. Velasquez (1992) provided an excellent example of a modern textbook that focuses on ethical practices in business. It is noteworthy because it did not simply leap into discussions of cases, ethical systems, and what organizations should do. Instead, Valasquez took the time and devoted the effort to place ethics within a detailed psychophilosophical conceptual framework. He suggested that to understand business challenges, leaders need to be capable of engaging in the difficult tasks of moral reasoning. Valasquez outlined a three-step process to frame these issues. First, a leader must be aware of and sensitive to the issue of moral standards. Second, he or she then develops factual information about the policy, behavior, or organizational practice being considered. Finally, executives then pass moral judgment of the rightness or wrongness of the policy, behavior, or organizational practice. Organizations do not have ethics or engage in moral reasoning; their leaders do, or, as in the Anderson–Enron case, do not.

We can only imagine what would have been the historical outcome if Enron's board of directors had insisted that each of the off-the-books transactions that were proposed by the executives of the company had been rigorously scrutinized through the lens of moral reasoning. Even in 2001 before the obstruction of justice took place in his company, it is interesting to speculate what would have happened if Joe Beradino had asked himself a version of Alexander's question, such as, "What would I choose to do in this situation if I thought there were a better-than-even chance that the Anderson company would be criminally indicted and convicted for the actions we are about to undertake?"

Systems of business ethics are firmly and historically rooted in considerations of the principles of moral philosophy and theories of justice. Rachels (2003) stated succinctly that

> morality is, at the very least, the effort to guide one's conduct by reason—that is, to do what there are the best reasons for doing—while giving equal weight to the interests of each individual who will be affected by what one does. (p. 14)

In his Socratic dialogues, Plato explicitly explored the issue of justice in the deliberations of leaders and raised it to the level of a virtue that he believed must be cultivated by societies as a whole. Lebacqz (1986) explored the issue of justice from the perspective of the systems of philosophical and theological thought. Her provocative summary started with the utilitarian views expressed by John Stuart Mill and then proceeded to examine those fundamental problems from perspectives of contractual obligations (John Rawls), entitlements (Robert Nozick), Catholic doctrine (The National Conference of Catholic Bishops), Protestant alternatives (Reinhold Niebuhr), and the challenges of liberation theology (Jose Porfirio Miranda).

Psychological science has pursued key questions concerning moral development and moral reasoning for many decades. Kohlberg's (1981) model of the six stages of moral development and types of moral reasoning elaborated on the ground-breaking work of Piaget (1965) and has provided a conceptual foundation for much of the research that has followed. His system divides the moral evolution of humans into three major epochs with six identifiable subcomponents. He labeled the first two stages *preconven-*

tional, the second set *conventional*, and the third set *postconventional*. He called Stage 1 the *punishment and obedience orientation*. Children are taught and learn to defer to authority and to avoid punishment. They do not truly recognize the rights and needs of others. He labeled Stage 2 the *instrument and reality orientation*. Here children become aware that other people have rights and needs and that the children's right actions can meet both their own desires and those of others. He identified Stage 3 as the *interpersonal concordance orientation*. At this point, children develop an internal concept of what it means to be a good son or daughter and person, and they understand what others expect of them. They work to live up to those expectations of themselves and others. He called Stage 4 the *law and order orientation*. Youngsters come to understand that they live in a social system with laws, rules, and norms for behavior, and they are able to see the rules of the system as separate from their own relationships and thoughts about right and wrong.

Kohlberg (1981) described the postconventional stages as involving the social contract orientation and the universal ethical principles orientation. In Stage 5, the *social contract* form, individuals come to understand and value that different people have different systems for moral- and reality-based decision making, and they strive to develop and use agreements, contracts, and due-process approaches to resolve differences and establish relationships. In Stage 6, *universal principles*, individuals come to choose right action as a function of moral, religious, or philosophical approaches that they consistently value and use to help them solve the complex problems that life throws at them. They use their moral and ethical principles to evaluate the systems of norms, ethics, values, and morals of other people and institutions and to determine the right thing to do in any situation.

Gilligan (1982) provided a profound critique of some of Kohlberg's (1981) assertions and findings, claiming that a variety of different studies conducted by many investigators had yielded fairly consistent results that girls tended to score at earlier, and hence "lower," levels of moral development than boys within Kohlberg's classification system. In a closely reasoned reexamination of a number of these studies and others like them, she concluded that rather than saying that girls' results were "lower" and hence inferior to those of boys in terms of their moral development, she believed that they based their reasoning in these experiments on altogether different ways of thinking. She contended that those approaches were not morally inferior to those of the male gender but rather that they represented a separate and equally valid way of considering moral conflicts and problems. According to Gilligan, the central focus of feminine moral reasoning holds the nature of the relationship between the people as the most important feature of the situation and subordinates all other issues to that priority. She and many others since then have demonstrated that the values and morals of U.S. society and organizations tend to be dominated by the men who lead them (Rachels, 2003), and they have hypothesized that organizations led by women might well be operated according to and by different moral precepts and principles.

The Moral Compass at Arthur Anderson

It is clear that leaders of every organization are routinely confronted with challenges that require them to use moral reasoning. If one examines the case example that started this chapter through the lens of moral reasoning, it is impossible to believe that Joe Beradino did not wrestle intensely with the fundamental issues confronting Arthur Anderson as it faced the demise of Enron. His nuanced leadership of the intense negotiations with the SEC in the late 1990s and his efforts to create an effective assessment of the risk profiles of Anderson's clients suggest strongly that he fully understood at least the technical and political issues in making correct accounting choices. In the absence of explicit conversations with him that would reflectively visit the nature of his thinking process during the Enron catastrophe, one would be hard pressed to state the exact nature of those internal deliberations. However, Byrne's (2002) report does offer several clues concerning the values he chose to clearly and publicly express during his brief term as CEO of that ill-fated company. Byrne reported Barbara Lee Toffler, a former Anderson partner from 1995 through 1999, as saying that

> when Beradino would get up at a partners meeting, all that was ever reported in terms of success was dollars . . . . Quality wasn't discussed. Content wasn't discussed. Everything was measured in terms of the buck . . . . Joe was blind to the conflict. He was the most aggressive pursuer of revenue that I ever met. (Byrne, 2002, pp. 55–56)

Byrne also suggested that several others had similar things to say about what drove the executive decision-making processes led by Beradino. Despite the historical and deeply rooted aspects of Anderson's accounting culture and what is known about Beradino's capacity to lead in complex crisis situations, we can reach a reasonable conclusion about the core value that had come to form the foundation of his leadership and the expectation of perhaps most of the senior decision-making partners at the Anderson company. The name of that value was *profit*.

Byrne (2002) also reported that the four historical cornerstones of the Anderson company were to provide good client service, produce quality audits, manage staff well, and produce profits. In response to Byrne's questions about whether profits had stifled considerations of the other three values, Beradino said, "Some of the partners thought that that was happening, I didn't" (p. 55). At a minimum, there is clear evidence of major conflict among at least some of the partners at Anderson over whether the issue of profitability had completely overtaken the culture of the company.

Values and Moral Reasoning

The *Oxford English Dictionary* (Simpson & Weiner, 1998) defined *values* as "the personal or societal judgment of what is valuable and important in life" (p. 2212). Kirschenbaum, Howe, and Simon (1972), in their classic book on values clarification, provided more than 30 different exercises to help people come to an understanding of the principles by which they do, should, or want to govern their lives. Many corporations, including the defunct Enron, have values statements that their leaders presumably use to guide their decisions and actions. In what must be a monumental piece of irony, the *1998 Annual Report* of the Enron Corporation listed their four principle values as follows:

> RESPECT We treat others as we would like to be treated ourselves. We do not tolerate abusive or disrespectful treatment. Ruthlessness, callousness and arrogance don't belong here. COMMUNICATION We have an obligation to communicate. Here, we take the time to talk with one another . . . and to listen. We believe that information is meant to move and that information moves people. INTEGRITY We work with customers and prospects openly, honestly and sincerely. When we say we will do something, we will do it; when we say we cannot or will not do something, then we won't do it. EXCELLENCE We are satisfied with nothing less than the very best in everything we do. We will continue to raise the bar for everyone. The great fun here will be for all of us to discover just how good we can really be. (Enron Corporation, 1998, p. 73)

In retrospect, we can only imagine what happened among Ken Lay, Jeffrey Skilling, and Andy Fastow, the chairman, CEO, and CFO of Enron, respectively, as they labored intensively to hide billions of dollars in losses due to bad business deals in the offshore, special vehicle accounting schemes they created. Juxtaposing what is known about their decisions and actions against the above values statement, one can only shake one's head in wonderment at the level of denial and rationalization that must have been going on in their deliberations and those of the company board of directors.

It is clear that the values driving the execution of their choices were not treating staff, customers, and shareholders with respect; practicing open communication; dealing honestly and openly; or demonstrating excellence in their leadership performance. If they had made any reasonable effort to examine the situation that they faced and their choices through these four related value lenses, they may well have made different decisions resulting in something other than the liquidation of the company's assets and a string of federal criminal indictments leading, at least in Fastow's case, to the imprisonment of both him and his wife. Again, if they had asked Alexander's question soon enough, one hopes they might have courageously dug themselves out of their extraordinary business problems using different means.

These cases take us to a fundamental issue in the domain of moral reasoning and ethical behavior that has been debated repeatedly for over 2,000 years. On the one side of the controversy are Socrates, Aristotle, Plato, Confucius, and a number of other classical philosophers who argued passionately that morality and honor in the world rest on the shoulders of people of virtue. Plato's *Republic* (trans. 1999) went so far as to provide a detailed curriculum for the development of virtuous leaders and explicitly stated that the process of creating virtue in statesmen took a lifetime of education and experience. Plato also suggested that just societies created the circumstances and structures through which leaders could be developed systematically. Confucius was renowned not only for his teaching but also for creating a school of leadership that continued to provide a steady stream of administrative executives for the various emperors who ruled China for thousands of years. One could argue that the principles of Confucius continue to pervade the thoughts and actions of the people and leaders of China even today. These founding fathers of both Eastern and Western thought and philosophy believed firmly that moral behavior resided in and was created by virtuous individuals. As I suggested in chapter 2, Plato stated that there were four key virtues that any leader must possess: (a) courage, (b) temperance, (c) justice, and (d) wisdom. In the Socratic dialogues, it was clear that individuals who did not possess these virtues were thought unlikely to be able to create and rule over a just and temperate society.

Rachels (2003) provided a succinct overview of both sides of this debate and how the clash of views has been rekindled in modern philosophical thought. In his estimation, the challenge to virtue ethics started with Augustine's 4th-century account of his conversion to Christianity (Pusey, 2003). Rachels suggested that following the appearance of Augustine's *Confessions*, a profound shift began in the consideration of right action in human affairs. If the classical views of Plato, Aristotle, and Confucius can be summarized as the belief that right thinking and right action come from well-developed and virtuous individuals, then Augustine provided a fundamental challenge to that position by stating that humans are incapable of creating right thinking and right action outside of the laws of God. In the Augustinian universe, essentially the Christian universe, the laws of God as delineated in Holy Scripture constitute the only true map to human goodness and right behavior. It is the duty of moral people to study and abide by those laws. Within those boundaries, and only within them, just and harmonious societies can be established. It is interesting that this view is completely in accord with traditional Jewish thought and religious practices (Epstein, 1978; Twerski, 1999), which originated centuries before Socrates and Confucius.

Rachels (2003) went on to suggest that Augustine's challenge had a profound influence on the Western philosophy, moral reasoning, and ethical systems that came afterward. These subsequent developments have been based on the view that humans behave best when they have a set of rules, laws, or norms to guide them. The work of countless thinkers since then has been to create deeper insights into the will of God as expressed in Scripture, the works of humans derived from considerations of Scripture, and the efforts to create what one can think of as the evolved secular versions of these laws in and through moral philosophy. Rachels suggested as well that virtue ethics have made a significant comeback in the halls of academic philosophy and that there has been an emergence of "neo-classic virtue advocates" who are once again challenging what could be called the "religious rule-givers."

Psychological research and practice are now mirroring these developments in philosophy. Seligman (2002) and a group of other researchers and practitioners are seriously challenging classic clinical conceptions of psychopathology and interventions that are based on the medical model, in which disordered behaviors are diagnosed and ameliorated with professionally correct forms of treatment. C. R. Snyder and Lopez (2002) provided a wonderful collection of papers summarizing much of the current thinking of positive psychologists whose work at its core appears to return to the fundamental stances taken by Plato, Aristotle, Confucius, and others who advocated the systematic development of virtue in human beings. This is not to say that *virtue* ever has disappeared from the lexicon of philosophy, psychology, or religion but that the relative degree of public emphasis on the topic has waxed and waned through the centuries.

Clifton and Nelson (1992) anticipated much of the move toward positive psychology. In their book, they referenced a fundamental question posed by Don Clifton some 50 years ago: What would happen if we studied what is right with people versus what is wrong with people? That question led to an extensive investigation by the Gallup Organization and the evolution of a strengths-based approach to developing people (Buckingham & Clifton, 2001). Clifton and Nelson created the StrengthsFinder, a psychological test composed of 180 items that yields a profile of 34 different strength themes. Clifton and Nelson summarized their strengths-based approach to building people and organizations with a simple aphorism: "Focus on strengths and manage the weaknesses" (p. 19). As an example of the effectiveness approach, they tell the story of the Chinese coach of their 1984 Olympic championship Ping Pong team. Describing the game of the gold metal winner, the coach said,

Here is our philosophy: If you develop your strengths to the maximum, the strength becomes so great it overwhelms the weaknesses. Our winning player, you see, plays only his forehand. Even though he cannot play backhand and his competition knows he cannot play backhand, his forehand is so invincible that it cannot be beaten. (Clifton & Nelson, 1992, pp. 19–20)

Most recently, there have been significant additions to the psychological literature on the issue of virtues. Chang and Samna (2003) provided a wonderful collection summarizing recent personality psychology research that has examined both virtues and their complementary vices through the lens of strategies that humans adopt in their adjustment. These chapters examined the historical evolution of personality theory as well as provided interesting examples of current research into such topics as the nature and maintenance of self-esteem, optimism and pessimism as fundamental forces in human character, control dynamics, intelligence, and the pros and cons of neuroticism in human behavior. They take a position close to Aristotle's (trans. 1908) that the definitions of virtue and vice can be found in the perceptions and behavior of individuals. For example, an expression of self-confidence by one person can be seen and experienced by another as an act of extreme arrogance; the perpetually self-critical thoughts of a person could be assessed as a symptom of pathological depression by a therapist, whereas the individual him- or herself interprets them as a way of learning in complex situations.

Other examples of the resurrection of the study and advocacy of virtue in the psychological literature can be found in Jordan and Meara's (1990) article, in which they formally proposed the addition of the study of virtue ethics to the training of psychology practitioners. They contrasted this approach with principle ethics by raising two fundamental questions. When applying principle ethics to any situation, the core issue is, "What shall I do?" They proposed that the same situations can be approached by means of virtue ethics in which the question becomes, "Whom shall I be?" Walker and Hennig (2004) recently conducted a series of three studies that further pursued the illumination of a character strength- or virtue-based understanding of moral psychology. They focused on three types of what they called *moral exemplars*—just, brave, and caring—trying to integrate them into the Big Five factors of personality (Extraversion, Agreeableness, Conscientiousness, Emotional Stability, and Openness to Experience). They concluded that moral excellence can be identified in many different ways and that the psychological understanding of moral behavior could be extended significantly by incorporating additional measures of these kinds of virtues.

More recently, Peterson and Seligman (2004) provided an initial classification system of character strengths and virtues and a comprehensive review of the available literature on each of them. Their classification delineates six principal character strengths, (a) wisdom and knowledge,

(b) courage, (c) humanity, (d) justice, (e) temperance, and (f) transcendence, along with 24 components that they believe are identifiable characteristics of the six basics. The system is outlined in Exhibit 7.3.

Peterson and Seligman's (2004) book represents an effort by them and their contributors to provide a fundamental challenge to the classification of human behavior solely based on psychopathology (American Psychiatric Association, 1994) and to encourage even more extensive efforts on the part of the psychology community to provide both research and practical interventions to build human strengths. This then can be seen as a confirmation of the historical work of Don Clifton and others who have been advocating such a shift in perspective in how we try to change behavior.

In his recent book entitled *Virtue and Psychology: Pursuing Excellence in Ordinary Practices*, Blaine Fowers (2005) welcomed Peterson and Seligman's (2004) classification system while simultaneously criticizing their utter dependence on objectivism, individual fulfillment, and instrumentalism in providing the fundamental conceptual underpinnings of their typology. Throughout his book, Fowers advocated that modern psychology should return to its classical Greek heritage and extend itself to consider what is truly good for human beings. He relied heavily on Aristotle's ethics to provide a flexible framework within and through which he explored many of the findings and conclusions of scientific psychology. Fowers stated that

> the first and most central thing that we need to understand about virtues is that they are the character strengths that make it possible for human beings to pursue uniquely human aims or goods successfully. I use several terms to refer to what is good. The terms *good* and *goods* refer to relatively abstract accomplishments or states of affairs that are worthwhile. Examples include knowledge, democracy, well-being, flourishing, and mutual understanding. (Fowers, 2005, p. 29)

Throughout his book, Fowers (2005) emphasized that character is and can be acquired by humans only through extensive practice: "Acting well consistently in the ordinary activities of life is one of the hallmarks of character" (p. 39). It is through the consistent enactment of virtues that an individual develops what is commonly referred to as a "good character." Flowers also went to considerable length to emphasize that perhaps the most important building block for the development of character is the individual person's ability to create and use practical wisdom in daily life. Again, he drew heavily on Aristotle's views by describing practical wisdom as

> choosing and acting well in the pursuit of what is good in our daily activities. I focus on three complementary components of wisdom: the moral perception of what is at stake, deliberation about what is possible and what actions are called for, and the reasoned choice of the best course of action. (Fowers, 2005, p. 117)

EXHIBIT 7.3

Classification System of Character Strengths and Virtues

Wisdom and knowledge	Courage	Humanity	Justice	Temperance	Transcendence
Creativity	Bravery	Love	Citizenship	Forgiveness and mercy	Appreciation of beauty and excellence
Curiosity	Persistence	Kindness	Fairness	Humility	Gratitude
Open-mindedness	Integrity	Social intelligence	Leadership	Prudence	Hope
Love of learning	Vitality			Self-regulation	Humor
Perspective					Spirituality

Note. From *Character Strengths and Virtues* (Table 1.1, pp. 29–30), by C. Peterson and M. E. Seligman, 2004, Washington, DC and New York: American Psychological Association and Oxford University Press. Copyright 2004 by Values in Action Institute. Adapted with permission.

I found Fowers's (2005) book at the 2005 Annual Convention of the American Psychological Association just as I was finishing the final editing on the present volume. Although his approach focused largely on the more general issue of how individual humans and societies can develop virtuous characters and through them pursue the good life, as one can see from the passages I have quoted above, his ideas are wholly in keeping and remarkably similar to those presented in this volume. I have never met Blaine Fowers, but it seems entirely reasonable that his ideas about individuals living in society are nearly identical to those that I believe can and should be applied to the executives who live in and lead modern organizations and nation-states. For in order for their enterprises to flourish, I believe executives must be virtuous people. And although this book has necessarily focused almost exclusively on executive wisdom, you as readers must understand that it is most likely that this most ephemeral and important characteristic of leadership can only take consistent root in the bedrock and deep soil of a person of virtuous character.

Executives can and must consistently try to nurture themselves; create high expectations for their behavior and for those whom they lead; and practice, practice, practice at trying to improve both what they do and how they do it. Peterson and Seligman (2004) did society a tremendous service by making the effort to summarize what is known in the psychological literature about virtuous behavior, but any careful reader of that book knows that there is an enormous, multimillennium foundation of philosophy, theology, history, and literature that informs each and every one of the findings that science has described in the past century or so. These academic traditions need not be in conflict. Throughout this book I have tried to demonstrate that if we are to make progress in how we develop leaders and the art of leadership, we must undertake the arduous attempt to integrate these various bodies of knowledge, skill, and experience. For it is only in the integration of humanity's experience and explorations that we can make the leap toward more consistently wise executive action. Our increasingly small world, with its increasingly large populations of humans, its diminishing base of natural resources, and its ever-expanding technological sophistication, demands such breakthroughs.

Applying Peterson and Seligman's (2004) classification system to the material presented in this book so far, I find that I am in agreement with most of what they have included, even if I might quibble with some of their labels and placements (e.g., prudence as a subcomponent of temperance) and with the notion that there are 24 independently identifiable virtues (an issue that in all probability will be decided by extensive factor analytic studies to come in the future, which may lead to the exposition of the equivalent of the "Big Five virtues" in human behavior. Perhaps, after a decade or more of interdependent studies, experimental psychology may

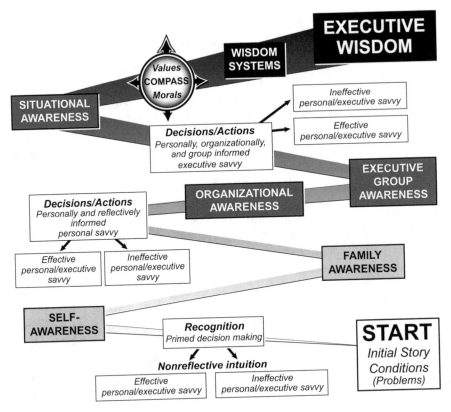

Figure 7.1. The full wisdom-mapping process.

find itself perilously close to adopting Plato's "Big Four"). Furthermore, I agree wholeheartedly, along with Socrates, Plato, Aristotle, and Confucius, that the greatest of these virtues is wisdom. I believe it is the lens through which the human experience and the challenges that all leaders face must be examined. To the extent that executives and their coaches can become better scholars and practitioners of wisdom and its various arts, they will serve their organizations and all of humanity more effectively.

Figure 7.1 shows the entire pathway that constitutes the wisdom mapping process. The final steps in the process apply situational awareness along with moral and value compasses and wisdom systems. Wisdom processes themselves were summarized in chapters 2 and 3 and can be succinctly described as involving the application of highly nuanced discernment, intuitive and analytically derived decision making, and courageous right action. When all of these components come together for a leader, then that leader becomes more likely to exercise Executive Wisdom. The absence of one or more components of the mapping process does not necessarily mean that an executive automatically cannot be wise in his or her assessments, decisions, or actions; instead, such gaps create risks that that the individual may well be overlooking something of extreme importance in the complexity of the particular situation that is being confronted or in his or her response to it. The case of Joe Beradino and his colleagues at Arthur Anderson introducing this chapter makes that point excruciatingly clear. In the presence of a profit-driven moral compass, they failed to see the risks inherent in their discernment, decisions, and actions. It cost them everything that they professionally valued.

To phrase it metaphorically, the wisdom-mapping process becomes an equivalent of the pilot's preflight checklist. Such procedural safeguards in aviation safety were developed only after research on pilot errors demonstrated that individuals with responsibility for the lives of their passengers were capable of making simple procedural mistakes that could kill and maim hundreds of people at a time. Can we truthfully say that the leaders of modern organizations have lesser responsibilities? Can we continue to watch highly effective executives like Joe Beradino and the leaders of Enron, Ken Lay and Jeffrey Skilling, literally crash their organizations and the lives of tens of thousands of employees, customers, and investors without trying to help improve their performances? Wisdom mapping has the potential to help leaders and their coaches improve their performances significantly.

ACTIVITIES TO DEVELOP LEADERSHIP AND COACHING ABILITIES: DEVELOPING A MORAL POINT OF VIEW

Imagine you are going to be interviewed for a 2- to 3-minute spot on the evening news concerning your personal and professional morals. You will be asked to give a succinct statement in front of a television audience to summarize your thoughts. In preparation for this event, please take 15 to 20 minutes and answer the following questions as best as you can. Then summarize your own individual moral point of view.

1. In what, if any, religious, ethical, or moral tradition were you raised, and what do you believe those experiences contributed to your own moral perspective?
2. Who is the person in your life who provided you with the best moral, ethical, or values guidance? Why was he or she so effective?
3. In your personal experience, who best represents someone who both has and abides by a moral- or values-based position in life? Briefly describe why you believe this is so.
4. Who is the most immoral person you personally know or have known? How did you discover the lack of morality? What did you learn from him or her?

5. What three books, plays, movies, or other sources of learning have most instructed you in moral reasoning or moral conflict? How and why did they influence you?
6. In your training as a leader or as a coach, what enables you to best identify and manage ethical values and moral issues?
7. Identify three of the most important issues or moral principles that you believe a leader should keep in mind.
8. On the basis of your answers to the above questions, please provide a brief synopsis (50–100 words) of what you believe best describes your current moral point of view.

8

REFLECTIVE ENGAGEMENT AND ADAPTIVE WORK: A MODEL AND METHODS FOR EXECUTIVE AND COACHING ACTION

The person of virtue makes the difficulty to be overcome the first business, and success only a subsequent consideration.

—Confucius

Socrates teaches that the important thing is the knowledge that one does not know.

—Gadamer (1986/1994, p. 365)

Perhaps the most visible aspect of the modern business world is the speed with which it is conducted. Formal memos and letters now take the form of e-mails. Contracts, complex budget documents, and lengthy conceptual papers are PDF files attached to the e-mails, which are sent instantly. Telephones are now kept in pockets and used in every conceivable public and private space 24 hours a day. We have created an expectation of immediacy in our dealings with each other that has produced an approach to managerial execution that I have called "fire, ready, aim." In essence, we are driven by our technologies; our accompanying business processes; the nature of the global competitive economy; and our tendency as humans to be impatient creatures, deciding and acting quickly and often without careful consideration of the consequences of what we say or do. When our intuitively guided decisions and actions are correct, we move through the world in a seemingly magical way. Everything we touch turns out well.

Every relationship seems to function smoothly. We succeed at whatever we do. When intuition fails us, disaster can strike.

As I have stated repeatedly so far, I believe the fundamental issue to focus on in the development of effective and wise leaders is how a man or woman can learn how to absorb the huge amounts of information that flow through modern organizations; focus on what is crucial to the future of the enterprise, its people, and society at large; make choices efficiently; and enact them effectively. I have come to believe that it is not speed that leads people to evolve such abilities. Instead, developing wise leaders who can act quickly and correctly depends most centrally on encouraging them to learn how to stop—even if only momentarily—and reflect carefully on what they are facing, what they are learning, what is possible for them to do, what they know and do not know and why such knowledge is present or absent, and what is wise or foolish in the various courses of action available to them. History is replete with example after example of the failures of rash action taken with no consideration of consequences. It is equally full of failed executions of carefully considered policies or strategies, because as important as these abilities are, developing the ability to reflect well does not guarantee that the results of such processes will automatically be successful.

This chapter focuses entirely on the issue of how leaders and those who coach them can both understand and use the reflective arts that I have been emphasizing throughout this book. I begin with a complex case study that I hope illustrates what the arts of reflection can accomplish when they are successfully applied. It is drawn from my consulting practice and involves an organization's senior executive team that had to make crucial decisions in the middle of an enormous crisis in order to save their company. The individuals in the case were able to make superb use of reflective methods that helped them make and enact wise choices. The chapter puts reflective practice in an appropriate historical context and succinctly provides access to and overviews of key components of the psychological and sociological literatures on how people and their organizations both reflect and take action. It presents a model of reflective engagement to guide practitioners in how they can think about these issues in their work along with a continuum of the kinds of actions that can be taken in the situations that they face.

The chapter also embeds these elements in the proposition that the central aspect of leadership work is how leaders enable their organizations and colleagues to do what Ron Heifetz (1994) called *adaptive work*. For him, the most difficult task facing executives and their coaches is how to make effective change occur for individuals, groups, and whole organizations. An effort is also made to put the case study in this conceptual context. As with the other chapters in the book, I offer at the end some practical suggestions for further developing reflective ability.

So, let us now turn to an interesting case example of how a leadership team effectively used the art of reflective engagement to guide themselves and their organization through a crisis that severely threatened their future. Because it involves a complex cast of characters in a succinct vignette, I start with a list of the principal individuals and groups who were involved in pulling this company through a trying time.

A CASE OF FOREGONE REGRET

The major players involved in this brief case example include the following:

- Alan Boseman (CEO)
- Jim Faisone, new chief operating officer (COO)
- Donna Saperstine, quality engineer in North American operations
- Tom Parkington, chairman of the board
- Alex Sanchez, influential board member
- Asian sourcing team
- Project launch team
- Research and development team
- External design experts
- Third-party sourcing consulting organization
- Asian manufacturing partners
- Advertising consultants
- The executive team: CEO, Alan Boseman; COO, Jim Faisone; Chief Financial Officer, Norman Letusky; Chief Information Officer, Linda Amundsen; and Executive Vice President for Sales and Marketing, Harriet Chen

The candle on the dinner table flickered silently between Tom, Alex, and me. The process of ordering, eating salads, and checking in with each other had drawn to a natural close. The main course was about to be served. Tom Parkington was the chairman of the board of a modest-sized, privately owned, consumer products company, and Alex Sanchez was his most experienced and knowledgeable board member. We had gathered together for the third time over a good meal to discuss their approach to what they perceived to be a threatening situation that the company had been facing. In the previous 2 years, the board had authorized their new CEO, Alan Boseman, and his executive team to spend a substantial portion of the working capital of the company to develop and bring to market a series of new products to create a fourth brand for the organization. This had been done with the enthusiastic support of everyone involved and with the goal of trying to double the size of the company over a 4-year period.

The existing product lines of the organization, although still profitable, had gotten a bit stale in design and were experiencing increased competitive pressure from both domestic and foreign companies. The leadership of the enterprise knew they had a limited period of time to respond to these threats before they faced an even more difficult set of challenges as their margins on existing products thinned. They had examined the possibility of making an acquisition in a related industry or in a completely different segment of the market and, after careful study, rejected it as being fraught with even more risk than further developing their own product line.

In the desire to create additional initial margin on their products, increase barriers to entry for competition, and preempt the competitive pressure of foreign companies, the board had required the management team to take their American marketing, design, and engineering expertise and marry it to the low-cost manufacturing infrastructure found with increasing frequency in the countries of Asia. With the full approval of the board, Alan had hired a small, new team of professionals to lead the creation of their Asian sourcing and supply chain, pulled in a superb set of design consultants to work with their own small research and development team to develop the new products, created a full-blown marketing and sales plan, and trained their experienced sales force to take the new products into existing distribution channels. Six months before our dinner, the company, with the full review and approval of the board and virtually the entire management team, had launched the new product line. The launch proved to be a major disaster for the company.

Problems had arisen early in the creation of the Asian manufacturing and sourcing team. In the haste to secure cost-effective manufacturing facilities and also check rapidly rising project costs, Alan and his executive team had decided to use a third-party company to help them create their sourcing strategy, choose a manufacturing partner, and maintain their Asian communications and decision-making infrastructure. The negotiations had gone smoothly, and the team had visited their newly acquired partners and facilities in southeast Asia early in the process. Alan made sure that the third-party sourcing company and their manufacturers were involved at each step of the design process and that the initial challenges identified in quality control and shipping were ironed out. The manufactured test samples of their new products had had many flaws, and the challenges of communicating in different languages with people from different cultures using a third-party company had been daunting. Nevertheless, Alan and his teams had persevered with patience and courage. They had kept their attention where it needed to be throughout the entire initial process. Their marketing and sales strategy had been built in conjunction with a top-tier advertising company, and they had planned the brand launch for early fall to take advantage of the holiday sales flood that so typifies the American retail market.

Throughout that process, I had been intimately involved with Alan and his executive team, coaching them as individuals and as a group. The stresses of running the company, managing their existing brands, and competing in a cutthroat market, on top of creating their new products, were extraordinary. They had created a product launch team representing all of the key organizational components involved in the new brand, and the members of that group had worked tirelessly to simultaneously do their existing jobs and to lead the new initiative. Alan provided consistent support to that launch team even as he drove them relentlessly to bring the process to a successful conclusion. Although the launch group was breathing hard and was fatigued with all of the work that it had to accomplish, its members had held themselves together; stayed focused; and, normal strains aside, seemed to be getting the job done. In the middle of the process, Alan and the board together decided that they needed to strengthen the management team, and so they conducted a search for a COO. They selected Jim Faisone, an experienced man who they thought could eventually succeed Alan, and brought him on board about 8 months prior to the brand launch.

The first hint of major trouble occurred late in the process, when one of the members of the product launch team, Donna Saperstine, a quality engineer from the company's North American manufacturing operations, made a tour of the sourcing partner's Asian offices and had gone on to visit the manufacturing facilities. In a summary meeting with the sourcing partners, Donna found herself reciting a litany of troubles she had uncovered in their operations. As it was later reported by both Donna and the sourcing partners, the meeting had started out cordially, but under Donna's incessant and determined questions and the list of problems that she had documented on her trip, the exchange grew defensive and hostile. Donna herself had told Alan when she returned that she had lost her temper, and at a subsequent meeting she went on to publicly criticize the whole project team for letting the sourcing and manufacturing activities get so out of control. At the outset of the project, Alan had known that Donna had a reputation in the company for being both defensive and abrasive at times, but he also had felt he needed to have her expertise on the team.

After lengthy consultations with the other members of the product launch team, and a face-to-face meeting including himself, Tom, and the sourcing partners in which they reviewed all of the issues on Donna's list, Alan reluctantly removed Donna from the new product team. After several extremely tense months, the entire management team then met with the board to discuss the launch. The board conducted a withering assessment, probing deeply into as many issues that they could imagine. Alan and his team performed beautifully in that board meeting. From all reports to me afterward, they answered every question and creatively responded to every challenge the members of the board threw at them. After that exhaustive review, the board members expressed their unqualified support for the leadership team's efforts, and the decision was made to proceed with the launch of the new products. The company then initiated an advertisement and sales campaign to their extensive base of established customers, took millions of dollars in orders for the holiday season, and then pushed the start buttons on the supply chain and manufacturing operations.

The first hint of trouble came out of the distribution center, a large, centralized, stateside operation in the company that reported that the products coming from Asia were being mislabeled. Alan and his team attacked that problem quickly, creating a unit to go over all of the orders as they were received in the major warehouse facility before they were shelved in preparation for working the holiday rush later in the fall. This put additional pressure on the leadership and launch teams as they traveled to and from the distribution center, worked the phones to the sourcing partners and the manufacturing facilities, and tried to figure out what was going wrong. In the background, Donna was being heard throughout the American facilities broadcasting to whoever would listen that she had told everyone this would happen.

When the time came to ship products for the holidays, the launch team had solved the labeling problem, and the new brands were sent to customers along with their traditional orders. Alan, Tom, Jim, Alex, and the rest of the company watched with deep satisfaction as the new brand caught on and their sales figures for the holiday season met their projections. They had all enjoyed a much-earned rest in the few days prior to Hannukah. They were anticipating a happy holiday party until the second day of Hannukah, when the company's customer service unit started to get a series of calls from both individual consumers and many of their corporate customers complaining about flaws in the products. After 1 day, Alan had to put extra people on the customer service lines, but they were not enough. The phone traffic got so heavy that major customers started to call their sales representatives directly. The sales reps called their managers, and they in turn called the senior vice president for sales and marketing. By the time Hannukah was over, some retail customers were pulling the products from their shelves and sending them back to the warehouse. Some of their customers simply sold the products, hoping that they could get through Christmas. Even though the sales numbers for the entire holiday season remained well within their realistic expectations, the week after Christmas proved to be an even bigger customer service nightmare. Alan and his team had to issue a revised, emergency credit policy for the products. By the 1st week of the new year, they had pulled all of the new brand products off the shelves.

Their initial assessment showed that as many as 40% of some of the batches of products had problems. The maddening thing for everyone was that there were about a dozen different flaws that were identified as they looked at the returns. Although the majority of the production runs came through without any problems and customers who bought those items reported being pleased with their purchases, the company's long-term retail partners claimed that there had been so much damage to their relationships with their own customers that they were considering pulling the traditional product lines off of their shelves as well. Managing the embarrassed anger of people who had bought the new products for holiday gifts and then had to return them for their loved ones was also exhausting their own customer service teams. That this combination of problems occurred during the most important period of the retail sales year was very threatening to the leaders of these companies because it was a situation that each of them had to explain to their own boards of directors.

Tom, Alex, and the full board had been kept up to date by Alan throughout the entire disaster. They concurred with the decisions made by Alan and his team in managing the actual crisis, but an atmosphere of tension, frustration, and suppressed anger permeated the corporation's headquarters. Alan had kept me involved after the holiday disaster and, at his request, I met with each of the individual members of the leadership team in the middle of the crisis. They were exhausted and extremely anxious and angry, and several of them reported to me privately that they had agreed with Donna Saperstine's initial assessment. When I asked them why they had not spoken up before the final decision had been made to go ahead with the product launch, several of them wept as they described their fatigue, the pressures to conform to what they saw as the launch team's desire to have a success, and their own troubles at home because of the sacrifices that they and their families had made throughout the development process. What had started out as a tremendously exciting opportunity for many of them had ended up as simply an anvil tied to their necks sinking them in an ocean of unrelenting, hyperdemanding work. In the early part of the new year, the halls of company headquarters then started to echo with whispering recriminations against Alan, the leaders of the launch team, the sourcing partners, and their Asian manufacturing facilities. The American manufacturing and supply chain folks were sitting in their offices alternating between feeling smug that the overseas sourcing and manufacturing strategy had failed and simultaneously feeling terrified that their own jobs might well be in jeopardy because of the widening retaliatory response from some of their retail customers.

I met with Alan, Jim, and Tom immediately at the end of my day with the members of the management and launch teams in the middle of the crisis. As I reported my results, none of them seemed surprised by anything I said, with the exception of the number of people who had stated in confidence to me that they had agreed with Donna's criticisms and had kept silent. On the basis of my feedback, the three of them immediately convened an emergency conference call with Alex and a couple of other members of the board while I was still there. Although it is impossible to describe in detail what happened on the call, all of the information available was reviewed, and a preliminary strategy for managing the crisis was established.

When asked what I thought they should do, I emphasized several issues. First, I told them they needed to focus on restoring customer confidence in their existing product lines and focus on making their financial numbers for the first quarter—absent the projected gains and losses related to the new brands launch. Second, I suggested that they would need to rest the staff who had been centrally involved in the development and launch processes. Many of them were the most talented, dedicated, and committed members of the company's management team, and I thought that some of the most gifted of their staff, if not given a degree of respite, would become flight risks. Finally, I encouraged them to be vigilant about the rise in levels of frustration, anger, and humiliation throughout the company. I suggested that these emotional states often lead leaders and governance members to regress into a kind of lynch mob that is satisfied only when an individual or a group is publicly held accountable for the disaster and fired. I said that given the size and relative sophistication of the senior management team of the company, taking such precipitous aggressive action seemed to me unwise and that they would be better served by concentrating on restoring order in the organization, limiting the financial damage, and then taking the time to conduct a thorough review of what had transpired.

In our first dinner meeting, about a month after I had made those recommendations, Tom, Alex, and I reviewed the situation in the company. At the time of the dinner meeting, Alex and several others on the board had started to press Tom for a vote of no confidence in Alan. Although paying lip service to my coaching regarding the deleterious effects of scapegoating their CEO, they wanted to move him out of the organization as quickly as possible and felt that they could promote Jim, the new COO, or go out to the market and get another CEO within a matter of months. At that dinner, I counseled them as much as I could to go slow with that effort, because I believed that Alan had unique knowledge of their business and industry and I knew the difficulty the company had had with finding Jim, whom they had brought in from outside of their core industry. There was also the possibility that in the middle of their business restoration efforts, signaling a change at the top might undermine their efforts.

After that dinner meeting, despite my coaching, the board subsequently did decide that it wanted a leadership change. As the chairman of the board, Tom drew the task of talking to Alan, and he asked me for advice about how to handle the conversation. Again, I counseled him to be as flexible as possible with the arrangements and to keep the change quiet initially because both Tom and many other members of the board were not sure that Jim could take over as CEO if Alan left precipitously. I also raised the concern that the business restoration effort was actually going much better than anyone had thought that it would and that Alan's knowledge of and relationships with their core customers had proved very helpful in that process. The sales force had done a remarkable job of using their long-term relationships with customers to absorb most of the shock. Alan and the rest of the organization had created finance and sales incentives to keep the existing brands moving, and the rest of the company had functioned nearly flawlessly in that first quarter, so the major impacts of the disaster were confined to the loss of business and capital from the new product launch.

Weeks later, at a second dinner, Tom and Alex reported to me that Alan had taken the news well and that they were on a path to achieve a changeover in leadership in a 6- to 12-month time frame. They had asked Jim, as the new COO, to lead an effort to examine the entire launch effort and to evaluate the performance of the launch team. In quiet conversations, they had also asked him to come up with a set of recommendations about the leadership structure of the organization. Jim had done a good job in conducting that review; had discussed his recommendations with Alan and me; and had handled himself well with Tom, Alex, and the rest of the board. Momentum was growing to make a change in CEOs sooner rather than later. We discussed the pros and cons of what they were proposing to do, and again, I urged caution and sensitivity in how they were proceeding. I suggested as strongly as I could that although Jim was performing well in the tasks that he was being assigned, he was still new to the business and the industry, and that if the board did not treat Alan appropriately they might be in a position in which they would lose Alan, Jim might leave because the board ultimately did not have enough confidence to give him the CEO job outright, and other members of the company's executive team could leave, resulting in a tremendous loss of executive talent and experience when they were still in the crisis.

The reports they provided on the business itself seemed to indicate that the sales numbers on their traditional products had stabilized and that they were back to making money. I gently but firmly encouraged the two of them to examine why they were in such a hurry to push Alan out and to consider that taking another 6 to 12 months to mentor and test Jim could prove to be most helpful to him and everyone else. I also suggested that they needed to be attentive to how they managed the public situation with Alan. I had grown to know him pretty well, and I believed that if they handled his transition with tact and sensitivity and did not publicly humiliate him that he would continue to serve the company loyally. Because I knew a lot about the leadership team itself, I also believed, but did not say, that the board's desire to change senior executives might not be the best strategy and that the company might need Alan to serve longer than the board currently believed was prudent.

My decision not to confront them was informed by a series of confidential conversations with Alan, Tom, Jim, and the other members of the executive team of the company that I had had throughout this period of time. As a result of those discussions, it became clear to me that although Jim was bringing enormous knowledge and skill to the job and that he was attacking problems with vigor and high energy, he was also proving to be difficult to work with for a variety of people. I strongly encouraged everyone with whom I talked to bring these challenges to Jim and Alan's attention, and several members of the group had been able to do this courageously.

It was clear to me from my discussions with Tom and Alex that the board felt the need to take some kind of public action in response to the failed launch out of their own concern; frustration; and, ultimately, personal embarrassment. And because most boards wisely stay out of the day-to-day management of their companies, their actions during or in response to a crisis are often constrained to how much trouble they can cause for or pressure they can put on their CEOs. Thus, knowing that the board was determined to act against Alan and simultaneously knowing that their major leadership alternative, to quickly promote Jim, would be problematic at best, I simply tried to help them apply the brakes to their propensity to act precipitously rather than either confront them directly or remain silent. In my experience, there are times when consultants must be completely candid with clients and still other times when such candor, especially if it does not support the client's thinking or decisions, can actually reduce one's influence because of the likelihood that a client can perceive such feedback as nonsupportive, politically naive, and fundamentally unwise. Knowing what not to say and when to keep silent in consulting and coaching engagements can ultimately serve to maintain the working relationship with a client and thus allow for many other opportunities to intervene when hotter emotions of the moment cool, additional data and experience are obtained, and people can open themselves to considering alternatives that they might not examine in what can be thought of as the heat of battle. In addition, in these complex coaching and consulting engagements in which a practitioner may be talking to many different people, the freedom to speak out can be significantly constrained by what is known; how that knowledge was obtained; who must be protected; and the whole complex of individual, group, and organizational dynamics that typically accompany such situations.

As our main courses were served, Tom started the business conversation with a review of the current status as he saw it. Over the last two quarters of the fiscal year, the company had gotten itself back on track with its operations budget minus what had been predicted in revenue for the new brand and the launch cost losses that would need to be realized by the end of the fiscal year. Its customers had remained loyal, and the credit and sales promotions seemed to have been effective. The staff had settled down and was working reasonably well together, even though there were still many more tensions in the group than before the new brand initiative. Tom and Alex seemed genuinely relieved and pleased with how the management team and the entire organization were performing. Then the discussion turned to the leadership situation. Tom summarized the recent developments, including the professionalism of Alan's response to his continued conversations with him about stepping down, Jim's continued energetic attention to the details of the business, and the feedback that he was getting from a variety of sources about Jim's leadership style. We discussed these issues in detail, and I was continuously mindful of having talked privately to everyone involved with the exception of Alex. I had maintained my distance from Alex because the consulting agreement I had negotiated with the company did not extend to working with board members other than Tom. Tom trusted Alex greatly and brought him in on many of his discussions, but I had no real reason to talk to him separately.

My assessment of the situation continued to be that the question of leadership succession needed to be handled cautiously, that the verdict on whether Jim could successfully lead the company during the next 5 to 10 years remained unsettled, and that the board would be most wise if it found a way to keep Alan involved with the organization at least for another year. During the conversation, Alex turned to me and asked, "Dick, what do you think of Jim? What's your take on this situation?"

I said, "As you've heard from Tom, Jim has many, many strengths. The board has asked him to do a lot in the past 6 months or so, and he has performed these tasks quite well. He has made great strides in understanding the business, its customers, the people in the organization, and the board. However, there are several areas that remain concerns. As you've heard from Tom, he seems to rub some people the wrong way. Although I think it's early yet and impossible to tell whether people in the company are just tired and raw, whether the challenges that the board have given him create natural tension between him and other folks in the organization, or whether he's a person who must grow in his interpersonal skills, I do think it could be a long-term problem if it were left unaddressed. In addition, he still lacks an in-depth understanding of the industry, and he has never had the full responsibility for competitively positioning and leading a corporation over time. With the business coming back to what can be thought of as a normal state of operations, I think the board can afford to go a little more slowly until some of these questions have clearer answers."

Alex, a businessman with enormous experience across a range of industries who had sat on the boards of a variety of other companies, took a bite of his pasta and several moments to respond.

"Now I know why you urged us several months ago to be so careful in how we managed Alan's self-respect."

I nodded at Alex, nonverbally acknowledging his recognition that my previous advice to them had been sound. Alex turned to Tom and said, "Well, at least we have an alternative if Jim doesn't work out. What do you think we should do?"

The rest of the meal and the conversation proceeded uneventfully. After talking things over thoroughly, Tom and Alex, who had a superb working relationship, quickly came to the conclusion that they would need to collect some more detailed information both about how the company and Jim were performing, delay any public announcements about leadership changes, and let the board know that they were proceeding cautiously but with all due speed. I was relieved that I had been able to intervene with them over the course of several months in a way that did not undermine their roles as leaders Alan (who as the CEO was my principal client), Jim (who was still growing as a leader), and the other members of the company's leadership team (who were also my clients). I had tried to protect the company and all of its human assets without violating any confidences or other professional standards.

I revisit this case at the end of this chapter, but first I want to make sure that readers have a firm grasp on the basic concepts and some of the historical background underlying the coaching interventions described in the above material. I have come to believe that through the work of a wide variety of scholars, we now have a strong foundation for the practice of reflection by leaders and their coaches.

THE ARTS OF REFLECTIVE ENGAGEMENT AND LEADING ADAPTIVE WORK

I cannot do justice to the intensity of emotions and the professional obligations that my involvement with the company described in this case study produced for me. Working at the top of organizations with the senior leaders as individuals and their management teams as groups requires highly nuanced judgment; the ability to contain strong emotional states; understanding of how businesses and other kinds of organizations operate, the role of governance in corporations, group and organizational dynamics, psychodynamics, macro- and microeconomics, and careful attention to professional boundaries and ethics; and many other skills. These assignments are among the most complex, challenging, and exciting coaching and consulting engagements that it is possible to obtain. Professionals who are hired for these kinds of jobs become a kind of special partner with the senior business leaders of the organization and experience directly many, if not most, of the highs, lows, and challenges of running enterprises in the modern global economy. The company described in this case study is not much different from many others in the American economy. Past success, even yesterday's success, is no guarantor of survival tomorrow. A leader can be toasted as a genius immediately following a company victory and in a matter of months become figurative "toast" that is mindlessly and heartlessly tossed into the global economic sea from the deck of the corporate ship when a small number of influential people lose faith in his or her judgment or actions.

The situation in this case was particularly difficult, because Tom and Alex both were fond of and friends with Alan. Their relationship up until the product launch disaster was superb. They saw themselves as intimate partners in the success of the business; consulted each other frequently; managed disagreements with professionalism and grace; and were completely aligned on the future of the company, their roles, and the day-to-day operations of the enterprise. To my knowledge, there had never been a period of time when they mistrusted each other or when their relationship was threatened in any way. The speed with which the governing board both lost confidence in Alan and then moved specifically to try to have him leave the company surprised me. I found myself working hard to help them consider the consequences of such rapid action, think through how they would implement this decision, and develop options that they might need to access should things not go as they initially imagined. The small comment made by Alex at dinner provided a signal to me that my efforts to slow them down, make them reflect carefully about what they proposed to do and the consequences of those actions, and protect their options had been successful as well as helpful to these men as leaders and, ultimately, to the organization. Nevertheless, I frequently felt in this process like I was standing in front of an onrushing locomotive with only the power of persuasion to try to move it onto a different track. I also knew that my work with them was in jeopardy because I was strongly identified with Alan, his team, and the process that they had used to implement the product launch. However, despite my best efforts and those of everyone involved, the launch failed and cost the organization millions of dollars. The disaster humiliated everyone involved and enraged owners, executives, customers, and many people in the company. The entire experience taught me once again how complex and difficult leading organizations and getting them to change can be.

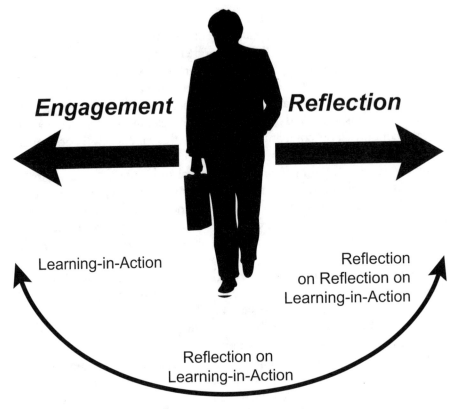

Engagement   Reflection

Learning-in-Action   Reflection
                                  on Reflection on
                                 Learning-in-Action

Reflection on
Learning-in-Action

Figure 8.1. The leader's learning and attention dance.

The Tao of Reflective Engagement

So the core question becomes how leaders and those who help them develop can increase the likelihood that they will succeed in this complex, difficult, and sometimes dangerous world that exists in modern organizations. Are there approaches in addition to wisdom mapping that can reliably improve the odds that wisdom will prevail and that folly will be avoided? Can leaders implement such approaches without the aid of coaches or consultants, and how can such professionals be even more effective when they are brought in by organizations that are facing the kind of trouble described in the case study above?

Figure 8.1 illuminates the central process that executives and their coaches can use to significantly increase the likelihood that they will discern, decide, and act wisely within the right time frames. I call it the *dance of reflective engagement*. At its core is the Taoist notion of life being composed of a complementary dynamic—for our purposes here, the yin and yang of executive and organizational (and therefore of coaching and consulting) life. In Taoist philosophy, *yin* is the force of stillness, the intuitive mind, the dark, the receptive, the earth, whereas *yang* is the light, creative heaven, reason and action. Yin has been linked to the feminine approach to life, whereas yang is seen as encompassing the masculine. The process of being involves ceaseless dynamic interaction between these complementary, even polarized, forces and processes (Legge, 1962).

The dance of reflective engagement captures the core aspects of Taoism by focusing on two intimately and dynamically related types of activity that executives and their coaches need to be able to master; they also must demonstrate superb judgment about which of them should be exercised at any given moment in the life of a leader and his or her organization. Most modern texts on leadership and executive function emphasize that the central role of executives is to take decisive and concerted action on behalf of the organization in order to have it succeed. In those terms, then, it is through the consistent implementation of action that leaders preserve and extend the well-being of their organizations.

Theories of action have been created in philosophy, economics, political science, anthropology, religion, sociology, biology, physics, and psychology. In a sense, virtually every learned discipline has been struggling for millennia to determine why things happen; why life and the universe work the way they do; why humans behave the way they do; and what, if anything, can be done about it. Theories of action abound in the academic disciplines and provide the grist for much of the discovery mill of humankind. To understand the totality of ideas and knowledge about action that have been created through the centuries would require an intimate study of each of these disciplines and of their relationships to each other. Such integrative efforts have periodically been undertaken, but nearly all of them have ended with the authors making selections from the vast menu of choices. Indeed, much of the ferment and creativity of academic pursuit comes from individuals who begin to ask questions about how the boundaries of knowledge states and disciplines relate (Kuhn, 1977).

In the last century, perhaps the foremost scholar of and advocate for a formal theory of human action was Talcott Parsons (1949), whose effort to create a general theory paralleled the rise of Einstein's (1961) general theory of relativity and the emergence of von Bertalanffy's (1968) general systems theory. The middle part of the 20th century was a time of creative ferment and grand integrating ideas. For his part, Parsons tried to pull together the various strands of utilitarian philosophy and economics, logical positivism, learning and behavioral psychology, classical sociology, and Darwinian biology. It was a breathtaking effort.

Working with a distinguished group of social scientists of their era, Parsons and Shils (1951) tried to summarize their efforts at theory-building in sociology and psychology even as they acknowledged, but did not explicitly try to include in depth, coverage of economics, political science, biology, and many of the other academic disciplines. The core of the social psychological theory of action rests on the study of individual actors or a collectivity of actors who are seen as physiological organisms that have needs and goals. They engage actions toward physical and social objects to meet their needs and reach their goals. They select strategies that enable them to pursue these actions and evaluate the effectiveness of their approaches on the basis of cognitive, appreciative, or moral standards. In Parsons's (1949) world, motivational states of actors are confined to individuals, although, as we have seen in the emergence of group theory, collectives of humans can also be said to have motives. In general, individuals and groups look to pursue gratifying experiences and avoid or reject noxious ones—in political terms, they want to make gains and avoid losses.

Individuals and collectives are also seen as pursuing strategies of adaptation to social, psychological, economic, and political realities; attain goals in the sense of political, economic, or personal objectives; maintain their own social and cultural identities; and simultaneously achieve a degree of social integration that allows them to live together in relative harmony. In this context, the human world is best thought of as pursuing a rational approach to living while simultaneously coping with the presence of the irrational, illogical, and even pathological forms of human behavior. The formal theories emerged into two different schools of thought: the theory of rational action and the theory of normative action (Joas, 1996).

Parsons's (1949) work has been extensively studied, criticized, and extended in recent years by Habermas (1981, 1987) and Joas (1996). These scholars have made an extensive effort to incorporate the empirical and theoretical contributions of communications theory and the human creativity literatures as they reviewed the conceptual developments of the early and middle parts of the 20th century. In these efforts one sees the systemic logical positivist and utilitarian approaches of Parsons extended within the postmodern frame, because Habermas and Joas both criticized the holes created in and by the original conceptual work while simultaneously acknowledging the extensive contributions made by those theories.

Psychology has also been extremely vocal in this global discussion of human action, contributing psychodynamic, psychopolitical, social, learning, developmental, cross-species comparative, and now even behavioral–genetic and psychoevolutionary views of the structures and processes underlying human action. One and only one example of a psychological approach to action theory can be seen in the work of Winter (1973), who made an effort to explore the power motive as a source of social action in society and in small groups. His studies extended to the uses of various forms of power (Kipnis, 1976); individuals having either a fear of others having power over them or the hope of exercising power for themselves; and how these behaviors expressed themselves in various forms in individuals, groups, and larger social collectives.

Cocivera and Cronshaw (2004) made an effort to integrate some of this theoretical work into a conceptual approach to executive coaching that they called *action frame theory*. The core components of their approach consist of a five-element process through which executives act and practitioners coach. The process begins with the set of conditions or constraints that exist for the executive, his or her organization, the environment in which the leader and the enterprise are functioning, and the coach who is working with him or her. The leader and the coach are thought not to have any direct control over the conditions. The second component of the process consists of the means that are available to the leader and the coach to try to influence the organization, the environment, and the conditions. These means are enablers that could be brought to bear in any action sequence and include the decisions a leader could possibly make to affect the conditions. The third aspect of the process consists of the specific actions that a leader or coach takes on a voluntary basis in the psychological, social, or physical world aimed at influencing the state of the systems with and within which they are working. In a sense, a leader or coach chooses and executes an approach from the total menu of ideas and responses (means) available in the moment. Actions produce the fourth component of the process, which Cocivera and Cronshaw labeled *results*. These outcomes can be effective or ineffective, wanted or unwanted, by the individuals or organization. They presumably are visible and at times even measurable, but this is not always the case. The final component involves evaluation, in which the impacts of the results are assessed and consideration is given to the starting conditions, means available, and actions that were taken or might be taken in response to the consideration of the evaluation. Although this action process might seem deceptively simple and perhaps even obvious, it is embedded in and takes account of more than a century of model-building and empirical examination of various theories of action.

Technical and Adaptive Work: The Yang of Executive Life

On the surface, then, the yang of executive life consists of what seems to be eternal pressure to take action. Bossidy and Charan (2002) devoted an entire book to the issue of execution in the modern business world:

> Most often today the difference between a company and its competitor is the ability to execute. If your competitors are executing better than you are, they're beating you in the here and now, and the financial markets won't wait to see if your elaborate strategy plays out. So leaders who can't execute don't get free runs anymore. Execution is the great unaddressed issue in the business world today. Its absence is the single

biggest obstacle to success and the cause of most of the disappointments that are mistakenly attributed to other causes . . . . Here is the fundamental problem: people think of execution as the tactical side of the business, something leaders delegate while they focus on the perceived "bigger" issues. This idea is completely wrong. Execution is not just tactics—it is a discipline and a system. It has to be built into a company's strategy, its goals, its culture. And the leader . . . cannot delegate its substance. (Bossidy & Charan, 2002, pp. 5–6)

Bossidy and Charan provided an interesting update of Mintzberg's (1973) classic book in which he also described the essence of managerial work as involving the perpetual demand for action rather than the more traditional ideal of the leader as reflective strategist who floats above the enterprise and sees the future path that it needs to take.

Elaborating on this core notion of the importance of execution, Heifetz (1994) and Heifetz and Linsky (2002) made the distinction between *technical work* and *adaptive work* in organizations. Technical work, which usually requires little or minimal learning, is described as involving problems for which the definition and the potential solutions, as well as who bears the responsibility for implementing them, are reasonably clear. This kind of work can be difficult, even arduous at times, for leaders, followers, and organizations. Delivering a contracted service or product, performing a complex manufacturing process, or conducting a routine audit of a major corporation can be thought of as involving technical work.

Adaptive work, on the other hand, involves problems that require learning by leaders and organizations to define the challenge and to create and implement solutions. The leader and his or her subordinates and partners share the responsibility for adaptive work. Heifetz and Linsky (2002) made it clear that adaptive work is fraught with difficulty and in many situations even physical peril. They pointed to historical examples of the leaders of nation-states who were assassinated while in office, such as Abraham Lincoln, Gandhi, and John F. Kennedy. Attempts were also made on the lives of Gerald Ford and Ronald Reagan. One only needs to read the headlines of newspapers and business magazines to see individuals who are routinely deposed from their leadership positions in government, for-profit, and not-for-profit enterprises for nonperformance, public scandals, and even criminal behavior. Heifetz and Linsky, along with Argyris (1993), suggested that when individual humans or groups of them face problems, issues, or challenges that make them anxious; have the potential for causing embarrassment; threaten to or actually create losses; require that they actually need to learn something new; or change beliefs, values, or behaviors, adaptive work is required and defensive behavior is to be expected.

The work of organizational change, market adaptation, and executive growth is therefore adaptive in nature and always difficult. Overcoming the natural tendencies toward self- and organizational protection, engaging the awkward and challenging actions leading to new and different behavior, and coping with the emotional responses of everyone involved are among the most dangerous activities a leader can undertake. I consistently maintain that the most dangerous animal on planet Earth is a human being who is extremely anxious, humiliated, and enraged. Most of the disasters in human history have started with an individual or a human group who dwelled in that emotional state. For coaches, adaptive work comprises the essential core of their engagement with leaders in organizations. In both the technical and adaptive arenas, the major difference between executives and enterprises that succeed and those that fail is how well they execute.

Heifetz (1994), Heifetz and Linsky (2002), and Argyris (1993), have provided a great many examples of organizations and individuals who confronted and either succeeded or failed at adaptive challenges. They also have provided a variety of suggestions for action steps that a leader or a coach can consider in order to improve the odds of success in taking on such problems. Heifetz specifically recommended identifying the nature of the adaptive challenge being confronted, regulating the distress that automatically comes with taking on these problems, staying focused on the nature of the problem and the steps being taken to solve it, and making sure that the work of change and of dealing with the challenges are shared extensively with others in an organization. He also discussed extensively the need for a leader to use an appropriate combination of providing challenges to subordinates while simultaneously discerning what kind and how much support they might need to complete adaptive assignments successfully. Heifetz and Linsky (2002) elaborated on these basic approaches and provide a variety of additional ideas and case examples regarding how to manage adaptive work.

In a recent book, Howard Gardner (2004) continued his efforts to extend cognitive concepts and methods to the problems of changing human behavior. He defined the core of the adaptive challenge as involving changing minds, which he described as "the situation where individuals or groups abandon the way in which they have customarily thought about an issue of importance and henceforth conceive of it in a new way" (p. 2). He identified seven factors, what could be considered in the context of this discussion as action or execution strategies, that can be used in the work of changing minds:

1. *Reason*—identifying the factors involved; weighing their importance; and arguing, including formal rhetorical exchanges and debates, for a particular approach.
2. *Research*—collecting an appropriate body of information and data relevant to the change to help assess what action steps

might be best and providing this information to individuals in ways that enable them to put it to productive use.

3. *Resonance*—accessing and using the wisdom of emotional reactions and information to help determine the feel of a change, challenge, approach, or solution and then taking appropriate action on the basis of what is discovered.

4. *Representational redescriptions*—finding different ways of thinking about, considering, or assessing the problem or issue being addressed.

5. *Resources and rewards*—providing reinforcements, recognition, or other approaches that increase the likelihood that a change will take place. Rewards can also be withheld to motivate change.

6. *Real world events*—recognizing that life happens; history, nature, fate, the actions of economies, societies, other humans over whom one has no control can power significant changes in thoughts and feelings.

7. *Resistances*—engaging the real work of changing minds involves overcoming previously developed, often cherished ways of thinking, feeling, and behaving.

Gardner (2004) examined the use of these mind-changing methods in six different arenas in which change can take place:

1. Large changes involving diverse groups and populations: nation-states.
2. Large changes with more homogeneous groups or organizations.
3. Changes stimulated through art, science, and scholarship.
4. Changes created in formal settings, such as schools.
5. Changes fermented in intimate relationships with friends and families.
6. Changing one's own mind.

Finally, Gardner (2004) used his revolutionary multimodal framework for human intelligence to examine just how different approaches can enable change in these different venues. These forms of intelligence can be used by leaders in their efforts to formulate strategic approaches to adaptive and technical work. The primary forms that Gardner described in his framework are linguistic, logical–mathematical, musical, spatial, bodily–kinesthetic, naturalistic, interpersonal, and existential intelligences. He suggested that they can be used independently or in various sophisticated combinations to create the means and the actions—in Cocivera and Cronshaw's (2004) terms, to change human minds. Within Heifetz's (1994) framework of adaptive and technical work, such mind-changing technologies can be thought of as major tools that leaders must master.

Leading Adaptive Work: A Continuum of Methods

Figure 8.2 provides a framework for conceptualizing a continuum of strategies and methods that leaders can use for managing adaptive work. At one end of the continuum lies the position in which an executive is in complete denial that such work must be undertaken and therefore no decisions are made and no actions taken. However, in the paradoxical world of leadership no decision is a decision, and no action is action. To put it affirmatively, every behavior of a leader is an act of social construction, even those behaviors in which he or she simply sits and observes or even ignores what is occurring. As Bossidy and Charan (2002) described, all too often in executive life it is the lack of appropriate and timely action that brings about the downfall of leaders and their organizations.

Confrontation anchors the other end of the continuum. In its extreme form, this can take the shape of overt or covert acts of war. Examples of

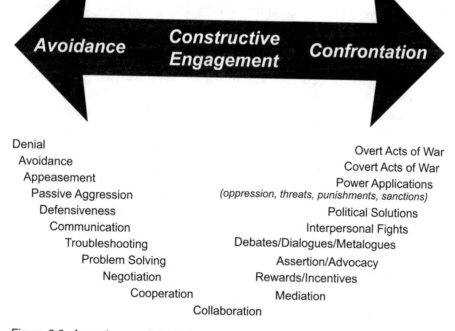

Figure 8.2. A continuum of strategies and methods for managing adaptive work.

this can be seen throughout history and reflect von Clausewitz's (1896/ 1986) view that war represents the extension of the policies of a nation-state by means other than negotiated agreements, economic exchanges, and diplomatic relationships. Threats, promises, sanctions, and oppression of various sorts are other forms of confrontation, just as appeasement and passive aggressive and defensive responses are alternative approaches to avoidance. The heart of the continuum comprises the arts of constructive engagement, in which leaders do not deny or avoid adaptive work but move assertively with a variety of tools to try to do what is necessary to create the required changes. Communications, troubleshooting, negotiations, cooperation, collaboration, mediation, building reward and incentive systems, engaging in debates and dialogues, and applying political strategies and approaches are all examples of the technical means and actions that leaders can use to address the challenges of adaptive work. Executives, if they are to be consistently wise, must—I repeat, must—have the sophistication to diagnose the situations that they face, take the appropriate decisions, and then execute the right actions in the right way and within the right time frames. Making the determination of when and how to fight, when and how to negotiate, and when and how to leave a situation alone and being able to implement effectively such decisions represents the essential core of leadership work.

The Reflective Arts and Adaptive Work: The Yin of Executive Life

The other dimension of leadership work presented in Figure 8.1 involves developing and using the arts of reflection, which is the core of the wisdom mapping process discussed in the last several chapters. If effective engagement represents the active mind, the yang of executive action, then its complementary partner is the more passive, observing mind, the yin of executive reflection—in psychodynamic terms, the experiencing and observing egos of the leader. The figure also depicts the three forms of reflection identified by Schön (1987): (a) learning-in-action, (b) reflection on learning-in-action, and (c) reflection on reflection on learning-in-action. Schön (1987) and Argyris (1993) have argued that leaders are almost always in some form of reflective state. For executives, learning-in-action consists of that persistent frame of mind that accompanies virtually every form of human behavior. It is a state of doing an activity while simultaneously watching that process. As that dynamic interaction takes place, humans engage in a sometimes obvious but often subtle mental, emotional, and behavioral exchange in which an action is taken, the effects are observed, and modifications are made in the activity, sometimes without conscious intervention. These forms of reflective action are most often seen in over-learned sequences of behavior such as typing, riding a bike, conducting the opening part of a routine staff meeting, or driving a car. At any point in such a sequence, a person can become consciously aware of what he or she is doing and make significant modifications. Most often, there is a quiet, well-schooled part of the mind that watches what is happening and makes micro adjustments as needed in the moment to keep the activity going in a normal way. However, action in these situations is rarely completely interrupted.

In the middle of the continuum of reflective engagement rests the process that Schön (1987) called *reflection on learning-in-action*. As the label suggests, in this form of reflection a person steps further back from the activity or action as it is occurring or has recently occurred and tries to assess how well it is going or has gone. Again, this kind of reflection can be largely unconscious, as can be seen in a simple comment, like "That was a good meeting" or "That did not go well," as a leader thinks about an event during a busy day. In more formal situations, such as strategy retreats or quality review meetings, this level of reflection is engaged deliberately to examine carefully what is going on in the daily life and actions of a leader, leadership team, or organizational unit to make determinations of effectiveness and, in Heifetz's (1994) and Gardner's (2004) senses, determine whether adaptive work is needed or if there are minds to change. Often, data are evaluated, even if this involves only replaying mentally what recently happened in events like a meeting, a sales promotion, or an effort to refinance part of a corporation's infrastructure. Mentally and emotionally, reflection on learning-in-action involves being able to see the acts as physical or mental objects of which a leader can develop mental models and then operate on and imagine just how they can be changed. For a more detailed consideration of this representational process, review chapter 3.

At the far end of the continuum rests the most complex level of reflection imagined by Schön (1987), which he called *reflection on reflection on learning-in-action*. Problems with the complexity of labeling this phenomenon aside, this is an elaborate mental and emotional process that requires a leader and his or her coach to actually see, hear, imagine, and otherwise sense what is happening when the act of reflection on learning-in-action is taking place. Once that perception or discernment occurs, it becomes available for the executive and coach to examine and to question; in its most sophisticated forms, it serves as a basis on which to create mental simulations and experiments. It consists of being able to ask questions such as the following:

> Just how well did we evaluate that strategy or activity? What did we miss? What conclusions did we draw? Did our approach cloud our assessment? Are we about to embark on a new course of action based on our careful assessment that is fundamentally flawed because of errors in how we created our mental models, assessed the data we had available, and evaluated the effectiveness of our own actions?

In the context of a metacognitive understanding of Executive Wisdom, this third order of reflection involves building and examining models of the models we construct of reality and models of how we construct those models themselves. Such assessments, when they can be done, allow for highly detailed and careful considerations not only of what has been or might be done by a leader but also of how he or she is coming to think and decide what to do. Such mental activity enables someone to address questions such as, "How do I know what I know? Why do I know what I know? What don't I know? Why don't I know what I don't know?" In the hurly-burly, hustle-bustle, nearly frantic world of leaders, making time for such higher order reflection is difficult, and many leaders have neither the patience nor the skill to practice such an art. Nevertheless, such reflective processes often mean the difference between how well a leader learns and therefore executes and, as a result, performs.

Reflective knowledge and skill are key components in any leader's efforts to consistently discern, decide, and act wisely. Without reflective skills it is possible for an executive to act wisely in a given situation. With reflective skills, it is much more possible for an executive to repeat deliberately the process of acting wisely. Executive development activities, including coaching, not only need to be geared to helping leaders learn to take effective actions but also must provide opportunities for them to develop the ability to reflect on the actions that they take.

Schön (1983, 1987) has called this process *reflective practice* and the results of professional training as producing *reflective practitioners*. His research and teaching speak directly to the central conundrum of leadership, which is how a person can learn how to be a better executive while being completely immersed in the swirling, confusing, and sometimes terrifying actions that they are always being pushed, prodded, and otherwise drawn to take. Heifetz and Linsky (2002) and Heifetz (1994) used a different term and metaphor to describe the same process. They called it "getting on the balcony," and they suggested that leadership is very much like a dance to which an individual becomes completely committed, but in that process of commitment he or she loses perspective for what is happening on the entire dance floor. These authors suggested that leaders must disengage from the act of dancing in and with their organizations and retreat to a balcony from which they can observe what is happening on the whole floor. Once they have a different; more nuanced and complex; and therefore, one would hope, more accurate, understanding, they can return to the dance with a renewed sense of intelligently informed strategy. Heifetz and Linsky suggested that this ability "to get perspective in the middle of action" (p. 51) has an intellectual and practice history going back to the Buddhist and Hindu traditions of "karma yoga" or mindful meditation. Any decent reading of the history of human thought and contemplative practice readily reveals just how deeply some of the greatest human minds have considered this subject.

In a more recent treatment of the same subject in the context of creating practitioners of care, Polkinghorne (2004) emphasized the Aristotelian foundations of thought that specified *techne* and *phronesis*, which I briefly described in chapter 2. *Techne* involves "knowledge about how nature operates . . . the art of applying human intelligence to control nature" (Polkinghorne, 2004, pp. 99–100). *Phronesis*, on the other hand, "is the excellence by which one deliberates well about what to do in the human realm" (Polkinghorne, 2004, p. 111). In these definitions one can again clearly see a reprise of the fundamental philosophical roots of the effort in this book to define and elaborate on the phenomenon of Executive Wisdom. Polkinghorne deepened his approach to both conceptualizing and training practitioners of care by relying on Gadamer's (1960/1975) description of *reflective understanding*.

Polkinghorne (2004) described reasoning based on reflective understanding as involving

> a dialogic engagement with a situation in which a practice is being carried out. It results in an increased understanding of the unfolding situation. From this enlarged understanding, other possible actions become apparent. The reflective–understanding mode of practice fits best with human situations in which practitioners of care make action choices. (p. 163)

He contrasted this approach with *technical–rational reasoning*, which "calls for the use of conscious, deductive thought to determine correct practices. Through the technical–rational mode, one arrives at decisions about practical actions by employing inference to move from scientifically validated knowledge statements to conclusions about what to do" (p. 163). From this foundation, Polkinghorne then added a summary of a four-step process that Gadamer (1986/1994) suggested as a pathway for creating reflective understanding:

a. A problem occurs within a practice;
b. one questions the prior understanding of the situation;
c. new understandings are considered and deliberated about; and
d. a new understanding is appropriated and serves to inform practice. (Polkinghorne, 2004, p. 164)

Most important, both Polkinghorne (2004) and Gadamer (1986/1994) emphasized that this entire process rests on one of the fundamental principles introduced by Socrates, *docta ignorantia*. The literal translation of the Latin is "he knows that he does not know" (quoted in Polkinghorne, 2004, p. 164). Regarding this principle, Gadamer (1986/1994) wrote the following:

Recognizing that an object is different, and not as we first thought, obviously presupposes the question whether it was this or that. From a logical point of view, the openness essential to experience is precisely the openness of being either this or that. It has the structure of the question . . . the knowledge of not knowing. This is the famous Socratic *docta ignorantia* which amid the most extreme negativity of doubt, opens up the way to true superiority of questioning. (p. 362)

It is thus easy to see the parallels between what Polkinghorne (2004) proposed as the mental foundations for the practice of care and what I have proposed here as the arts of reflective engagement that must be used by leaders in organizations. He also relied heavily on Schön's (1987) ideas and methods for educating reflective practitioners in industries as diverse as music, architecture, and psychotherapy. One can also see the direct parallels between what Polkinghorne suggested for practitioners of care with what Fowers (2005) called for in helping people develop virtuous characters through which they pursue what is good in life and what is good for humanity as a whole. I firmly believe that these basic philosophical, psychological, and educational principles can be applied equally well by executives as they do their work and by the individuals who help to develop them. Thus, the art of reflection, of engaging fundamental doubt, of pursuing a rigorous inquiry of what they do not know and why they do not know what they do not know, constitutes the Taoist, fundamental opposite to what is ordinarily described as the essential component of successful leadership, namely, the art of action. In the language of the Tao, successful leaders must be trained rigorously in both if they are to serve their organizations well. In becoming masters of reflective engagement, executives will take many positive steps toward developing more virtuous characters and, through those processes, become ever more likely to find the right things to do and the right ways to do them in and for their organizations.

A Short Historical Review of Human Reflective Practices

According to the best anthropological, archeological, and historical information currently available, *Homo sapiens* as a separate species evolved on the continent of Africa some 7 million years ago (Diamond, 1999). For what is as yet an unknown reason, our distant ancestors began a massive diaspora to the Middle East and Europe approximately 1 million years ago. There is evidence that by the year 2000 B.C., *Homo sapiens* had colonized every land mass on the planet save Antarctica. That same scientific record documents the systematic development and use of tools by *Homo sapiens* approximately 400,000 years ago. There is evidence of religious ritual in the burial practices of known tribes of our ancestors 200,000 years ago, and the rise of representational art in the form of cave drawings and artistic carvings began approximately 40,000 years ago.

As rapid and fantastic as these developments were in our species' history, the real race for civilization started in the first agricultural settlements in Mesopotamia and southeastern China at approximately 11,000 B.C. Diamond (1999) and others have suggested that the rise of agriculture allowed for time for the specialization of work, which in turn pushed the evolution of knowledge and technology. Villages gave rise to cities, and evidence for the art of writing has been documented as far back as 5000 B.C. in the Middle East as well as in South America. Similarly, mathematics seems to have started at about 4000 B.C. in Egypt and Babylon, and formal philosophy rose in China, Mesopotamia, and Greece between 1200 and 400 B.C.

Looking back on that breathtaking pace of development of the species and therefore the human mind, we can trace the formal rise of reflective cognitive capacity at least to the creation of tools some 400,000 years ago. It is easy to imagine primitive humans with stones in their hands experiencing learning-in-action for the first time as they perceived the effects of using them for various purposes. The first human to actually approach and try to understand fire must have been one courageous and smart person.

For 97% of the time between the age of stone tools and the development of agriculture, our human ancestors were hunters and gatherers. However, once *Homo sapiens* invented writing, mathematics, and philosophy, it took us only 7,000 years to land on the moon, create nuclear power plants, and develop string theory. I insert this extraordinarily brief history to make a point. I believe it has been the evolution of the reflective capacity of the mind of *Homo sapiens* that, in the end, accounts for all that we have accomplished. Tools to religion to art took approximately 360,000 years. Art to agriculture took 30,000 years. Agriculture to writing and mathematics took 5,000 years. Math to philosophy and formal education took a little less than 2,000 years. With philosophy and education, we then see the rise of Chinese, Greek, Egyptian, and Persian culture, and the formal written history of humankind and of leadership development began. It is a breathtaking and awe-inspiring pace of invention.

Within this relatively recent history of the evolution of reflective states of mind one can trace early roots in the Jewish tradition of *teshuvah* (Agnon, 1948), which began after they escaped their enslavement from the Egyptians. During approximately 1250 to 1200 B.C., after Moses descended from Mount Sinai with the tablets of commandments, the Jews as a people and as a tribe of humans created a religious tradition in which they retreated for a day and reflected on their history, their deliverance, and their relationships to God and to each other. Their collective reflective practice continues today on the holiday of Yom Kippur, when they gather to remember and ponder their culture and collective spiritual life. Such collective reflective practice has been extended to many other religions. It has been routine for 4,000 years or more for large groups of *Homo sapiens* to collect together in a church, synagogue, mosque, or physical equivalent to ponder the nature of human existence, questions of moral rightness, the will of God, and the future of the species. Today, every Saturday and Sunday throughout the world billions of people gather to enact these same traditions and rituals.

In China, perhaps the most convincing evidence for the emergence and consistent practice of reflective states of mind can be found in the *Analects of Confucius* (Waley, 1989). Confucius, the ancient genius and master developer of executive talent, lived between 551 and 479 B.C. As described earlier, his ideas about the nature of leadership and how to live a virtuous life continue to inform much of the daily living in the Eastern world of humanity today. Confucius was a contemporary of Buddha, who lived from 563 to 483 B.C. and established an approach to human living based on mindfulness meditation (Hanh, 1975; Langer, 1989; Newman, 1996). Buddhist thought, reflective practices, and moral traditions have now penetrated every continent of the human world. Mindfulness approaches have also made their way into the mainstream of psychological interventions for a wide variety of disorders (Bishop et al., 2004; Hayes & Feldman, 2004).

Socrates (470–399 B.C.), Aristotle (384–322 B.C.), and the other Greek philosophers took up where Confucius and Buddha left off, establishing schools for the education of leaders, pushing the envelopes of reason and science, and creating much of the foundation for Western thought. Overholser (1993) systematically applied the core approaches of Socratic reasoning to the work of psychotherapy and demonstrated that the Greek master's approach to rational investigation can in fact be seen as supporting much of what happens in psychological approaches to behavioral change. Nozick (1997) provided an interesting set of puzzles and problems designed to help readers develop their ability to reason with the Socratic method.

The traditions of the Greek philosophers were taken up by the Romans, which in turn led to the establishment of Christian forms of reflective practice. One of the largest single steps taken early in that religion is represented in the *Confessions* of St. Augustine (Pusey, 2003), in which he documented his agonizing review of the life he had lived in pagan Rome and, through the acts of contemplative reflection, his turn toward Christianity and the foundation of the society of reflective Augustinians. Mottolo (1989) documented the later but equally influential meditative practices of St. Ignatius, the founder of the Jesuits, who brought an even more rigorous discipline to spiritual reflection that is still being enacted in the schools, churches, and retreat centers operated by that religious order.

The initial studies of modern psychology in the laboratory of Wilhelm Wundt were based in what was then a new "scientific" methodology of introspection and led to his fundamental theories of the human mind (Boring, 1950; Watson, 1963). For Wundt, psychology began with scientifically conducted introspection, and it led to his laws of mental association. In his theory of actuality, he stated that "the mind, as actual, is immediately phenomenal and is thus not substantial" (Boring, 1950, p. 335), which, when one carefully considers that statement, predates and predicts many of the rather extensive findings of modern cognitive psychology by a century. Wundt went on to demonstrate how thoughts formed, related, and changed each other in his principles of association, fusion, assimilation, and complication. His association work provided a scientific base for the practices of Freud's psychoanalysis and continuing inspiration for successive generations of psychologists interested in just how the human mind works.

Reflective practices and the nature of thinking itself have informed and tremendously influenced the rise of 20th-century concepts of education. Beginning with Dewey's (1910) examination of how humans think, educational researchers and practitioners have continuously pushed for deeper understanding of these processes and for the application of this knowledge to classroom instruction. Kolb (1984), Mezirow and Associates (1990), and Schunk and Zimmerman (1998) have provided specific examinations of modern methods of reflection that they recommend to assist students with the acquisition of knowledge and to learn the essential processes of thinking.

M. Snyder (1974, 1979), Graziano and Bryant (1998), and a large number of other social psychologists have thoroughly demonstrated that both children and adults routinely engage in self-monitoring activity. In essence, they perceive and reflect on the ways in which they express themselves and how they present themselves. They try to observe and control how they think and feel and how they display the results of those internal states to others. The research demonstrates at least two prototypical approaches to self-monitoring and self-control. The *high self-monitor* appears to be guided by the question, "What does the situation want me to be, and how can I be that person?" The *low self-monitor*, on the other hand, asks, "Who am I, and how can I be me in this situation?" These forms of internal mental processes and their influences on social behavior thus appear to be constants in human behavior and have been consistently documented in empirical studies.

Efforts to enable practitioners of management to think, learn, and act in real-time situations with the capacity for critical, creative, and reflective imagination were documented by Burgoyne and Reynolds (1997). In this extremely interesting and comprehensive set of collected papers, they made a significant effort to summarize and critically examine what is known about how managers learn and how those who help them develop conduct those processes. Throughout these papers there are many explicit expositions of the value of and methodological approaches to the reflective enablement of managerial learning and practice.

In his summation contribution in that volume, Reynolds (1997) strongly suggested that managerial pedagogy must be tied to developments in 20th-century critical theory and that those ideas create three levels of reflective practice within which managerial development efforts can and should be examined. In the first level, which he called the *instrumental* mode of reflection, knowledge that is assumed to be objective and value free is unleashed to help practitioners and educators control their environments and to create solutions to real problems. He identified the second as the *consensual* mode of reflection, through which people identify the values and assumptions that form the foundation of their beliefs and behaviors. They jointly engage in this type of reflection to try to ensure that the individuals engaged in any organized effort properly align their own attitudes and approaches with what they and their colleagues are trying to accomplish together. The third and final level is the *critical* mode of reflection, in which participants in any activity question their core assumptions about practice, their organization, and their environments. In these challenging acts of learning, individuals and groups are expected to examine the purposes, conflicts, individual and group motivations, and effects of their organized efforts on their environments, thus putting managerial learning and practice in larger social, political, economic, and even spiritual contexts (Reynolds, 1997, p. 314).

Reynolds (1997) went on to suggest that managerial development itself must create and enact the capacity to be self-examining and self-challenging. Quoting Reed and Anthony (1992), he suggested that management education itself must rest on three critical pillars:

> First, . . . it must be focused on how managers must negotiate the actual rather than abstract realities of organizational order.

> Second, . . . management practice is fundamentally about moral issues and ethical examinations of them as they are manifested in organizational realities.

> Third, . . . management education must develop "critical and skeptical responses." (Reynolds, 1997, p. 323)

Thus, both Reynolds (1997) and Reed and Anthony (1992) can be viewed as extending the work of Schön to managerial education and as strong proponents of this complementarity-focused, morally grounded, reflective engagement approach to the practice of leadership and the development of its performing artists.

Methods of Active and Proactive Reflection: Tools for Developing Leaders

These lines of educational and managerial research and practice have been explicitly tied to scientific efforts to assess how executive and management development programs can be systematically improved. Siebert and Daudelin (1999) conducted a set of experiments that examined the specific impact of including what they called *active* and *proactive* reflective practices in educational programs for managers. In the monograph in which they presented their studies, they provided a very interesting and fairly thorough summary of the roots of reflective practices. They then went on to describe active reflection as taking place during actual development experiences and to provide a process map that emphasizes the activation of the curiosity of the learning leader to inquire about the nature of the work being done and the interpretation of the learning that is taking place about that work. During active reflection, five types of questions are systematically raised and the responses thoroughly examined while the individual is actually involved in the development activity. They describe questions of fact, function, approach, purpose, and self. Through this form of reflection, students of leadership come to develop deeper understanding of and competency in the practice of management while simultaneously pushing forward just how their concepts of themselves as leaders need to change to accommodate the learning.

In proactive reflection, Siebert and Daudelin (1999) outlined different processes that can be applied to development experiences after they have taken place. They reported a study that compared three forms of reflective examination: (a) a leaderless group debriefing, (b) a telephone interview with someone who conducted more or less a structured inquiry, and (c) a mentor-led group investigation of development experiences. They identified a four-phase process for the reflective exercise: (a) identification of the problem, (b) analysis of the challenge, (c) formulation of a working theory of the problem, and (d) identification of actions to be taken in the future. They focused their analysis of the problem through the use of what they call their "seven questions":

1. What happened (what did you see, what were you feeling, what was the most important thing)?
2. What is the fundamental likeness of this problem or challenge to others?
3. What is the fundamental difference?
4. Why was that significant to you?
5. Why do you think it happened?

6. How can you do it differently next time for different results?
7. How can you use this information? (What concepts and principles will guide your future approach?). (Siebert & Daudelin, 1999, p. 148)

In this inquiry-based methodology, "what" questions are followed by "why" questions. The process ends with "how" questions focused on the issues of performance improvement and learning. For these scientific practitioners, questions form the heart of reflective approaches to executive development.

The results of Siebert and Daudelin's (1999) studies strongly suggest that reflectively grounded development efforts yield better educational results for leaders. Their results also suggest that more structured reflective efforts using both the leaders in development and mentors or people who can use an interview guide produced systematically better results in the form of higher rates of reported lessons learned by the participants in the experiments. Thus, in the results of their studies, we are beginning to see the emergence of an empirical literature that provides support for using explicitly reflective approaches in leadership development initiatives.

Conclusions and Applications of the Reflective Arts in the Case of Foregone Regret

What can be concluded from this succinct overview of the literatures on action and reflection as applied to the model of reflective engagement that I, along with a number of others, am suggesting is the necessary foundation for effective executive and coaching practice? The first and obvious point is that many of the finest minds in human history have been wrestling with these issues and have more or less reached the same conclusion. People learn best when they both do things and then think systematically about what they did, what happened, why those things took place, and how future actions could be different based on the experiences. Objective, scientific evidence coexists along with the explicit and tacit knowledge of philosophy and religious practices that reinforces the fact that this is the case. Second, neither systematic action nor systematic reflection alone are sufficient to yield the best results. Both are necessary, and in different forms, if executive learning and practice are to reach the highest possible levels of performance. Third, the emergence of executive coaching as a specific subdiscipline of the field of consultation, although resting on a thin, explicit foundation of scientifically designed and executed outcome studies, actually has much broader and deeper historic roots to which its practitioners can turn for both inspiration and practical suggestions. Fourth, effective leadership and effective coaching of leaders must rest on a foundation of doubt, on a willingness to admit that everything is not already known, and on the determined ability to engage in processes of systematic inquiry to reduce human ignorance. Finally, any executive who wants to increase the likelihood that he or she will do a good job for an organization and become an increasingly wise leader over time must become superbly adept at both the arts of execution and the arts of reflection. It is in the systematic and creative synthesis of both of these forms of executive activity that the wisest answers and actions will be found for the dilemmas facing most modern organizations.

Returning to the case study that opened this chapter, I can illustrate this model of reflective engagement somewhat more concretely. The immediate crisis that faced this company was based on an expensive set of mistakes that it made in the launch of a new product. Although new products and services fail in the global market every day, and their effects are often chronicled in the mass and academic media (Hartley, 2003), these reports seldom do justice to the complexities involved in managing them. Boards of directors in the early part of this new century are under tremendously increased scrutiny and pressure to take rapid, protective action on behalf of owners, government, and other stakeholders. In addition, the speed of business enabled by modern telecommunications, computers, and transportation systems has increased tremendously along with corresponding expectations for the performance of businesses. The results are an enormous increase in the preference for executives to take effective action and in a predisposition to act with extraordinary swiftness both by leaders inside of their organizations and by enterprises out in their competitive environments. This has in turn reduced the time, energy, and other resources available for reflection in the lives of executives, and that has led to the "fire, ready, aim" approach to leadership and management I described at the beginning of this chapter. Confirming evidence for this observation comes from the experience I have often had in which executive clients admit somewhat sheepishly that the time they spend in their coaching sessions with me is the only place in their professional lives in which they truly have the opportunity to think about what they are doing and why.

As I look back on the series of dinners, phone calls, and e-mails that I exchanged with this client organization during and immediately after its crisis, I can see several major forces in action. The board and the executive team knew that to save their business, they had to discern the situation they faced, make critical choices quickly, and execute those choices with ruthless efficiency. This was all well and good and appropriate to stem the losses from the failed product launch. However, the board then extended their action orientation to the question of leadership of the organization and, in the legitimate desire to make sure that their enterprise was in the right executive hands, they moved to undercut their chief executive. They did this despite not having a truly viable alternative executive who was immediately prepared to step into the job—leadership succession is another largely unseen and unmanaged crisis in most organizations. As a result, they destabilized their existing leader and loaded additional responsibilities on the person whom they were getting ready to take over that job, and then, not surprisingly, they encountered performance problems in their leader-to-be.

My efforts with them were focused almost entirely on trying to enable them to be more reflective about what they were trying to do. Coaches and consultants can take various stances with their clients, and my own strong preference is to avoid providing explicit prescriptions for action. Although I will often talk to clients about things that they could do and actions that I would be inclined to take if I had leadership responsibility in the situation, I always do so against the backdrop of reflectively examining the situations they are in and the various responses they can make to them. In this case, at our third dinner, Tom and Alex clearly acknowledged in quiet ways that my efforts had indeed slowed them down, made them more reflective, and caused them to act in ways that protected their future options and that they could see what I had tried to do with them and why.

For me, however brief, such a conscious and deliberate acknowledgement of my coaching work was an extraordinary moment and one that explicitly illustrates the value of reflective engagement. These men wanted and absolutely needed to take action in and on their company. The call to immediate action in the form of fighting a major organizational conflagration was clear and nearly terrifying in its ramifications. However, if they had simply been guided by their propensity to act, they may well have made their intermediate and longer term problems worse in the legitimate desire to take quick and decisive action to put out their fires. A series of reflective engagements with me were sufficient to help them discern and decide on a wiser course of action. They created a variety of new and positive leadership and organizational options for themselves because they reflected on the why and how of what they had done and could do to solve their problems. This, then, illustrates the pure essence of both reflective engagement as a key component of leadership and coaching practice and just how it can enable the emergence and advancement of Executive Wisdom in the heat of commercial battle. In my experience, when leaders can force themselves to take the time to balance the need to act with carefully measured and crafted reflection, they are much more likely to play "ready, aim, fire" and thus to hit the competitive targets at which they are aimed.

ACTIVITIES TO DEVELOP LEADERSHIP
AND COACHING ABILITIES

Questions for Constructionist Inquiry

Social constructionism has several core assumptions, including the following:

- Humans build their representations of the world and their interactions with it through a process of cocreative discourse or dialogue, and the process of doing so is a game with its own rules, structures, processes, and contents.
- Meaning is created by humans during the process of dialogue, and such meanings help the participants to understand, interact with, and have effects on the world around them.
- Ultimately, meaning is reduced to language, constructed of words. The words are the pieces of the game of dialogue, the game of creating meaning.
- Dialogues can privilege and grant power to certain players, concepts, rules, structures, processes, and contents. Dialogues can also withdraw privilege and power.
- Humans are well served by both understanding how such dialogues are created and the effects they have.

One way of learning to see the social construction of reality is to learn to conduct inquiries and ask questions that illuminate the underlying game within the words of a dialogue. What follows are some questions and ways of asking questions that may help you as a leader or, if you are coaching a client, deconstruct the representations of the world as it is being presented or experienced. Describe a challenge, problem, or opportunity that you face in your organization or have your client do so. If possible and desirable, record the description. Then reexamine that description using the framework and a number of the questions that are provided below.

- Assume the words being used are parts of a game. Your job is to use the words to understand the game that is being played—that is, constructed—by the client and the actors with whom the client is currently or historically has been engaged.
- Assume the words are "binaries" consisting of "the words" and "the not words" and immediately begin to observe the meaning of the words that are present and the words that are not present.
- As you listen and explore, ask yourself for whom these words and meanings create power and privilege. Also ask yourself

whom these words and meanings disempower and from whom they remove privilege.

- As you listen and explore, ask yourself if there are alternative ways of describing the person, situation, problem, group, organization, and why they have not been considered or considered and rejected.

Here are some other questions you can ask:

- Am I [are you], aware of lenses, filters, biases, attitudes, beliefs, values, experiences, attachments that are affecting the choice of words and meaning I [you] are making?
- What do I [you] stand to gain by the use of these words, selection of this meaning in this situation?
- What do I [you] stand to lose by the use of these words, selection of this meaning in this situation?
- What do I [you] value? Hold fast to?
- What do I [you] devalue? Abandon?
- What is worth doing? Not worth doing? Why?
- What is the origin of my [your] ideas? Why do you choose to insert them now? What are you not choosing to insert? Why? What do these choices have to do with power and privilege?
- What are your favored vocabularies? From where do they originate? What power and privilege do they create/suppress/destroy?
- How do you know if you are or your client is telling the truth?
- Who sets and enforces the rules in this relationship? Why? Who gains? Who loses?
- Will I [you] hurt/help you [me]?
- How can I understand and portray your inner experience accurately?
- What pictures, metaphors, values, ideas, interests, needs, wants, beliefs, attitudes, dimensions of diversity, and so on, are my [your] words conveying? Why? What is not being conveyed? Why?
- What have I [you] left out of the description?
- What patterns of action do these words lead us to, and why? What patterns of action are suppressed or avoided, and why?
- Are the assumptions underlying this dialogue based on Darwinian individualism or communalism? Why? With what consequences?
- Are the assumptions underlying this dialogue based on cocreating communal constructionism? Why? With what consequences?
- What is behind my [your] mask? What am I [are you] hiding?

- How can we rely on each other?
- What do I [you] truly think, feel, desire, need, fear?
- What would make me [you] feel safe, joyful, angry, sad, humiliated, unsafe, peaceful, proud, curious, bored, and so on?
- What do I [you] gain or lose in this situation?
- From whom or what did I [you] learn the best and worst lessons?
- What are the most memorable dialogues you have ever had? Why were they so important and useful?
- What dialogues do you wish you would have had?
- What was the most important, useful, hurtful, kind, loving, hateful, useless thing someone ever said to or about you? Did to you? Why was this so?
- What was the most important, useful, hurtful, kind, loving, hateful, useless thing that you ever said to or about someone? Did to someone? Why was this so?
- How do you [does the client] perform curiosity, fear, joy, anger, shame, guilt, sadness, surprise, sadness, sex? How would a stranger know you [he or she] was performing this?
- How do you [does this group, this organization] think? Act? Why? What is the history of this pattern? What are your vocabularies of thinking and action?
- Who have you [has the leader] invited to the table in this situation? What is on the table?
- Are there words, subjects, ideas, and feelings that are not spoken, under the table?
- How do we understand each other?
- Can I [you/we] create an imaginary moment and invent meaning for and in it?
- Who is the author of your story? What are its most important chapters?
- Can I [you/we] speak deliberately with the voices of others not here?
- Are you curious about the stories of others?
- What is the best or worst way to challenge you? For you to challenge me?
- Are there areas of uncertainty, things about which I [you/we/they] lack confidence?
- Can I [you/we/they] suspend the preferred way of seeing and interpreting the world?
- Can I [you/we/they] see and interpret the world in a different way?
- Are you working to expand your "repertoire of descriptions?"
- Are you as a coach listening hard for your client's vocabularies of meaning?

- Is your client listening, getting, willing to act on the vocabularies of meaning that you have shared?
- What resources do you need to solve this problem?
- Can you come together with someone else to create a solution to this problem?
- Can you separate the problem from yourself? Create a more objective view of what has happened?
- Do you [does your client] have a "consciousness of construction?" Are you able to witness your own acts of meaning making, reflect on them, change them deliberately, change them as you speak?
- Can you locate or create a different voice inside you with regard to your perspective on this problem or situation?
- Are there voices of internalized others inside of you that influence how you think, feel, act in these situations?
- How does your family, group, or organization make meaning? What vocabularies of meaning making are favored? Are suppressed?
- How do you [does your family, group, organization] test the reality of your meaning-making?
- Do you see problems and issues as a sickness that needs a cure, things that are broken and need to be fixed, puzzles that need solutions, challenges that must be overcome, or as efforts by humans to make meaning in a particular way?
- Do you see, inquire, and challenge with an appreciating eye and spirit or with a criticizing, demeaning eye and spirit?
- Do you seek and appreciate the narratives of others?
- Do you seek and demean the narratives of others?
- For what do I [you] search? For what can we search together?
- Can I [you/we/they] identify the challenge, the hidden curriculum here?
- Do I [you/we/they] encourage an active inquiry and critique?
- Are you asking and seeking answers to your own questions?
- Can I [you/we/they/the family/the group/the organization] manage disagreement or open conflict?
- Can I [you/we/they/the family/the group/the organization] manage multiple realities?
- Can I [you/we/they/the family/the group/the organization] solve problems?
- Can I [you/we/they/the family/the group/the organization] communicate effectively?
- Can I [you/we/they/the family/the group/the organization] manage multiple emotions?

- Can, should, do, and could you write, speak, and act from a realist position, a critical position, an appreciative position, a liberal position, a traditionalist position, an ism position?
- Can you lead, speak, write, and act from a position different from the one that you usually take?
- Do you know for whom and to whom you speak?
- What organizations, groups, individuals do your ideas, feelings, and actions feed? Starve?

9

FACILITATING THE EMERGENCE OF WISDOM IN EXECUTIVE GROUPS

In our every deliberation, we must consider the impact of our decisions on the next seven generations.

—From the *Great Law of the Iroquois Confederacy*

The top tier of most large, modern organizations is composed of a small group of senior executives who are charged by their boards of directors with ensuring the effective performance of their enterprises. In the vernacular of modern business, this is now known as the "C" level in the institution. Chief financial officers (CFOs); chief counsel; chief information officers; chief human resources officers; chiefs of marketing and sales; and, of course, the CEOs, or their equivalents, plus the heads of various strategic business units, most often constitute these groups. The fate of any enterprise rests largely on the ability of their senior executive teams to both lead their own units, often enormous organizational subunits, as well as to function effectively together to guide the whole business.

Over the past 50 years, researchers in the behavioral sciences have learned a huge amount about just how human groups work as well as how they become dysfunctional. A growing body of group literature has been developed that focuses on how these group dynamics and accompanying variables influence the performance of top management teams. Given the importance of these senior executive groups to the futures of their organizations and the fact that they are present in virtually every large, modern organization, any treatment of the subject of Executive Wisdom must provide at least some modest examination of how Executive Wisdom can emerge, disappear, or never surface in such leadership teams.

In this chapter, I provide brief overviews of many of the key issues that affect the development and performance of groups of executives. The topics covered range from classic themes of how groups are defined and developed, the emergence and management of organizational regression, the complexity of conflict dynamics, and the application of catastrophe and field theories to top management teams. As I have emphasized throughout this book, special attention will also be given to the issue of the impact of cognitive development and functioning in individuals and the ramifications of these capacities for the effective performance of these groups.

Components of group functioning will be used to help the reader understand the complex array of forces that influence the ability of the senior leaders to work together and to create what I see as an extraordinary event, namely, the emergence of Executive Wisdom in top leadership groups. The material is set against a case study that describes how unconscious, unspoken patterns of behavior in these executive teams can virtually guarantee that they will rarely deliberate and execute wisely. Throughout this chapter, I allude to the coaching implications of this material, but the major applications of coaching theory and practice with executive groups are covered in chapter 10. Readers are encouraged to work through the material in this chapter because of the relevance of the concepts to what determines the performance of top teams and consequently to what coaches and consultants must pay attention as they work at this level in major organizations. Now, let us examine how a long-standing leadership group that really wanted to improve its performance discovered that they had colluded for years to sabotage their collective work.

THE CASE OF THE UNCONSCIOUS COMMANDMENT

"I don't think this organization can really move forward unless we change the way we relate to Jim," Sally Morton, the CFO of a medium-sized financial services firm, said to her colleagues. The business provided a variety of financial services to customers in a large, multistate region. We were gathered in one of the conference rooms of the company where we had been having a series of quarterly leadership development meetings for a little less than a year. The format for the sessions usually consisted of the entire group of senior people, seven in all, taking a few minutes to check in with each other about the major events that had occurred during the previous several months, how their portions of the business were faring in the business climate of the early 21st century, and how they themselves as individuals were doing. That was followed by a presentation from me on a mutually selected topic touching on aspects of leadership, management, organizational and group dynamics, or interpersonal skills. We would then spend the rest of the day working together on the implications of the presentation for the functioning of the leadership group and for the organization as a whole.

At this point in my work with this group and this company, we were in the middle of my 2nd year of activity. The consultation had started with a team-building session with the top dozen leaders of the organization that focused on interpersonal style, organizational learning, and barriers to more effective organizational functioning. That successful day had led to a series of other activities in that 1st year and to a contract for a 2nd year of work that included these quarterly development sessions for the top seven executives in the organization. Seated around the table were several people. John Norton, the chief operating officer of the company, had been brought in when they acquired a competitor some 5 years before. John had been publicly given the additional role of CEO-in-waiting. Jim Wentworth, the CEO to whom Sally had addressed in her remark, sat in the corner of the room, away from the table. He had made a visible and tangible commitment to developing his leadership group with the construction of an annual review process that served partly as a performance review and partly as an examination of the future development path of the top 25 managers in the company. Wendy Benedict, Andy Roseman, Mel Peterson, and Carl Yousner, all in similar vice presidential operating roles in the various states served by the company, completed the leadership team. This exchange took place at the second development session during that year and the fourth meeting that I had attended with the entire group.

As one can imagine, Sally's remark electrified the group. She had put it out there as part of an exchange we were having on the factors that were inhibiting leadership and company performance. From his seat in the corner of the room away from the other six executives, Jim had just finished making a long, critical statement in response to a question from me regarding what he was most worried about as he considered stepping down as the CEO and transferring the leadership of this venerable company to John. Jim had focused most of his remarks on the group in the room, criticizing them for their overall lack of initiative, their unwillingness to take responsibility in times of crisis, and the general weakness of the management group underneath the vice presidents. He said in all sincerity that he really was ready to retire, a fact that many of the professionals in the room privately disputed, but that his departure, planned for about 18 months in the future, was contingent on his trust in the leadership team's capacity to take charge of the business. He was especially concerned about their seeming inability to be willing to make difficult choices in the midst of a crisis.

Sally's remark sat in the room like a heavy, spicy meal lying undigested in everyone's stomach. Initially, no one wanted to follow up on the remark, although there were one or two nods and a couple of faded smiles in response to what she had said. At first, I simply let the group try to deal with it, because I was curious about the growing ability to handle conflict and controversy that we had nurtured together during the past year. Eventually, Jim could no longer bear the tension. He was a direct, hands-on kind of leader who was accustomed to taking things on straightforwardly.

"Do you mind me asking you what you mean by that, Sally?" he asked.

I was pleased that someone had taken up the challenge but concerned a little for Sally because she was the one person besides John who seemed both strong enough and willing to push Jim a little bit. Having had conversations with Jim privately about this matter, I knew that he rather relished these types of confrontational exchanges and wished fervently that more members of the senior group would feel strong enough to challenge him. I watched Sally gather herself for the response to Jim. She took a breath or two first and seemed to compose herself; then she turned to face him in the corner of the room.

"Well Jim, we've talked about this before, and I just think that you can be pretty intimidating. Someone needs to be very self-assured to be able to talk directly with you."

"Does anyone else feel this way when you interact with Jim?" I asked before Jim could respond.

Both Wendy and Andy answered in quick succession that they often felt put on the defensive when talking with Jim. John smiled broadly. He was the most self-assured member of the group behind Jim. Calm, experienced, with almost 30 years in the industry, and confident that he would eventually take over from Jim, he talked routinely and privately to him about nearly every aspect of the business.

"Well, you can be a handful," John said, smiling, and in support of Sally.

"This is interesting, because I don't think I'm that hard to approach. I'm here, my door is open, and I think everyone knows that I'm interested in their opinions about the business."

"That's not the point I'm making," Sally answered as she looked now directly at me.

"Well, what are you trying to say?" I asked her.

"Jim is very good at being willing to sit down and talk to anyone about the business. That's not the hard part."

"What is?"

Sally's blue eyes closed for a second, and her face drew itself tightly together almost as though she were expecting a blow in response to what she was about to say.

"In every discussion I have with Jim, it's like I have to prove to him he's wrong."

Having said this, Sally hunched her shoulders in expectation of Jim's reply.

"Does this ring true for anyone else at this table?" I asked, noting the dramatic increase in tension in the room and acting again before Jim could jump in.

"Oh yeah," Wendy answered. "Any conversation I have with him is more like an argument than a discussion. He's always prepared to debate you, and his skill with words and his knowledge and experience with the business are so extensive that he often just shuts you down with a comment like, 'You don't know what you're talking about.'"

Andy chimed in as well, giving a concrete example of a situation about which he had approached Jim in his region. "You didn't really even give me a chance to offer any suggestions or tell you what I was thinking. I gave you the facts, and you told me what to do."

"Well, that's not what I was trying to do," Jim said, responding to Andy and finally managing to get himself into the conversation.

"What do you see yourself trying to accomplish in these exchanges?" I asked.

"I'm trying to test them, to see how well they've thought things through, to determine if they have the courage of their convictions and can stand up for what they believe. I'm also trying to see if they are right in what they propose, because often they are not."

"So, you don't dispute what Sally has said."

"No, I guess I don't."

"Does everyone at the table agree that Jim has been behaving like this pretty routinely?" I asked the group.

"I've known him for 20 years, and he's always been like that," Mel answered quietly.

"What's been the effect on you of interacting with him in this way?"

"I learned a long, long time ago never to argue with Jim. It doesn't do any good because he has to have it his way anyway. So I guess you'd say, I just do what he tells me to do."

At this point the entire room went silent. The juxtaposition of Jim's lament about the lack of individual and executive group initiative, Sally's challenge, Mel's quiet observation of his own standard operating procedure, and the concurrence of the rest of the team with Sally's observation was extremely powerful. It was one of those defining moments that one occasionally has in a consulting engagement where an elemental truth about an organization, an executive team, or a leader is uncovered and the opportunity for change is presented very clearly. I seized the opportunity to reinforce one of the major themes I had introduced to this leadership group during our first meeting. At that event, I had discussed Chris Argyris's (1993) concept of espoused theories versus theories in use in leadership groups and the defensive operations of organizations.

I took them back immediately to that point by asking Jim if he was deliberately trying to intimidate the members of his leadership group with his questions and use of his experience when he talked with them. He replied that he was not trying to intimidate but that he wanted to challenge them. He reiterated his concerns for the future of the business and the need to have leaders who could make tough calls and take difficult actions when needed. He said with quite a degree of passion that he really wanted and needed to have the group step up to the challenges of leading the business and that he would look forward to working with an assertive, tough-minded team of colleagues. The response of the other leaders in the room amounted to a collective, "Then you need to give us a chance to make some calls and take some risks instead of not listening, shutting us down, and trying to have your own way all of the time."

We spent several hours together talking about the implications of the pattern we had uncovered thanks to Sally's courageous action and Jim's willingness to both listen and respond without being overly defensive. I have rarely seen a group of executives quite so animated. They gave example after example of their interactions with Jim over the years of their work together and walked through what happened and why. Jim talked passionately about what he was trying to do in those exchanges, and it became clear that despite his conscious desire to have an aggressive, independent-minded, and able group of executives, all of his efforts to lead and train them instead had created a group whose primary mode of interacting with him was one of dependency. I pointed out to all of them how this group dynamic, largely under the table, rarely discussed by anyone, and never explicitly confronted, kept them all behaving in ways that no one liked and that the business could ill afford. By the end of the day together, the group had made an explicit commitment to each other and to Jim to communicate when they believed that they were behaving in the old way. I asked Jim to commit to the group members that he would tell them explicitly when he was trying to challenge them for the purpose of helping them grow. I also suggested to Jim and the rest of the group that they would need to take some risks together in the coming months to try to make and implement decisions in a different way.

That day proved extraordinarily decisive in the history of the company. It led to a number of individual coaching sessions with Jim about how he was trying to develop his team and the nature of his behavior both in groups and with individuals. The follow-up sessions with the group in turn enabled me to push them to discuss how they were doing in their interactions with Jim. Reluctantly, they all got better at talking more openly about what was really going on between them. Over the course of the next 9 months, two of the members, Mel and Andy, left the organization for positions in other corporations. They were replaced with vigorous new executives, Anita Stromberg and Harry Jameson.

In January, at the beginning of the next fiscal year, the business began to suffer some sales declines. By the middle of February, it was clear that they would miss their first-quarter numbers by a wide margin. Normally, Jim would have jumped all over the group to ensure that they developed a plan to curb costs and push sales, but this time, with the support of John, Jim kept himself on the sidelines. It was difficult for him, but he managed to do so. For his part, John rallied the group and set them to work on a short-term strategy to hold the business together.

The entire leadership team met repeatedly and formulated a complex plan to address the crisis. They pushed their initiatives into operation as soon as they collectively agreed on what to do, and the effects were amazing. They not only halted the slide but also discovered a variety of questionable business practices that were contributing to a number of long-standing problems. It turned out that they had inadvertently created financial incentives for their marketing and sales teams that favored business volume over profit margins. As a result, they were selling a lot of services but were making less money because they were not pushing their higher margin programs. Once they figured that out, they adjusted their incentive systems, and the impact on the bottom line was nearly immediate. These changes pushed them over their profit goals for the first half of the year. By the end of that second quarter, they had turned the company completely around, largely without Jim's usual direction. Rather than being upset for not directing this effort, Jim found himself both feeling and saying how relieved and pleased he was that the team seemed to really understand what was needed to lead the business. At the development session with the management group that June, he publicly reiterated his commitment to retire that fall. Although one of the management team members used the newly created atmosphere of freedom of expression to state that he would believe Jim's retirement when he saw it, Jim's spontaneous laughter and response to "hang around until October" was met with good-natured understanding and a lot of kidding among the members of the whole group.

By October, Jim was feeling so confident in the leadership group that he did move forward with his retirement. John stepped in as the new CEO, and the organization began a whole new chapter in its long leadership history. The company continued to grow under John, and as of this writing, the leadership group is still meeting and working on improving its ability to function together. During the final 18 months of Jim's term as CEO, he demonstrated a degree of flexibility of which no one in the organization thought him capable. As he modified his behavior and basically ceased to act as the grand inquisitor and dictator, the members of his executive group progressively found their own voices and ideas. They began to participate more fully, and as they did so the business responded with better profits even in tougher market conditions.

Now we will take a quick look at many of the key issues and dynamics that were embedded in the functioning of Jim's team and are present in every other leadership group. In my experience, an understanding of these complexities is crucial for anyone wishing to coach or consult with senior executives and is equally critical for the members of these leadership teams as well. Leadership groups that master the basics of their own operations are far less likely to run into trouble with their fundamentals and therefore are better able to focus continuously on mastering the challenges of global economic competition. I return to a consideration of the case material once the essentials of the concepts are covered.

DEVELOPING HIGH-PERFORMING EXECUTIVE TEAMS

Current conventional approaches to the design, development, and management of work teams, dedicated work units, and executive groups emphasize rational, reality-based, problem-solving models (Dyer, 1987; Katzenbach, 1998; Katzenbach & Smith, 1994; Mohrman & Mohrman, 1997; Nadler, Spencer, & Associates, 1998; Quick, 1992; Sundstrom & Associates, 1999; Tjosvold & Tjosvold, 1991; Varney, 1989). These approaches provide concepts, assessment methods, intervention techniques, and general advice to leaders and consultants who usually engage in the design, training, and management of teams. Nadler et al. (1998) also discussed the likelihood of conflict about and within executive groups and provided methods for the assessment of such situations and the approaches that CEOs can take to intervene and prevent these circumstances from becoming destructive.

Consulting practice in many, if not most, team and group settings is often limited to short-term engagements designed to assist with the initial design and start-up of groups; the resolution and management of conflicted or unproductive circumstances in teams; or other specific problems associated with performance, such as redeveloping corporate strategy, managing mergers and acquisitions, or integrating new members. This is often because the life spans of teams are short by design. As the average tenure of CEOs continues to decline, this has become even more typically the case. In a few situations, leaders of dedicated work or executive groups that exist more or less permanently within an organization have the courage to engage a consultant for a longer term assignment that focuses on routinely engaging in developmental or process-oriented work (Argyris, 1993; Schein, 1988). Consultants have been slowly evolving a body of concepts and practices to build and maintain successful, ongoing, working relationships in these engagements.

The central thesis of this chapter is that executives who lead or participate in these long-term management groups can benefit greatly from many of the ideas and methods being developed by consultants who focus on coaching individual executives and others who have specialized in the adaptation of psychodynamic theory to work groups and organizational settings. In particular, and in keeping with the focus of this book, I believe that consultants working with such groups must begin to advocate formally that these teams endeavor to improve their capacities for the use of wisdom, the key virtue in effective executive performance. Given that wisdom takes time to develop (Sternberg, 1990), one is most likely to see it emerge in leadership groups that have a long-term commitment to their organizations and the willingness to develop themselves both as individuals and as a working team through time. This represents a major paradox for globally competitive enterprises, in which major changes in the membership of leadership teams is a routine aspect of their operations.

APPLYING COACHING THEORY AND PRACTICE TO TEAMS AND DEDICATED GROUPS

Gilley and Broughton (1996), Kilburg (1996a, 1997, 2000), Hargrove (1995), Voss (1997), and many others have been evolving the theory and practice of coaching as applied to individuals and teams. Lowman (2002) provided several explicit chapters that included wonderful and recently updated overviews of current approaches to group development. In this chapter, I distinguish between teams that are more short-term, project-oriented configurations of individuals and dedicated, executive work groups that constitute long-term organizational structures through which leadership work is accomplished. This chapter and the next focus on these types of long-term structures. Even in cases in which I refer to executive teams in this chapter, unless otherwise specified, I am not discussing short-term project teams.

As you will recall, Figure 2.1 depicted the six foci for executive coaching that contribute to the emergence of Executive Wisdom as part of the overall model advocated in this book. This framework illustrates the three specific and interrelated zones that I introduced in earlier works (Kilburg, 1996b, 2000) that coaches most often penetrate in their work with individual executives: (a) the individual leader, (b) the organization itself, and (c) the mediated interface between them. The central concern in this chapter involves the mediated focus between the leader and the organization, presented in somewhat more detail in Figure 2.3, that is composed of the relationships and the interpersonal structures that make up organizations, especially work groups, subunits, and teams. For it is most often in and through these substructures that individuals do their work for organizations, and it is in these substructures that most problems arise for institutions. The figure also illustrates that these mediated behavioral and structural elements interact strongly with the internal components of individuals and with the processes, structures, and contents of the larger organizational supersystems along with the other components of the wisdom model.

CRITICAL FACTORS IN COACHING INDIVIDUALS

A listing of some of the critical factors consultants need to consider when coaching individual members of teams is provided in Exhibit 9.1. These continue to be relevant when a professional assignment specifically focuses on a team or work group, because the coachability of the individual members of the group can greatly affect the process, progress, and ultimate outcomes of these challenging assignments. Severe, debilitating patterns of psychopathology, including major character disorders, are particularly important to identify and address in coaching because of the sustained negative impact that they can have on other leaders in an organization and the general processes of a group. As I discussed briefly in chapter 7, for organizations to prosper, their leaders must continuously try to behave virtuously and, through those behaviors, refine their characters and capacity for doing good in the world. Leaders who insist on behaving in ineffective and even destructive ways will ultimately create harmful effects for their

EXHIBIT 9.1
Critical Factors to Consider in Coaching Individuals

- Personality structure and type
- Dimensions of diversity
- Physical and psychological health
- Psychosocial stressors and trauma history
- Unconscious conflict structures and processes—compromise formations and adaptive behavior patterns
- Unconscious defenses, emotions, cognitive structures and processes
- Psychosocial and relationship history; current life matrix
- Cognitive complexity
- Level and order of human consciousness and wisdom
- Level of self-awareness and reflective capacity
- Knowledge, skills, abilities, and experience in leadership and management, life skills, emotional management, interpersonal relations, and diversity management
- Empathic ability and skill and predisposition to group identification
- Receptivity to coaching—cognitive, emotional, and behavioral flexibility and curiosity

colleagues and institutions. If all the members of an executive group possess reasonable levels of skill, emotional maturity, cognitive complexity, and emotional intelligence and are fairly receptive to coaching, a practitioner can be reasonably confident that a team development assignment will go well even if it is challenging. With deficits in any of the areas identified in Exhibit 9.1 in all or even in some crucial members of a group, coaching assignments can be extremely difficult at best and, in the end, often prove impossible.

THE MAJOR FACTORS INFLUENCING LONG-TERM EXECUTIVE GROUP PERFORMANCE

A Coaching Model for Executive Groups

An illustration of my coaching model (Kilburg, 2000), applied to a group of four individuals, is provided in Figure 9.1. The systemic factors of

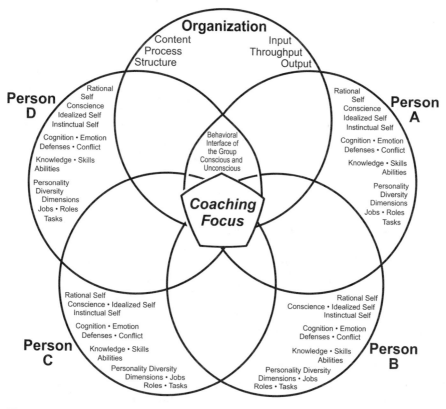

Figure 9.1. The coaching model applied to an organization and a four-person group.

the home organization appear in one of the five overlapping circles. The interpenetrating zones of the four individuals represent their working relationships, the structural and process features of their organization, and the interactions of their internal dynamics as depicted in Figure 2.1. The center of the figure, where all elements of the team and the organization converge, represents the site where a coach can best and most consistently focus his or her attention. In this zone, the psychodynamics, skills, and interpersonal relationships of the individual members create the leadership group's dynamics and interact with the larger culture, dynamics, and organizational systems of the parent enterprise. These subtle patterns, interaction effects, and crossover influences are often difficult to detect but very important to helping groups unravel the difficult challenges that such complexity can produce (Koortzen & Cilliers, 2002). Coaches must be able to maneuver their attention readily among the individuals in the group; their dyadic relationships, coalitions, or other subgroup dynamics; whole-group behavior patterns; the interactions with the superstructures of the core organization; and processes and contents of the actual work assigned and expected to be accomplished. Interventions can then be attempted that take this complexity into account.

Four Key Concepts for Coaching Teams and Groups

When coaching in these settings, practitioners must be well versed in the wealth of research and practice knowledge regarding groups that has evolved through the past 60 years (Cartwright & Zander, 1968; Forsyth, 1990; Gibbard, Hartman, & Mann, 1988; Thibaut & Kelley, 1959; Zander, 1981, 1983). It is impossible to review all of the material that is often relevant in these situations; however, I believe four key concepts are worthy of some brief discussion because of the routinely high value they provide to consulting practitioners and leaders working with teams and dedicated work groups.

Bales's Symlog and the Analysis of Group Behavior

First, I believe that coaches must be familiar with the core Symlog conceptual framework for analyzing behavior in groups developed by Bales and his colleagues (e.g., Bales & Cohen, 1979). This approach flows from the original work of Lewin (1997), who created and applied field theory to the function of groups. Using Bales and Cohen's (1979) three-dimensional model, observers can classify the behavior of individuals in groups along three continua: (a) negative/unfriendly–positive/friendly, (b) backward/ emotionally expressive–forward/instrumentally controlled, and (c) downward/submissive–upward/dominant. Rating scales are available to help categorize the observations into the 26 different cells of the model. Repeated observations of intact work groups can reveal consistent patterns of behavior by individuals, and these patterns can in turn be arrayed to describe the overall behavioral configurations displayed in a group. Observing consistent behavior, dominant patterns, and patterns that are absent regarding friendliness, emotional expression–instrumental control, and dominance and submission can greatly aid coaches and leaders in assessing group and team performance and in developing potential avenues for interventions. Awareness of these fundamental polarities as frameworks for assessment helps to orient practitioners and executives in the complex space depicted in Figure 9.1. No effort will be made here to describe Symlog methodology in detail, but coaches would be wise to become generally familiar with it if they wish to work regularly with groups and teams.

Usually, when I begin to work with leadership groups, I find it critical to be able to rapidly organize the way in which I think about them as a functional unit. The Bales and Cohen (1979) model is an efficient and effective way to consider the broad challenge of classification. Without becoming overly technical or elaborate in conceptual terms, this model can suggest whether the team seems friendly or hostile; focused on emotional expression or instrumental control of its environment; or is dominant or submissive in the ways in which it relates to leaders, other groups, and organizational structures. Consultants who can orient quickly in these engagements will make fewer mistakes. For example, working with a friendly, emotionally expressive, yet dominant executive team requires far different coaching methods than intervening with a hostile, control-oriented, and submissive group. At a minimum, a consultant can reasonably expect to manage more passive–aggressive conflict with a hostile, control-oriented, and submissive team than with a friendly and emotionally expressive leadership group.

Argyris's Loop Learning Model

Second, the work of Argyris (1993) and Schön (1987) in developing their double-loop learning theory is of special importance to coaches working with groups. Figure 9.2 (Kilburg, 2000) presents a modification of their basic flow model, incorporating the notion of a third learning loop first introduced by Hargrove (1995). In the Argyris model, the environmental context for the organization, group, or individual produces tasks of external adaptation and internal integration (Schein, 1990) that interact with and are informed by the culture and history of the organization and the identities of the individual members of the organization. In addressing these internal and external challenges, the members of the organization and its various teams and dedicated work groups engage both learning and defensive routines. These routines then result in implementation strategies and specific actions,

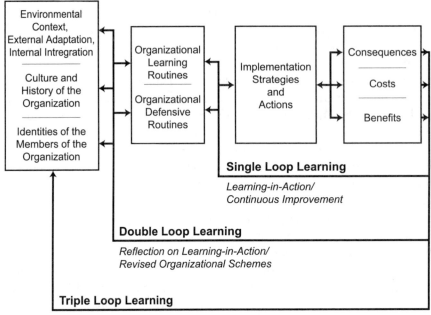

Figure 9.2. Triple-loop learning for organizations, groups, and individuals.

some of which are conscious and intentional, whereas others are entirely unconscious and can be either intentional or unintentional. These actions in turn produce consequences in the form of costs and benefits for individuals, groups, and the organization as a whole. I discussed this model in some depth in chapter 8.

In the context of working with executive groups, the single-learning loop, which uses learning-in-action activities for continuous improvement (Schön, 1987), applies feedback from these learning-in-action routines immediately to directly influence the strategies and actions that are being used to address the current challenges. In the double-learning loop, efforts focus on reflecting on the learning-in-action, a second-order exercise of self-, group, and organizational awareness and are used by senior teams to influence the learning and defensive routines that were initially selected to work on the problems being addressed. In the final, triple-learning loop, which creates a third level of self-, group, and organizational awareness, reflection on reflections on learning-in-action are used by leadership groups to examine the initial starting conditions of their challenges and can lead to the emergence of revised forms of organizational and group culture, individual identity, enterprise vision, and relationships with the external environment.

The value of this model to coaches is immediately apparent in its ability to direct their attention simultaneously to the learning and adaptive processes in play in any client system(s) and to the type and level of interventions available. Choices are immediately clear concerning what can be addressed and the types of reflection and change strategies that are most likely to be of optimal assistance. It is apparent that work on continuous improvement most optimally uses the learning-in-action type of reflection, whereas changing significant aspects of organizational schemes and routines requires the second level of reflection. To be sure, some continuous improvement efforts necessitate an examination of learning and defensive routines, but the model and practical experience suggest strongly that other methods must be used to do the work of organizational restructuring successfully. Similarly, when comprehensive change efforts are aimed at cultural transformation, repositioning an organization strategically in relation to its environment and markets, or reshaping the identities of individuals or groups, feedback loops involving the third level of reflection are necessary.

Using this model can help coaches and consultants avoid intervention strategy selection errors as well as help to orient them to the place, process, and issues in the organization, group, or individual to which assistance is being targeted. This model also makes clear that conflicts and defensive routines cannot be avoided in organizations, groups, and individuals. They are at the heart of the adaptive process that guides all living entities and of the kind of learning emphasized by Heifetz (1994). Coaches must embrace these fundamental principles of human learning and defensive behavior if their efforts on behalf of their clients are to have long-term, constructive impact.

The Stages of Group Development

Exhibit 9.2 summarizes the classic five-stage model of group development found in virtually every textbook devoted to group dynamics and organizational learning (Forsyth, 1990; Voss, 1997). The stages follow a flow format, beginning with the initiation of a group and the first meetings of its members that start its formation. This is usually followed by a period of *storming*, in which some conflict over roles, goals, task assignments, relationships, and power often lead to the experience and expression of strong negative emotions by members of the group. Successful work during this stage leads to the third set of tasks, in which the group *norms* itself by establishing roles, goals, procedures, accountabilities, authority and affiliation relationships, and so on. This sets the stage for the work of the group during its period of real performance. Finally, in many settings, the work group dissolves and adjourns itself during the last stage of its existence.

EXHIBIT 9.2
Five Stages of Group Development

1. *Forming*—Initiation of the group; establishing task identity and relationships; polite social interaction and dialogue; concerns about ambiguity and ambivalence; initial dependency, anxiety
2. *Storming*—Conflict over procedures, boundaries, roles, resistances; debates, open criticism and hostility; often polarized and fractured into coalitions; group regression; anxiety and anger
3. *Norming*—Establishing norms, roles, performance standards, procedures, group culture; dialogue used to establish agreements, reduce ambiguity, increase cohesion and conformity; curiosity
4. *Performing*—Task performance and goal achievement, productive exchanges; dialogue, problem solving, creative interaction; resilient adaptation; curiosity and joy
5. *Adjourning*—Task completion; termination of group agenda; dissolution of group; leave-taking withdrawal, sadness, grief; reemergence of independence and autonomy

Senior executive teams rarely dissolve completely, but their membership can shift often as individuals enter and leave the organization.

Similarly, this flow or stage model can provide some useful feedback to intact groups as they shift their attention from task to task. I have frequently seen stable groups that work together on a variety of projects and problems move in and out of these different stages of development depending on the specific issue on which they are working. At times, intact groups can display effective levels of performance on one task at the same time as they start a new project and begin to struggle with their roles, task assignments, norms, and behavioral expectations. This can be a source of tremendous confusion and conflict in executive groups, because they experience themselves simultaneously as both well organized and effective and as simply inept. In such circumstances, defensive routines often emerge that make sustained performance across a number of tasks and activities difficult.

These five stages are most in evidence in the project-oriented work teams now seen in almost every significant organization in the world. As these short-term groups form, organize, work, and dissolve, sometimes at blistering speeds, one can often see compressed cycles of the five stages occurring in days or weeks. Indeed, some organizations are making efforts to structure themselves around project teams as the very core of their identities. In these enterprises, the issues of work group identity are forever pressing into the consciousness of the employees through the absence of sustained and tangible attachments. Often, individuals can have assignments on multiple project teams that may be at various stages of development.

This places a premium on the emotional maturity and intelligence, psychological and behavioral sophistication, and the interpersonal and organizational knowledge and skill of individual employees. However, most institutions tend to make simultaneous use of project teams, dedicated work groups, and executive groups. These semipermanent organizational environments are no less complex or challenging for individuals. Employees can have an equal or greater number of group assignments in these more traditional organizations with the same kinds of psychological and professional challenges.

The identification and management of boundaries are of special importance in the dynamics of group formation and function (Aldefer, 1987). Particular attention to who is in the group, why they are present, their external allegiances and political obligations, and the histories of the individuals and their constituencies can provide clues as to what may be impeding work or growth. In addition, it is important to discern the permeability of the boundaries—whether they are loose, and allow for many influences to percolate into and through the deliberations and processes of the group, or tight, and prevent such external influences. Groups need to manage these aspects of their developmental process with great care to ensure their initial and ongoing success, because their boundary conditions may well need to change depending on the nature of the tasks they are confronting at any particular point in time.

This model is also helpful for coaches to use in their assessments of the functioning of any team or group. Asking a few simple questions concerning the roles, goals, norms, boundaries, and qualities of the interpersonal relationships among group members along the lines of the suggested forms of inquiry provided in chapter 6, when used along with objective information about task performance, can provide a quick and relatively accurate picture of where a group is in its development and why it may be having troubles. Again, the model can help a coach orient toward the kinds of interventions that might be optimally useful and effective at given times or in particular stages of development. For example, processing what may be clearly signaled anxiety about its ultimate adjournment will usually not be helpful to a group if it has not even begun to storm about the basic nature of its goals, roles, procedures, and so on. Similarly, when groups try to jump into the performance of actual tasks without providing clarity on boundaries, procedures, performance standards, the management of conflict, or the delegation of authority and responsibility, they are unlikely to be successful in any sustained way. Coaches armed with this conceptual knowledge can remain oriented themselves in these confusing and often conflicted situations and help the members of a team or dedicated work group do the same.

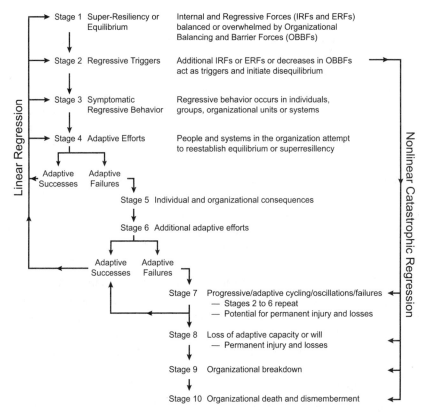

Figure 9.3. Stages in the management of organizational regression.

Understanding Organizational Regression

Fourth and finally, Figure 9.3 provides a 10-stage flow model for the management of organizational regression introduced by Kilburg, Stokes, and Kuruvilla (1998; Kilburg, 2000). The loop learning model illustrated in Figure 9.2 and described both above and in chapter 8 demonstrates that individuals, groups, and organizations are under constant adaptive pressure to change and learn and that defensive routines are regularly engaged as a result. When defensive operations predominate—or, as Kilburg et al. (1998) described in their model, when organizational balancing and barrier forces are temporarily or permanently overwhelmed by regressive forces—adaptive failures and even organizational death and dismemberment are frequent outcomes. The flow model of regression management emphasizes that adaptive efforts within organizations can restore effective functioning and growth. It also illustrates that regression can be either linear and sequential or nonlinear and catastrophic in nature.

Regression in teams and groups is experienced very often in organizations, but it is rarely described outside of the mental health literature. Exceptions are found in a seminal article by Lewin (1997) and most notably in the writings of Kernberg (1978, 1979, 1998), Bion (1961), and Jaques (1976, 1989). Consultants and coaches are often called in when a team or group has entered into a regressive process that overwhelms the adaptive capacity of its members, accountable leaders, or other internal organizational resources. Moderately and severely regressed groups can provide some of the most challenging practice assignments imaginable. The most primitive human emotions and interpersonal, group, and organizational dynamics are often on display. As detailed beautifully by Kernberg (1998) and Fromm (1973), it is frequently these regressed human group environments that give rise to some of the most destructive and despicable human behavior imaginable. Knowledge of such regressive patterns and processes arms the coach or consultant and enables him or her to be on guard against the worst of the consequences of these patterns. It is especially important to note here that practitioners should take steps to protect themselves when moving into these assignments by doing so with teams of colleagues, structuring clear contracts and boundaries, and backing themselves up through the use of shadow consultants (Kilburg, 1998; Schroder, 1974). In this way, professionals may be able to withstand the rigors of these challenges without suffering physical health, mental health, reputational, or economic consequences. Failure to anticipate the corrosive nature and potential adverse effects of regressive processes can produce profound negative effects for groups, their individual members and parent organizations, and coaches alike.

Critical Factors in Coaching Teams and Groups

Along with the four major concepts just discussed, four other critical factors influence coaching efforts with teams and groups: (a) individual and group psychodynamics, (b) discontinuous or catastrophic change, (c) field effects, and (d) levels of human consciousness or orders of mind. All of these factors interact with the major concepts outlined thus far to increase the complexity of the behavior that can be observed in these executive group settings. The interaction of these domains creates many, if not most, of the challenges faced both by leaders of these groups and by the consultants who work with them.

Individual and Group Psychodynamics

The first factor that affects coaching efforts in these settings consists of the underlying psychodynamic patterns of the individuals in the dyad or group. Figure 9.4, which I have discussed previously (Kilburg, 1997, 2000),

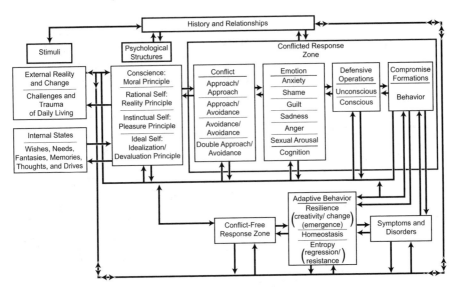

Figure 9.4. The structure and process of individual psychodynamic conflict and adaptation in individuals.

presents the structure and underlying process of the shadow system of behavior of individuals. As with the model for groups and organizations presented in Figure 9.1, shadow systems are stimulated by adaptive pressures from outside of the individual and by various internal states, such as values, needs, memories, wishes, drives, thoughts, and the shaping forces of past experiences, such as trauma. These stimuli are assessed and mediated by psychological structures and the individual's history and interpersonal relationships. If the internal structures of conscience, rational self, and instinctual self are not conflicted about the response necessary to adapt to the stimulus, then the individual enters the conflict-free response zone and creates adaptive behavior that can be resilient, homeostatic, or regressive in nature. However, when the individual is in conflict about a response, strong emotions and various less mature forms of cognition and emotion are often aroused, and defensive operations are activated. The interaction of conflicts, emotions, defenses, and cognition produces compromise formations in behavior. These can result in symptoms and disorders associated with mental and physical illness or adaptive patterns similar to those produced by conflict-free behavior.

Coaches must be mindful that this shadow system operates constantly in every individual he or she meets in professional circumstances as well as in him- or herself. Every human being is frequently coping either consciously or unconsciously with conflict and the defensive behavior patterns associated with it. There is no escape from the ever-present reality of conflict. Under-

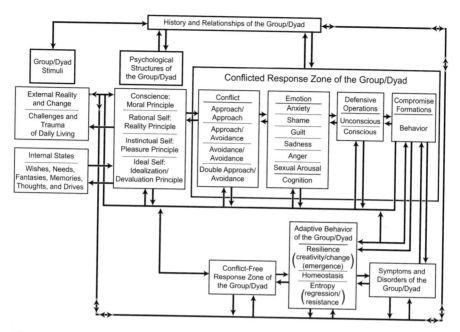

Figure 9.5. The structure and process of individual psychodynamic conflict and adaptation in groups and dyads.

standing how such processes operate in individuals gives a coach significant information and many tools for intervening during assignments. I have come to appreciate how such awareness can tremendously improve a coach's ability to intervene with clients and how the absence of such understanding can often produce either suboptimal outcomes or outright failure.

For example, it is often critical for a coach to know how his or her client has responded in the past to teachers; parents who were trying to help him or her learn; athletic coaches; ministers, rabbis, and imams; and other authority figures who related to the client in a developmental capacity. Such knowledge can alert both the coach and the client to past patterns of relating, learning, or defensive behavior that might affect their work together. The absence of a conscious exploration of these kinds of experiences can in turn lead both coach and client to re-enact ineptly or destructively pieces of history that negatively influence their ability to learn and grow. The reverse is equally true: The development of a mutually conscious understanding of some of these psychodynamic forces can enable a coach and his or her client to diagnose trouble long before it creates any destructive impact on their efforts.

Figure 9.5 provides the model of structures and processes of individuals; Figure 9.6 represents an effort to apply these individual shadow systems to those of dyads and groups. Jung (1989); Bion (1961); A. K. Rice (1963,

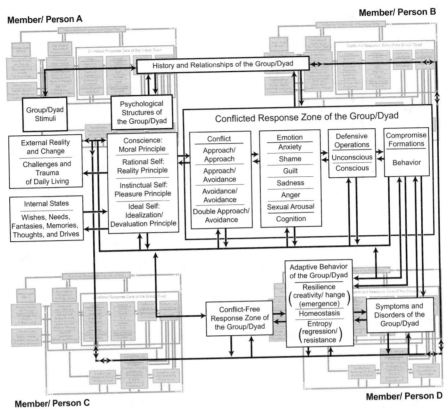

Figure 9.6. Individual contributions to the collective unconscious/shadow system of a four-person group.

1965); Kernberg (1998); Yalom (1970); and Gibbard, Hartman, and Mann (1988), among others, have suggested that human beings, when functioning in groups, create a collective group unconscious that activates and incorporates partial aspects of the individual shadow systems of the assembled and involved individuals plus certain psychodynamic patterns that arise only when more than one person is involved. In Figure 9.6, I am suggesting that the underlying psychodynamic structures and processes of dyads and groups can duplicate or interact with those of the individuals involved. However, the main effect of the interactions of the psychodynamics of individuals in groups is to produce a metadynamic shadow system, which was first discussed by Jung (1989) as the *collective unconscious.*

Figure 9.6 illustrates the point that this meta-state or collective unconscious is produced out of the shadow substrates and interactions of the individuals in the group. However, it is important to note that the collective shadow system can and does develop its own properties that are interdependent with those of the individuals and significantly interact with and influence both the conscious and the shadow systems of the individual members of a group. Levi (2001) provided a complex and thorough review of many of the major dynamics that any team confronts during the time that it exists. Every leadership group must master the basics of communication, cooperation and competition, conflict, the processes involved in power and social influence, decision making, problem-solving, conformity and deviance, and the management of diversity. As the case examples in this book have demonstrated, problems in any one of these areas of group function and dynamics can lead to even more difficult challenges for an organization. For example, Bion (1961) described three basic assumption groups—dependency, fight–flight, and pairing—that illustrate such collective problems. Similarly, Jaques (1976, 1989) has described paranoiagenic groups and organizations. Kernberg (1998) made the most systematic effort to date to discuss the influences of these collective dynamics on organizations and their individual members that I could find. Kernberg emphasizes and illustrates brilliantly the emotional and behavioral corrosion and severe negative consequences that can occur when malignant narcissism and significant paranoid processes arise and operate in a group or organization.

Coaches entering into group settings organized and regulated by such dynamics must be aware of the possible existence of such collective shadow systems in order to both function effectively and to survive professionally and personally. Coaches must be especially alert to these patterns and to the basic assumption dynamics of dependency, fight–flight, pairing, paranoiagenesis, and malignant narcissism that are often encountered in teams and groups. Again, this critical psychodynamic factor has major diagnostic and intervention implications for coaches working with dyads and groups.

The case study that opened this chapter is a wonderful illustration of how an unstated yet powerful group dynamic adversely affected an entire leadership team for nearly 2 decades before it surfaced and was able to be managed in a different and more productive way. Despite all of the efforts of the CEO and his colleagues to consciously perform effectively together, for years they had continued to enact a much stronger although unstated and largely unconscious pattern that inhibited their relationships and work outcomes. However, once they were able to consciously discuss the pattern and to operate on it together in the ways in which we discussed in chapter 3, they were then able to learn to relate and perform differently and more effectively.

Influence and Importance of Complexity and Chaos in Executive Groups

The second critical factor influencing coaching assignments with groups and teams consists of the likelihood that discontinuous or catastrophic change processes will appear. As described earlier, in the section on regressive

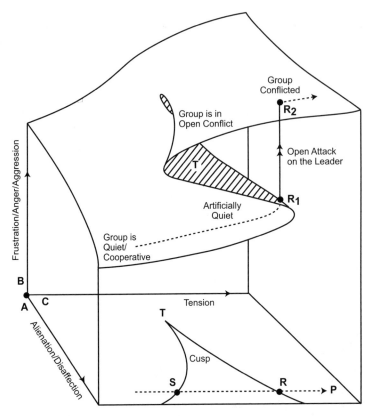

Figure 9.7. A simple cusp catastrophe in a group. T = the point at which the tension peaks and open aggression breaks out with an attack on the leader; B = the degree of frustration, anger, and aggression experienced and expressed in and by the group; C = the level of tension experienced and expressed in and by the group; R_1 = the point at which there is an open attack on the leader; R_2 = the point at which tension, aggression, anger, frustration, and alienation have risen high enough so that the entire group is engulfed by conflict; S = the point at which tension begins to rise noticeably; P = when the equilibrium is stabilized and the group has become one that is in constant conflict; A = the dimension of the degree of alienation and disaffection in the group.

dynamics, a catastrophic change can occur with blinding speed and often catches the members of a group by complete surprise. The associated shock and trauma can significantly affect the capacity of a team to adapt and even survive. Figure 9.7, introduced in an earlier work (Kilburg, 2000), illustrates a change occurring in a group called a *cusp catastrophe*. Cusps are one of the simplest forms of catastrophic change, but there are many others that can involve larger numbers of variables. This example involves three major dimensions: (a) the tension in the group; (b) the degree of alienation and disaffection felt by the members; and (c) the extent of frustration, anger, and aggression. As these pressures mount in this group over time, the team

Attractors

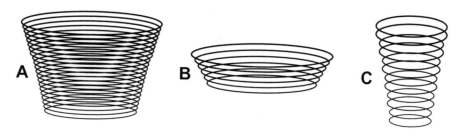

Repulsors

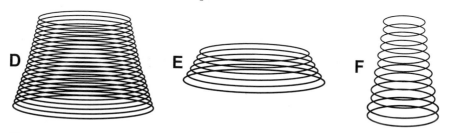

Figure 9.8. Visual representations of chaotic attractors and repulsors.

moves progressively from the zone of quiet cooperation, depicted as the area of the illustration labeled "Group is Quiet/Cooperative," toward the center. These types of movements are often undetectable by the members of a group unless they are extraordinarily sensitive to their inner dynamics and emotional states. As the group enters into the cusp, a point, symbolized by T in Figure 9.7, is reached when the members explode into what was to them completely unpredictable open conflict, which, in this example, leads to attacks on the group leader. The group is now in a dramatically different state, and the members probably have no conscious understanding of how they got there. This is represented graphically by the group and its leader now functioning on the higher plane above the cusp fold in the illustration, in which they collectively must manage the consequences of the explosion. These catastrophic patterns occur often in human organizations and frequently lead to calls for consultation and coaching.

Figure 9.8 visually represents chaotic attractors and repulsors (Kilburg, 2000). These are patterns of systemic function or behavior in groups and teams that can readily be discerned by coaches. Attractors and repulsors can consist of either positive or negative patterns of behavior. For example, in Figure 9.7, the group initially operates in an attractor consisting of a virtuous circle of cooperative and peaceful behavior. Work gets done, relations among members are reasonably harmonious, and behavior toward the leader is largely cooperative and supportive. Attractors in Figure 9.8 are represented by downward-directed helixes to illustrate the quality of human attention and behavior being pulled into them, much like whirlpools in a body of water. Figure 9.8 also illustrates that attractors and repulsors can have different qualities, such as depth, width, and intensity, such that some of them are easily entered and left (Attractor B) whereas others are more difficult to access and, once accessed, are much more difficult to exit (Attractor C). Chaotic repulsors act in the reverse way. These patterns of behavior seem to consist of whirlpools in reverse in that they are hard to get into and, once accessed, stay in, depending on their height, width, and intensity.

Attractors and repulsors can be used to help explain the phenomenon depicted in Figure 9.7. As the catastrophic change occurs in Figure 9.7, the group undergoes a dramatic reconfiguration, leaving one virtuous, cooperative attractor and entering into another that represents a vicious circle of aggression and attacking behavior directed toward the leader. Depending of the strength of this attractor, the ability of the leader to handle the change in behavior, and the emotional intelligence and flexibility of the group and its individual members, the result can be a short visit to open or passive–aggressive conflict, a permanent shift into conflicted guerilla warfare types of behavior, an oscillating pattern of fight–flight between the two attractors, or another even more complex form of conflict.

Figure 9.9 combines Figures 9.7 and 9.8 to illustrate what might happen in a situation in which the open aggression and conflict represents a repulsor for the group. In this example, the behavior of open conflict is much more difficult to enter into by the members of the group because of the existence of group norms against open conflict, leadership that is attuned to the morale and emotional tenor of the group, or the lack of a specific flash point that catalyzes the attack. In such circumstances, the catastrophic shift might not occur because the point (T) might be significantly changed, requiring much higher levels of tension and alienation to trigger an openly aggressive exchange. Although passive–aggressive behavior or individual incidents of anger might appear, the wholesale, sudden shift of the group into open combat will probably be avoided in a case such as this.

Figure 9.10 provides a different illustration of the first case example, in which the open aggression represents another attractor state for the group that is easily accessed once the flash or transition point is passed (T). In such situations, a group can move almost instantly from a virtuous circle of behavior into a vicious one. These circumstances are disconcerting; often traumatizing; and most disruptive to teams and dedicated groups in terms

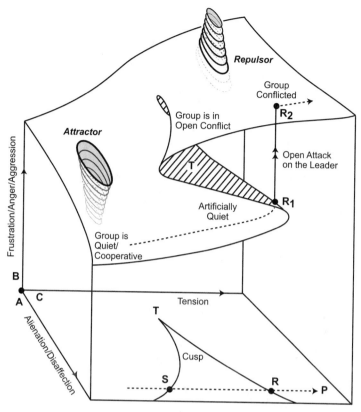

Figure 9.9. A cusp catastrophe in a group with an attractor and repulsor. T = the point at which the tension peaks and open aggression breaks out with an attack on the leader; B = the degree of frustration, anger, and aggression experienced and expressed in and by the group; C = the level of tension experienced and expressed in and by the group; R_1 = the point at which there is an open attack on the leader; R_2 = the point at which tension, aggression, anger, frustration, and alienation have risen high enough so that the entire group is engulfed by conflict; S = the point at which tension begins to rise noticeably; P = when the equilibrium is stabilized and the group has become one that is in constant conflict; A = the dimension of the degree of alienation and disaffection in the group.

of morale, individual well-being, and collective productivity. They also represent likely scenarios in which coaches and consultants are called for assistance. Understanding catastrophic change processes and the functions of attractors and repulsors can significantly aid coaches in these types of circumstances in the conduct of both assessment and intervention activities. Making determinations as to whether catastrophic change has occurred or could occur will orient the coach to the current urgency or impending sense of doom encountered when meeting with clients and how an assignment should be contracted and carried out.

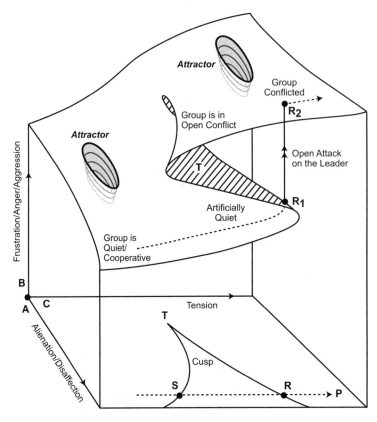

Figure 9.10. A cusp catastrophe in a group with two attractors. T = the point at which the tension peaks and open aggression breaks out with an attack on the leader; B = the degree of frustration, anger, and aggression experienced and expressed in and by the group; C = the level of tension experienced and expressed in and by the group; R_1 = the point at which there is an open attack on the leader; R_2 = the point at which tension, aggression, anger, frustration, and alienation have risen high enough so that the entire group is engulfed by conflict; S = the point at which tension begins to rise noticeably; P = when the equilibrium is stabilized and the group has become one that is in constant conflict; A = the dimension of the degree of alienation and disaffection in the group.

Coaches should be alert in such situations that progress can be rapidly, if not instantaneously, undermined when a negative attractor such as open warfare between a leader and his or her followers claims the attention, motivation, and overt behavior of a group client. Moving client teams from vicious attractors into virtuous ones is the fundamental strategy that should guide coaches in these assignments. Often, a coach may need to work assiduously with the client group to develop a virtuous attractor, such as professional collaboration, if it has not existed in a stable configuration in the past life of the group. In addition, trying to aid client groups in turning vicious attractors into repulsors represents another strategy. It should also be noted that although this example focuses on a regressive shift to unproductive aggression in this group, the same model could be used to illustrate a group that moves into a virtuous attractor of executive group wisdom that I describe at the end of this chapter. Assisting teams in making virtuous repulsors into attractors represents another vital coaching strategy.

In an interesting and relevant study that examined the relationship between the expression of positive emotions and the performance of business teams, Losada and Heaphy (2004) demonstrated empirically that catastrophic changes could be identified in intact business teams and that their performance could be modified for the better by introducing a control parameter—read: virtuous attractor—that involved raising the rate of positive emotional communications in the groups. In their meta-learning model, teams that had a ratio of close to three positive communications to one negative communication tended to create improved performance that seemed to become self-maintaining. They also demonstrated the reverse, namely, that the presence of a ratio of positive to negative communications of one to one or less appeared to create a vicious attractor that seemed to permanently mire the teams in lower levels of performance. They suggested that the creation or simple presence of such positive emotional processes expands the behavioral repertoires of the members of business groups, in keeping with Fredrickson's (1998, 2001) broaden-and-build theory of positive emotions.

In Fredrickson's (1998, 2001) model and research, the presence of positive emotions such as joy, interest, love, and contentment contribute significantly to improving psychological resilience, individual health, and creative thinking as measured by various types of behavior. These streams of intervention-oriented research are highly confirmatory of both the importance of understanding catastrophic models of human behavior and the underlying role that positive emotions play in individual and group performance.

Field Effects in Leadership Groups

The third critical factor involves the existence and influence of what can be thought of as *behavioral fields* for teams and groups. Kurt Lewin (1997) introduced the application of many basic concepts in physics and mathematics to the study of individual and group behavior. His field theory represents a complex effort to describe a geometry of the human mind. It has been widely influential as applied to groups through the work of many of his colleagues. No effort will be made here to explore this work, but it represents the foundation for understanding the third critical factor to which I believe coaches should be alert in their work with teams and dedicated work groups.

EXHIBIT 9.3
Definitions of *Field*

- A space within which forces are in operation
- Anything that changes or tends to change the state of rest or motion in a body
- Power exerted on any resisting person or thing; the quality of anything that produces an effect on the mind or will

Exhibit 9.3 presents a summary of several definitions of *field*. Conventional dictionaries provide multiple listings for the word (e.g., *Funk & Wagnalls Standard College Dictionary*, 1975). However, the major interest I have in the term is in how it has been applied in physics, psychology, and other branches of science (Adair, 1987). When looking at the definitions listed in the exhibit, one can see two core components. First, a field exists as a geometrically defined space. Second, within that space forces operate and produce effects on whatever exists inside or enters into the space. These are simultaneously simple and yet complex ideas. As an example, one could examine the operation of a simple, three-dimensional field if one looked at a pool table with its collection of balls arrayed randomly. As a player introduces a forcefully directed pool stick striking the cue ball, the positions of various balls on the table are changed, depending on the pattern of their interactions with the moving cue ball. When all of the balls come to rest at the end of the play, the surface of the table or field is completely reconfigured. If one or more balls have landed in a pocket, they disappear from the active field. Yet because the game of pool is also controlled by the scoring field to which the players agree at the outset of the match and the fact that the table is a three-dimensional space, those balls in the pocket continue to exert a enormous influence on what will happen on the table and in the behavior of the players. This example describes the fundamental nature of a field and how it can influence whatever exists within it.

Lewin (1997) and others have suggested that human groups create behavioral fields within which the members function. As people interact with each other in various ways, the dynamics, forces, and ultimate behavioral outcomes constantly shift within the field. A summary of 11 examples of what I have come to see as fields operating in teams and dedicated work groups is presented in Exhibit 9.4. Each field creates its own effects in the complex psychological space that exists within and among the members of a group.

Thom (1972) described the geometry of *N* dimensional space, illustrating that the conventional human understanding of space and time as existing in four dimensions is fundamentally flawed. In space, with no limits on the numbers of its dimensions, the number and type of catastrophic folds and effects rise to infinity. The case illustrated in Figure 9.8 becomes simple in

EXHIBIT 9.4
Examples of Behavioral Fields Operating in Human Groups

- Leadership—Styles, methods, behaviors
- Followership—Styles, methods, behaviors
- Organizational and group cultures—Assumptions, values, beliefs, attitudes, expectations, norms, rituals, signs, symbols
- Goals—Teleological causality
- Communication—Exchanges of information
- Transactions—Exchanges of matter and energy, time, attention, money, goods, services
- Human motivation—Individual, group, organizational (power, achievement, affiliation, transcendence, Maslow's hierarchy [Maslow, 1954])
- Organizational and group strategies and tactics—Behavioral expectations, alignment, direction of resources
- Core technologies—Hardware, software, brainware
- Learning—Capacity to generate and use new information
- Group and organizational dynamics—Conformity, cohesion, deviance, resistance, defenses and regressive patterns, compromise formations, symptoms and disorders, patterns of resilience, adaptive functioning, diversity dynamics ("isms," collusion, privilege, scapegoating, injustice, patterns of differences and opposites)

these new terms because only the four dimensions need to be described. In a complex behavioral system such as a group with 11 fields operating, one can see the enormous problem of trying to understand and predict what will happen at any point in time. In reality, there are probably many other types of fields operating in the spaces that emerge within a functioning senior executive group. It is a central task of the leaders of these groups and those who coach them to try to determine what fields are operating, how they are interacting to inhibit positive performance, and to intervene in positive ways to unleash the potential of the group for creative and constructive work.

In human behavior and other natural systems, the probable number of catastrophic shifts and fields in actual operation that one is likely to see is significantly less than infinity, but I believe that it is extraordinarily large. I do not believe that psychological science has evolved sufficiently to let us use these powerful mathematical tools of non-Euclidian geometry to understand most of what we do in practice. Fortunately for coaches, the patterns of behavior in the majority of the cases they take on are readily discernable. Nevertheless, every practitioner must be alert to the possibility that the behaviors in which their clients are engaged are at least influenced by the action of these complex field effects and that those effects may be largely undetectable through the normal mechanisms used in a consulting engagement.

Exhibit 9.4 demonstrates some of the large-scale variables that can act as fields within teams and groups. In classic physics, four fields act on matter and energy: (a) electromagnetism, (b) the weak force, (c) the strong force, and (d) gravity. Scientific efforts throughout the past several centuries have focused on the effort of discovering, describing, and learning how to control and use these basic forces in nature. In the complex psychological space of human groups, the fields identified here interact to produce the conscious and unconscious, observable and nonobservable behaviors that make up the interactions among the people coaches find there. Following this logic, then, leadership, followership, culture, goals, communication, and group dynamics involving conflict, among others, operate both separately and interdependently as definable fields within the psychological space created and occupied by a team. Each of these fields has major effects on the people within it, namely, the members of the group. The fields interact with each other to produce complex global outcomes that are described in Figure 9.5 as resilient–creative, homeostatic, and regressive–destructive.

In the context of field theory, coaching efforts are usually directed first toward assessing the strength and other characteristics of each of these fields in a group and then to designing interventions that will influence one or more of them in order to produce more desirable, creative, and productive outcomes for the client team. Loop-learning strategies, described in Figure 9.2, are among the most frequent strategies used as coaches work with their clients to try to discern the existence of defensive patterns of behavior and then intervene to create learning and then more constructive effects for them. Coaching with the individual executive managing the group can also be seen in this context as an intervention deliberately introduced to alter the leadership and hence followership fields in a top team. Similarly, culture change initiatives most often represent broad efforts to shift many fields within an organization simultaneously. The sweeping nature of these culture interventions and the nearly universal resistance to such broad changes by the members of organizations often account for how treacherously complex and difficult these initiatives can be to implement successfully.

It is impossible in the space of this chapter to describe these phenomena and their interactions completely, so a simple example will need to suffice for now. Let us briefly examine a project team in the storming stage of its development. As we know, during this stage, open conflict and struggles over boundaries, role definition, goals, and norms, all usually only vaguely defined, are common. If we insert a leader into such a situation who understands group dynamics, has excellent communication and problem-solving skills, considerable experience, and advanced emotional intelligence and is motivated to lead the team, it is likely that he or she will immediately exert constructive influences on the members of the team. These leadership forces in all probability will pressure the members of the group toward resolution of the conflicts via developing role clarity; goal specificity; norms for communication, conflict, and performance; and explicit expectations for overt behavior by the members of the team. Communication and transaction fields will be established that support these efforts as seen in the role modeling provided by such an effective leader.

In such a situation with effective leadership, the group begins to create active learning routines that also exert pressure toward performance. The underlying, unconscious dynamics of the team evolve quickly toward resilient adaptation, including reasonable conformity to the newly established norms, increased group cohesion, decreased destructive defensiveness, and so on. The group in this kind of situation then can pass relatively smoothly through forming and storming and into norming and thus avoid catastrophic negative shifts in behavior and performance. The leadership field established thus influences and helps create the followership field, and both pressure the members of the team toward successful resolution of the opening phases of team development as well as influencing the other fields identified in Exhibit 9.4. In a sense, this kind of effective leadership and followership can be said to create a virtuous attractor of effective group dynamics and positive work outcomes.

Similarly, the example can be reversed by simply extracting the experienced and gifted leader and letting the highly conflicted group wallow in its own initial forming and storming. If the maturity, talent, and knowledge to resolve this fundamental challenge in group development do not exist within any of the members of the group, then one can reasonably predict that the leadership and followership fields will be insufficient to enable the group to move successfully out of the storming phase of development. Efforts at performance will undoubtedly be made in such a situation, but it is relatively easy to predict that the outcomes will be less satisfactory than those from a group led by the experienced individual described above. Without the reasonable influences and positive pressures of role clarity, goal definition, and boundary setting established by good leadership, a team can often regress into a basic-assumption group that demonstrates fight–flight; dependency; pairing; paranoia; narcissistically defended entitlement; or other ineffective, unconscious, and potentially negative catastrophic dynamics.

Here again, the roles and goals of coaches become clear, although perhaps problematic to implement. Helping such a troubled team to assess and identify the problems and work toward a successful development sequence can be a fairly straightforward type of intervention when the group is motivated and has not regressed to the point of permanent injury to the working relationships of its members. If such regression and irrevocable injuries have occurred, a coach may need to recommend that the team disband and that some other effort be instituted to accomplish the task delegated to it. Familiarity and expertise in recognizing and intervening constructively in these psychological fields of team and group clients thus should be a core competency of coaches and consultants working in such settings.

Effects of Wisdom and Individual Cognitive Development on Executive Groups

The fourth and final critical factor involves the level of wisdom, human consciousness, cognitive complexity, or order of mind of the individual members of an executive team or dedicated work group. The work of Kegan (1994), Sternberg (1990), Jaques and Clement (1991), and many others as summarized in chapters 2 and 3, is crucial for coaches to understand in trying to unravel these influences on the effectiveness of group performance. For purposes of brevity, I use Kegan's (1994) framework to explore this issue, although at the outset it must be understood that the range of issues involved in the creation and use of advanced forms of human consciousness is in fact enormous.

A summary of Kegan's (1994) typology of five orders of mind that he asserts drive the human capacity to adapt to the demands of life made by relationships, families, organizations, and societies is presented in Table 9.1. These stages of mental and emotional development are reached slowly, through a number of processes. They emerge sequentially and in an orderly fashion. They are driven by the fundamental capacity to discern what Kegan and other cognitive scientists and philosophers call *subject* from *object*. Loosely defined, the *subject* is usually the individual person, or what can be called the *self*. *Objects* are those events, entities, people, and things that exist outside of the person. According to Kegan and his colleagues, the capacity to distinguish between the self and objects grows systematically in humans.

As outlined in Table 9.1, the first order of mind, the simplest and earliest to develop, is seen in children between the ages of birth and 7 years. During this time, a child slowly builds the ability to determine the difference between him- or herself and the outer world. Research has clearly demonstrated that in the first days of infancy, humans appear to have only rudimentary abilities to experience themselves as separate from their environments, especially their caretakers. Although by the end of the stage most children can distinguish reliably between the self and an external object, for the average 7-year-old, the world remains a mysterious and magical place in which the child is largely self-centered, lacks empathy for others, has difficulty remembering and conceptualizing rules, and possesses only the most basic understanding of him- or herself as a separate being. The child thinks largely in precategorical terms and uses defenses such as denial, splitting, projection, and rudimentary repression (Kilburg, 2000). Children have great

TABLE 9.1
Five Orders of Mind: Levels and Types of Human Meaning Making and Consciousness

Order of mind	Age group	Characteristics
First	Children: birth to 7 years	Lack of durable objects or categories World as magic and mystery Precategorical thinking Splitting, denial, projection, repression Self-centeredness Sees others as extensions of self Lack of or minimal empathy Can't conceptualize or remember rules Absence of internally constructed self
Second	Children: 7 years through adolescence; some adults	Durable objects and categories Categorical thinking Possesses beliefs, rules, coherent feeling states Sees others as instruments Instrumental and self-centered empathy Obeys rules for fear of retaliation, being caught, punishment Absence of internally constructed self
Third	Most adults	Durable objects and categories Cross-categorical thinking Problematic empathy—great differences and distance between minds Constant attitudes, values, beliefs, feelings, preferences Obeys rules out of loyalty to family, organization, village; concerns for not letting others down Sees others as separate humans Capacity to subordinate desires and beliefs to those of others Capacity for abstract thinking Capacity for self-reflection Absence of a consistent and coherent internally constructed self Difficulty in making hard choices when in conflict—feels "torn in two"
Fourth	Some adults	Durable objects and categories Systems thinking Internally constructed self Internal rules and regulations—a self-governing, self-regulating system Use of self-system to make judgments, decisions, choices Human empathy used in reality testing, problem-solving, decision making Own their work Can create and protect rules, limits, boundaries Relates to others as independent people with their own identities, values, ideas, and feelings

(continued)

TABLE 9.1 *(Continued)*

Order of mind	Age group	Characteristics
Fourth	Some adults	Capable of "reauthoring" the self-system Capable of making difficult choices Some difficulty in using empathy to see and feel different approaches to what is right Does not necessarily value diversity
Fifth	Very few adults	Durable objects and categories Incorporation of dialectics, polarities, and paradox in transsystemic thinking Internally constructed self Recognizes limits in the self-system; seeks and solicits others' ideas, experiences, feelings Able to see systems of rules, limits, boundaries, why they are useful, when they are not, how they can be changed and protected Relates to others as interdependent people, able to appreciate and value their differences and similarities, sees them as necessary extenders of the self Capable of "reauthoring" self-system and mutual relationships Universally applied accurate empathy Owns his or her work and sees its relationship to that of others Curious about and values diversity

Note. From Kegan (1994).

difficulty negotiating the complex, external world and are largely dependent on adults to help them understand and survive in it.

As each child moves toward adolescence, he or she slowly gains the ability to create an understanding of the world as being made up of durable and lasting objects and categories of objects. Mom and Dad come to be accepted and understood as people, separate from the child, who function as parents. The child evolves a set of permanent feelings about categories of objects, such as "I like ice cream and I hate homework," and "I love my friends and dislike my teachers and other authority figures." Other people are treated largely as instruments that help him or her get things done in the individual world of the child. During this stage, children learn to conceptualize rules, and they tend to obey them largely out of a desire not to be caught, punished, or retaliated against. Categorical thinking largely consists of the logical operations of identity and disjunction. In other words, the objects encountered in the world can be clearly labeled for what they are and can be distinguished from other objects. For example, ice cream can be distinguished from music; the categories are either food–ice cream or music. This ability to categorize provides a powerful new tool for encountering and mastering the world. Pre-, mid-, and late adolescents possess an ability to empathize with others, but this ability is flawed because they still largely lack a firmly constructed, internal sense of a self as separate from family or peer influences.

The evolution of the third order of mind marks in most people the emergence of young adulthood. The most distinguishing characteristic is the ability to think across categories. Objects can now be seen as either this or that or this and that. Empathy exists but is somewhat problematic because the differences between people are often experienced as very great. Most adults can think abstractly; reflect about themselves fairly accurately; and have constant attitudes, beliefs, feelings, and preferences. They obey rules out of a consistent understanding of their effects and their sense of loyalty to the family and community or their desire to not let others in the social group down. They see other people as separate human beings and can, if they desire, subordinate their own wishes and desires to those of others. When they experience significant interpersonal, intrapsychic, or social conflict, most adults feel torn and can find it difficult to resolve the differences experienced. Kegan (1994) defined the *third-order mind* as being adept at dealing with the traditional world, in which social institutions provide strong rules and limits that individuals are expected to follow. He also suggested that the third-order mind can move out of its depth when confronted with the demands of the modern world. To be effective there, a person must evolve a fourth-order mind.

Table 9.1 defines the *fourth-order mind* as being able to define itself as a separate entity and as one that has the capacity to understand and re-create or "reauthor" itself according to the circumstances that it encounters in the world. A person functioning with a fourth-order mind thinks systemically, not only possessing the ability to think within and across categories but also able to reason about multiple categories and their hierarchical and interpenetrating relationships to each other. He or she is able to create rules, limits, and boundaries and defend or change them for their own sake, make complex and difficult decisions without being emotionally torn in two, own his or her own work, and have internal rules and regulations. Such individuals become self-regulating, self-managing, and self-creating systems who can also change themselves, their rules, their decisions, and their behaviors when they recognize the need to do so. Fourth-order minds are able to meet other people and experience them as separate, independent, unique, and thus different from themselves. They use empathy reasonably well, but they can continue to struggle with the issues of understanding others. They do not necessarily value diversity in the world. Kegan (1994) expressed the opinion that modern relationships, organizations, and society as a whole demand that individuals be able to operate minimally within the fourth order of mind to be successful. He also suggested that only some adults develop this level of consciousness. This hypothesis is supported by some research that is based on the use of the Subject Object Interview in experiments with various populations (Lahey, Souvaine, Kegan, Goodman, & Felix, 1988).

Finally, Table 9.1 describes Kegan's (1994) fifth order of mind, reached, according to him, by only a few modern adults. A person operating at the fifth order possesses a self-regulating mental system but also recognizes the limitations of his or her own mind. In other words, a fifth-order mind first and foremost is self-aware and self-regulating. A person with such a mind can deliberately know what he or she knows and does not know. Such a person thinks dialectically in transsystem terms, creating, valuing, and containing polarities and paradoxes; possesses accurate empathy for others as separate humans; and values and seeks their differences as enhancements to those possessed by the all too limited self. He or she owns his or her own thoughts, feelings, behaviors, and work and sees them in relationship to those of others. He or she creates rules, boundaries, and limits and is able to see why they are useful and when and how they must be changed. A person functioning in a fifth-order mind values diversity and becomes a seeker of others' experiences and a creator of new ways of seeing and doing things. Kegan and his colleagues suggested that fifth-order minds are rare. However, they also suggested that the postmodern world is rapidly emerging and will require fifth-order mental and emotional capacity for successful negotiation of the complexities of a global, transcultural, collective conscious experience.

The requirement for possessing fourth- and fifth-order levels of mind is especially true for leaders in the transglobal, business enterprises that have emerged rapidly in the world. Teams and dedicated executive groups in these kinds of organizations are increasingly diverse and must successfully negotiate across multiple national, cultural, and enterprise boundaries to design, manufacture, market, and deliver goods and services. Without fifth-order capacity, individuals and teams are often left struggling across differences, able to define and distinguish them but unable to incorporate, re-create, and transcend them. If Kegan (1994) and his colleagues were correct, coaches themselves will need fifth-order minds to be able to work successfully with these leadership groups.

I encountered a clear-cut case of this challenge a few years ago when I was called in to coach a manager in a major company who had been promoted to lead a multidisciplinary and multinational team of technical experts to solve a major problem for the enterprise. This individual had distinguished himself in the U.S. operations of the organization, leading productive teams at a variety of levels in the company and in several different geographic locations in the country. However, in the assignment he had recently been given, his team was composed of approximately 20 men and women from all over the world. They had come together with initial good spirit and commitment to attack the problems they had been given to solve as creatively and quickly as possible.

However, despite everyone's best efforts, the group quickly disintegrated into a nightmare of miscommunication, open conflict, and ineffective performance. When I met with the client, it quickly became clear to me that he did not understand the multicultural dimensions of his team or the nuanced forms of leadership that were required of him. Our initial conversations were full of comments on his part about how troubling he found it that the Korean, Japanese, and Chinese members of the team had such difficulty talking to each other and getting along. He was devoid of any historical information about the nature of the conflicts between these cultures and countries, let alone understood their different approaches to interpersonal relationships, authority and decision-making processes, and the expression of emotions. At one point early on, he said in an exasperated tone, "I don't understand why they can't get along together!"

In that assignment, it quickly became very clear to me that the individual did not possess sufficient cognitive, interpersonal, or social skills to know what his assignment required. I made a number of efforts to coach him about the impact of diversity dynamics on team performance, the need for him to think and behave with much more sensitivity and flexibility, and the changes he had to make in the organization and operations of the group in order to succeed. Although he tried hard to change, at the end of several months of effort, his boss said to me, "He just doesn't get it." The organization then found him an assignment in their U.S. operations and promoted an experienced British woman who had lived in Asia and worked for the company for a number of years to lead the team. Both of these executives succeeded in their new roles.

This case vignette demonstrates that in modern global corporations, many, if not most, of the senior leadership assignments require leaders to possess and use fourth- and fifth-order minds to succeed. Thinking and behaving in systemic and transsystemic models is a requirement when leaders face the kind of complexity that global competition produces. The lack of such development in an executive or in any coach trying to work in such settings can produce profound deficits in function and often creates the circumstances for public and thus spectacular failure.

Facilitating the Emergence of Wisdom in Executive Groups

In addition to the foregoing set of key concepts and factors influencing the operation and coaching of executive groups, the core models describing Executive Wisdom introduced in chapters 2 through 8 also can and should be applied to them. Because the majority of senior leaders in organizations usually have a group of colleagues through and with which they operate the organization, it becomes crucial that all of the members of the group demonstrate Executive Wisdom as individuals. They also operate as a group together to manage the organization, and as the case study that opened this chapter aptly demonstrates, many complex issues can get in the way of the group as a whole exercising their collective wisdom at any point in time.

As I have consistently pointed out, the emergence of Executive Wisdom in any individual leader represents the outcome of a complex process involving potentially a huge number of variables. When the additional nuances of a number of executive team members and their group dynamics are added to the rich mixture of factors and forces that constitute life at the top of most organizations that I have explored thus far in this chapter, it is easy to see why wisdom remains such an elusive phenomenon either for individuals or for leadership groups to produce consistently in these environments. This is not to say that it never or rarely happens because, in fact, history is replete with many examples of what I have described in this book as Executive Wisdom emerging in leadership groups. However, any leadership group that aspires to the consistent creation and expression of such wisdom needs to be determined to address the barriers to its achievement and to facilitate the conditions from which it can more easily arise.

For me, Executive Wisdom as expressed and experienced in leadership groups follows the same definition I have applied to individual executives. It involves discerning and doing the right things, in the right way, against the right time frame for the organization. When executive groups meet, each of the individuals brings with him or her all of the components of the wisdom models. Figure 9.11 depicts a typical executive group composed of six individuals, each of whom can be thought of as encompassing the base model of the components of wisdom described in Figure 2.1. For the sake of argument, I am going to assume that each of the members of this group is well motivated to perform and desires to deploy his or her highest levels of individual Executive Wisdom but may or may not strive in each and every interaction with colleagues in the group to do so. Figure 9.11 demonstrates that unless the leader of the executive team, the group as a whole, or a subgroup of its membership actively engages Executive Wisdom, for the most part it does not emerge out of the team. They continue to operate more or less as individuals and function more or less effectively as a group, but they do not rise to the level of superb performance that modern organizations need from their senior teams.

If we modify the scenario and create one in which several of the members of the group are willing and able to enact their own individual Executive Wisdom at least part of the time and then are able to develop a partial integration of these individual capacities, one sees the modification

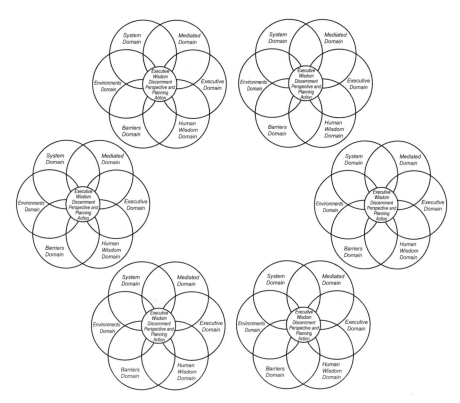

Figure 9.11. A six-person group with no shared Executive Wisdom.

of the group as presented in Figure 9.12. Here, several group members are at least partially engaged in rising to individual Executive Wisdom and in creating a subgroup level version of it. The figure also suggests that the size of the leadership outcome—and, also for the sake of the argument, the quality of the wisdom outcome—is limited by the number of individuals involved, what they are able to do, and by the absence of involvement of some of the other members of the leadership group. In essence, in such a scenario one sees the emergence of some group Executive Wisdom but not what might be possible if everyone were fully engaged and had enabled their individual wisdom systems.

If we further modify the scenario by allowing all of the members of the group to participate in creating the group wisdom effect, one can see an illustration of this in Figure 9.13. With all of the members of the group now participating at least in part, the figure displays an expansion of what could be thought of as the *wisdom field*. If everyone is involved creatively and constructively in creating group wisdom, the odds are likely to improve that Executive Wisdom will emerge out of the group as a whole.

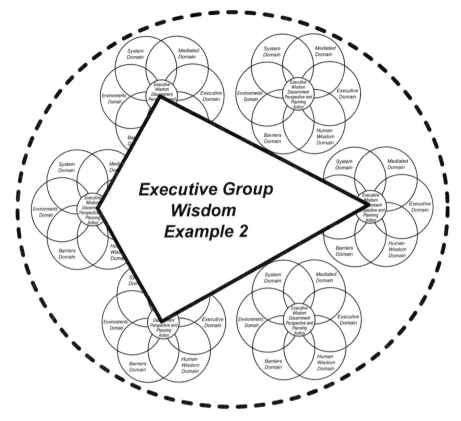

Figure 9.12. A six-person group with four members partially sharing their wisdom.

Finally, in Figure 9.14, one sees a scenario in which each and every member of the executive team is fully engaged in the exercise of creating wisdom as a group. The wisdom field is depicted by the dotted line surrounding the whole group instead of occupying a smaller space between the individuals. This scenario represents the optimum situation for executive groups, one in which everyone does their best in every way to enable both individual and group wisdom to emerge and constructively influence their collective and individual work. In such a scenario, one can imagine that both the individual members of the group as well as the group as a whole are both capable of and actually perform the tasks of wisdom mapping described in chapters 4 through 7. In addition, such an executive group can usually be seen in the act of nimbly engaging in the dance of reflective engagement examined in chapter 8. Such executive groups become self-monitoring, cocreating, environmentally responsive entities that possess both individual and group wisdom. They actively strive to become more effective and wiser, using the capacities of fourth- and fifth-order minds,

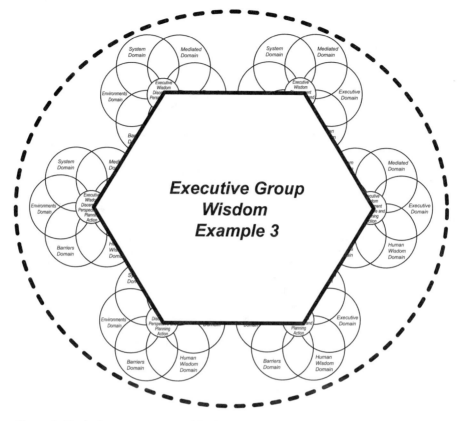

Figure 9.13. A six-person group with six members partially sharing their wisdom.

and if they do so, they continuously evolve in response to the presence of this kind of virtuous performance, and they avoid the destructive effects of group and organizational defensiveness and organizational regression described earlier in this chapter. In effect, they become virtuous groups of leaders pursuing good on behalf of their organizations and of society as a whole.

In my experience, such wise leadership groups are rare, but they do exist. Also in my experience, they do not arise as a result of accidental evolution. They are cocreated by their members, who deliberately engage all of their collective capacities to improve their performance as individuals, as a leadership group, and thereby as an organization. In terms of Fowers's (2005) models of character development, virtuous teams are made, not born. They are the result of a lot of hard work on the part of their individual members and even more hard work in putting their collective knowledge, skill, experience, and virtue together on a day-to-day basis. For as much as it takes a great deal of practice to produce an individual with a good

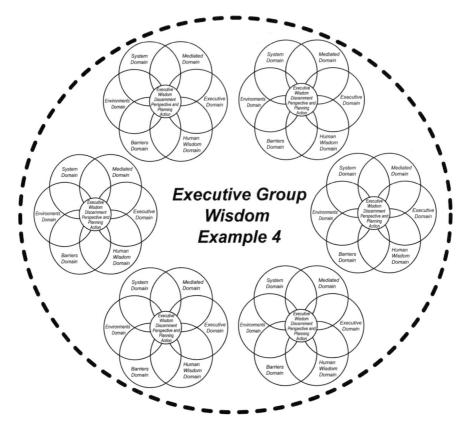

Figure 9.14. A six-person group with six members fully sharing their wisdom.

character, it can take even more effort to create a group that behaves in a consistently virtuous fashion.

In my experience, coaching and consulting interventions with intact executive groups can use any or all of the types of reflection and awareness exercises enumerated in this book to increase the likelihood that group wisdom will emerge. However, I also believe that it takes time for this to occur. It is extremely unlikely that the kind of one-of-a-kind, in-and-out development events that often characterize leadership initiatives with senior teams will promote the conditions and the changes that are needed for consistently wise performance. The teams that I have seen develop and sustain this kind of capacity most often have the goal of becoming increasingly better at individual, group, and organizational functioning. They make their individual, group, and organizational development a routine part of what they devote time, energy, and other resources toward. They regularly assess how they perform as individuals and as groups and come to value feedback that enables them to improve. They rapidly address defensive routines together to reduce their adverse impacts. Entering such organizational and interpersonal environments, any coach or consultant becomes immediately impressed with the energy, drive, and motivation to achieve outstanding results that seem to permeate these groups. Helping to cocreate such progressively developing organizations is the most challenging and rewarding assignment a coach can obtain.

Group Wisdom: Research and Practice Support

Two recent books have addressed the phenomena of executive group wisdom effects in somewhat different ways. Salas and Fiore (2004) put together a collection of conceptual, research, and methodological papers that described what a subset of psychological investigators is now calling *team cognition*. On the basis of an emerging body of knowledge that is aimed at trying to further refine just how teams can be enabled to achieve even higher levels of task performance, these authors suggested that effective groups appear to develop a group-level understanding of their tasks, roles, challenges, and overall situation. They enact their group strategy and individual task components while simultaneously keeping both their individual- and group-level understandings in conscious awareness.

Similarly, Rentsch and Woehr (2004) suggested a social relations foundation for the formation of what they call "team member schema similarity" (p. 14). A *schema* refers to "the cognition to be organized—structured knowledge that enables individuals to understand, interpret, and give meaning to stimuli" (Rentsch & Woehr, 2004, p. 14). They further suggested that there are at least two components of this schema similarity, congruence and accuracy:

> The degree of team member schema congruence that exists is indicated in the degree of match between team member's schemas in content, structure, or both. . . . . When team member schema congruence exists among team members and the schema content is functional, they are likely to engage in smooth interpersonal interactions and constructive task behaviors. . . . . Team member schema accuracy refers to the degree to which a team member's schema is similar to a pre-specified target value or "true score." (p. 15)

Rentsch and Woehr (2004) went on to discuss a social relations foundation for the development of these schemas that is based on the dyadic interactions between the members of a team organized around such issues as the degree to which they see each other as similar or different and the amount of overlap between their mutual perceptions of each other. These ideas, in addition to opening new avenues for the investigation of group dynamics and effectiveness, provide at least some encouragement to the ideas expressed above that the emergence of Executive Wisdom could well be an outcome for an effectively organized and led leadership group.

Furthermore, Hinsz (2004), in the same volume, provided a succinct summary of a parallel body of research that demonstrates that groups can develop and use metacognitive mental models in their work. Hinsz, Tindale, and Vollrath (1997) provided an extensive review of the research literature that examines how groups process information in the service of decision making and task performance. This growing body of work demonstrates that many of the metacognitive phenomena described in chapter 3 of this book are possible to investigate in either intact or ad hoc groups. Furthermore, the research strongly suggests that groups can and do use metacognitive processes for memory, problem-solving, and decision-making functions. Indeed, there has been significant work done for years on what I described in chapter 2 as executive ignorance or blindness within the "groupthink" framework described by Janis (1982). What one could think of as the more dysfunctional aspects of group cognition have been much more thoroughly explored in a large variety of studies exploring this phenomenon.

Surowiecki (2004) also made a recent and more popularized effort to address the question of why groups seem to outperform the smartest of individuals in many different situations. Starting with Francis Galton's earliest recorded experiment, in which he documented just how accurate group estimations could be as opposed to those of individuals, Surowiecki provided intriguing case examples in the context of easy-to-read summaries of relevant decision-making and group problem-solving literature that demonstrated the superiority of groups.

In one instance of this phenomenon, he cited the response of the New York Stock Exchange to the news of the destruction of the space shuttle *Challenger* in 1986. Four American companies—Rockwell International, Lockheed, Martin Marietta, and Morton Thiokol—were the major contractors involved in the construction of the shuttles (the shuttle and its main engines, ground support, the external fuel tank, and the solid rocket boosters, respectively). Within 21 minutes of the news hitting the wires, the stock of each company was down by an average of 4%. However, by the time the market closed, Morton Thiokol's stock had lost 12%, but the other three company's losses were limited to 3%. It took the National Aeronautics and Space Administration an enormous investigative effort over a 6-month period to determine that the O rings on Morton Thiokol's solid rockets were defective. The collective wisdom of the New York Stock Exchange came to the roughly same conclusion about a problem with the solid rockets in less than 6 hours.

In his book, Surowiecki (2004) explored three kinds of problems—cognitive, coordination, and cooperation—suggesting that in each of them, under the right circumstances, groups could exceed the performance of individuals. For example, he identified having a group composed of diverse members with different views, allowing them to influence and educate each other but decide about problems individually, and providing them with a vehicle for aggregating their opinions as specific interventions to improve their performance. Under such conditions, groups can perform remarkably well and often much better than the best effort of the most effective individual member. However, Surowiecki also provided ample evidence for how stupid groups can be when they are misled or "misorganized" or when they misunderstand what they are trying to do. Although an in-depth discussion of this literature is beyond the scope of this book, it is apparent from these and other available resources that there is a realistic scientific basis on which to suggest that Executive Wisdom can and does emerge in groups as well as in individuals. There certainly is ample evidence to suggest that it is easy to induce ignorance and stupidity in groups of humans.

Throughout this chapter, I have attempted to provide an overview of the major domains of executive group behavior and factors that can influence performance as a way of establishing a conceptual foundation for understanding what can, and often does, determine whether and how wisdom or stupidity emerges in leadership teams. Most modern organizations are managed by what amounts to an oligarchy of individual executives. They are almost always structured as representational groups that, according to Berg's (2005) recent article, create unique organizational and individual dynamics that significantly influence the effectiveness of their behavior. It is the fundamental thesis of this chapter—indeed, of the book taken as a whole—that the best of these groups master the challenges of learning and defensive routines, unconscious group processes, organizational regression, the stages of group development, chaotic dynamics in their operations, and creating constructive field effects. They evolve progressively as individual leaders within these groups to be able to consistently deploy self-monitoring, self-awareness, and constantly growing fourth- and fifth-order minds. These groups also become increasingly able to create and use wisdom as a whole. When they are able to lead modern, complex, globally competitive enterprises with and through such wisdom, their organizations, the people in them, and the world at large consistently improve.

As with Executive Wisdom in individuals, wise executive teams also become metacognitively sophisticated, self- and group aware, cocreating, postmodern, fifth-order thinking and acting entities that are capable of knowing themselves, their organizations, their environments, and also determining what they do not know and why they do not know what they should. They function with high levels of moral and ethical awareness that inform their processes of discernment, decision making, and action. They are not born in the instant of their formation; instead, they evolve progressively and with careful attention to the details of their development and with a great deal of practice and reflective learning on and about that practice. I believe that these kinds of wise executive groups are currently rare, but I also believe that many more leadership teams are capable of further evolving their capacities for deploying wisdom and other virtues as they cope with the perpetual struggles of life at the top of institutions. In addition, coaches and consultants can improve the likelihood that they too will be able to act more wisely and display more consistent human virtue as they do their work with both individuals and executive teams.

In the next chapter, I look a little more closely at what coaches and consultants can do with executive groups to promote the emergence of more wisdom in their ongoing exchanges. I also revisit the case study that started this chapter and try to apply some of the ideas I have explored here to better understand what was happening in that particular leadership team. In those passages, I hope you as readers will continue to grow in your understanding of how the development of human virtue in individual leaders and executive groups can and must be given a higher priority in our modern organizations.

ACTIVITY TO DEVELOP LEADERSHIP AND COACHING ABILITIES: WISDOM CHECK-UP EXERCISE

Given the amazing array of processes and factors that appear to influence whether wisdom arises and can be deployed in executive group settings, readers might be wondering if there is an easier way to encourage teams to consider their behavior and activities through the lens of human wisdom. What follows is a series of questions that I have used with both individual leaders and with executive teams to help them examine themselves and to become more sensitized to the complex nature of wisdom. Asking the questions does not guarantee that wisdom will emerge in a group; however, taking each in turn at the end of a meeting or after a difficult decision has been reached will force people to think a little differently about what they have done or what they are about to undertake.

1. Is this the wisest course of action to undertake in this situation that we face?
2. Is this the correct time to take these steps?
3. Are we going to implement this plan in the right way?
4. Have we carefully examined the individual, group, organizational, situational, and moral factors and influences that have led us to this course of action?
5. Are our personal, political, economic, and moral motivations that power this decision and action plan clear to us?

6. Have we explored whom we will privilege, and perhaps whom we will exploit, as a result of this course of action?

7. Have we considered the long-term consequences of our choice(s)? How far into the future have we projected our estimates of the consequences? Are those projections sufficient?

8. How will we evaluate whether this course of action succeeds or fails?

9. How will we keep ourselves true to our values, honest with each other, and committed to the exercise of human virtue as we implement our plan of action (behaving with courage, temperance, and pursuing both justice and goodness)?

10. What are we doing or will do routinely to ensure that we are becoming wiser and more virtuous as individuals, as leaders, and as an executive group?

11. What will we do and how will we feel, think, and change if we fail? How will we know if we have failed? How can we behave now to increase the likelihood that we can face and work through a failure with courage, dignity, modesty, temperance, and wisdom?

10

CONCLUSION

In short, there is no algorithm for life. We have to use our judgment continually to decide how best to act in a given state of affairs.
—Fowers (2005, p. 13)

Imagine for just a moment that you were a coach or consultant hired by the now-defunct Enron Corporation to work with the company's senior leadership group in the 6 months prior to its complete implosion. Consider the issues and dynamic forces described in the last chapter—unconscious psychodynamic conflict, defensive behaviors, vicious chaotic attractors, regressive behaviors, and categorical thinking abound. On the surface, the company appeared sound, and your check from them cleared the bank. However, as you began to assess the situation and really started to talk with the members of the team, you discovered the degree to which the culture had deteriorated beyond anyone's control; that the chairman of the board seemed more interested in the purchase of the latest jet for the company than in paying attention to the real problems in the organization; and that the newly appointed CEO, although overtly confident and bragging brashly about the future of the enterprise, had lost touch completely with the chief financial officer. You also discovered that the meetings of the senior executive group were in essence scripted farces during which there was no serious discussion of the issues facing the institution. At some point as well, one of the senior team members confided in you that he was truly worried for the future of the organization because he believed there was real financial trouble brewing and that the leadership team was not dealing with it in an open and honest fashion. What would you do? What could you do?

Although Enron was indeed a special and spectacular case, all too often coaches and consultants face similar conditions and challenges in their assignments. In a sense, this fact is the main reason that the disciplines of coaching and consulting have arisen. The worlds of corporate leadership and global economic competition produce incredible pressures and difficulties for both individual executives and the groups within which they work. In the absence of a consistent commitment to growth and development, executive teams are all too prone to create and experience symptoms of psychodynamically influenced conflict and organizational regression. Knowing how to maneuver in these environments is crucial for anyone who wants to be a leader at the top of an organization and for any practitioner who believes that he or she can assist such people in the conduct of their offices.

In this chapter, I attempt to provide some clarity about how interventions with senior leadership groups can be conceptualized and focus on the issue of what activities are more likely to lead them to become wiser and therefore more virtuous in their relationships, deliberations, and actions. I briefly explore how confidentiality can be managed in such engagements. I also revisit the case that introduced chapter 9 and attempt to understand it through the various concepts that we have explored thus far. At the end of the chapter, I try to bring some closure to the journey we have made together by summarizing some of the principal themes of the book.

COACHING, CONSULTING, AND COUNSELING: UNDERSTANDING INTERVENTIONS WITH EXECUTIVE GROUPS

Over the past few years, I have struggled somewhat in trying to determine what would distinguish coaching activities from those of the other typical kinds of interventions that have evolved and are used often with groups. Currently, I see three overlapping and systematic forms of activities being used with leadership teams: what we have come to identify as (a) psychotherapy or group counseling (Yalom, 1970), (b) team building (Dyer, 1987, and others), and (c) organization development and process consultation (Schein, 1988). Therapeutic interventions focus on the amelioration of regression and dysfunction in individuals and groups. Team-building activities typically provide education and training in order to build new knowledge and skills as well as to identify challenges and problems and work on them in a group setting. Organization development and process consultation focuses structured interventions to improve team and enterprise performance over time. Organization development efforts are usually the most extensive interventions in the repertoires of consultants. These larger projects often focus on and result in restructuring enterprises, reshaping elements of organizational culture, or refocusing the competitive strategy of an institution as typical projects.

I believe that coaching can be distinguished from these other activities in two ways. First, it usually involves a longer term relationship with the executive group or team than a typical organization development or team-building intervention. In longitudinal types of engagements, a coach can see and support a team through a full cycle of normal development. He or she acts in some measure as a therapist does, providing a stable, committed, professionally informed and conducted emotional containment (Kilburg, 2000) within which the members of the group can explore and evolve with each other and do so with reasonable safety. The coach may well need to help the group manage some forms of regressive or dysfunctional behavior, but most often these efforts stop significantly short of providing a classic, therapeutic group environment that focuses historically on improving the mental health and social relationships of the individual members. Some highly dysfunctional executive groups might well need and benefit from such an intervention, but this is normally beyond the scope of a coach's agreement and, often, his or her ability. In my experience, the leadership environments of family businesses are the most likely to create the kinds of dynamics and pressures that might push a coach to consider making a referral to a family therapist for more in-depth assistance with those problems.

Figure 10.1 presents a Venn diagram that contains these three major forms of traditional interventions with groups. The center of the diagram, the nexus where all three intervention domains overlap, is where the process of coaching executive teams resides. The distinction between the three different forms or types of interventions may seem like an artificial one, but I think that a coach will often select from the array of concepts and tools in all three forms of traditional, group-based interventions to help a client team or group. In the context of a longer term relationship, he or she is free to experiment with team-building; process consultation; individual coaching; and even limited, therapeutically informed interventions using techniques such as confrontations and selective interpretations. Long-term coaching relationships do not necessarily require a coach's constant presence with a team. Indeed, in my experience such intervention relationships often stretch over years and consist of periodic engagements with a leadership group that remains largely intact through time. Argyris (1993) provided probably the best and most elaborate description of such an ongoing coaching relationship with a dedicated executive team.

Second, in my coaching work with executive groups I have found it both useful and necessary to loosen some of the traditional role boundaries that consultants usually negotiate in such interventions. One of the main practice issues that is always present in working with groups has to do with whether a consultant will talk with individuals about other individuals on the team without formally disclosing that such conversations have taken place. This is usually a wise role and process boundary to negotiate, and

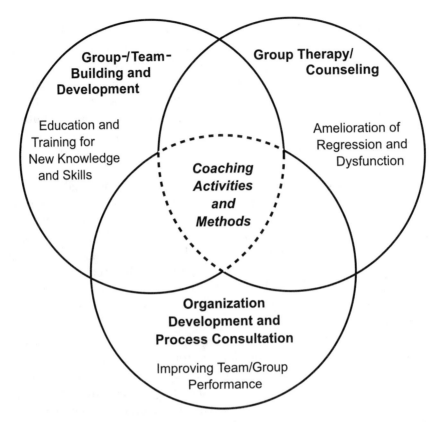

Figure 10.1. The coaching interface to executive groups.

doing so tends to provide clarity and reassurance to all of the members of the group that the practitioner is not playing favorites or plotting against someone. However, what I have found in long-term engagements with executive teams is that with some minor modifications of the usual boundary and role negotiations, clients appear to be able to tolerate and make gains from a mixture of individual and group-oriented interventions.

In a significant number of client organizations over the past couple of decades, I have found myself coaching the CEO, executive director, or manager of record in the organization and his or her entire leadership group as well as individual members of that group. In the individual sessions with members of the leadership group, I have often discovered problems, issues, and developmental challenges for the entire group, the senior executive, and for other members of the team that would never be surfaced otherwise. As we know, in group settings individuals do not always explicitly and overtly disclose what they are thinking and feeling. In working one on one with members of the team, I have found that I can often encourage and support them in getting their thoughts and feelings more directly expressed with the rest of the group or with other individuals and that the process of doing so can be extraordinarily useful to the individuals and the team. Similarly, in working with the senior leader as well as the group as a whole, it becomes possible to process together what is happening in the team and its individual members as well as how the team itself is responding to the leader's management efforts. As complex and difficult as this kind of work often becomes, I am much more confident in my diagnostic and interventional judgments in the engagements in which I am working with the whole group as opposed to an individual member of an executive team, even if it is the CEO, because I have much more data with which to assess any situation.

MANAGING CONFIDENTIALITY WHILE COACHING LEADERSHIP GROUPS

In the engagements in which a coach does end up working with a leader, his or her whole team, and individual members of the team, it is important to provide explicit ground rules about what will and will not be disclosed and the framework for the coaching. I have three working rules of engagement that typically guide my actions in these situations. First, I tell the members of the group that I will not disclose the explicit content of their individual discussions with me to other members of the group, including the CEO, unless I believe that there is an issue that represents a potential violation of laws or major company policies and procedures. However, I also tell them that I will be using the information that is provided in the individual sessions to improve my ability to work with the other members of the group and the team as a whole. Second, I tell them that I will not use the information I get in the individual sessions to participate in any performance evaluation process. The work with the group as well as the individuals must be seen and experienced as developmentally oriented. Finally, I make clear to them that I believe firmly that executive teams and their individual members perform much better when the issues, challenges, and problems that they have with their work and with each other are on the table, open to public scrutiny and discussion, and become part of their collective efforts to lead the organization and improve their performance.

Under this last guideline, I am nearly always discussing with clients how they are going to take their thoughts, feelings, and the results of our individual coaching work and put them into practice in the group or in their relationships with colleagues. In the situations in which I have negotiated and managed these boundaries following the above guidelines, I believe I have managed to be of considerable assistance to both the individuals and the group as a whole and have largely stayed out of major trouble with clients. I must also caution, however, that working in this way requires the utmost tact, extraordinary diplomatic skill, an ability to find ways to describe and explore issues without revealing explicit sources of information, and a steely determination to both maintain one's boundaries and steadily push the clients to work on their own issues by taking explicit and public actions.

RULES OF THUMB FOR COACHING DYADS AND GROUPS

Exhibit 10.1 presents 28 suggested rules of thumb for coaches working with dyads and groups that I have distilled from my experience and that are suggested by the various concepts and key factors described above. For purposes of brevity, I need not go into each of them in any depth, for I believe they are stated plainly enough to speak for themselves. Careful attention to them can assist anyone working with a dyad, team, or dedicated work group to develop a consistent and coherent approach to many, if not most, of the common troubles and developmental challenges they encounter. The rules can also help a coach to keep him- or herself oriented to the boundaries of the coaching role and to be successful in what are often the most complex and difficult assignments.

Throughout this book and the one I wrote previously on executive coaching (Kilburg, 2000), I have repeatedly and insistently emphasized that the single best thing that a coach can do with a client or a group of clients is to enable them to surface what is troubling them, their team, and their organization and to then make careful, reflective determinations about what could be done to improve the situation. In this conviction and advocacy, I find myself keeping some distinguished company with other scholars and practitioners who have struggled with the same issues. A careful reading of these rules of thumb will disclose these clear biases on my part.

Leaders in modern organizations are, in a sense, pioneers. Each and every day, they go to work and proceed to face complex, uncertain, ambiguous, and anxiety-arousing circumstances. Even in the perpetual, often stifling and never-ending meeting and communication rituals of corporate life, executives must remain vigilant. They must constantly scan the stimuli to which they are exposed to determine what is significant, what is dangerous, what requires an immediate and forceful response, and what can be safely ignored. Although the dangers of living among predators in the canopied jungles of the tropical rainforest are well behind most human beings, we know well that organizations fail and are liquidated, leaders derail, and executive teams implode. We know that the brilliant strategies of yesterday rapidly unravel in the face of unanticipated technological breakthroughs, turmoil in global financial markets, and upheavals in the world's geopolitical landscape. In other words, the art of leadership begins when the rules disappear and an executive then must determine what to do in a situation

Rules of Thumb for Coaching Dyads and Groups

Coach toward the following:

1. Creating and maintaining the coaching containment through contracting and adherence to sound coaching practice.
2. Identifying and maintaining boundary clarity, stability, and control.
3. Setting and enforcing healthy limits.
4. Increasing knowledge and skills in the areas of group dynamics, management of interpersonal relations, continuous and discontinuous change processes, and task performance in groups and dyads.
5. Increasing self-, dyad, and group awareness and the skills of reflection.
6. Improving the ability to recognize, correct, and prevent patterns of regressive behavior.
7. Creating the ability to identify and implement resilient and adaptive patterns of behavior.
8. Providing increased role clarity and specific task delegation.
9. Creating appropriate delegation of task authority and responsibility.
10. Improving goal clarity and professional alignment to the goals for the group as a whole and for individual members of the group: "Why are we here?"
11. Verifying and aligning the organization's vision, mission, values, strategies, and goals with the administrative structures and processes operating within the group: "We are here to increase value, make goods, provide services in the following ways."
12. Improving constructive paranoia—anticipate crises, catastrophes, problems, risks, potential opportunities, and creative solutions.
13. Pursuing requisite power and political behavior—development of power and political influence necessary and equal to the needs of task performance in the group.
14. Providing adequate resources or clarity about priorities for the allocation of available resources to the dyad or group.
15. Improving effective leadership and followership behaviors in the members of the group or dyad—reality testing, honesty in communication and professional dealing, getting problems on the table, not acting out, not playing the "shame–blame game," "the emperor's new coat," "playground bully," or engaging in other defensive routines.
16. Demonstrating healthy narcissism through sufficient self-esteem to protect individuals from overly dependent behavior and corrupting influences from subordinates, peers, superiors, and outsiders.
17. Identifying conflicting interests, values, and needs and pushing them toward the common good and task accomplishment.
18. Identifying, creating, and improving cooperative and collaborative behavior between members of the dyad and group and between groups within organizations.
19. Identifying and providing tangible benefits for the members of the group, including emotional and interpersonal support and freedom from harassment, coercion, and the other negative effects of "isms" operating within the dyad or group.
20. Using effective moral reasoning and creating justice for all members of the group.
21. Ensuring appropriate participation in decision making within the group tied to levels of information available and the necessity for group member commitment to implement any decision made.
22. Assisting the evolution of higher orders of consciousness and wisdom for individual members of the group and for the group as a whole.

(continued)

EXHIBIT 10.1 *(Continued)*

23. Assisting the functions of the observing egos of the members of the group.
24. Providing consistent support for objectification of the tasks, processes, structures, relationships, and other features of the operation of the dyad or group.
25. Provoking shifts of attention toward objectification—helping dyads and groups improve their ability to view themselves and to reflect on their reflections about themselves.
26. Assisting members of the dyad or group to engage in the learning and development that are needed and are taking place.
27. Supporting the development of awareness of the dimensions of diversity of the members of the group and their potential contribution to increasing either regressive or resilient patterns of behavior.
28. Remembering and acting on the knowledge that the dyad or group will be limited in its creative and adaptive potential by the orders of mind, cognitive complexity, creativity, knowledge, skills, abilities, and the regressive and resilient potential of the individual members.

in which he or she knows very little, the stakes are high, and the consequences for his or her life can be extreme. The same is true for leadership teams as a whole.

In a sense, these rules of thumb serve as an elaboration and emphasis of Gadamer's (1986/1994) method for discovering the truth in the kinds of cloudy, ambiguous, and complex environments in which executives work. Polkinghorne's (2004) description of that method suggested

> that uncovering the truth about a situation is a more open and creative process than simply following the algorithmic steps laid out in a method. Understanding is more likely to be clouded or distorted than it is to be enlarged by strictly following the requirements of a predetermined method. Gadamer again emphasized that openness is essential to all aspects of hermeneutic reflection: (a) openness to the problematic of a background interpretation; (b) openness to a reappraisal of all aspects of the initial background understanding; (c) openness to framing questions that show up different aspects of the situation; and (d) openness to how the testing of questions is to be carried out. (p. 167)

Within this framework, it becomes clear that the true focus in coaching executive teams consists of helping them to create these same processes so that they themselves can master them in order to lead their organizations. Following Gadamer's (1986/1994) method, leadership groups must practice the art of dialogue with each other and with the situations that they face to determine the truth of those often foggy and indeterminate circumstances. In other words, leaders, executive groups, and their coaches must become experts in conducting exploratory and creative discussions. Gadamer (1986/1994) described it in the following way:

To conduct a conversation means to allow oneself to be conducted by the subject matter to which the partners in the dialogue are oriented. It requires that one does not try to argue the other person down but that one really considers the weight of the other's opinion. Hence it is an art of testing. But the art of testing is the art of questioning. For we have seen that to question means to lay open, to place in the open. As against the fixity of opinions, questioning makes the object and all of its possibilities fluid. . . . Dialogue consists not in trying to discover the weakness of what is said, but in bringing out its real strength. It is not the art of arguing (which can make a strong case out of a weak one) but the art of thinking (which can strengthen objections to the subject matter). (p. 367)

These words are an eerie echo of Lee Nichol's description of Bohm's (2000) work on dialogue, which Bohm began in 1970. In the foreword of that book, Nichol, the editor of the collection of papers, provided a crucial summary that enables readers to see clearly the parallel efforts of philosophical pioneers who were struggling to understand the same problems in the human condition. Nichol (2000) said in part about Bohm,

We find here a pivotal definition: dialogue is aimed at the understanding of consciousness per se, as well as exploring the problematic nature of day-to-day relationship and communication. This definition provides a foundation, a reference point if you will, for the key components of dialogue: shared meaning, the nature of collective thought; the pervasiveness of fragmentation; the function of awareness; the microcultural context; undirected inquiry; interpersonal fellowship; and the paradox of the observer and the observed. . . . As Bohm himself emphasized however, dialogue is a process of direct, face-to-face encounter, not to be confused with endless theorizing and speculation. In a time of accelerating abstractions and seamless digital representations, it is this insistence on facing the inconvenient messiness of daily, corporeal experience that is perhaps most radical of all. (p. xi)

The rules of thumb identified in Exhibit 10.1 point the way for coaches and executives to create such safe and exploratory spaces for their leadership teams. These quotes illuminate how complex, unique, and difficult it is for any group of people, let alone one struggling with making critical and sometimes life-and-death decisions in real time with all-too-limited information, to engage in the kind of extremely human exchange from which truth and thus wisdom can emerge. The commitment and dedication to create such dialogues and to craft wise, long-lasting decisions and actions as outcomes of them represents the true call to leadership and the true challenge of coaches and consultants who want to help executives with that work. I also believe that the more practice executive teams have in creating and using such dialogic, wisdom-generating processes, the more likely they are to behave routinely as people of virtue and as virtuous groups. The fate of organizations and nation-states has in the past, does now, and always will in the future depend on the capacity of their leaders to develop and routinely engage in such processes.

REVISITING THE CASE OF THE
UNCONSCIOUS COMMANDMENT

If we return to the case that opened chapter 9, we can see that most of the issues and factors I have described that influence executive groups are covered. To begin, Jim Wentworth, the long-term CEO of the company, had unconsciously developed an executive group dynamic and culture that in the Symlog framework could be described as overtly friendly, backward in its emotional expression, and predominantly submissive to him as the leader. Individual discussions with Jim and public discussions with the group as a whole made it clear that Jim was frustrated with the lack of forward momentum in the organization and the seeming unwillingness of the group members to express directly their thoughts and feelings. He had no conscious idea that he had inadvertently created a submissive and dependent leadership team through his own analytic brilliance, assertive engagement on nearly every facet of the business, hard work, long hours, and extraverted personality. In essence, the personal virtuous attractor of his leadership style and the field that it created pushed his entire executive team into a vicious attractor of a dependency-based followership field. Any crisis or significant challenge to the business routinely elicited the best from Jim and the regressed worst from his team. In psychodynamic terms, this was an unconscious pattern of conflict that produced conscious manifestations such as the mutual and pervasive dissatisfaction that Jim felt with his team and they with him.

Dissatisfied as they all were, they could hardly do anything but point at each other as the source of discomfort and dysfunction. Any intervention designed to change such well-established patterns of behavior needed to be both sophisticated and conducted over a period of time, for this team had done other short-term activities in the past to try to change their performance for the better. Obviously, all of them had failed.

The second year of the consulting and coaching work created enough knowledge, skill, and trust for us to be able collectively to identify these issues and make them public for Jim and the rest of the team to manage overtly. In the end, it was Sally Morton's ability to both reflect at the second level on the nature of the group and its relationship with Jim that led her to pronounce the keystone summary of their collective culture: "Prove to Jim that he's wrong." That verbalization and our subsequent work on its implications allowed the group to do some double-loop learning and to begin to modify the ways in which it had historically operated. It also demonstrated the long-term benefits of the reflective-engagement methodologies discussed in chapter 8, because the development sessions that had preceded it were systematic efforts on my part to push the group to the balcony (Heifetz, 1994) to try to gain perspective on its performance.

Finally, it represented first and foremost an expression of the virtue of courage on Sally's part, for without her willingness to take the public risk of eliciting a negatively defensive reaction from Jim the team would never have been able to create the dialogue that we used to move them forward. It also represented a similar level of courage expressed by Jim, who took Sally's observation as a serious effort to try to improve the team and solve the problems that they faced and not as a personal attack. It would have been all too easy for him to respond sharply, critically, sarcastically, and defensively and thereby shut down the entire group. Instead, he simply listened and watched as I further probed the rest of the team for their observations and reactions. In that process, the whole pattern began to surface and, as that happened, Jim began to see that he had been contributing to create and maintain the very behaviors that most frustrated him as a leader. In a tribute to his own virtues of temperance and courage, he decided to ask questions and explore the situation and his contribution to it as opposed to trying to explain his actions, attack Sally, and thereby defend the status quo.

When examining what happened through the lens of the process of group development, Sally's comment essentially correctly identified the central component of the norms by which that leadership team operated. Her verbalization, along with Jim's dissatisfaction with what had been happening, was sufficient to allow the group members to publicly discuss their unconscious norms for the first time and to try to renegotiate them. It also allowed Jim to realize what his own character strengths were doing paradoxically to undermine his long-term goals for the organization and its leadership team. As he began to change some of his behavior, the members of the team responded and became more publicly expressive of their individual views, more assertive in what they thought needed to be done to manage the organization, and much less submissive. Over time, the group successfully renegotiated a new set of norms that allowed its members to work far more productively together. As the team progressed, Jim found it easier and easier to engage in the new patterns in his own leadership approach.

It is interesting that this executive group had been able to avoid any significant public regressive behavior over time. However, it was mired in this oscillating pattern in which Jim pushed people to be more assertive and then wore them down as he forced them to examine critically what they thought and felt. As a result, the members of the group became avoidant and tended to wait until Jim told them what to do. For them, the emotional carrying costs of waiting to hear the "word from Jim" were much lower than taking independent action and then being required to defend themselves in what felt to them like a toxic exchange. For Jim, the leadership and organizational costs had become enormous, and it was clear that the business was not reaping the benefits of its investments in leadership. Renorming the group had the effect of reducing those oscillations and allowing the team to become much more functional. They began to exhibit routinely the ability to think about their business and their teamwork in systemic forms. Their deliberations became more animated; more informed by different sources of information and opinions; more open to considering other choices; and, in the end, wiser.

In psychodynamic terms, this team had been mired in both fight–flight and dependency dynamics that were known, experienced, and even discussed in dyads. The hidden aspects of the patterns consisted of the emotional reactions of shame, anxiety, and rage experienced by everyone, the avoidant, passive–aggressive, and triangulated types of communications and problem-solving activities in which they engaged, and intense, if not overtly displayed, conflicts over identity, performance, control, power, competition, and loyalty (Wurmser, 2000). Surfacing the norms and the patterns freed the group to examine these ways of relating and ultimately led to triple-loop learning in the form of changes in the culture of the group and in the attitudes and behaviors of the individual members and the organization as a whole.

Similarly, Sally's comment, which crystallized and illuminated their core dynamic, had the electrifying effect of creating the possibility for catastrophic positive change in the group. Jim's historical way of leading and his strengths had effectively created what one could also call *behavioral repulsors* for the rest of the team. In essence, his own dominance, work ethic, and brilliance on the details of the business made it nearly impossible for the other leaders to express themselves. As a result, they fell into their own vicious behavioral attractor that consisted of passive, submissive, dependent behavior. They had been collectively locked into these patterns until routine engagement in active and retrospective reflective examinations of themselves and their organization allowed them to see what they had created. Once they discovered what they had been doing, together they invented a joint new attractor of supportive assertion; effective teamwork based on reflective engagement; and professionally collaborative, interdependent relationships.

Surprising everyone, Jim significantly reduced his own historical reliance on dominating debates and knowing everything, and he moved toward an increase in delegation; listening more to what his team members thought and wanted to do; and willingness to engage in dialogue with individuals, dyads, and the whole leadership team rather than competitive debates. As he did so, the team members responded, and John, the CEO-in-waiting, took much firmer executive control over the group. In a matter of a relatively few short months, Jim was sufficiently reassured that he moved forward with his retirement plans.

With regard to field effects, the effect that this leadership–followership dynamic had on the group, its performance, and the entire organization was palpable. The entire culture of the enterprise had been built around Jim's knowledge, work ethic, demandingness, and analytic abilities. Everyone expected him to perform that way and conformed their own behavior accordingly. In the classic way that these fields affect individuals and groups, everyone in the entire organization was unconsciously and consciously frozen into their places in the structures and processes of the enterprise. Once reflective learning took place, it was possible to begin to modify the fields.

Finally, this case also illustrates the constraints that defensive and regressive executive group dynamics can exert on the use of the cognitive capacities of its members and the adverse impact on group performance that such effects can have. If one thinks about Jim's executive team in terms of the orders of mind they routinely used in their meetings and work, it seems clear in retrospect that their dynamics, fields, and processes more or less forced them into second-order states of mind. They largely stayed within their individual, categorical silos; managed what was in front of them; and waited for Jim to tell them what to do. In the arenas in which their areas of responsibility overlapped, Jim was nearly always drawn in to help conceptualize the problems and issues as well as to make final determinations of the actions that would be taken. Even if team members had the ability to think cross-categorically or systemically, it was almost impossible for them to express their views without going through a vigorous and, most would have said, onerous and often toxic exchange with Jim.

The tragic irony, of course, was that Jim saw himself as heroically trying to exhort, teach, and encourage the group to do the job of systematically examining and leading the business. Almost immediately after Sally made her remark, and with the work that we did with it in the team, everyone began to express themselves more directly and in more complex ways. As it turned out, every member of the team could in fact think about their organizational systems and their interactions in more creative ways. In and through the crisis that arose for the business, they proved their ability to work together to identify and change many aspects of the organization's infrastructure to improve performance. Their interventions worked so well that Jim and everyone else were shocked by the ability that had been there but long suppressed.

In the end, the journey with this executive team demonstrates most of the core concepts and intervention ideas presented throughout this book. At their best, Jim's group and Jim himself would periodically demonstrate periods of executive savvy. They got things done: They made money, competed fairly well in the environment, and had reasonable levels of personal and professional satisfaction. However, they were all dissatisfied, and they knew that they possessed tremendous untapped potential. After 2 years of progressively more sophisticated coaching and teamwork, their ability to express aspects of individual and group Executive Wisdom began to emerge more regularly. I do not want to imply that the pathway to the emergence of Executive Wisdom is linear or even predictable. I do want to suggest that with the consistent and dogged application of the ideas and methods identified in this book, executives and their coaches can significantly improve the potential that wisdom will be a more consistent presence in their lives. Such interventions can also exert considerable support for the simultaneous emergence of other forms of virtuous behavior in leaders and executive teams. The ability to act with courage, emotional intelligence, and considered moral judgment are often parallel outcomes of coaching engagements that are effectively conducted, for in the end, collective efforts, those of leaders and those who want to assist them, must be directed toward creating virtuous characters and right action with long-lasting and good effects for organizations and society as a whole.

A BRIEF HISTORICAL EXAMPLE

In his recent book, David Rothkopf (2005) has done students, consultants, and leaders of executive teams an enormous service by chronicling the 60-year history of the National Security Council (NSC) of the U.S. government. Following the global chaos of the second world war, the leadership of the United States underwent a tremendous shift as Harry Truman took over from the long-tenured Franklin Roosevelt. Truman faced a situation in which most of Europe, Russia, Japan, and significant parts of China lay in ruins. The government of Josef Stalin was proving itself to be both unreliable and a rising competitive threat ready to step into the power vacuum left by the destruction of most of the leadership infrastructure of European nations. Truman's own country was weary from the war effort, financially strapped from its costs, and eager to turn back to its own affairs.

In 1947, Truman's administration sponsored and passed the National Security Act, which in turn established the NSC. That organization has remained intact and grown in size and influence through 6 decades of service to nine successive presidencies. Its membership has shifted, the scope of its focus has broadened, and the threats that it has faced have varied, but it continues to be responsible for assessing the security problems of the United States and providing recommendations for action to the president and his cabinet.

Truman's group included George Marshall, Dean Acheson, George Kennan, Clark Clifford, James Forrestal, W. Averell Harriman, Arthur Vandenberg, Dwight Eisenhower, John McCloy, Robert Lovett, Charles Bohlen, Ferdinand Eberstadt, and others. As described by Rothkopf (2005),

> It was in a span of four months that Truman delivered his doctrine, Marshall unveiled "his" plan, and the National Security Act of 1947, which laid the groundwork for the modern national security mechanisms of the U.S. Government, was signed into law. In something like 120 days, the United States took the foreign policy stance that would define its role in the world through almost the end of the century. (p. 40)

Rothkopf quoted Arnold Toynbee's evaluation of this period of history in the United States:

> It was not the discovery of atomic energy, but the solicitude of the world's most privileged people for its less privileged as vested in Truman's Point IV and the Marshall Plan . . . that will be remembered as the single achievement of our age. (pp. 40–41)

We have no clearer example in recent American history of the rise of the phenomenon of collective Executive Wisdom in a senior leadership group than what took place in the deliberations and subsequent actions of that first NSC. The steps that they undertook in 1947 systematically shaped the destiny of the entire world for half a century. The long-term consequences of those strategies and actions led to the reconstruction of Europe and Japan and the containment of Communist ideology, and they were largely responsible for the prevention of a third global war in the 20th century. The creation of the European Union; the reintegration of eastern and western Europe; the emergence of a more democratic and peaceful Russia; the deconstruction of the Soviet Union; and the new, historical rise of China, India, and the other countries of Asia in the early 21st century were made possible because of the wisdom that group of people exercised at that time.

Rothkopf's (2005) history also provides evidence of another major thesis put forth in this book, namely, that Executive Wisdom is the emergent property of a complex set of interacting systems. Although the NSC can rightfully claim credit for those early triumphs, it also played a role in the fiasco that led to the Bay of Pigs, the tragedy of the Vietnam War, the absence of effective action to prevent the genocidal madnesses in Cambodia and Rwanda, and the inability of the United States to protect itself from the terrorist attacks of September 11, 2001, in New York and Washington, DC. It is thus clear that having smart, well-resourced people in a room who have lots of information about their world, a clear mission to pursue, and the motivation to do whatever it takes to succeed may be necessary but are nonetheless insufficient conditions for wisdom to arise. As I have explored in these last two chapters, a large number of complex variables interact in mind-numbingly chaotic patterns that can interfere with or facilitate the emergence of wisdom. The NSC is but one such leadership group in a convoluted, global web of such leadership teams, all of which are trying to make sense and meaning for their organizations in the world. They are led by individual executives who may or may not consciously be striving for wisdom, building and using virtuous character traits, or creating good in this world.

IN CONCLUSION

I hope the foregoing chapters help coaches and consultants who are currently working in these situations with individual leaders and their teams think more consistently not only about the means of their work but also about the ends. I also hope that individual leaders who have chosen to make this reading journey can see the benefits of consciously and steadily working toward producing wisdom in their executive lives. I believe strongly that we have the capacity to integrate much of what we have learned about leadership, organizational dynamics, and group functioning in ways that can systematically help executives perform more effectively. It seems clear to me that as has always been the case, *Homo sapiens* needs wise leadership to ensure the continued development of the species. Over the course of the last 5,000 years, the responsibility for exercising such leadership has rested on the shoulders of kings, queens, despots, rebels, and now the democratically elected heads of modern nation-states. In the past century, we have seen the rise of privately owned corporations with global capacities, many of which rival and even exceed the reach and abilities of nation-states themselves. Modern telecommunications, information management, and transportation technologies enable leaders to do what was impossible even 50 years ago.

If current trends continue to evolve, we may see some of these private organizations begin to challenge nation-states themselves for dominance in the world. In an era in which weapons of mass destruction are slowly and surely diffusing through the world, humanity will need its leaders to be wiser and more virtuous than ever as they cope with the complexity and threats of this rapidly evolving world. It is not enough that leaders be able to conceive and execute strategies that enrich their nations and enterprises in the short run. In the end, history has and always will be the judge of the quality of any individual's term in an office with leadership responsibility. History requires leaders to find and do the right things, in the right way, and against the right time frame. It requires them to develop the capacity for Executive Wisdom and the ability to deploy it. It absolutely requires that they both see and systematically pursue the development of virtue in their own characters. As I hope we have seen, this is much easier to say and describe than it is to do.

The quote that opened this chapter indicated that human leadership groups routinely face situations for which they have no rules to guide them and all too often for which they have little or no knowledge. In these circumstances, they are always anxious and face incredible pressures to behave badly because they most often do not know what they do not know. Almost nothing is more difficult, anxiety arousing, and humiliating than for a leader to admit that he or she does not know the right thing to do.

Humans have had an intuitive sense of the need for wisdom and virtue for millennia. As I described in the opening of this book, in the first major moral challenge to the human race identified in the Bible, Eve listens to the serpent say "Ye shall not die: for God doth know that in the day ye eat thereof, then your eyes shall be opened, and ye shall be as gods, knowing good and evil." The passage continues,

> And when the woman saw that the tree was good for food, and that it was pleasant to the eyes, and a tree to be desired to make one wise, she took of the fruit thereof, and did eat, and gave also unto her husband with her, and he did eat. And the eyes of them both were opened and they knew that they were naked. (Genesis, 4:4–7)

Regardless of whether you believe this to be the revealed word of God or a brilliantly and intuitively insightful, metaphoric literary passage describing the emergence of the prefrontal cortex of *Homo sapiens*, it captures the complexity of the dilemma of our species and of our leaders. For wise leaders have been and are likely to continue to be our best way of determining good and evil and of deciding the courses of action that we will take on this increasingly small planet of ours. And if there is one thing about which my work with leaders has made me certain, it is that they often—yes, all too often—feel extremely naked, alone, and so very vulnerable when they have no rules to guide them and no real idea about how to gain new knowledge that would help them in their work. They replicate the history of those first humans who looked out into their complex world with wonder, awe, and fear as they truly saw it for the first time and asked, "Now what should we do?"

When we combine the wisdom of the philosophers and leaders of ancient times with what we now know from modern studies of leadership, organizational and group behavior, economics, politics, sociology, anthropology, and individual psychology, perhaps we can improve the odds that individual executives and dedicated executive groups will be better able to think, feel, and act wisely more routinely. Such information can and should also inform the deliberations of those of us who believe that we can help them in this most difficult activity.

I hope that this book will inspire others to go in search of wisdom and other virtues in themselves and in their clients, for it is clear that the most prestigious figures in human history are those individuals who strove throughout their lives to learn how to be virtuous and how to help others develop these abilities themselves. We have many models, methods, and historic mentors. Despite the availability of these materials, I do not believe that the average leader is either trained in or aspires to virtue. However, most of them do aspire to improved performance, and it is this desire for progressive development that holds the key for those who would become virtuous leaders and for those who would help them along this path. Developing wisdom and other virtues takes time, as does developing true expertise in any domain of human activity. Formal education, executive-development programs, coaching, and life experience can contribute, but it takes a determined spirit and a well-honed mind many years to get there. I believe that leaders and those who would help them develop must devote themselves to such a pathway of longitudinal, progressive development. I hope that the resources summarized in this volume are of assistance to you as you pursue your own journey toward wisdom, a more virtuous character, and the pursuit of the good life.

REFERENCES

Adair, R. K. (1987). *The great design: Particles, fields, and creation.* New York: Oxford University Press.

Adizes, I. (1988). *Corporate life cycles.* Englewood Cliffs, NJ: Prentice Hall.

Agnon, S. Y. (1948). *Days of awe: A treasury of Jewish wisdom for reflection, repentance and renewal on the high holy days.* New York: Schocken Books.

Aldefer, C. P. (1987). An intergroup perspective on group dynamics. In J. Lorsch (Ed.), *Handbook of organizational behavior* (pp. 190–222). Englewood Cliffs, NJ: Prentice Hall.

American Psychiatric Association. (1994). *Diagnostic criteria from DSM–IV.* Washington, DC: Author.

Aquinas, T. (1981). *Summa theologica* (Fathers of the English Dominican Province, Trans.). Allen, TX: Bartlett Publishing.

Argyris, C. (1990). *Overcoming organizational defenses.* Englewood Cliffs, NJ: Prentice Hall.

Argyris, C. (1993). *Knowledge for action: A guide to overcoming barriers to organizational change.* San Francisco: Jossey-Bass.

Bales, R. F., & Cohen, S. P. (1979). *Symlog: A system for the multiple level observation of groups.* New York: Free Press.

Baltes, P. B., Gluck, J., & Kunzmann, U. (2002). Wisdom: Its structure and function in regulating successful life span development. In C. R. Snyder & S. J. Lopez (Eds.), *Handbook of positive psychology* (pp. 327–347). New York: Oxford University Press.

Baltes, P. B., & Staudinger, U. M. (2000). Wisdom: A metaheuristic (pragmatic) to orchestrate mind and virtue toward excellence. *American Psychologist, 55,* 122–135.

Baltes, P. B., Staudinger, U. M., & Lindenberger, U. (1999). Lifespan psychology: Theory and application to intellectual functioning. *Annual Review of Psychology, 50,* 471–507.

Bandura, A. (1977). Self-efficacy: Toward a unifying theory of behavioral change. *Psychological Review, 84,* 191–215.

Bandura, A. (1982). Self-efficacy mechanism in human agency. *American Psychologist, 37,* 122–147.

Bandura, A. (1997). *Self-efficacy: The exercise of control.* New York: Freeman.

Barron, J. W. (Ed.). (1993). *Self-analysis: Critical inquiries, personal visions.* Hillsdale, NJ: Analytic Press.

Bazerman, M. (1998). *Judgment in managerial decision making* (4th ed.). New York: Wiley.

Becker, B. E., Huselid, M. A., & Ulrich, D. (2001). *The HR scorecard: Linking people, strategy, and performance.* Boston: Harvard Business School Press.

Bedeian, A. G., & Zammuto, R. F. (1991). *Organizations: Theory and design.* Chicago: Dryden.

Bennis, W., Brown, T. L., Champy, J. A., Crainer, S., Davis, S., Edwards, H., et al. (Eds.). (2002). *Business: The ultimate resource.* Cambridge, MA: Perseus.

Berg, D. N. (2005). Senior executive teams: Not what you think. *Consulting Psychology Journal: Practice and Research, 57,* 107–117.

Bierly, P. E., III, Kessler, E. H., & Christensen, E. W. (2000). Organizational learning, knowledge and wisdom. *Journal of Organizational Change Management. 16,* 595–618.

Bion, W. R. (1961). *Experiences in groups and other papers.* London: Tavistock.

Bishop, S. R., Lau, M., Shapiro, S., Carlson, L, Anderson, N. D., Carmody, J., et al. (2004). Mindfulness: A proposed operational definition. *Clinical Psychology: Science and Practice, 11,* 230–241.

Boemeke, M. F., Feldman, G. D., & Glaser, E. (1998). *The Treaty of Versailles: A reassessment after 75 years.* Cambridge, England: Cambridge University Press.

Bogdan, R. J. (2000). *Minding minds: Evolving a reflexive mind by interpreting others.* Cambridge, MA: MIT Press.

Bohm, D. (2000). *On dialogue* (L. Nichol, Ed.). New York: Routledge.

Boring, E. G. (1950). *A history of experimental psychology* (2nd ed.). New York: Appleton-Century-Crofts.

Borkowski, J. G., Chan, L. K. S., & Muthukrishna, N. (2000). A process-oriented model of metacognition: Links between motivation and executive function. In G. Schraw & J. Impara (Eds.), *Issues in the measurement of metacognition* (pp. 1–41). Lincoln, NE: Buros Institute of Mental Measurements.

Bossidy, L., & Charan, R. (2002). *Execution: The discipline of getting things done.* New York: Crown Business.

Bowlby, J. (1988). *A secure base.* New York: Basic Books.

Bronson, M. B. (2000). *Self-regulation in early childhood: Nature and nurture.* New York: Guilford Press.

Brown, W. S. (2000). *Understanding wisdom: Sources, science, and society.* Philadelphia: Templeton Foundation Press.

Bruner, J. (1986). *Actual minds, possible worlds.* Cambridge, MA: Harvard University Press.

Buckingham, M., & Clifton, D. O. (2001). *Now, discover your strengths.* New York: Free Press.

Burgoyne, J., & Reynolds, M. (Eds.). (1997). *Management learning: Integrating perspectives in theory and practice.* London: Sage.

Butterfield, E. C., Albertson, L. R., & Johnston, J. C. (1995). On making cognitive theory more general and developmentally pertinent. In F. E. Weinert &

W. Schneider (Eds.), *Memory performance and competencies: Issues in growth and development* (pp. 181–206). Hillsdale, NJ: Erlbaum.

Butz, M. R. (1997). *Chaos and complexity: Implications for psychological theory and practice*. Washington, DC: Taylor & Francis.

Byrne, J. (2002, August 12). Fall from grace. *Business Week*, 50–56.

Campbell, J. (Ed.). (1971). *The portable Jung*. New York: Viking.

Cartwright, D., & Zander, A. (Eds.). (1968). *Group dynamics research and theory*. New York: Harper & Row.

Carver, C. S., & Scheier, M. F. (1998). *On the self-regulation of behavior*. Cambridge, England: Cambridge University Press

Cavanaugh, J. C., & Green, E. E. (1990). I believe, therefore I can: Self-efficacy beliefs in memory aging. In E. A. Lovelace (Ed.), *Aging and cognition: Mental processes, self-awareness, and interventions* (pp. 189–230). Amsterdam: Elsevier.

Cavanaugh, J. C., & Perlmutter, M. (1982). Metamemory: A critical examination. *Child Development, 53*, 11–28.

Chang, E. C., & Sanna, L. J. (2003). *Virtue, vice, and personality: The complexities of behavior*. Washington, DC: American Psychological Association.

Chase, W. G., & Simon, H. A. (1973). The mind's eye in chess. In W. G. Chase (Ed.), *Visual information processing* (pp. 215–281). New York: Academic Press.

Church, A. H. (1997). Managerial self-awareness in high-performing individuals in organizations. *Journal of Applied Psychology, 82*, 281–292.

Clausewitz, C. von (1986). *On war*. Middlesex, England: Penguin Books. (Original work published 1896)

Clifton, D. O., & Nelson, P. (1992). *Soar with your strengths*. New York: Dell.

Cocivera, T., & Cronshaw, S. (2004). Action frame theory as a scientific and practical model for the management of the executive coaching process. *Consulting Psychology Journal: Research and Practice, 56*, 234–245.

Collins, J. D. (1962). *The lure of wisdom*. Milwaukee, WI: Marquette University Press.

Conger, J. A., & Benjamin, B. (1999). *Building leaders: How successful companies develop the next generation*. San Francisco: Jossey-Bass.

Conner, P. E., & Lake, L. K. (1994). *Managing organizational change* (2nd ed.). Westport, CT: Praeger.

Cooperrider, D. L. (1996). The child as agent of inquiry. *OD Practitioner, 28*(1–2), 5–11.

Cyert, R. M., & March, J. G. (1963). *A behavioral theory of the firm*. Englewood Cliffs, NJ: Prentice Hall.

Czander, W. M. (1993). *The psychodynamics of work and organizations: Theory and application*. New York: Guilford Press.

Damasio, A. (1999). *The feeling of what happens: Body and emotion in the making of consciousness*. New York: Harcourt.

Darwin, J. (1996a). Dynamic poise: A new style of management—Part 1. *Career Development International, 1*(5), 21–25.

Darwin, J. (1996b). Dynamic poise: A new style of management—Part 2. *Career Development International, 1*(7), 12–17.

Davis, J. W., Jr. (2000). *Threats and promises: The pursuit of international influence.* Baltimore: Johns Hopkins University Press.

de Bono, E. (1999). *Six thinking hats.* Boston: Back Bay Books.

de Waal, F. (2000). *Chimpanzee politics: Power and sex among apes* (2nd ed.). Baltimore: The Johns Hopkins University Press.

Dewey, J. (1910). *How we think.* Boston: D.C. Heath.

Diamond, J. (1999). *Guns, germs, and steel: The fates of human societies.* New York: Norton.

Dimitrov, V. (2003). Fuzziology: A study of fuzziness of human knowing and being. *Kybernetes, 32,* 491–510.

Dotlich, D. L., & Cairo, P. C. (2003). *Why CEOs fail: The 11 behaviors that can derail your climb to the top—And how to manage them.* San Francisco: Jossey-Bass.

Dubrin, A. J. (1978). *Winning at office politics.* New York: Ballantine.

Dyer, W. G. (1987). *Team building: Issues and alternatives* (2nd ed.). Reading, MA: Addison-Wesley.

Einstein, A. (1961). *Relativity: The special and the general theory.* New York: Three Rivers Press.

Endsley, M. R., & Garland, D. J. (2000). *Situational awareness, analysis, and measurement.* Mahwah, NJ: Erlbaum.

Enron Corporation. (1998). *1998 annual report.* Houston, TX: Author.

Epstein, P. (1978). *Kabbalah: The way of the Jewish mystic.* Boston: Shambhala Publications.

Ericsson, K. A. (Ed.). (1996). *The road to excellence: The acquisition of expert performance in the arts and sciences, sports and games.* Mahwah, NJ: Erlbaum.

Ericsson, K. A., & Lehmann, A. C. (1996). Expert and exceptional performance: Evidence of maximal adaptation to task constraints. *Annual Review of Psychology, 47,* 273–305.

Ericsson, K. A., & Smith, J. (Eds.). (1991). *Toward a general theory of expertise: Prospects and limits.* New York: Cambridge University Press.

Erikson, E. H. (1963). *Childhood and society* (2nd ed.). New York: Norton.

Everitt, A. (2003). *Cicero: The life and times of Rome's greatest politician.* New York: Random House.

Ferrari, M., & Sternberg, R. J. (Eds.). (1998). *Self-awareness: Its nature and development.* New York: Guilford Press.

Fiedler, F. (1967). *A theory of leadership effectiveness.* New York: McGraw-Hill.

Finkelstein, S. (2003). *Why smart executives fail and what you can learn from their mistakes.* New York: Portfolio.

Fitzgerald, C., & Kirby, L. K. (1997). *Developing leaders: Research and applications in psychological type and leadership development: Integrating reality and vision, mind and heart.* Palo Alto, CA: Davies-Black.

Flavell, J. H. (1977). *Cognitive development*. Englewood Cliffs, NJ: Prentice Hall.

Flavell, J. H. (1979). Metacognition and cognitive monitoring: A new area of cognitive–developmental inquiry. *American Psychologist, 34*, 906–911.

Fleck, L. (1979). *Genesis and development of a scientific fact* (F. Bradley & T. J. Trenn, Trans.). Chicago: University of Chicago Press. (Original work published 1935)

Fogarty, R. (1994). *How to teach metacognitive reflection*. Arlington Heights, IL: SkyLight Training & Publishing.

Forsyth, D. R. (1990). *Group dynamics* (2nd ed.). Pacific Grove, CA: Brooks/Cole.

Fowers, B. J. (2005). *Virtue and psychology: Pursuing excellence in ordinary practices*. Washington, DC: American Psychological Association.

Fredrickson, B. L. (1998). What good are positive emotions? *General Psychology, 2*, 300–319.

Fredrickson, B. L. (2001). The role of positive emotions in positive psychology. *American Psychologist, 56*, 218–226.

Freud, S. (1964). The future prospects of psychoanalytic therapy. In J. E. Strachey (Ed. & Trans.), *The standard edition of the complete works of Sigmund Freud* (Vol. 11, pp. 139–151). London: Hogarth Press. (Original work published 1910)

Freud, S. (1964). The ego and the id. In J. E. Strachey (Ed. & Trans.), *The standard edition of the complete works of Sigmund Freud* (Vol. 19, pp. 3–66). London: Hogarth Press. (Original work published 1923)

Freud, S. (1964). The dissection of the psychical personality. In J. E. Strachey (Ed. & Trans.), *The standard edition of the complete works of Sigmund Freud* (Vol. 12, pp. 3–82). London: Hogarth Press. (Original work published 1932)

Fromm, E. (1973). *The anatomy of human destructiveness*. New York: Holt, Rinehart & Winston.

Funk & Wagnalls standard college dictionary. (1975). New York: Funk & Wagnalls.

Gadamer, H. G. (1975). *Truth and method* (G. B. R. Cumming, Trans.). New York: Seabury. (Original work published 1960)

Gadamer, H. G. (1994). *Truth and method* (J. W. D. G. Marshall, Trans., 2nd rev. ed.). New York: Seabury Press. (Original work published 1986)

Gardner, H. (2004). *Changing minds: The art and science of changing our own and other people's minds*. Boston: Harvard Business School Press.

Gelade, G. A., & Ivery, M. (2003). The impact of human resource management and work climate on organizational performance. *Personnel Psychology, 56*, 383–404.

Gergen, K. J. (1991). *The saturated self: Dilemmas of identity in contemporary life*. New York: Basic Books.

Gergen, K. J. (1999). *An invitation to social construction*. London: Sage.

Gerten, J. E. (2001). *The mind of the CEO*. New York: Basic Books.

Gibbard, G. S., Hartman, J. J., & Mann, R. D. (1988). *Analysis of groups: Contributions to theory, research, and practice*. San Francisco: Jossey-Bass.

Gilley, J. W., & Broughton, N. W. (1996). *Stop managing, start coaching! How performance coaching can enhance commitment and improve productivity.* New York: McGraw-Hill.

Gilligan, C. (1982). *In a different voice: Psychological theory and women's development.* Cambridge, MA: Harvard University Press.

Glickauf-Hughes, C., Wells, M., & Chance, S. (1996). Techniques for strengthening clients' observing ego. *Psychotherapy, 33,* 431–440.

Goldberg, E. (2001). *The executive brain: Frontal lobes and the civilized mind.* New York: Oxford University Press.

Goleman, D., Boyatzis, R., & McKee, A. (2002). *Primal leadership: Realizing the power of emotional intelligence.* Boston: Harvard Business School Press.

Gottschalk, L. A. (1989). *How to do self-analysis and other self-psychotherapies.* Northvale, NJ: Jason Aronson.

Gray, P. (1994). *The ego and analysis of defense.* Northvale, NJ: Jason Aronson.

Graziano, W. G., & Bryant, H. M. (1998). Self-monitoring and the self-attribution of positive emotions. *Journal of Personality and Social Psychology, 74,* 205–261.

Greenspan, S. I. (1989). *The development of the ego: Implications for personality theory, psychopathology, and the psychotherapeutic process.* New York: International Universities Press.

Greenspan, S. I., & Benderly, B. L. (1997). *The growth of the mind and the endangered origins of intelligence.* Cambridge, MA: Perseus.

Greiner, L. E. (1972, July/August). Evolution and revolution as organizations grow. *Harvard Business Review,* 37–46.

Gupta, G. C. (1992). *Ecology, cognition, metacognition and mind: A developmental perspective.* Delhi, India: B. R. Publishing.

Habermas, J. (1981). *The theory of communicative action: Vol. 1. Reason and the rationalization of society* (T. McCarthy, Trans.). Boston: Beacon Press.

Habermas, J. (1987). *The theory of communicative action: Vol. 2. Lifeworld and system: A critique of functionalist reason* (T. McCarthy, Trans.). Boston: Beacon Press.

Hambrick, D. C. (1994). Top management groups: A conceptual integration and reconsideration of the "team" label. In *Research in organizational behavior* (Vol. 16, pp. 171–213). Greenwich, CT: JAI Press.

Hambrick, D. C., & Mason, P. A. (1984). The organization as a reflection of its top managers. *Academy of Management Review, 9,* 195–206.

Hamel, G., & Prahalad, C. K. (1994). *Competing for the future.* Boston: Harvard Business School Press.

Hammer, M., & Champy, J. (1993). *Reengineering the corporation: A manifesto for business revolution.* New York: HarperBusiness.

Hanh, T. N. (1975). *The miracle of mindfulness: An introduction to the practice of meditation.* Boston: Beacon Press.

Hargrove, R. (1995). *Masterful coaching: Extraordinary results by impacting people and the way they think and work together.* Johannesburg, South Africa: Pfeiffer.

Hariman, R. (1995). *Political style: The artistry of power*. Chicago: University of Chicago Press.

Harrison, M. I. (1994). *Diagnosing organizations: Methods, models, and processes*. Thousand Oaks, CA: Sage.

Hartley, R. F. (2003). *Management mistakes and successes* (7th ed.). Hoboken, NJ: Wiley.

Hartmann, H. (1958). *Ego psychology and the problem of adaptation*. New York: International Universities Press.

Hartmann, H. (1964). *Essays on ego psychology: Selected problems in psychoanalytic theory*. New York: International Universities Press.

Hawking, S. (2001). *The universe in a nutshell*. New York: Bantam Books.

Hayes, A. M., & Feldman, G. (2004). Clarifying the construct of mindfulness in the context of emotion regulation and the process of change in psychotherapy. *Clinical Psychology: Science and Practice, 11*, 230–241.

Heifetz, R. A. (1994). *Leadership without easy answers*. Cambridge, MA: Harvard University Press.

Heifetz, R. A., & Linsky, M. (2002). *Leadership on the line: Staying alive through the dangers of leading*. Boston: Harvard Business School Press.

Herrmann, D. J. (1990). Self-perceptions of memory performance. In K. W. Schaie (Ed.), *Self-directedness and efficacy: Causes and effects throughout the life course* (pp. 199–211). Hillsdale, NJ: Erlbaum.

Hersey, P., & Blanchard, K. H. (1977). *Management of organizational behavior: Utilizing human resources* (3rd ed.). Englewood Cliffs, NJ: Prentice Hall.

Hertzog, C., Hultsch, D. E., & Dixon, R. A. (1989). Evidence for the convergent validity of two self-report metamemory questionnaires. *Developmental Psychology, 25*, 687–700.

Hinsz, V. B. (2004). Metacognition and mental models in groups: An illustration with metamemory or group recognition memory. In E. Salas & S. M. Fiore (Eds.), *Team cognition: Understanding the factors that drive process and performance* (pp. 11–31). Washington, DC: American Psychological Association.

Hinsz, V. B., Tindale, R. S., & Vollrath, D. A. (1997). The emerging conceptualization of groups as information processors. *Psychological Bulletin, 121*, 43–64.

Hogan, R., Curphy, G. J., & Hogan, J. (1994). What we know about leadership: Effectiveness and personality. *American Psychologist, 51*, 469–477.

Hogan, R., & Hogan, J. (2001). Assessing leadership: A view from the dark side. *International Journal of Selection and Assessment, 9*, 40–51.

Hogan, R., Raskin, R., & Fazzini, D. (1990). The dark side of charisma. In K. E. Clark & M. B. Clark (Eds.), *Measures of leadership* (pp. 343–354). West Orange, NJ: Leadership Library of America.

Holliday, S. G., & Chandler, M. J. (1986). *Wisdom: Explorations in adult competence*. Basel, Switzerland: Karger.

Horney, K. (1942). *Self-analysis*. New York: Norton.

Howard, A., & Bray, D. W. (1988). *Managerial lives in transition: Advancing age and changing times*. New York: Guilford Press.

James, W. (1950). *The principles of psychology*. New York: Dover. (Original work published 1890)

Janis, I. (1982). *Groupthink* (2nd ed.). Boston: Houghton-Mifflin.

Jaques, E. (1976). *A general theory of bureaucracy*. Portsmouth, NH: Heinemann.

Jaques, E. (1989). *Requisite organization: The CEO's guide to creative structure and leadership*. Arlington, VA: Cason Hall.

Jaques, E., & Clement, S. D. (1991). *Executive leadership: A practical guide to managing complexity*. Arlington, VA: Cason Hall.

Joas, H. (1996). *The creativity of action*. Chicago: University of Chicago Press.

Jordan, A. E., & Meara, N. M. (1990). Ethics and the professional practice of psychologists: The role of virtues and principles. *Professional Psychology: Research and Practice, 21*, 107–114.

Jung, C. G. (1989). The concept of the collective unconscious. In W. McGuire (Ed.) & R. F. C. Hull (Trans.), *The collected works of C. G. Jung*. Princeton, NJ: Princeton University Press. (Original work published 1936)

Kampa, S., & White, R. P. (2002). The effectiveness of executive coaching: What we know and what we still need to know. In R. L. Lowman (Ed.), *Handbook of organizational consulting psychology* (pp. 139–158). San Francisco: Jossey-Bass.

Kampa-Kokesch, S., & Anderson, M. (2001). Executive coaching: A comprehensive review of the literature and comparison to a general consultation and general coaching model. *Consulting Psychology Journal: Practice and Research, 53*, 205–228.

Katzenbach, J. R. (1998). *Teams at the top: Unleashing the potential of both teams and individual leaders*. Boston: Harvard Business School Press.

Katzenbach, J. R., & Smith, D. K. (1994). *The wisdom of teams: Creating the high-performance organization*. New York: HarperBusiness.

Kegan, R. (1982). *The evolving self: Problem and process in human development*. Cambridge, MA: Harvard University Press.

Kegan, R. (1994). *In over our heads: The mental demands of modern life*. Cambridge, MA: Harvard University Press.

Kegan, R., & Lahey, L. L. (2001). *How the way we talk can change the way we work: Seven languages for transformation*. San Francisco: Jossey-Bass.

Kernberg, O. F. (1978). Leadership and organizational functioning: Organizational regression. *International Journal of Group Psychotherapy, 28*, 3–25.

Kernberg, O. F. (1979). Regression in organizational leadership. *Psychiatry, 42*, 24–39.

Kernberg, O. F. (1998). *Ideology, conflict, and leadership in groups and organizations*. New Haven, CT: Yale University Press.

Kilburg, R. R. (1995). Integrating psychodynamic and systems theories in organization development practice. *Consulting Psychology Journal: Practice and Research, 47*, 28–55.

Kilburg, R. R. (Ed.). (1996a). Executive coaching [Special issue]. *Consulting Psychology Journal: Practice and Research, 48*(2).

Kilburg, R. R. (1996b). Toward a conceptual understanding and definition of executive coaching. *Consulting Psychology Journal: Practice and Research, 48*, 134–144.

Kilburg, R. R. (1997). Coaching and executive character: Core problems and basic approaches. *Consulting Psychology Journal: Practice and Research, 49*, 281–299.

Kilburg, R. R. (1998, August). *Shadow consultation: A reflective approach for preventing practice disasters.* Paper presented at the 106th Annual Convention of the American Psychological Association, San Francisco.

Kilburg, R. R. (2000). *Executive coaching: Developing managerial wisdom in a world of chaos.* Washington, DC: American Psychological Association.

Kilburg, R. R. (2001). Facilitating intervention adherence in executive coaching: A model and methods. *Consulting Psychology Journal: Practice and Research, 53*, 251–267.

Kilburg, R. R. (2004). Trudging toward dodoville: Conceptual approaches and case studies in executive coaching. *Consulting Psychology Journal: Practice and Research, 56*, 203–213.

Kilburg, R. R. (Ed.). (2005). Trudging toward dodoville—Part 2: Case studies in executive coaching. *Consulting Psychology Journal: Practice and Research, 57*, 3–96.

Kilburg, R. R., & Siegel, A. W. (1973a). A developmental study of feature analysis in reflective and impulsive children. *Memory & Cognition, 1*, 413–419.

Kilburg, R. R., & Siegel, A. W. (1973b). Formal operations in reactive and process schizophrenics. In R. Cancro (Ed.), *Annual review of the schizophrenic syndrome* (Vol. 4, pp. 142–151). New York: Brunner/Mazel.

Kilburg, R. R., Stokes, E. J., & Kuruvilla, C. (1998). Toward a conceptual model of organizational regression. *Consulting Psychology Journal: Practice and Research, 50*, 101–119.

King, P. M., & Kitchener, K. S. (1994). *Developing reflective judgment: Understanding and promoting intellectual growth and critical thinking in adolescents and adults.* San Francisco: Jossey-Bass.

Kipnis, D. (1976). *The powerholders.* Chicago: University of Chicago Press.

Kirschenbaum, H., Howe, L. H., & Simon, S. B. (1972). *Values clarification.* New York: Warner Books.

Klein, G. (1999). *Sources of power: How people make decisions.* Cambridge, MA: MIT Press.

Klein, G. (2003). *Intuition at work.* New York: Doubleday.

Kohlberg, L. (1981). *The philosophy of moral development: Moral stages and the idea of justice.* New York: HarperCollins.

Kolb, D. A. (1984). *Experiential learning: Experience as the source of learning and development.* Englewood Cliffs, NJ: Prentice Hall.

Koortzen, P., & Cilliers, F. (2002). The psychoanalytic approach to team development. In R. F. Lowman (Ed.), *Handbook of organizational consulting psychology: A comprehensive guide to theory, skills, and techniques* (pp. 260–284). San Francisco: Jossey-Bass.

Kotter, J. P. (1996). *Leading change*. Boston: Harvard Business School Press.

Kuhn, T. S. (1977). *The essential tension: Selected studies in scientific tradition and change*. Chicago: University of Chicago Press.

Küpers, W. (2005, July). *Phenomenology and integral phenol-practice of wisdom in leadership and organization*. Paper presented at the Critical Management Conference, University of Cambridge, Cambridge, England.

Lahey, L., Souvaine, E., Kegan, R., Goodman, R. F., & Felix, S. (1988). *A guide to the subject–object interview: Its administration and interpretation*. Boston: Author.

Lancel, S. (1997). *Carthage: A history*. Oxford, England: Blackwell.

Langer, E. J. (1989). *Mindfulness*. Reading, MA: Addison-Wesley.

Laswell, H. (1936). *Who gets what, when, and how*. New York: McGraw-Hill.

Lebacqz, K. (1986). *Six theories of justice: Perspectives from philosophical and theological ethics*. Minneapolis, MN: Augsburg.

Lee, S. K. J., & Yu, K. (2004). Corporate culture and organizational performance. *Journal of Managerial Psychology, 19*, 340–359.

Legge, J. (1962). *The texts of Taoism: The sacred books of China (Part I)*. New York: Dover.

Levi, D. (2001). *Group dynamics for teams*. Thousand Oaks, CA: Sage.

Levine, P. A. (1997). *Waking the tiger: Healing trauma*. Berkeley, CA: North Atlantic Books.

Levinson, H. (1981). *Executive*. Cambridge, MA: Harvard University Press.

Levinson, H. (2002). *Organizational assessment: A step-by-step guide to effective consulting*. Washington, DC: American Psychological Association.

Lewin, K. (1997). *Resolving social conflicts and field theory in social science*. Washington, DC: American Psychological Association.

Little, J. (Ed.). (2002). *Will Durant: The greatest minds and ideas of all time*. New York: Simon & Schuster.

Losada, M., & Heaphy, E. (2004). The role of positivity and connectivity in the performance of business teams: A nonlinear dynamics model. *American Behavioral Scientist, 47*, 740–765.

Lovelace, E. A. (1990). Aging and metacognitions concerning memory function. In E. A. Lovelace (Ed.), *Aging and cognition: Mental processes, self-awareness, and interventions* (pp. 157–188). Amsterdam: North-Holland.

Lowman, R. L. (2002). *Handbook of organizational consulting psychology: A comprehensive guide to theory, skills, and techniques*. San Francisco: Jossey-Bass.

Luria, A. (1976). *Cognitive development: Its cultural and social foundations*. Cambridge, MA: Harvard University Press.

Lustiger-Thaler, H., & Salee, D. (Eds.). (1994). *Artful practices: The political economy of everyday life*. Montreal, Quebec, Canada: Black Rose Books.

Luthans, F., & Peterson, S. J. (2003). 360-degree feedback with systematic coaching: Empirical analysis suggests a winning combination. *Human Resource Management, 42*, 243–256.

Machiavelli, N. (1961). *The prince* (G. Bull, Trans.). New York: Washington Square Press. (Original work published 1514)

Magna Carta. (1986). In *Encyclopaedia Britannica* (Vol. 7, pp. 673–677). Chicago: Encyclopedia Brittanica.

Marks, M. L., & Mirvis, P. H. (1998). *Joining forces: Making one plus one equal three in mergers, acquisitions, and alliances*. San Francisco: Jossey-Bass.

Marlatt, G. A., & Gordon, J. R. (Eds.). (1985). *Relapse prevention*. New York: Guilford Press.

Maslow, A. H. (1954). *Motivation and personality*. New York: Harpers.

McCullough, D. (1992). *Truman*. New York: Simon & Schuster.

McLean, B., & Elkind, P. (2003). *The smartest guys in the room: The amazing rise and scandalous fall of Enron*. London: Portfolio.

Mearsheimer, J. J. (2001). *The tragedy of great power politics*. New York: Norton.

Meichenbaum, D., & Turk, D. C. (1987). *Facilitating treatment adherence: A practitioner's guidebook*. New York: Plenum Press.

Metcalfe, J., & Shimamura, A. P. (Eds.). (1996). *Metacognition: Knowing about knowing*. Cambridge, MA: MIT Press.

Mezirow, J., & Associates. (1990). *Fostering critical reflection in adulthood: A guide to transformational learning*. San Francisco: Jossey-Bass.

Michalisin, M. D., Karau, S. J., & Tanpong, C. (2004). Top management team cohesion and superior industry returns: An empirical study of the resource-based view. *Group & Organization Management, 29*, 125–140.

Miner, A. C., & Reder, L. M. (1994). A new look at feeling of knowing: Its metacognitive role in regulating question answering. In J. Metcalfe & A. P. Shimamura (Eds.), *Metacognition: Knowing about knowing* (pp. 47–70). Cambridge, MA: MIT Press.

Mintzberg, H. (1973). *The nature of managerial work*. New York: Harper & Row.

Mintzberg, H., Ahlstrand, B., & Lampel, J. (1998). *Strategy safari: A guided tour through the wilds of strategic management*. New York: Free Press.

Mohrman, S. A., & Mohrman, A. M. (1997). *Designing and leading team-based organizations*. San Francisco: Jossey-Bass.

Moore, G. A., Johnson, P., & Kippola, T. (1998). *The gorilla game revised edition: Picking winners in high technology*. New York: HarperBusiness.

Morgan, R. E., & Strong, C. A. (2003). Business performance and dimensions of strategic orientation. *Journal of Business Research, 56*, 163–176.

Mottolo, A. (1989). *The spiritual exercises of Saint Ignatius*. New York: Doubleday.

Nadler, D. A., Spencer, J. L., & Associates. (1998). *Executive teams*. San Francisco: Jossey-Bass.

Natsoulas, T. (1991). The concept of consciousness: The personal meaning. *Journal for the Theory of Social Behavior, 21*, 339–367.

Natsoulas, T. (1998). Consciousness and self-awareness. In M. Ferrari & R. J. Sternberg (Eds.), *Self-awareness: Its nature and development* (pp. 12–33). New York: Guilford Press.

Neisser, U. (1967). *Cognitive psychology*. New York: Appleton-Century-Crofts.

Nelson, T. O., & Narens, L. (1994). Why investigate metacognition? In J. Metcalfe & A. P. Shimamura (Eds.), *Metacognition: Knowing about knowing* (pp. 1–25). Cambridge, MA: MIT Press.

Neustadt, R. E. (1970). *Alliance politics*. New York: Columbia University Press

Neustadt, R. E. (1990). *Presidential power and the modern presidents: The politics of leadership from Roosevelt to Reagan*. New York: Free Press.

Neustadt, R. E., & May, E. R. (1986). *Thinking in time: The uses of history for decision makers*. New York: Free Press.

Newman, J. W. (1996). *Asian thought and culture: Disciplines of attention: Buddhist insight meditation, Ignatian spiritual exercises, and classical psychoanalysis*. New York: Peter Lang.

Nichol, L. (2000). Foreword. In D. Bohm, *On dialogue* (L. Nichol, Ed.; pp. vii–xvii). New York: Routledge.

Nozick, R. (1997). *Socratic puzzles*. Cambridge, MA: Harvard University Press.

O'Bannon, D. P., & Gupta, A. K. (1992). *The utility or homogeneity versus heterogeneity within top management teams: Alternate resolutions of the emerging conundrum*. Paper presented at the 52nd Annual Meeting of the Academy of Management, Las Vegas, NV.

Orlitzky, M., Schmidt, F. L., & Rynes, S. L. (2003). Corporate social and financial performance: A meta-analysis. *Organizational Studies, 24*, 403–441.

O'Toole, J. (1996). *Leading change: The argument for values-based leadership*. New York: Ballantine.

Overholser, J. C. (1993). Elements of Socratic method: I. Systematic questioning. *Psychotherapy, 30*, 67–74.

Parsons, T. (1949). *The structure of social action* (Vols. 1–3). New York: Free Press.

Parsons, T., & Shils, E. A. (Eds.). (1951). *Toward a general theory of action*. New York: Harper & Row.

Pearce, J. A. II, & Robinson, R. B. (1997). *Formulation, implementation, and control of competitive strategy* (6th ed.). Chicago: Irwin Press.

Perry, W. G. (1999). *Forms of intellectual and ethical development in the college years: A scheme*. San Francisco: Jossey-Bass.

Peterson, C., & Seligman, M. E. (2004). *Character strengths and virtues: A handbook and classification*. Washington, DC and New York: American Psychological Association and Oxford University Press.

Pfeffer, J. (1983). Organizational demography. *Research in Organizational Behavior, 5*, 299–357.

Pfeffer, J. (1992). *Managing with power: Politics and influence in organizations.* Boston: Harvard Business School Press.

Piaget, J. (1965). *The moral judgment of the child.* New York: Free Press.

Piaget, J. (1971). *Biology and knowledge: An essay on the relations between organic regulations and cognitive processes.* Chicago: University of Chicago Press.

Picken, J. C., & Dess, G. C. (1997). *Mission critical: The 7 strategic traps that derail even the smartest companies.* Chicago: Irwin.

Plato. (1999). *The republic* (A. D. Lindsay, Ed., & T. Irwin, Trans.). London: Everyman.

Polkinghorne, D. E. (2004). *Practice and the human sciences: The case for a judgment-based practice of care.* Albany: State University of New York Press.

Porter, M. E. (1980). *Competitive strategy: Techniques for analyzing industries and competitors.* New York: Free Press.

Pusey, E. B. (Trans.). (2003). *The confessions of St. Augustine.* New York: Barnes & Noble.

Quick, T. L. (1992). *Successful team building.* New York: American Management Association.

Rachels, J. (2003). *The elements of moral philosophy* (4th ed.). New York: McGraw-Hill.

Reed, M., & Anthony, P. (1992). Professionalizing management and managing professionalization: British management in the 1980's. *Journal of Management Studies, 29* 591–613.

Rentsch, J. R., & Woehr, D. J. (2004). Quantifying congruence in cognition: Social relations modeling and team member schema similarity. In E. Salas & S. M. Fiore (Eds.), *Team cognition: Understanding the factors that drive process and performance* (pp. 11–31). Washington, DC: American Psychological Association.

Reynolds, M. (1997). Towards a critical management pedagogy. In J. Burgoyne & M. Reynolds (Eds.), *Management learning: Integrating perspectives in theory and practice* (pp. 312–328). London: Sage.

Rice, A. K. (1963). *The enterprise and its environment.* London: Tavistock.

Rice, A. K. (1965). *Learning for leadership.* London: Tavistock.

Rice, E. F., Jr. (1958). *The Renaissance idea of wisdom.* Cambridge, MA: Harvard University Press.

Robinson, D. N. (1990). Wisdom through the ages. In R. J. Sternberg (Ed.), *Wisdom: Its nature, origins, and development* (pp. 13–24). New York: Cambridge University Press.

Ronell, A. (2003). *Stupidity.* Chicago: University of Illinois Press.

Rothkopf, D. (2005). *Running the world: The inside story of the National Security Council and the architects of American power.* New York: Public Affairs.

Rothschild, B. A. (2000). *The body remembers: The psychophysiology of trauma and trauma treatment.* New York: Norton.

Rothwell, W. J., & Kazanas, H. C. (1999). *Building in-house leadership and management development programs: Their creation, management, and continuous improvement.* Westport, CT: Quorum Books.

Roy, A. (2001). *Power politics.* Cambridge, MA: South End Press.

Rubin, N. (1992). *Isabella of Castile: The first Renaissance queen* (2nd ed.). New York: St. Martin's Press.

Sambasivan, Z. A. R., & Johari, J. (2003). The influence of corporate culture and organizational commitment on performance. *Journal of Management Development, 22,* 708–728.

Salas, E., & Fiore, S. M. (Eds.). (2004). *Team cognition: Understanding the factors that drive process and performance.* Washington, DC: American Psychological Association.

San Segundo, R. (2002). A new concept of knowledge. *Online Information Review, 26,* 239–245.

Schein, E. (1988). *Process consultation* (Vol. 1). Reading, MA: Addison-Wesley.

Schein, E. (1990). Organizational culture. *American Psychologist, 45,* 109–119.

Schön, D. A. (1983). *The reflective practitioner: How professionals think in action.* New York: Basic Books.

Schön, D. A. (1987). *Educating the reflective practitioner.* San Francisco: Jossey-Bass.

Schore, A. N. (1994). *Affect regulation and the origin of the self: The neurobiology of emotional development.* Hillsdale, NJ: Erlbaum.

Schraw, G., & Impara, J. C. (Eds.). (2000). *Issues in the measurement of metacognition.* Lincoln, NE: Buros Institute of Mental Measurements.

Schroder, M. (1974). The shadow consultant. *Journal of Applied Behavioral Science, 10,* 579–594.

Schunk, D. H., & Zimmerman, B. J. (Eds.). (1998). *Self-regulated learning: From teaching to self-reflective practice.* New York: Guilford Press.

Scott, W. R. (2004). Reflections on a half-century of organizational sociology. *Annual Review of Sociology, 30,* 1–21.

Seligman, M. (2002). Positive psychology, positive prevention, and positive therapy. In C. R. Snyder & S. J. Lopez (Eds.), *Handbook of positive psychology* (pp. 3–9). New York: Oxford University Press.

Senge, P. M. (1990). *The fifth discipline: The art and practice of the learning organization.* New York: Doubleday.

Shimamura, A. P. (1994). The neuropsychology of metacognition. In J. Metcalfe & A. P. Shimamura (Eds.), *Metacognition: Knowing about knowing* (pp. 253–276). Cambridge, MA: MIT Press.

Siebert, K. W., & Daudelin, M. W. (1999). *The role of reflection in managerial learning.* Westport, CT: Quorum.

Simpson, J. A., & Weiner, E. S. C. (Eds.). (1998). *The Oxford English dictionary* (2nd ed.). Oxford, England: Clarendon Press.

Slywotzky, A. J., Morrison, D. J., Moser, T., Mundt, K. A., & Quella, J. A. (1999). *Profit patterns: 30 ways to anticipate and profit from strategic forces reshaping your business.* New York: Random House.

Small, M. W. (2004). Wisdom and now managerial wisdom: Do they have a place in management development programs? *Journal of Management Development, 23,* 751–764.

Smith, R., & Emshwiller, J. R. (2003). *24 days: How two Wall Street Journal reporters uncovered the lies that destroyed faith in corporate America.* New York: HarperBusiness.

Snyder, C. R., & Lopez, S. J. (Eds.). (2002). *Handbook of positive psychology.* New York: Oxford University Press.

Snyder, M. (1974). The self-monitoring of expressive behavior. *Journal of Personality and Social Psychology, 30,* 526–537.

Snyder, M. (1979). Self-monitoring processes. *Advances in Experimental Social Psychology, 12,* 86–128.

Srivastva, S. (Ed.). (1983). *The executive mind.* San Francisco: Jossey-Bass.

Stacey, R. D. (1992). *Managing the unknowable: Strategic boundaries between order and chaos in organizations.* San Francisco: Jossey-Bass.

Stacey, R. D. (1996). *Complexity and creativity in organizations.* San Francisco: Berret-Koehler.

Staudinger, U. (1999). Older and wiser? Integrating results on the relationship between age and wisdom-related performance. *International Journal of Behavioral Development, 29,* 641–664.

Stern, D. N. (1985). *The interpersonal world of the infant: A view from psychoanalysis and developmental psychology.* New York: Basic Books.

Sternberg, R. J. (Ed.). (1990). *Wisdom: Its nature, origins, and development.* Cambridge, England: Cambridge University Press.

Sternberg, R. J. (1999). A balance theory of wisdom. *Review of General Psychology, 2,* 347–365.

Sternberg, R. J. (2003). *Wisdom, intelligence, and creativity synthesized.* Cambridge, England: Cambridge University Press.

Sternberg, R. J. (2005). WICS: A model of leadership. *The Psychologist Manager Journal, 8,* 29–43.

Sundstrom, E., & Associates. (1999). *Supporting work team effectiveness: Best management practices for fostering high performance.* San-Francisco: Jossey-Bass.

Surowiecki, J. (2004). *The wisdom of crowds: Why the many are smarter than the few and how collective wisdom shapes business, economies, societies, and nations.* New York: Doubleday.

Swartz, M., & Watkins, S. (2003). *Power failure: The inside story of the collapse of Enron.* New York: Doubleday.

Tedlow, R. S. (2001). *Giants of enterprise: Seven business innovators and the empires they built.* New York: HarperCollins.

Tenner, A. R., & DeToro, I. J. (1997). *Process redesign: The implementation guide for managers.* Reading, MA: Addison-Wesley.

Thibaut, J. W., & Kelley, H. H. (1959). *The social psychology of groups.* New York: Wiley.

Thom, R. (1972). *Structural stability and morphogenesis: Essay on a general theory of models.* Reading, MA: Benjamin.

Tjosvold, D. W., & Tjosvold, M. M. (1991). *Leading the team organization: How to create an enduring competitive advantage.* New York: Lexington Books.

Trice, H. M., & Beyer, J. M. (1993). *The cultures of work organizations.* Englewood Cliffs, NJ: Prentice Hall.

Twerski, A. J. (1999). *Visions of the fathers.* Brooklyn, NY: Shaar Press.

Valliant, G. E. (1993). *The wisdom of the ego.* Cambridge, MA: Harvard University Press.

VanLehn, K. (1996). Cognitive skill acquisition. *Annual Review of Psychology, 47,* 513–539.

Varney, G. H. (1989). *Building productive teams: An action guide and resource book.* San Francisco: Jossey-Bass.

Velasquez, M. G. (1992). *Business ethics: Concepts and cases* (3rd ed.). Englewood Cliffs, NJ: Prentice Hall.

Von Bertalanffy, L. (1968). *General systems theory.* New York: Braziller.

Voss, T. (1997). *Sharpen your team's skills in coaching.* Berkshire, England: McGraw-Hill.

Vygotsky, L. S. (1962). *Thought and language.* Cambridge, MA: MIT Press.

Waley, A. (1989). *The analects of Confucius.* New York: Vintage Books.

Walker, L. J., & Hennig, K. H. (2004). Differing conceptions of moral exemplarity: Just, brave, and caring. *Journal of Personality and Social Psychology, 86,* 629–647.

Wall, T. D., Michie, J., Patterson, M., Wood, S. J., Sheehan, M., Wall, T. D., et al. (2004). On the validity of subjective measures of company performance. *Personnel Psychology, 57,* 95–118.

Watson, R. I. (1963). *The great psychologists: From Aristotle to Freud.* New York: Lippincott.

Weisbord, M. R. (1978). *Organizational diagnosis: A workbook of theory and practice.* Reading, MA: Addison-Wesley.

Wiersema, M. F., & Bantel, K. A. (1992). TMT demography and corporate strategic change. *Academy of Management Journal, 35,* 91–121.

Winter, D. G. (1973). *The power motive.* New York: Free Press.

Wurmser, L. (2000). *The power of the inner judge: Psychodynamic treatment of the severe neuroses.* New York: Jason Aronson.

Yalom, I. D. (1970). *The theory and practice of group psychotherapy.* New York: Basic Books.

Yammarino, F. J., & Atwater, L. E. (1993). Understanding self-perception accuracy: Implications for human resource management. *Human Resource Management, 32*, 231–247.

Yukl, G. (1994). *Leadership in organizations* (3rd ed.). Englewood Cliffs, NJ: Prentice Hall.

Yzerbyt, V. Y., Lories, G., & Dardenne, B. (Eds.). (1998). *Metacognition: Cognitive and social dimensions.* London: Sage.

Zaccaro, S. J. (2001). *The nature of executive leadership: A conceptual and empirical analysis of success.* Washington, DC: American Psychological Association.

Zander, A. (1981). *Groups at work.* San Francisco: Jossey-Bass.

Zander, A. (1983). *Making groups effective.* San Francisco: Jossey-Bass.

Zenger, T. R., & Lawrence, B. S. (1989). Organizational demography: The differential effects of age and tenure distributions on technical communication. *Academy of Management Journal, 32*, 353–376.

INDEX

effects of wisdom/cognitive development on, 296–301
facilitating emergence of wisdom in,
  301–307
field effects in leadership, 291–296
and loop learning model, 275–277
model for coaching, 273–274
psychodynamics of, 281–285
regression in, 280–281
research on wisdom of, 307–310
Groups, coaching, 318–322
  activities to develop abilities in,
    310–311
  concepts for, 274–281
  factors in, 281–301
  model for, 273–274
Groupthink, 202, 308
Group wisdom, 307–310
Gupta, A. K., 176
Gupta, G. C., 98, 99

Habermas, J., 238
Hambrick, D. C., 176
Hamilcar Barca, 13, 14
Hannibal of Carthage, 13–15, 21, 33, 43
Hargrove, R., 275
Hariman, R., 205
Harrison, M. I., 177
Hasdrubal, 14
Heaphy, E., 291
Heifetz, Ron A., 134, 204, 224, 240–242,
  245, 246, 277
Hennig, K. H., 216
Henry IV, King of Castile, 19
Henry VI, Holy Roman Emperor, 15
Heraclitus, 189
Heuristics, 129
Hindsight, 131
Hinsz, V. B., 308
Historical leadership, 11–23
  basic questions of, 12–13
  central thesis of, 21–23
  Hannibal's example of, 13–15
  Queen Isabella's example of, 19–21
  King John's example of, 15–16
  Harry Truman's example of, 17–19
  Woodrow Wilson's example of,
    16–17
Hitchcock, John, ix
Hogan, R., 120, 139

Holliday, S. G., 4, 31–32
Homo sapiens, 248–249
Horney, Karen, 155
Howe, L. H., 213
Human blindness, 57
Human consciousness, 96–100
Human knowledge, 27–28
Human performance, 78–79
Human wisdom, 37–42, 47, 98
Huselid, M. A., 177

Idealized self, 88
Ignatius, St., 250
Ignorance, realization of own, 32
Immediacy, expectation of, 223
Individual psychodynamics, 281–285
Individuals, coaching of, 272–273
Ineffective savvy, 139
Information
  absorbing large amounts of, 224
  necessary/sufficient, 59, 60
Information collection, 204
Inner awareness, 152
Innocent III, Pope, 15
Inquisition, 20
Insensitivity to base rates, 130
Insensitivity to sample size, 130
Instinctual self, 88
Instrumental mode, 252
Instrument and reality orientation, 211
Insufficient anchor adjustment, 131
Intelligence, forms of, 242
Interpersonal concordance orientation,
  211
Introspection, 70
Intuitive decision making, 53
Invulnerability fallacy, 31
Iroquois Confederacy, 263
Isabella, Queen of Spain, 19–22
Ivery, M., 175

James, William, 93, 151
Janis, I., 308
Jaques, E., 101–103, 281, 285
Jesuits, 250
Jewish tradition, 214, 249
Jews, 20
Joan of Castile, 19, 20
Joas, H., 238

Merton, Thomas, 189
Mesopotamia, 249
Metacognition, 63–114
    basic model of, 79–80
    behavioral geography/psychological
        geology in, 84–96
    definitions of, 71
    development of, 100–103
    evidence of emergence of, 108,
        112–113
    examples of, 64–70
    and executive mind, 79–84
    in executives, 75–76
    exercise to stimulate, 111, 113–114
    and human consciousness, 96–100
    literature about, 74–75
    principles for developing, 103–106
    process-oriented model of, 72
    psychodynamic/human performance
        contributions to understanding,
        76–79
    and self-regulation, 70–84
    teaching, 72–74
    techniques for stimulating, 106–111
    as term, 69
Metacognitive level, 52, 73, 94–95, 98
Methods of inquiry, 201
Mezirow, J., 251
Michalisin, M. D., 175
Micromanaging, 121
Mind, five orders of, 296–300
Mintzberg, H., 126, 240
Model(s) of Executive Wisdom, 25–62
    ancient, 25–29
    Baltes–Staudinger's Berlin paradigm,
        31
    barriers domain of, 42–43
    behavioral geography/psychological
        geology in, 50–54
    Bierly–Kessler-Christensen's four-
        level paradigm, 32
    case study of, 48–50
    continuum in, 56–58
    Darwin's uncertainty paradigm, 32
    Dimitrov's fuzziness theory, 32
    domains contributing to, 33–34
    emergence of wisdom in, 58–60
    environments domain of, 43–45
    example of, 54–56
    executive domain of, 36–37
    Holliday–Chandler's, 31–32

    human wisdom domain of, 37–42
    leadership/coaching activities in,
        60–62
    mediated domain of, 35–36
    postmodern, 29–30
    Sternberg's balance theory, 30–31
    structures/processes in, 46–48
    system domain of, 34–35
Molotov, Vyacheslav, 17, 18
Monitoring processes, 90, 91, 94
Moors, 20
Moral awareness, 141–143, 208–222
    activities for developing, 221–222
    at Arthur Anderson, 212–213
    in leaders, 190
    psychological/philosophical contribu-
        tions to business, 209–212
    stages of, 210–211
    values and reasoning in, 213–221
Moral exemplars, 216
Morgan, J. P., 118
Morgan, R. E., 175
Morrison, D. J., 95
Morton Thiokol, 308
Moser, T., 95
Mottolo, A., 250
Mundt, K. A., 95
Muthukrishna, N., 72

Nadler, D. A., 178, 270
Narens, L., 79, 82, 83
National Aeronautics and Space
    Administration, 308
National Security Act (1947), 326, 327
National Security Council (NSC),
    326–328
Natsoulas, T., 151–152
Nelson, P., 215
Nelson, T. O., 79, 82, 83
Neustadt, R. E., 124, 199, 201, 205
New York Stock Exchange, 308
Nichol, Lee, 321
Nicholas of Cusa, 27–28
Nitze, Paul, 18
No Man Is an Island (Thomas Merton),
    189
Nonreflective intuition mode, 138
Normal knowledge, 57
Normandy, 15
Norming stage, 277, 278

ABOUT THE AUTHOR

Richard R. Kilburg received his PhD in clinical psychology from the University of Pittsburgh in 1972. He attended a postgraduate program in mental health administration at the Community Psychiatry Laboratory at Harvard University and obtained a master's degree in professional writing from Towson State University in 1992. He has held positions in the Department of Psychiatry at the University of Pittsburgh as an assistant professor, as the director of the Champlain Valley Mental Health Council (a community mental health center in Burlington, Vermont), at the American Psychological Association's (APA's) Offices of Professional Affairs and Public Affairs, and in private practice as a clinician and consultant. Currently, he is the senior director of the Office of Human Services, The Johns Hopkins University, a multiprogram service component of human resources that meets the developmental needs of the faculty and staff of the university. He was the 2005 recipient of the Harry and Miriam Levinson Award for Exceptional Contributions to Consulting Organizational Psychology.

He has published widely in the fields of management, professional impairment, and executive coaching. His three previous books, all published with the APA, are *Professionals in Distress: Issues, Syndromes, and Solutions in Psychology* (1986); *How to Manage Your Career in Psychology* (1992); and *Executive Coaching: Developing Managerial Wisdom in a World of Chaos* (2000). He was the founding president of the Society of Psychologists in Management and is a fellow of APA's Division 13 (Society of Consulting Psychology). He has one son, Benjamin, and currently lives in Towson, Maryland.